Cultural and Heritage Tourism in Asia and the Pacific

The Asia Pacific region's enormous diversity of living cultures and preserved heritage sites has significant appeal to many tourists. However, tourism has grown so rapidly that many issues associated with the incorporation of cultural and heritage experiences in tourist itineraries (such as authenticity verses commodification, exploitation of national cultures, impacts on local communities, and the management of heritage resources) have not been adequately addressed and must be debated.

This revealing book reviews recent developments in cultural and heritage tourism in the Asia Pacific region and provides a discussion on how communities have faced and overcome significant challenges to develop and market their culture and heritage resources. A range of models and case studies are used to deepen the reader's understanding of heritage and cultural issues, to illustrate many of the more controversial issues, and to examine new evaluative, and planning tools.

This book is based on two special issues of the *Asia Pacific Journal of Tourism Research*.

Professor Bruce Prideaux is at the School of Business, James Cook University, Australia

Professor Dallen J. Timothy is in the Department of Geography, Brigham Young University, USA

Professor Kaye Chon is at the School of Hospitality and Tourism Management, Hong Kong Polytechnic University, Hong Kong

Cultural and Heritage Tourism in Asia and the Pacific

Edited by Bruce Prideaux, Dallen J. Timothy and Kaye Chon

Routledge
Taylor & Francis Group

LONDON AND NEW YORK

First published 2008
by Routledge
2 Park Square, Milton Park, Abingdon, Oxon, OX14 4RN

Simultaneously published in the USA and Canada
by Routledge
270 Madison Avenue, New York, NY 10016

Routledge is an imprint of the Taylor & Francis Group, an informa business

© 2008 Bruce Prideaux, Dallen J. Timothy and Kaye Chon

Reprinted 2008

Typeset in Sabon by Techset Composition, Salisbury, UK
Printed and bound in Great Britain by MPG Books Ltd, Bodmin, Cornwall

British Library Cataloguing in Publication Data
A catalogue record for this book is available from the British Library

Library of Congress Cataloging in Publication Data
A catalog record for this book has been requested

ISBN10: 0-415-36673-9
ISBN13: 978-0-415-36673-1

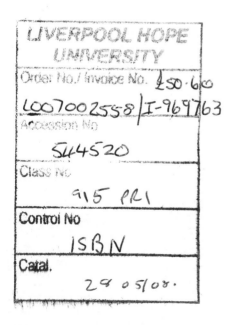

Contents

Contributors

R.J.S. Beeton, Associate Professor, School of Natural and Rural Systems Management, The University of Queensland, Australia

Anna Carr, Senior Lecturer, Department of Tourism, University of Otago, Dunedin, New Zealand

R.W. (Bill) Carter, Associate Professor, Faculty of Science, Health and Education University of the Sunshine Coast, Australia

Ilika Chakravarty, Associate Professor, Master of Tourism Administration Department, Garden City College, Bangalore, India

Malcolm J.M. Cooper, Professor of Asia Pacific Studies, Formerly Dean, Wide Bay Campus, University of Southern Queensland, Ritsumeikan Asia Pacific University, Beppu, Japan

Ros Derrett, Office of the Pro Vice Chancellor (Research), Southern Cross University, Lismore, Australia

Hilary du Cros, Professor, Institute for Tourism Studies, Macao

Dianne Dredge PhD, Griffith School of Environment, Griffith University, Australia

Jeremy S. Eades, Professor, Ritsumeikan Asia Pacific University and Senior Honorary Research Fellow, Department of Anthropology, University of Kent at Canterbury, UK

Warwick Frost, Senior lecturer, Department of Management, Monash University, Australia

Paul Leung Kin Hang, School of Hotel and Tourism Management, Hong Kong Polytechnic University, Hong Kong

Donald E. Hawkins, Eisenhower Professor of Tourism Policy, School of Business and Public Management, The George Washington University, USA

Steve Hill, Professor of Journalism, University of Wisconsin-Stevens Point, USA

Pamela S.Y. Ho, Senior Lecturer, Chinese University of Hong Kong

Chang Huh, Assistant Professor, Department of Parks, Recreation and Hospitality Administration, Arkansas Tech University, USA

Tazim Jamal, Associate Professor, Recreation, Park and Tourism Sciences, Texas A&M University

Angela Kah, Research Affiliate, University of Manitoba, USA

Eric Laws, Visiting Professor, School of Business, James Cook University, Queensland, Australia

Sarah Leonard, Associate Director of Philanthropy, The Nature Conservancy, Alaska, USA

Sandra Leong, Singapore Tourism Board, Invited Professor Institute For Tourism Studies, Macao

Jing Li, Center for Folklore and Ethnography, The University of Pennsylvania, Philadelphia, USA

Alison J. McIntosh, Associate Professor, Department of Tourism Management, The University of Waikato, Hamilton, New Zealand

Bob McKercher, Professor, School of Hotel and Tourism Management, Hong Kong Polytechnic University, Hong Kong

Hirini Matunga, Department of Tourism Management, The University of Waikato, Hamilton, New Zealand

Masakatsu Ogata, Professor of Asia Pacific Studies, Formerly Executive Vice-President, Japan National Tourism Organisation, Ritsumeikan Asia Pacific University, Beppu, Japan

Grace Wen Pan, ACNielsen China, Adjunct Professor, Department of Travel, Leisure, Sport and Hotel Management, Griffith University, Australia

Douglas G. Pearce, Professor of Tourism Management, Victoria University of Wellington, Wellington, New Zealand

Shane Pegg, Senior Lecturer, School of Tourism and Leisure Management, The University of Queensland, Ipswich, Queensland, Australia

Bruce Prideaux, Professor, School of Business, James Cook University, Cairns, Australia

Glenn F. Ross, Adjunct Professor of Business-Tourism Program, James Cook University, Cairns, Australia

Norma J. Stumbo, Professor, Director, Midwest Alliance, University of Illinois at Urbana-Champaign, USA

Raewyn Tan, former Research Fellow, Victoria University of Wellington, Wellington, currently International Marketing Coordinator for Positively Wellington Tourism, New Zealand

Dallen J. Timothy, Department of Geography, Brigham Young University, Utah, USA

Christine A. Vogt, Associate Professor, Department of Community, Agriculture, Recreation and Resource Studies, Michigan State University, USA.

Justin St Vincent Welch, Office of the Pro Vice Chancellor (Research), Southern Cross University, Lismore, Australia

Frania Kanara Zygadlo, Department of Tourism Management, The University of Waikato, Hamilton, New Zealand

Themes in Cultural and Heritage Tourism in the Asia Pacific Region

Bruce Prideaux and Dallen J. Timothy

Cultural and Heritage Tourism in Asia and the Pacific is the result of lengthy discussions between the editors and colleagues in many countries and is based partially on a double special issue of the *Asia Pacific Journal of Tourism Research*. The call for papers for the special issue generated such a large response in submissions that two issues of the Journal (Vol. 9(3), *Heritage in the Asia Pacific* and Vol. 9(4), *Cultural Tourism in the Asia Pacific*) were required to publish some of the papers submitted. There were still a number of excellent papers remaining, and given that there is an ongoing debate occurring on many of the issues raised, the editors decided to publish the collection of papers from the special issue with a number of new chapters as a book. We believe that collectively the contributions provide a benchmark of current scholarly research into the main issues of heritage and culture in the Asia Pacific Region. While we acknowledge that the collection of chapters is not a definitive statement of the breath of research currently underway, it does provide a useful summary and highlights the ongoing nature of the issues that are the subject of scholarly debate.

The overall aim of the book is to create a collection of work that both enhances current understanding and provides a guide to future research. In developing this book the editors were mindful of the need to include chapters by scholars within the region, as well as those who observe from afar, to provide a range of contrasting perspectives. This introductory chapter outlines the structure of the book before undertaking a review of some of the many issues raised by contributing authors.

The Structure of the Book

Cultural and Heritage Tourism in Asia and the Pacific is organized into four parts that collectively contain 22 chapters. The book is organized in a format that introduces readers to many of the key questions, such as authenticity, before challenging them to consider how authenticity can be retained in the face of the demands of the tourism industry to manage and market cultural heritage. The first part of the book, *Authenticity: The Search for the Real*, consists of seven chapters that examine a range of issues that encompass the debate surrounding the meaning of authenticity and how this can be achieved in a changing world. The issues canvassed in this part of the book influence the structure of cultural heritage tourism and include themes that are examined in greater detail in this chapter.

In the second part of the book the impacts of tourism on heritage and culture are examined in five chapters. It is apparent that many of the issues surrounding the debate on retaining authenticity are dependent on the degree to which the contemporary world is changing and how that change affects traditional expressions of culture and uses of place. Even traditional music undergoes change when it is played by traditional instruments but in non-traditional settings, such as hotels and cultural centres. Similarly, the use of places that have strong heritage values is often contested, as new uses seek to supplant or replace traditional ones.

In Part 3, *Planning, Managing and Enterprise*, five chapters consider issues relating to managing cultural and heritage assets, as well as their planning, and for many organisations involved in bringing culture and heritage to the tourism industry their ability to engage in the establishment and running of successful sustainable businesses. Issues raised in this part of the book have strong links back to the issues raised about authenticity in Part 1, as well as the impacts that cultural exhibitionism may have on culture and heritage as noted in Part 2.

The book's final section deals with issues of marketing. In a competitive world where many attractions seek to maximize their returns from tourism dollars, marketing has become a key activity that organizations must understand and successfully engage in. Marketing in this sense includes promotion and engaging with the distribution system to maximize exposure to potential clients in market regions. The book concludes with a summary and synthesis of the major issues relating to heritage and culture, as well as the identification of some priorities for future research in this challenging area of tourism research.

The Significance of Heritage and Culture

In tourism settings, heritage and culture may be used for a variety of purposes, including entertainment, preservation, information, education, profit and propaganda. For the society whose culture and heritage is the object of presentation to visitors, the themes may be ordinary and familiar, but to visitors these same themes may be unique, exotic and extraordinary, and characterized by differentness from the visitors' own normal environment. Heritage and culture therefore serve a variety of purposes, and the study of these purposes is important both from the perspective of providing a focus for guests to learn about the hosts' culture and for the hosts as a means of preserving and sharing their unique past and way of life with others. In recent decades, as the pace of tourism has increased, heritage has become an important selling point, but it is often sold to buyers who have little real interest in, or concern for, the meaning of the culture they are gazing upon. This book examines a range of issues that impact on the use of heritage and culture by the tourism industry in the Asia Pacific region. This chapter introduces a new

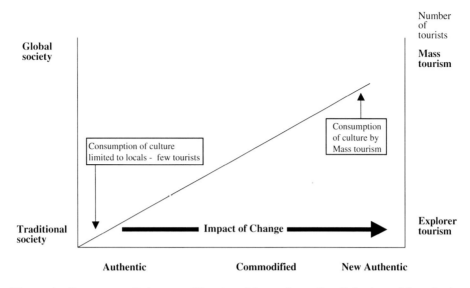

Figure 1   Impact on Culture as Tourism Moves from Small Scale to Mass Scale.

explanatory model that may be used to examine how culture is affected by tourism. Issues discussed in this chapter include authenticity, interpretation, heritage contestation, social exclusion, contested space, personal heritage, control and preservation. The heritage model, illustrated in Figure 1, may be used to classify heritage destinations and visitors using a spectrum that commences with the authentic and then plots the evolution of the authentic through commodification and ultimately the metamorphosis of the authentic into a new authenticity.

The breadth and depth of cultural heritage issues that communities in the Asia Pacific are involved with is enormous, evolving, and in some cases controversial. In many instances even the meaning of heritage and culture is disputed. In recent decades a substantial literature on heritage and cultural issues has emerged, paralleling the growth in recognition of the place that heritage and culture now hold in the tourism industry. The study region has an enormous variety of people who express

themselves through their culture and reflect on their patrimony through both cultural expressions and preservation of relics of the past. The ensuing complex mosaic of cultural expressions has provided the tourism industry with a rich well of experiences on which to draw as an increasing number of countries, and regions within countries, recognize the potential of the tourism industry to create employment and wealth.

Tourism is, however, only one of many actors on the stage of national economic, social and cultural development. Tourism works best when uniqueness becomes a point of differentiation from competitors and creates an experience that is marketable because it is not easily substitutable by other places and events. Thus, for the tourism industry, heritage and culture must exhibit uniqueness and marketability; yet culture is rarely static, and the symbols of heritage may be needed for other more contemporary uses, creating tensions that must be resolved. Culture is a living expression of a way of life and people's relationships with each other, the environment in which they live, the religious expressions which give meaning to their life, and manners in which they cope with the forces of nature and politics.

Globalisation and its associated demands for modernisation offer many improvements in material welfare and health but often at the expense of traditional forms of economic organization and lifestyle. The process of globalization demands change and creates a tendency towards uniformity rather than diversity. Culture is often one of the victims of progress, and the rhythm of daily life that for millennia was determined by the demands of seasons must now change and be determined by a new rhythm created through membership in the global economy. As people migrate from the country to the city the need for harvest festivals and other symbols of rural life are replaced with more impersonal, globalised festivals. Thus, the impersonal experience of watching the soccer World Cup on a television set in one's lounge room has replaced the far more personal experience of participating in a harvest festival with one's neighbours. For these reasons culture is rarely static, as it responds by adapting to the many social, economic and political changes that shape and then reshape society. At which point in time a culture should be frozen to be packaged and exhibited to tourists is therefore an important question that will ultimately be decided by the major stakeholders and the level of demand by tourists for specific cultural experiences.

The dilemma facing communities attempting to attract visitors through their cultural uniqueness is that the changing nature of life is creating uniformity between diverse peoples on a global scale; however, the retention of uniqueness requires participation in traditional experiences that no longer reflect contemporary society. The arguments about authenticity thus take on new meanings because the present is often vastly different from the past. Tourism interest usually focuses on uniqueness, which was apparent in the past but which has been lost to the increasing uniformity of the present. Commodification thus becomes a necessity, and in the process authenticity is typically lost.

Against this background of cultural change communities must seek to build images and attractions that rely on cultural heritage and other elements of tourism interest to fashion a tourism experience. To model this process of change and provide a tool that can be used to measure change to culture quantitatively, Figure 1 illustrates how traditional culture, identified as authentic, undergoes a process of commodification as culture is adapted for exhibition to an increasingly mass tourism market. The left hand vertical axis represents the shift from traditional to global society while the horizontal axis measures change in consumption of culture from traditional forms of cultural expression that can be described as authentic to commodified forms of expression that appeal to mass markets. The curve illustrates the change in the consumptive pattern of culture. In its original form, where culture represented traditional values, tourism interest was low and confined to those who sort out unique cultures in their authentic form. As tourism grows the authentic undergoes change via a process of commodification to reach a new authenticity that represents the new form of cultural expression that is acceptable to the tourist and also fits into the newly globalised form of culture that the local community has adopted.

The patterns described here can be illustrated by examining cultural change in Bali. Traditional forms of dance such as the Legong and Sanghyang trance dances were central to village culture in the period before modernization and mass tourism. At that time tourists were able to view these dances but no allowances were made for the benefit of the tourist spectator. With modernization and the introduction of new entertainment media such as radio, motion film and television, the place once held by traditional forms of dance changed. Simultaneously, tourist interest in these forms of dance has increased with the presentations requiring considerable modification to fit the demands of tourism. Commodification occurred and the dance in a sense metamorphosed from a traditional form to a new tourist focused form.

As tourism reaches into more distant areas, bringing with it change and in some respects being changed, it is important for researchers, policy makers and the tourism industry to recognize the impacts that are occurring, to be conversant with strategies to manage change and to be sensitive to the needs of destination communities (Singh *et al.*, 2003). This chapter explores some of these issues.

Several authors (e.g. Carter in this volume; Prideaux, 2003) have reported on aspects of the use and adaptation of national and regional heritage and culture in the Asia Pacific region. Carter for example models the impact of tourism as an agent for social and cultural change, noting that many communities face the temptation to trade cultural expression for the economic benefits that tourism can provide. The adaptation and elevation of elements of culture as marketing icons is one example of this trend. In Australia, Aboriginal dances and the didgeridoo, the Aborigines' unique musical instrument, have been largely removed from their tribal settings and promoted as an iconic expression but specifically packaged to meet the needs of the tourism industry. Conversely, cultures must adapt if they are to survive (Harrison, 1996), and to do otherwise may ultimately lead to extinction. In these and other ways discussed later in this chapter, national cultures and heritage are under pressure from the tourism industry. Some face the danger of trivialization and exploitation while others have responded by changing to meet the demands of the contemporary world. Without some form of education, tourists exposed to packaged culture and heritage experiences may return to their homes with little knowledge of the significance of the sites visited or of the cultures experienced.

Management of heritage and cultural sites has become an important issue in many nations as stakeholders have become aware of the difficulties of managing the preservation and development of sites while accommodating visitor needs and the interests of hosts (Vogt *et al.*, this volume). Other issues that may occupy the attention of stakeholders include conflicting land uses, funding, ownership, interpretation and exhibition arrangements. Rejuvination and the need to build sustainable tourism industries are other issues that have received attention (Dredge and Carter in their respective chapters). Carter, for example, argues that a shift in tourism planning is required from outcome-focused to process-orientated where there is greater consideration between the market, product and destination community. The following discussion canvasses a range of issues that require extensive debate within destination communities, as well as in the commercial organizations that profit from these experiences and places.

Current Trends in Heritage Tourism

Authenticity

Despite its widespread popularity as a topic of debate in heritage tourism studies, authenticity is an elusive concept that lacks a set of central identifying criteria, lacks a standard definition, varies in meaning from place to place, and has varying levels of acceptance by groups within society. What is consistent in the debate on authenticity is its inconsistency. Timothy and Boyd (2003: 244–254) created a five-part typology of distorted pasts, which are indicative of the types of inauthenticity that exist most typically within the realm of heritage. The first type is *invented places*, wherein replicas of historic places, non-original renditions of the past, and imaginary or contrived places, people and events are created. In many cases, tourists travel in search of places that never really existed (e.g. the Land of Oz in Kansas, or Peter Rabbit's garden in England). As a result, tourism takes these expectations and marks places and creates spaces that will satisfy tourists' need to consume these make-believe locations (Herbert, 1995; Raivo, 2000).

The second form of inauthentic pasts is *relative authenticity*. Authenticity is a relative concept, influenced and defined by individual experience, social and cultural influences, politics, and official histories. In most cases, the meanings of historic artifacts derive from people's collective and personal experiences rather than from the objects themselves (Burnett, 2001; McLean, 1998, Derrett and St Vincent Welch this volume). Lowenthal (1975: 18, 26) noted that "Much of our aesthetic pleasure in the ancient lies in the belief that such objects really do come from the remote past...because we feel that old things

should look old, we may forget that they originally looked new".

The third type of distorted past is described as *Ethnic intruders* and refers to the situation where actors in a so called authentic reproduction or ethnic display do not belong to the ethnic or cultural group they are representing. This is not uncommon. In an example from the USA, the re-created Bavarian village located in Leavenworth, Washington, is staffed by people dressed as Bavarians but who are not of Bavarian descent.

The fourth type of inauthentic past classed as *sanitized and idealized places and events* is very common. According to Barthel (1990), historical accuracy is not always in agreement with aesthetic and sensory harmony for people can only see representations of the past (e.g. museums, living heritage villages, etc) with eyes of the present. Thus the unpleasant aspects of smell, dirt and so on are sanitized to make them acceptable to the expectations of contemporary tourists (Burnett, 2001; Hubbard and Lilley, 2000; Leong, 1989).

Finally, the *unknown past* implies that it is impossible to achieve true authenticity because people in the current era find it difficult to understand how people lived in the past. Even the most carefully written and preserved archival records and diaries only provide glimpses into what life might have been like in the past. According to Lowenthal (1985: 215) "no account can recover the past as it was, because the past was not an account, it was a set of events and situations". The past is therefore enigmatic and can only be comprehended using imprecise and socially constructed interpretations (Hewison, 1991).

All of these types of distorted pasts in heritage tourism exist in the Asia Pacific region. For example, the Polynesian Cultural Center

(PCC) in Hawaii has been criticized because the performances, costumes, and handicrafts are inauthentic, having been extensively modified to be entertaining and involving performers who are not from the appropriate islands. Thus, the authenticity of the PCC experience is diminished when costumes donned by the actors are more ornate than in the islands, Samoans make Tahitian crafts, and Tongans perform Hawaiian dances (Balme, 1998; Douglas and Douglas, 1991). Taman Mini, an Indonesian theme park, depicts representative villages from throughout the archipelago but, like the PCC, suffers from inauthenticity. Not all interpreters in the Balinese village are Balinese, and how can one be certain that the Tana Toraja long house is in fact representative of all long houses? The many cultural parks, museums and historic sites found throughout the Asia Pacific region must each face these questions and determine what level of authenticity they will strive to achieve.

Cooper *et al.* (this volume) remind us that buildings are often adapted over time and in the Japanese tradition the built form of a particular building has much less importance than the uses of that building over time. It is not unusual, for example, to see shrines and other significant heritage buildings refurbished on a regular basis using modern building materials such as concrete. In a context of this nature authenticity is not seen to be a function of the fabric of the building but more the purpose and use of the structure over time.

Jamal and Hill's chapter addresses some of these issues by developing a typology for examining authenticity in cultural heritage tourism. Authenticity, they argue, can be viewed as multidimensional and include elements of time, space and theoretical approach in one dimension and the objective, constructive and personal in the other dimension. It is apparent that the debate on authenticity is ongoing and one that needs serious consideration by destination communities and other stakeholders.

In many areas cultures are facing two forces of change: globalization, which pushes towards uniformity, and tourism, which encourages commodification but still seeks uniqueness. In the first case, traditional material culture and self sufficiency are replaced by a new material culture based on interdependence, often on a global scale. Changing material culture creates a new authenticity. This can be illustrated by examining the use of the boomerang by Australian Aborigines. The authentic use of the boomerang is for hunting or as a weapon; however, in this setting the boomerang is neither visually attractive nor guaranteed to return to its owner after it is thrown. In the new authenticity, described as the new use of the boomerang as an object designed for tourism consumption, it is no longer used for hunting or as a weapon, but instead is used as a symbol to identify contemporary aboriginal culture and as an implement that can be thrown in the expectation that it will return. Thus, according to new authenticity, (see Figure 1) the boomerang has an entirely different use from its traditional purpose. This is demonstrated in Figure 2. The process of commodification of the old authenticity to create a new authenticity is a consequence of the tourism industry's need for new icons that can be promoted as points of differentness or uniqueness. This process may preserve some form of the original but in a highly commodified way. In the case of the boomerang, if it had not been adopted as a new symbol of indigenous

Figure 2   An Example of the new authentic – in this case a hand painted souvenir boomerang. (Photo by Bruce Prideaux.)

culture it would likely have been replaced by newer weapons and ultimately lost. Commodification therefore need not be a negative force as it refashions elements of culture to provide a new symbol that can be used as a marketing icon.

In the sense described above, commodification is a process of cultural adaptation that occurs where the object or place is reinterpreted to give it a new meaning within the cultural norms of visitors. Thus, a Balinese shadow puppet performance which may take many hours to perform in its traditional setting is transformed into a 30-minute presentation for visitors. The temptation for communities to commercialize their heritage and culture as a means of tapping into the growing demand of the tourism industry for new attractions is strong. Given the global context that cultural change is occurring in and the rapidity with which that process is transforming all societies, commodification is necessary and indeed may be one mechanism via which all communities can retain at least part of their traditional culture and heritage that otherwise might be lost in the march of modernization and its passengers of uniformity and conformity.

Interpretation

Interpretation – a process of communicating to visitors the meaning and significance of the place being visited – is an important part of heritage tourism and can be a useful tool for managing heritage visitors and their impacts. In the context of heritage and culture, interpretation plays at least three major roles (Timothy and Boyd, 2003). First, it is an educational tool. From this perspective, interpretation is important for increasing awareness and appreciation of the resources being presented, which in theory at least should result in higher levels of respect for and understanding of historic events, places and artifacts (Light, 1995; Prentice *et al.*, 1998; Tilden, 1977). Second, interpretation also includes an entertainment factor. Today, education specialists realize that entertainment and learning are not dichotomous terms; learning can in fact be very entertaining and needs to be recognized by heritage managers as an enjoyable experience (McAndrew, 1995; Schouten, 1995). Finally, interpretation is a useful tool for meeting conservation and sustainable development objectives through visitor management, positively influencing visitor spending and other economic benefits, promoting cultural heritage conservation, changing attitudes and values in positive ways, and involving destination communities in the provision of interpretation and other elements of the heritage product (Bramwell and Lane, 1993; Moscardo and Woods, 1998; Pearson and Sullivan, 1995).

In the Asia Pacific region, many issues can be identified in the provision of interpretive services for heritage and cultural tourists. Cultural differences are an important issue in the region, because there are so many different ethnicities, nationalities, and cultures involved in tourism as both consumers and producers of the heritage product. As part of this, bi- and multi-lingual interpretation is an important element of heritage management in places where visitors come from a variety of countries. All too often interpretive signs and other media are printed only in one language – usually the language of the destination. From a service quality viewpoint, this is a problem and reduces visitor satisfaction. From another aspect, the destination loses out because the guest has failed to understand the cultural or heritage significance of the experience. Rectifying these problems is relatively simple but often ignored. In her chapter on the Maori people of New Zealand, Carr (this volume) examines how interpretations of cultural landscapes is able to enhance the heritage experience and in so doing how it is possible to assist visitors to understand the significance of the culture they are observing.

Heritage Contestation

Heritage dissonance, according to Tunbridge and Ashworth (1996), is discord over a lack of agreement and consistency. Heritage is inherently a contested phenomenon, especially when communities are comprised of multiple ethnic groups, belief systems, cultures, and social mores. In this case, then, questions always arise regarding what heritage should be, or is presently, conserved, promoted and interpreted (Ashworth, 2003). Dissonance, or contestation, occurs between groups when multiple groups share the same heritage, when there are heritage divisions within one group, and where overlapping heritages exist in the same places (Olsen and Timothy, 2002). Administrations in power have a

tendency to support and portray the heritages and cultures that function best for their purposes. However, as Frost points out in his chapter about the heritage of the pearl industry in Broome, Western Australia, it is possible to integrate a number of cultural traditions and themes into an experience that adds to the understanding of the past while not excluding the history of minorities.

Social Exclusion

One of the most significant political implications of culture and heritage, and one of the most common forms of dissonant heritage, is the notion of social exclusion or societal amnesia. This political treatment of heritage typically entails the intentional forgetting or leaving out of some aspects of the past, wherein societies elect to ignore and eliminate certain elements of history that are embarrassing or uncomfortable (Timothy and Boyd, 2003). Ashworth (1995) terms this 'disinheritence', which means that certain non-powerful groups are written out of the libretto of history for a variety of ideological or political reasons. In the past, slavery and Native American heritages in the United States were good examples of this, although the climate is changing as heritage managers realize the need to include the pasts of African Americans and Native Americans, regardless of the painful reality of history in that country's national heritage (Bartlett, 2001; Morgan and Pritchard, 1998; Smith, 2000). Similar issues are coming to the fore in South Africa as a new struggle to recognize the contributions of native Africans in the building of the Republic emerges (Goudie *et al.*, 1996; Worden, 1997).

Where this issue has been confronted, the ethnic richness of the minorities has become a major selling point and in some instances elevated to iconic status. New Zealand has a strong Maori culture that has become a focal point of its cultural tourism industry and to a lesser extent Australia has also recognized the 'selling power' of its aboriginal cultures. Incorporating indigenous and other minority groups into mainstream tourism is an issue greater than the commercial value of the experience and, as noted in the chapter by McIntosh *et al.*, tourism of this nature must be sensitive to the culture on display.

Contested Space

Many significant cultural and heritage sites compete for space with growing populations and a range of land uses. Where this occurs, the value of the heritage site may be less than the value of competing land uses and as a consequence faces the possibility of damage or destruction. In Liang Zhu, China, for example, Dredge (this volume) notes the potential for conflict between residents and the need to preserve the area's rich Neolithic heritage and argues that there is a need to develop cooperative planning to mitigate these problems. As urbanization increases, particularly in areas where there is a long history of human habitation, these problems will continue and will need to be addressed by governments as well as the commercial users of these sites.

Personal Heritage

Attractions most closely related to personal heritage draw people who possess emotional attachments to a particular place, person or event. Often this entails genealogy-related travel to do family history research, to visit

communities where ancestors came from, and other places of significance to the individual and his/her family (Timothy, 1997). A recent manifestation of this that is beginning to receive considerable attention in the tourism literature is diaspora-related travel. This ranges from people of a specific race or ethnicity traveling from their present home country to visit the lands of their ancestors and can take the form of visiting friends and relatives if they are first- or second-generation migrants. For others, the trip tends to be one of discovery where people travel to find their roots, learn about their own heritage, or be able to find their place in modern society.

This form of heritage is particularly important in the Asia Pacific region, for there have long been transnational migrations between countries and islands in the region. Diaspora travel among overseas Chinese is an important element of tourism in China, for instance, wherein Chinese populations from Southeast Asia, Australia, New Zealand, North America and Europe travel back to China to visit the lands of their ancestors or to visit relatives who might still be living. Likewise, a growing portion of the urban populations of New Zealand and Australia is comprised of Pacific Islanders from various islands in the region. Fijians, Samoans, Tongans, and Cook Islanders, for instance, make up some of the largest non-Maori and non-European populations of New Zealand. Among these people, traveling back to the home islands is usually undertaken for family purposes, but these trips might also include elements of personal heritage. The same is true of the various diasporic populations in other countries in the region (Coles and Timothy, 2004; Hall and Duval, 2004; Lew and Wong, 2004; Nguyen and King, 2004).

Control

Control of cultural and heritage resources is a significant issue (Ho and McKercher, this volume). Restoration and preservation are expensive and many local communities find the task beyond their resources. While some sites of world significance, Borobudur Temple for example, may attract international funds (Hawkins, this volume), other smaller sites face challenges that may result in the loss of control of aspects of their culture and heritage to others. Li (this volume) cites a range of issues that have emerged as the central authorities in China have devolved power to the regions. In Xishuang Banna the Dai Yuan have struggled to retain control of aspects of their culture they wish to share with visitors. The power of tour operators to select which attractions are patronized has resulted in a de facto power transfer from the local community to commercial interests in a pattern found in other parts of the Asia Pacific. This trend needs to be reversed if local communities are to benefit form tourism development. Leong and du Cross (this volume) examine these issues from a Chinese perspective and emphasize the advantages of local empowerment in decision making. Chakravarty (this volume) also reinforces the need for community participation in tourism even if public participation demands considerable resources and time and may prolong the planning process.

Preservation

The growing engagement between dissimilar cultures on all levels with the forces of modernization and more recently globalization has placed enormous pressure on many traditional cultures. In an effort to preserve the past, some communities have turned to tourism as a means of preserving the past through a process of commercializing aspects of cultures and heritage that are threatened. However, the commercial imperatives of tourism, where products prosper or fail according to demand, mitigate against genuine preservation and encourage selective preservation of those elements that have a commercial value.

Moreover, cultures are not static and change over time in response to larger changes in society, the organization of the economic system and the form and reach of political organization. In one sense, culture is the contemporary telling of the stories of the present as well as the past. To label the authentic as only that which exists at a given point in time and is representative of all aspects of a target culture is to discount the need for culture to adapt and transform as the world that the culture represents undergoes change.

In a more general sense the issue of representing culture is significant. The neo-colonialist view that tourism is a destructive influence has been challenged but ultimately it is the owners of the culture and heritage who must decide how to present their culture and how much this presentation is representative of their core cultural values. In a discussion on the potential for using tourism as a vehicle to fund the preservation and development of traditional arts in Southern China, Hang's chapter points out that the design and then re-design of experiences may need to occur to meet changing visitor needs. Is this a case of culture being adapted for 'sale' as a tourism commodity or a process of a culture recognizing the pressure of the contemporary world on traditional society and adopting a solution that incorporates both?

Management

Management is an important issue particularly where the ability to present culture and heritage is dependent on financial sustainability. Selling heritage and culture will entail trade-offs as previously discussed. However, in the long run the trade-offs may mean the difference between preservation with commodification or loss because of lack of funds. This is an issue that must be grappled with by stakeholders and the customary custodians of culture. Aside from these issues, which have been debated previously in this chapter, other management issues need to be addressed. For example, Pegg and Stumbo (this volume) remind readers of the need to consider the needs of the disabled traveler. From yet another perspective, Ross (this volume) discusses the significance of identifying visitor motivations, in this case senior travelers.

Access

Access to heritage sites can be discussed from several perspectives, including physically traveling to the site and the ability of tourists to gain admittance once they have arrived at the site. Heritage sites may be located in a variety of settings that may not enjoy easy access to public transport. In Australia for example, many Aboriginal rock paintings are located in remote areas that have few roads and may require walking some distance. Similarly, in the Pacific Islands many cultural sites are located in remote regions that are poorly serviced, if at all, by public transport such as airlines. This is an issue that must be addressed by site managers as the ability of tourists to reach a site will often be the major factor determining the

ability of the site to attract tourists. Pegg and Stumbo (this volume) remind us that access not only includes transport access but also the ability of tourists to enter and move around a site. Exclusion from places or events may occur for a number of reasons including ethnicity, ability to pay, social status, physical impairments or personal economic circumstances. The growing demand for travel by disabled persons will lead to increased demand by members of this tourism sector to visit sites, and is a trend that should not be neglected by managers. Similarly, it is important that local residents also have access to their cultural heritage and are not excluded because of entry costs or social status. It is therefore important for site managers to identify barriers of the nature discussed and attempt where possible to implement policies to mitigate the impacts.

Conclusion

This chapter has summarized many of the major issues facing the development of cultural and heritage resources in the Asia Pacific region, although there are clearly many more which have yet to be addressed in detail. While no solutions are offered, the identification of these issues followed by education (Hawkins, this volume) in its broadest sense are necessary first steps towards resolution. The issues raised are being experienced in many countries of the Asia Pacific region. Other issues have not been covered, not because they lack importance but because of the enormity of the range of issues that surround the development of heritage and culture for tourism purposes.

A danger that many communities in the region face is the rush to modernize and exploit the unique heritage and cultural elements of the destination for short-term commercial gain. However, this approach is rarely sustainable in the long run. Conversely, living cultures and heritage sites do undergo change and the point at which authenticity is lost is an issue that needs additional debate. The many issues raised indicate the extent of the problem and breadth of research required to assist stakeholders to achieve a sustainable balance between competing forces, including conservation and commercialization.

It is apparent that there is considerable scope for future research in the area of culture and heritage in the Asia Pacific, both from a thematic approach and from the perspectives of specific countries. This collection should therefore be seen as an introduction to discussions on heritage and culture in the Asia Pacific, not the final word.

References

Amit-Talai, V. (1997) In pursuit of authenticity: globalization and nation building in the Cayman Islands. *Anthropologica*, 39(1/2): 53–63.

Ashworth, G.J. (2003) Heritage identity and places: for tourists and host communities. In S. Singh, D.J. Timothy and R.K. Dowling (eds) *Tourism in Destination Communities*, pp. 79–97. Wallingford: CAB International.

Ashworth, G.J. (1995) Heritage, tourism and Europe: a European future for a European past? In D.T. Herbert (ed.) *Heritage, Tourism and Society*, pp. 68–84. London: Mansell.

Balme, C.B. (1998) Staging the Pacific: framing authenticity in performances for tourists at the Polynesian Cultural Center. *Theatre Journal*, 50(1): 53–70.

Barthel, D. (1990) Nostalgia for America's village past: staged symbolic communities. *International Journal of Politics, Culture, and Society*, 4(1): 79–93.

Bartlett, T. (2001) Virginia develops African-American tourism sites. *Travel Weekly*, 4 June: 16.

Bramwell, B. and Lane, B. (1993). Interpretation and sustainable tourism: the potential and the pitfalls. *Journal of Sustainable Tourism*, 1(2): 71–80.

Burnett, K.A. (2001) Heritage, authenticity and history. In S. Drummond and I. Yeoman (eds) *Quality Issues in Heritage Visitor Attractions*, pp. 39–53. Oxford: Butterworth Heinemann.

Coles, T. and Timothy, D.J. (2004) 'My field is the world': Connecting tourism, diaspora and space. In T. Coles and D.J. Timothy (eds) *Tourism, Diasporas and Space*, pp. 1–29. London: Routledge.

Douglas, N. and Douglas, N. (1991) Where the tiki are wired for sound and the poi glow in the dark: a day at the Polynesian Cultural Center. *Islands Business Pacific*, 17(12): 60–64.

Goudie, S.C., Khan, F. and Kilian, D. (1996) Tourism beyond apartheid: black empowerment and identity in the "New" South Africa. In P.A. Wells (ed.) *Keys to the Marketplace: Problems and Issues in Cultural and Heritage Tourism*, pp. 65–86. Enfield Lock, UK: Hisarlik Press.

Hall, C.M. and Duval, D.T. (2004) Linking diasporas and tourism: Transnational mobilities of Pacific islanders resident in New Zealand. In T. Coles and D.J. Timothy (eds) *Tourism, Diasporas and Space*, pp. 78–94. London: Routledge.

Hang, P. (In press) "The southern sound" (Nanyin): Tourism for the Preservation and development of traditional arts,

Harrison, D. 1996 Sustainability and Tourism: reflections from a muddy pool, in L. Briguglio, B. Archer, J. Jafari, & G. Wall (eds), *Sustainable Tourism in Islands and Small State: Issues and Policies*, London: Pinter, 69–89.

Herbert, D.T. (1995) Heritage as literary place. In D.T. Herbert (ed.) *Heritage, Tourism and Society*, pp. 32–48. London: Mansell.

Hewison, R. (1991) The heritage industry revisited. *Museums Journal*, 91: 23–26.

Hubbard, P. and Lilley K. (2000) Selling the past: heritage-tourism and place identity in Stratford-upon-Avon. *Geography*, 85(3): 221–232.

Leong, W.T. (1989) Culture and the state: manufacturing traditions for tourism. *Critical Studies in Mass Communication*, 6(4): 355–375.

Lew, A.A. and Wong, A. (2004) Sojourners, Gangxi and clan associations: Social capital and overseas Chinese tourism to China. In T. Coles and D.J. Timothy (eds) *Tourism, Diasporas and Space*, pp. 202–213. London: Routledge.

Light, D. (1995) Visitors' use of interpretive media at heritage sites. *Leisure Studies*, 14: 133–149.

Lowenthal, D. (1985) *The Past is a Foreign Country*. Cambridge: Cambridge University Press.

Lowenthal, D. (1975) Past time, present place: landscape and memory. *Geographical Review*, 65(1): 1–36.

McAndrew, T.M. (1995) Making history: when historic site interpreters try to entertain visitors, do they make history come alive or do they reshape the past? *Illinois Issues*, 21(7): 18–20.

McLean, F. (1998) Museums and the construction of national identity: a review. *International Journal of Heritage Studies*, 3(4): 244–252.

Morgan, N. and Pritchard, A. (1998) *Tourism Promotion and Power: Creating Images, Creating Identities*. Chichester: Wiley.

Moscardo, G. and Woods, B. (1998) Managing tourism in the Wet Tropics World Heritage area: interpretation and the experience of visitors on Skyrail. In E. Laws, B. Faulkner and G. Moscardo (eds) *Embracing and Managing Change in Tourism: International Case Studies*, pp. 307–323. London: Routledge.

Nguyen, T. and King, B. (2004) The culture of tourism in the diaspora: the case of the Vietnamese community in Australia. In T. Coles and D.J. Timothy (eds) *Tourism, Diasporas and Space*, pp. 172–187. London: Routledge.

Olsen, D. H. and Timothy, D. J. (2002) Contested Religious Heritage: Differing Views of Mormon Heritage. *Tourism Recreation Research*. 27(2): 7–15.

Pearson, M. and Sullivan, S. (1995) *Looking after Heritage Places: The Basics of Heritage Planning for Managers, Landowners and Administrators*. Carlton: Melbourne University Press.

Prentice, R.C., Guerin, S. and McGugan, S. (1998) Visitor learning at a heritage attraction: a case study of Discovery as a media product. *Tourism Management*, 19: 5–23.

Prideaux, B. (2003), Commodifying Heritage: Loss of Authenticity and Meaning or an Appropriate Response to Difficult Circumstances? *International Journal of Tourism Studies*, 3(1): 1–17.

Raivo, P. (2000) Landscaping the patriotic past: Finnish war landscapes as a national heritage. *Fennia*, 178(1): 139–150.

Schouten, F.F.J. (1995) Improving visitor care in heritage attractions. *Tourism Management*, 16(4): 259–261.

Singh, S., Timothy, D.J. and Dowling, R.K. (eds) (2003) *Tourism in Destination Communities*. Wallingford: CAB International.

Smith, L. (2000) Slave cabin opens at Virginia plantation. *Washington Post*, 8 October: 16.

Tilden, F. (1977) *Interpreting Our Heritage*. Chapel Hill: University of North Carolina Press.

Timothy, D.J. (1997) Tourism and the personal heritage experience. *Annals of Tourism Research*, 34: 751–754.

Timothy, D.J. and Boyd, S.W. (2003) *Heritage Tourism*. Harlow: Prentice Hall.

Tunbridge, J. and Ashworth, G.J. (1996) *Dissonant Heritage: The Management of the Past as a Resource in Conflict*. Chichester: Wiley.

Worden, N. (1997) Contesting heritage in a South African city: Cape Town. In B.J. Shaw and R. Jones (eds) *Contested Urban Heritage: Voices from the Periphery*, pp. 31–61. Aldershot: Ashgate.

Part One
Authenticity – the Search for the Real

Developing a Framework for Indicators of Authenticity: The Place and Space of Cultural and Heritage Tourism

Tazim Jamal and Steve Hill

Introduction

At an international conference where a portion of this paper was presented in July 2002, a tourism scholar commented, upon hearing what the talk was to be about, that "authenticity is a spent issue" in tourism studies. But a social events brochure enclosed in the conference materials advertised a night trip in an "authentic paddle-wheeler" along the wide river that wound its way past the conference site in Brisbane (Australia). A few days later, a visit to the Tjapukai Aboriginal Cultural Park near Cairns (Australia) revealed a state-of-the-art facility where technology and tradition are woven seamlessly together to provide both a hands-on and visual cornucopia of cultural experiences. Authenticity, as one of the site's administrators said, is a combination of education and entertainment because tourists found education alone boring. Interestingly, printed on the admission ticket stub to the center alongside other information was the following:

WE SELL AUTHENTIC
ABORIGINAL ART
SUPPORT OUR CULTURE

So perhaps for some practitioners authenticity is not a spent issue. Neither is it so in the academic literature on tourism studies, where the concept's substantial role in the discipline has been noted by various scholars (e.g., Hughes, 1995; Uriely, 1997; Wang, 2000). Today, the issues attached to this concept extend urgently into the realm of cultural and heritage tourism. Today's social world is marked by the transformation of destinations and cultures worldwide due to highly mobile capital, labor and technology flows, as well as mobile populations (Urry, 2000). Understanding the tourist's perceptions and experience of objects, events and their properties, as well as understanding the role of the private and public sectors in the packaging and marketing of tourism attractions and destinations, is essential to responsible development and management of tourism. Whether explicitly or implicitly, the notion of authenticity is intricately entwined in this endeavor and yet, while a number of scholars have made key contributions to this study area, authenticity appears to remain an ill-defined and puzzling concept.

This paper therefore has a dual objective: (1) to examine the range of meanings that constitute researchers' understandings of "authenticity" in tourism, and (2) to compile a framework for categorizing various dimensions and aspects of authenticity from which useful management indicators might be developed. The overall aim of the framework and related discussion is to assist tourism managers and cultural groups to better understand and manage (1) the meaning of authenticity in cultural and heritage attractions, particularly with respect to how their own interpretation influences how the concept is described, studied, and used, (2) the role of place and space in the "authenticity" of the object, event or experience in tourism, and (3) the politics of authenticity, as related to the politics of identity and belonging in cultural and heritage places and spaces. By understanding how the general framework applies to specific sites and situations, both managers and scholars may develop effective indicators for monitoring and managing the historicizing, marketing and display of cultural objects, sites and destinations. It is not the purpose of this paper to present a single definition of authenticity, but rather to examine some of the meanings, dimensions and aspects associated with the term. Similarly, the framework does not intend to objectify or essentialize the notion of authenticity, or subvert the politically contested terrain in which it plays out. It is aimed to assist managers and scholars to develop effective indicators for monitoring and managing cultural objects, sites and destinations.

This task commences in the next section with a brief critique of tourism research, in relation to the assumptions associated with this term. The subsequent section draws upon this to propose a framework that responds to the typology of authenticity discussed by Wang (2000) and to the larger body of scholarship on authenticity. This framework is intended to help organize the task of developing indicators of authenticity in heritage-based areas and cultural destinations. The framework is then illustrated through examination of a range of indicators researchers have discussed, either explicitly or implicitly in various studies, as well as an examination of space, place, and "sense of place." An example of cultural centers and areas that are home to an Australian aboriginal people is then provided to illustrate some of the concepts presented through the framework. This example also addresses the politics of authenticity, as related to identity, ethnicity and interpretation of cultural and heritage places and spaces. The paper closes with a summary and comment on the embodied and interactive space in which the politics of authenticity is enacted.

Assumptions About Authenticity

Commencing a discussion on authenticity with MacCannell's seminal contribution, The Tourist (1976, 1989), quickly reveals the complexity of the term and its multiple uses. Tourist settings can be viewed as a continuum, with the first and frontmost region being the one that is most for show purposes ("staged authenticity") and the sixth or backmost region being the one that is most authentic and "motivates touristic consciousness" (MacCannell, 1976, p. 102). The dialectic of authenticity, as he points out, reflects an ontological anxiety of existence, about what we are, what it is that is genuine and objectively true about the human condition. By tying tourism to social structures, the tourist becomes a metaphor for social conditions and a victim of modernity:

The dialectic of authenticity is at the heart of the development of all modern social structure. It is manifest in concerns for ecology and front, in attacks on what is phony, pseudo, tacky, in bad taste, mere show, tawdry and gaudy. These concerns conserve a solidarity at the level of the total society, a collective agreement that reality and truth exist somewhere in society, and that we ought to be trying to find them and refine them.

(MacCannell, 1976, p. 155)

As opposed to contrived, "phony" or "pseudo" in the modern world, there is somewhere an "other" – reality and truth lie somewhere to be discovered. In the quotes above and below, MacCannell appears to identify some potential components of authenticity as well as inauthenticity or spuriousness – the everyday, the tasteless or tacky, the commercial – and a resulting societal discontent. Identifying "real" French homes and "actual" Dutch towns as "true" sights and genuine structure seems to suggest that there must be some essential property or objective quality that qualifies them as such. One might assume from the subjects chosen to illustrate authenticity – an ancient temple or quaint European homes, communities or establishments – that historicity or at least the suggestion of a tie to something in the past, like a previous era or a pre-modern culture or tradition, is part of what qualifies an entity as "authentic" in addition to not being a commercialized artifice (i.e., a copy):

Genuine structure is composed of the values and material culture manifest in the "true" sights. These true sights, real French country homes, actual Dutch towns, the Temple of the Moon at Teotihuacan, the Swiss Alps, are also the source of the spurious elements which are detached from and are mere copies or reminders of the genuine. The dividing line between structure genuine and spurious is the realm of the commercial.

(MacCannell, 1976, p. 155, emphasis original)

In the decades following MacCannell's original book, many other tourism scholars have integrated the notion of authenticity into their work. A review of this literature reveals how researchers' interpretations and assumptions contribute to almost mythical characterizations of authenticity in the tourism literature. In particular, there is a scholarly tendency to (1) ascribe characteristics such as "real" or "true" to an experience, object or event in the tourism domain in a way that suggests an undisclosed normative or personal bias, as well as revealing philosophical assumptions ranging from essentialism to realism, and (2) characterize tourism experiences as "authentic" or "inauthentic" often by implication rather than direct application of the term. The above example is illustrative of the first tendency, while the following example illustrates both. An examination of themed Iowa communities attempting to capitalize on tourism (Engler, 1993) cites The Tourist in its bibliography, but neither MacCannell's work nor the concept of authenticity were discussed in the article. Instead, the article was concerned with "desire to make the imaginary real" (Engler, 1993, p. 8) or sustaining "the priority of a place-rooted community over a tourist-based economy, a commercial fantasy land" (p. 17). It gave numerous suggestions for themes that "connect historical sensibilities" with the contemporary as a way of "restoring community identity" and "promoting the preservation and the historical continuity of the town landscape" while avoiding "the violent modification of the traditional small town landscape and culture" (Engler, 1993, p. 17). Among the suggestions were recycling abandoned farm structures (e.g., silos or grain elevators) into play structures, galleries or other public buildings; creating outdoor art from discarded farm machinery or other out-of-use materials; or constructing a field of abandoned farm windmills and "amusing weather-vanes" (Engler, 1993, p. 17).

Some might question how such contemporary uses of historic objects relate to authenticity, and others might question whether the article is about authenticity at all. Ultimately, however, the article's concerns – historicity, realness, identity, commoditization – are similar to those addressed in articles which more directly address authenticity in tourism. Wang's (2000) comprehensive study of the sociology of tourism and travel identifies and discusses three "types" of authenticity: "objective", "constructive" and "existential." He points out that discussions of authenticity in tourism could benefit by clearly distinguishing two areas of study, that of the authenticity of toured objects (i.e., "objective authenticity") and that of the experience of authenticity. Those coming from a geographical perspective often argue for greater attention to the situated place and space in which the object is experienced (e.g., Crouch, 2000). Increasingly discussed are the politics of identity and ethnicity in relation to authenticity (for example, see Fees, 1996). We build on these works by focusing on the relationship between object and experience as one that is integrally woven into a physical and cultural matrix. Time and space play vital roles here in situating the peoples and places of cultural and heritage destinations. The framework discussed in the next section reflects the importance of understanding the methodological and philosophical assumptions that influence researcher views and understandings of authenticity, as well as comprehending the scope and range of the study of authenticity in the tourism domain. It also emphasizes the fluidity and flexibility of the concept, and is based on the perspective that understanding various dimensions and aspects of authenticity is a more fruitful way of working with the concept than a perspective which considers authenticity to be broken down into discrete categories.

Situated Indicators: Heritage Time, Cultural Space

Leisure and tourism play an important role in shaping the way individuals come to know about the world in new and different ways, whether through liminal experiences or negotiating and reworking identity and meanings through simpler, embodied encounters with objects and events in situated spaces (such as a family holiday to a familiar destination). Value is conferred on the place through past and present activities, memories, knowledge and sociocultural relationships that occur in relation to that time and space. Kirshenblatt-Gimblett (1998) describes three types of time involved in heritage tourism: historic time, heritage time and visitor time. These help to situate the three dimensions of authenticity in the framework shown in Table 1. "Historic time" is the objective point or period in time at which an object or event being judged in terms of its authenticity takes place or took place in the real world (a realist view of authenticity). Historians and scientists are two key groups interested in objectively situating records in historical time; the former attempt to locate

Table 1 Dimensions and Aspects for Addressing Authenticity in Cultural-heritage Tourism*

Aspects of authenticity	Dimensions of authenticity		
	Objective (real)	Constructive (sociopolitical)	Personal (phenomenological)
Time Space	"Historic Time" MacCannell's (1989) "back stage"; real and genuine found in pre-modern locations, outside one's own spurious society. (e.g. sights, markers, 'scientifically' dated material artifacts, "genuine" objects [Bruner, 1994])	"Heritage Time" Production (manufacture) of attraction, community, destination; enclavic space (Edensor, 1998). (social-political landscape influencing nationhood, destination image, sense of place, heritage/historic reconstructions, etc.)	"Resident/Visitor Time" Interactive, performative touristic space; heterogeneous space (Edensor, 1998). (tourists and residents engage in sense-making, narrative and interpretive meaning-making encounters with situated place and contextual space)
Approach	Scientific and positivist paradigms. Realist; essentialist (authenticity is a fixed property of object/event); pre-modern as original/unique	Constructivisim and social constructionism; Postmodernism. Meanings negotiated and emergent; political contest among stakeholders; space is mediated by ideological & technological forces; symbolic and constructed authenticity (Wang, 2000)	Interpretive & narrative approaches. Psychological (perceptions/emotions); Experiential and existence-based, phenomenological, where meanings emerge through the social relations that are situated and embodied in the touristic space (and place)

*Adapted from Jamal and Hill (2002)

this objective moment in the historic record, while archaeologists, geologists and other scientists interested in dating scientific objects of interests will attempt to pinpoint the time, date and spatial location of certain events and objects in the natural world.

In contrast to this realist view of time and the site-specific, physically located space and material objectivity of historical time, "heritage time" is situated within a constructivist or social constructionist approach, where the object, event or site is embedded in an inter-subjective and discursive matrix, i.e., authenticity can emerge through negotiation or be enacted through substantive staging (Cohen, 1988, 1989). The objects and events of a particular time period may be appropriated to construct a story (or a myth) that conforms to the economic, social or political interests in a particular domain (Bruner, 1994). Here, authenticity in the heritage domain has to be evaluated within a sociopolitical context, particularly with respect to the role of public and private sector actions in historic preservation, heritage (re)construction and destination management. The parameters of examination of the constructed heritage space include the temporally situated symbolic or "virtual" objects, representations and material artifacts, as well as the people and the narratives of the place. These are all used to inscribe the heritage story in which a heritage plot constructs "heritage time" as the legitimate time frame by which the heritage site or setting is to be identified and interpreted by the visitor. Thus time, as much as space, becomes an important aspect of the contested narratives of heritage.

Finally, "visitor time" might be thought of as a transcendence of time. The tourist is aware that an event took place in another time, but also is aware of that moment's importance in relation to the tourist's own life, so that the experiential moment can be simultaneously in the past, present and even future. Of importance here to the notion of being a heritage tourist is the characteristic of time as something experienced by the visitor as being continuous from the past into the present (and future). This allows the tourist to evaluate the authenticity of a heritage attraction or the authenticity of a re-enacted site/object/event against various dimensions, including how well the sight or site being presented to the visitor represents the original sight or site. Note here that the focus of this aspect of authenticity is that of the experience of the visitor, which is discussed in Wang (2000) under "existential authenticity."

What is less clearly expressed in discussions about authenticity is the importance of the personal dimension in situating the other object-related and sociopolitical dimensions of the authenticity framework (Table 1). Meanings about touristic spaces, Lanfant (1995, p. 36) pointed out, lie in the "eye of the beholder." This requires some clarification, however. All that is objective, such as the "real" objects in the destination space, take on meaning in relation to the person, but meaning is not merely a bunch of social constructs derived through symbolic and social interaction. It involves activities of sense-making and identity-building through phenomenological encounters of the self in the destination space. Embodied existence and meaning-making constitute the "lived experience" of those who inhabit lived spaces for whatever period of liminal or extended time (Berger & Luckmann, 1967; Heidegger, 1996). This personal dimension includes visitors as well as those who live in the destination and work at the attraction; both interact with the objects and events of the destination space, and with each other over a particular moment or period in time. For cultural and heritage tourism, the dimension of "personal authenticity" (Table 1) has to include residents and other local participants since their stories and their lived existence are often woven into those of the tourists through narrative encounters and interactions in that lived cultural place. These storied existences are embedded within a wider geographical, bioregional space (Cheney, 1989; Jamal & Hill, 2002) that is also sociopolitical and negotiated (Cohen, 1988). Hence, such cultural sites are dynamic and performative, reinforcing and constituting personal and collective identity through narrative encounters and experiences with the objects in that destination place and space.

Indicators for Understanding Authenticity

The dimensions and aspects of authenticity outlined in the framework in Table 1 and discussed above reveal complex interrelationships between the objects, places and spaces of tourist destinations. While they may be viewed as always evolving, incomplete and partial, developing indicators for identifying and understanding authenticity as related to heritage and culture may be helpful to the challenging task of destination management and historic preservation. The notion of sense of place is particularly important to clarify here, for it requires a paradigm shift away from traditional conceptualizations of objective and apolitical views, towards showing the varied notions of space and the political concept of place as it plays out in identity, heritage and the "lived experience" of both tourists and residents. This has important implications for planning and marketing (e.g. with respect to the politics of destination image), since a destination's sense of place is

not one that is static and objective, but is one that is constructed, contested and lived within a performative space. The examples provided in Table 2 draw upon studies that either sought to assess authenticity directly through measurable indicators or less directly by emphasizing actions and activities that aimed to provide a meaningful cultural or heritage-based experience, or place-based identity. Accompanying the table is a discussion of the studies cited.

The importance of place relative to personal authenticity is reflected in Table 2, which attempts to identify indicators of place and "placeness" or a sense of place, as related to the personalized and situated use of space and objects or events within the destination area. Place, as Crouch (2000) notes, is negotiated socially – people define identities, friendships, cultural relationships through embodied encounters with other people and objects in spaces that then become places of memory and knowledge. Hence, three distinct dimensions for developing authenticity indicators (see Table 2) are the object, the experience and the in-between space and time in which these are located, a socially and politically constructed space (as noted in Table 1). Several examples from the literature reveal a range of indicators that may be helpfully applied to the notion of authenticity in cultural and heritage based destinations.

Moscardo and Pearce (1986) conduct a useful study using concrete examples of potentially authentic or inauthentic objects. Elements they examined with respect to authenticity included such categories as activities and demonstrations, buildings, people working in a town, overall setting, craftspeople, shops and refreshment areas, and steam equipment and other machinery. Technically, such items could be evaluated scientifically and categorized in Table 2 as part of the

Table 2 Developing Indicators of Authenticity: Some Topic Areas and Considerations

Topic area	Dimensions of authenticity		
	Objective (real)	Constructed (sociopolitical)	Personal (phenomenological)
Performative spaces and the politics of cultural sites	Buildings, machinery, demonstrations, cooking, crafts in heritage theme park (Moscardo & Pearce, 1986)	Experience theatre (Interpretation of aboriginal culture and history), enclavic spaces (Edensor, 1998, cited in Spark, 2002)	Performative and lived experience of identity, heritage and multiculturalism (Bruner, 1994; Kirshenblatt-Gimblett, 1998), heterogeneous spaces (Edensor, 1998)
Crafts purchased by Midwest tourists (Littrells, 1993); Ethnic art (Cohen, 1988)	Production technique; clearly identifiable origin; links to past in design, material, technique (Littrell et al., 1993)	Constructing self and the other's identity through 'substantive staging' and 'emergent authenticity' (Cohen, 1988), illustrating how meanings of authenticity change over time	Appealing or useful at home (Littrell et al., 1993)
San Angel Inns (Salamone, 1997)	Typical dress; elegant dress; elegant furnishings; Mexican high cuisine	Water ride through representation of three historic periods	Atmosphere perceived as refined, elegant
"Third Places" (Oldenburg, 1989)	Cars have not defeated pedestrians; conversation as main activity; plenty of places to sit; regular hours and appearance/attendance of patrons; accessible/accommodating	Relationships appropriate to realm of experience; everyone welcome; neutral ground; social levelers; playful mood reigns	Place is considered: (a) "home away from home," (b) different from home/work; (c) often plain or homely
The "geographical imagination" (Ryden, 1993)	Roadside markers as repositories of geographical meaning	The construction of destination image in relation to placeness, sense of place	Perceived mystery, dimension, depth to stimulate geographic imagination
Country music (Jensen, 1998)	Rural origins; stylized sets; cowboy hats/other suitable clothing; crowded & casual dances, fairs, outdoor concerts	"folksy" interviews/public events	Artists, concerts seen as: heartfelt, spontaneous, accessible
Living/working space	Warm colors; presence of old people; ample light; proximity to parks (Hiss, 1990) Natural light; geophysical energy; feng shui (Gallagher, 1993).	Contested use of sacred places, sites and artifacts; appropriation of public spaces by competing interests	Individual emotional/physiological reactions to light, energy (Gallagher, 1993); experience with feng shui (Gallagher, 1993)

objective aspect of authenticity. Noting that such objective elements as the buildings, machinery and activities had to be substantially reconstructed, thus rendering them inauthentic in objective terms, the researchers determined that visitors still found their experience to be authentic – perceptions that reflected meanings of "personal authenticity" for individual tourists (see Table 2).

Multiple dimensions of authenticity can be identified in Salamone's (1997) study of cultural and heritage negotiations through the hospitality space of Mexican inns. The original San Angel Inn in Mexico City is "original" because it stresses the romance and dignity of Old Mexico, efficiency and courtesy of service, and knowledge of when to allow visitors to linger – in a nutshell, a "coherent pattern of elegant and efficient living ... a Mexican variation of the modern good life, solidly based on the virtues of inherited elite status" (Salamone, 1997, p. 318). But the daughter inn also symbolically "romanticizes Mexico's past though imparting a message of classical Mexico's great achievements, one that combats stereotypes in a spirit of old-fashioned cultural pluralism" (Salamone, 1997, p. 319). Specifically, it integrates elements of "Ballet Folklorico" dress worn by wait staff, Mexican high cuisine (as opposed to a greater emphasis on American and Europeans variations in the Mexico City inn), and incorporation of a water ride that passes through exhibits focused on pre-Columbian, Spanish colonial, and modern Mexican culture (Salamone, 1997, p. 316). Here is an example by which the past is appropriated into the present as 'heritage' (Lowenthal, 1998), and provides a good example of the constructed aspect of authenticity in Table 2. But one can also see that each inn depends on a mixture of objective

actions or items (i.e., response time to requests, quality of furnishings, colorful dress), constructed presentations of history or social mores and status, and tourists' personal reactions to various elements of the inns' presentations. In other words, all three dimensions of authenticity come into effect in each inn.

Littrell, Anderson and Brown (1993), in their examination of what made crafts authentic for tourists, also developed a number of indicators. Focused on what they called the "real research question" of what characteristics authentic crafts possess, they found the answer varied according to tourist types. Some people needed external criteria (aesthetics, production techniques, or clearly identifiable reference of authenticity such as time/place of manufacture); others used internal criteria, such as whether crafts are appealing or useful when they arrive home. For some buyers, crafts must have links to the past in design, materials, technique, or content; in other situations, tourists are content with changing techniques as long as high quality materials and techniques are used. Other criteria related to authenticity were total number produced (with smaller numbers preferred), uniqueness to region, and whether crafts were made in new or different ways. "Active outdoor" tourists preferred functionality while "urban entertainment" tourists wanted a good shopping experience and viewing of craftmaking. "Arts, ethnic and people" tourists wanted high quality process and materials (Littrell *et al.*, 1993, p. 212). Here, it is clear that the authenticity of the crafts is being evaluated by touristic perceptions, an aspect of personal authenticity where meaning-making and identity-building are of paramount importance rather than scientific study and objective dimensions of authenticity (though they play a role, of course).

Issues of Place and Placeness

Since place and placeness, i.e., sense of place, are important to all three dimensions of authenticity, we focus the rest of Table 2 and discussion on this aspect. The meaning of "place" was noted earlier with respect to the work of Engler (1993). Other studies that have specifically examined the changing "sense of place" in tourism destinations include an analysis of impacts of gambling in small communities (Stokowski, 1990), and a look at social transformations in the Saariselkä tourism region in Finnish Lapland (Saarinen, 1998), as well as works by Dahles (1998) and Teo and Yeoh (1997). These reveal that the concern with authenticity in tourism destinations like these is also a concern with place identity. A number of elements of authenticity found in a range of literature related to tourism and place identity are thus listed in Table 2. Additionally, Table 2 includes examples that were identified as being about place, sense of place or placeness. Although definitions for place, sense of place and placeness vary, the three terms are used interchangeably in this paper because they deal very similarly with issues relevant to discussions of authenticity in these settings (including uniqueness, desirable experiences, history and heritage).

For instance, Dahles (1998), after analyzing Amsterdam's image as a tourist destination, recommended reshaping its image to one of a city with unique artistic and other related cultural and historic offerings, along with a celebration of its status as a meeting place with "a variety of cultural flows ... [a] sense of place ... established by a sense of the interrelation of local, national and global cultural products, mediated through a process of experiencing cultural practices by tourists" (Dahles, 1998, p. 66). Components

of authenticity in Amsterdam include a wide range of historic and modern offerings from art to food, with elements of the objective, the constructed and the personal included as noted in Table 2. This article is useful in pointing out an emphasis on different places themselves as a component of an overarching sense of place, a constantly evolving culture of cultures. It suggests that place authenticity is tied closely to sociopolitical global and spatial characteristics. The authenticity of a heritage site or place, we argue, should be examined within the broader context in which individual and site-specific places are embedded. The analysis should include, as noted earlier, the range of stakeholder interests that influence how places are constructed and positioned for experience (and consumption) by the viewing public.

Among well-known works about place is also The Great Good Place (Oldenburg, 1989), a sociological look at "third places" that received both ample scholarly attention and some commercial success. Third places, the "great good places" where citizens can gather and put aside their concerns about both work and home, are presented as an endangered type of place, but one that, with effort, can be rejuvenated or otherwise encouraged. Oldenburg's work is also useful because it is explicit in defining the characteristics that make good public places and spaces, like cafes, coffee shops, community centers, beauty parlors, general stores, bars or other "hangouts." The initial elements for such areas are that everyone is welcome and there are plenty of places to sit and commune with others. Cars have not "defeated" pedestrians, and relationships that are appropriate to the third place's "realm of experience" and democratic sensibilities are built and encouraged. These and other critical elements (thirteen in all, according to Oldenburg) are listed in

Table 2, as a reminder that such diminishing public spaces (in the face of increasing urbanization, globalization and corporatization) are cultural, perhaps even sacred, spaces in urban, industrialized centers and regions. Ensuring the survivability and use of such cultural spaces for the well-being of the local community is an important factor in 'sustainable tourism development'.

Ryden (1993), in his study of both oral folk narratives and written narratives pertaining to place, was concerned with elements of mystery, dimension and depth. Using oral stories collected in an Idaho mining district, as well as written works he termed "essays of place," he examined the ways people used words to give expression to significant meaning in the eyes of inhabitants. Yet these elements of mystery, dimension and depth are found in many ways, and one example Ryden cited is a roadside sign and granite marker at the entrance to a small park in the center of a New England village. Saying simply, "Adamsville/Rhode Island/1675," the sign raised for Ryden many questions about the ages of the buildings around him, what life was like in 1675, how the buildings in the village looked then, who the "Adams" in Adamsville was, and what exactly happened there. Although the only significant event detailed on the marker turns out to be development of the Rhode Island Red breed of poultry, an amused Ryden (1993, p. 7) noted that he had already enjoyed a "stimulant to the geographical imagination" that caused him to look around and "rebuild the countryside with landscapes of centuries gone by." This was because the park, deliberately set off from the rest of the village and calling attention to itself as a repository of geographical meaning, can color the view of the place by people who stop to take a closer look. Here, the experience of the larger situated space of the village has already commenced with a stop at a small touristic place (site) within it, i.e., the visit to a touristic attraction (the park) whose historic marker is an indicator and constructor of heritage (see also Lowenthal, 1998).

Intangible Contributors to Sense of Place and Authenticity

The above examples illustrate that the objects of leisure and tourism are encountered in many different ways by the cultural and heritage tourist, such as with the intangible and tangible indicators of place. Crouch (2000, p. 63) states these encounters may be with "other people, material space, with one's imagination, ideas, metaphors of place, of leisure and tourism, of nature and of the city. These encounters may with memory and people and places in other parts of one's life." Cultural and heritage places and spaces, like time, are always 'in the making' through the meaning constructing and participatory activities that occur within them, generating a variety of personal, heritage and identity relationships including sense of ownership or emotional attachment, empowerment, value, and feeling (Crouch, 2000, p. 65). The "sociopolitical" dimension of authenticity in Table 2 reflects indicators for discerning how personal and collective identities are negotiated through interaction with the material and symbolic cultures of that place and space. For example, Cohen's (1988) study of the Hmong of Cambodia showed how they departed from traditional symbols in their embroidery to depict more recent and difficult events in their history while still using traditional methods to produce their embroidery. This has also been considered authentic even though it is a new and evolving cultural expression. Hence, this indicator can be developed under a factor called "emergent authenticity" (Cohen, 1988, p. 380).

The above examples show that place, placeness, and sense of place, like authenticity, cover a spectrum from objects, events and experience, all of which are generally interrelated within a performance-based touristic space (Edensor, 1998) that shapes individual, collective as well as place-based identities. Consider, for instance the role of music in place identity, illustrated here by an examination of "Nashville sound" (Jensen, 1998). Identified with a specific city, Nashville sound is also representative of both a real and imagined landscape, the "country" of country music (Jensen, 1998). According to Jensen, key elements or "markers" in establishing country music authenticity are rural origins, stylized sets, seemingly spontaneous performance, accessible performers and heartfelt songs. Among the indicators of these elements are such routine accoutrements or activities as cowboy hats, western shirts, overalls and other suitable clothing; performers "dropping by" to perform with their friends in concert; appearances at dances, fairs, benefits and outdoor concerts that are crowded and casual; and "folksy" interviews and other publicity events. In this example, the experience to be considered is not only that of the tourists, but also that of the performers in the country music event, and the performer-tourists. Moreover, their experience is based closely on their situated activities within the specific place of the event and the overall space of the town, which is also a performative one – the town comes into being for the visitor through the activities, knowledge and interactions of the tourist with the geo-politically defined and, culturally situated, social concept called "Nashville." Jensen's (1998) study, although firmly rooted in media criticism and communication studies, has much in common with sociological and cultural studies of tourism (see Dann, 2002). It is, foremost and expressly,

an analysis of country music's authenticity and commercialization, both of which are crucial notions in MacCannell's original work. The object of Jensen's study is a product of Nashville, a place which is an important tourism destination in itself. Although it is neither stated as a study of place or tourism, Jensen's work is clearly related to both and thus serves as an appropriate vehicle for ideas one might apply to analysis of touristic authenticity.

Two other interesting works deserve a brief mention here, since they contribute tangible indicators to studying how "sense of place" may be enacted in cultural and heritage sites, particularly with respect to creating a suitable mood or ambiance related to that attraction. Hiss (1990) focused his work around a sense he calls "simultaneous perception," an ability to recognize and react to many stimuli from the environment at once. He cited a study in Berkeley, California, that identified 253 factors, including warm colors, the presence of many elderly people, and proximity of parks or open spaces as physical factors people react to positively when they themselves are in a place. Besides factors such as the construction of buildings and spaces around them (e.g., or the layout of natural areas), the use of light for creating an appropriate mood is an especially important consideration in this study. Gallagher (1993), like Hiss, spent a great deal of time examining the physical and emotional responses of humans to light or lack thereof, including tendencies toward depression or other disorders when natural light is in short supply. Gallagher also noted the presence of subtle geophysical energies that produce such phenomena as the "Marfa lights" of west Texas, as well as other effects that make places "sacred" to visitors, and devoted a chapter to the Asian art of feng shui and other practices that focus on positive or negative stimuli from objects in an environment (for instance, a picture that one sees when first entering a home). It is the perceiving and experiencing of these objective elements that locate the visitor-object relationship within the phenomenological dimension of personal authenticity in Table 2.

The range of elements discussed here is not meant to be comprehensive, but rather a partial look that illustrates how a range of concepts and studies related directly or indirectly to sense of place might contribute to developing indicators of authenticity for cultural and heritage attractions. Some of the concepts are almost as abstract as the notion of place or authenticity; for instance, the concept of sacred places, and notions of mystery, dimension and depth (Ryden, 1993). Despite this abstraction, they can be used as guideposts for developing more solid indicators or easily comprehended, measurable objects or actions, such as the village marker that raised questions about history for a traveler. Understanding the interactions between object and experience in the touristic place may help establish indicators of those micro-level characteristics that produce a sense of the sacred, of mystery, dimension, depth, and uniqueness to the individual. The place is always situated and interactive, for the experience is always personal and embodied. At the same time, situating these within a macro-level sociopolitical matrix reveals spatially embedded and contested discourses that make up the politics of authenticity. The following example illustrates this in the context of Tables 1 and 2, drawing upon our experience of aboriginal cultural sites in Australia.

The Politics of Authenticity: Aboriginal Cultural Areas

Aboriginal cultural sites like the Dreamtime Cultural Centre and Tjapukai Aboriginal Cultural Park in Queensland, the Brambuk living cultural centre in Victoria and the Minnumurra Rainforest Centre located in Budaroo National Park, New South Wales, offer valuable insights into the multidimensional aspects of cultural and heritage tourism management. This is particularly true for areas such as these where indigenous people hold significant moral claim over the stewardship of a land struggling to re-create individual, social and national identities. Here, as in many other countries, the influences of postcolonialism, globalization and multiculturalism are reshaping the economic, natural and cultural landscapes. Within these contested domains, struggles for both economic and cultural sustainability are closely related to the politics of authenticity and reveal two distinctive uses of place and space: (i) cultural sites as pragmatic sites that act as educational, art and commercial areas, and (ii) indigenous sites as contested sites of identity, legitimacy and belonging.

Places of Entertainment, Education and Commerce

Cultural Centers like the Dreamtime Cultural Centre (located on the northern outskirts of Rockhampton) and Tjapukai Aboriginal Cultural Park (located just outside of Cairns) are embedded within a larger Aboriginal landscape of sacred sites and cultural histories. The Dreamtime Cultural Centre (DCC) claims unique appeal by offering insights into both Aboriginal and Torres Strait Islander culture, with a management structure comprised of traditional people involved in a stand-alone venture where belief, knowledge and culture are shared with a paying public. A management brochure notes that one of the centre's aim is "to educate people in

Aboriginal and Torres Strait Islander culture while entertaining them." It also states that DCC is "the largest Cultural Centre of its type providing authentic and historically relevant displays to the local and wider tourist communities."[1] The Tjapukai Aboriginal Cultural Park (abbreviated TACP here) is also considered integral to protecting and preserving the culture of the Tjapukai people. As young people were brought together to participate at the site, the teaching of the Tjapukai language grew and the site became a locus for enabling cultural flourishing in the area.

The centre is 51% owned by the Tjapukai, and control over cultural education and commercial aspects related to their culture (e.g. the content and presentation of day and night shows at the site, sale of culturally determined souvenir within the Tjapukai Tribal Area in which TACP was located) is strictly in the hands of the Tjapukai elders. Cultural education and profit went hand-in-hand at this site, as evident from the very well-organized, state-of-the-art displays, choreography and facilities. A management representative summarized this well, saying that TACP was "a tremendous combination of theatre and authenticity", where cultural education and technology combined to provide a personal experience of authenticity, reinforced by the objective authenticity of the cultural artifacts, the personalized outdoor show at the Tjapukai Dance Theatre (set amidst the lush tropical landscape), the 'virtual' authenticity of the dreaming show held in the Creation Theatre, and the moving (and disturbing) film shown in the History Theatre towards the end of the organized tour. The words of a Tjapukai participant summarize a key cultural objective of the centre; she was

not angry about the historical genocide of her people, but said she wanted the visitors to understand and appreciate the Tjapukai culture, i.e., know that it is alive, know what's happened to it historically, and be able to respect it today. In this sense, such cultural sites act as places and spaces of "living heritage", enabling political survival and ethnic identity to flourish through sometimes deeply personal narratives of the site, its objects, its history and its people.

TAJC, however, has another story to share if one took a pleasant gondola ride from a rail operation located adjacent to TAJC up to the little hill town of Kuranda, nestles in the rugged tropical backdrop of the TAJC. One of the two interpretive stops provided us with a self-guided trail whose spectacular viewpoints were marked by narrative of some of the sacred sites and myths that imbue the Tjapukai landscape with rich meanings. Standing at the edge of a spectacular escarpment and gorge offers a different embodied experience of the natural landscape and its culturally constructed meanings than the carefully structured and timed tour of the TAJC. How aboriginal places and spaces are structured and interpreted have important consequences for the authenticity of experience, the appreciation of the intangible (e.g., the sacred), and the protection of cultural-heritage. Spark (2002) presents an instructive example of how time and space evolved at the Brambuk living cultural centre in Victoria. At one time, space was more heterogeneous (Edensor, 1998), allowing visitors more sensual encounters through touching, handling and feeling the tools, and pacing themselves, moving at their own time and mood. Spark's (2002) study indicates that as demands for economic rationalism

---

[1]Nature and History of Dreamtime Cultural Centre. *See section entitled: "Contributions to the development of tourism in Queensland/Australia".*

took over, the "soft control" of the tourism industry and state control of funds replaced the more equivocal and juxtaposing display with a more enclavic space (Edensor, 1998) of controlled movement and commercialization. Hence, in these living places of ethnic survival, aboriginal cultural identity is contested, shared and nurtured through the visible and political spaces of heritage tourist attractions.

Contested sites of Identity and Belonging

The social significance of heritage lies in its association with identity: it is fundamental in helping individuals, communities, and nations define who they are, both themselves and to outsiders.

(Sofield, 2001, p. 260)

The Tjapukai's cultural center is a "Park" (the TACP), an enclosed place producing a tourism experience through both "heterogeneous" and "enclavic" spaces. It is a careful balance of powerful experience, some "virtual," some "real," all carefully crafted and structured by theatre experts working closely with the indigenous people. The carefully controlled tourist movement, seating, and structuring of stopping places along the monitored and directed tour from one stop to another are softly authenticated by heterogeneous experiences at the stopping stations and the overall location of the park within traditionally Tjapukai land. Interpretation at such sites forms an important aspect of how the authenticity of the aboriginal culture is conveyed. Staiff *et al.* (2002) studied the politics of interpreting postcolonial and aboriginal cultural history within protected areas where environmental education and interpretation are subject to scientific management. They offer five critical questions for interpretation praxis that exhibit potential for indicator

development under the social/political dimension of "constructed authenticity" (Table 1 and 2): Who are the owners/custodians of the objects, collections, and natural areas? How are these objects or collections or landscapes represented or displayed? Who speaks for them? What is spoken and why? Who is looking at the objects or landscapes and who is listening to these messages?

The questions posed above illustrate the politics of authenticity that run through all the dimensions of authenticity in cultural sites like the ones noted above. A sustainability-based tourism approach would suggest that both scientific and traditional knowledge should be considered in discussions of the objective authenticity and preservation of artifacts and collections, which can lead to disputes over the legitimacy and accuracy of various knowledge forms. What to represent to the tourist – and how – is also a political task of choosing what aspects of the culture or heritage will be told and "preserved" or protected. For heritage site managers, providing a high quality, satisfactory experience also becomes a political task of choosing appropriate combinations of entertainment and education. A key indicator here might be the extent of local involvement, illustrated by the ability to own, control and interpret the cultural objects, collections and landscapes being shared with the visitors. Identifying and involving those who stand to be most impacted by the heritage decisions being made is an essential aspect of indicator development pertaining to stakeholder interests. In other words, the indicators must be able to help the locals and the managers to gauge the economic, social and cultural costs and benefits of putting their culture and heritage on display. The politics of authenticity, as Fees (1996) showed in his study of Campden, UK, is also the politics of identity and the politics of ethnicity. Good indicators that address these less tangible but crucial issues act as useful reminders for ensuring the well-being and sustainability of local communities, their public and private spaces, events, customs and traditions within the sociopolitical stage of the global tourism system.

Conclusion

The framework suggested by the typology (Table 1) and the listing of characteristic elements or indicators of authenticity under such a framework (Table 2) illustrate the broad range of meanings that have been associated with authenticity in tourism. A large and varied collection of elements needs to be considered in developing practical indicators of the places, spaces and experiences of authenticity, as discussed above. In addition to object-related authenticity, the sociopolitical and personal dimensions are crucial dimensions of the framework summarized in Table 1. The framework in Table 1 also includes spatial and temporal aspects as being integral to the study of authenticity and the development of indicators related to heritage and culture in tourism. Cultural and heritage areas come into being through the meaning-making activities of people interacting with objects, events and activities within historically, politically and culturally defined destination areas. This interactive experience includes residents and visitors engaging with the place and with each other through temporally and spatially influenced narratives.

Facilitating embodied encounters and personal interactions is particularly helpful in developing individual and collective meanings and memories, personal identities and narrative understandings of cultural heritage in

relation to self and the other. Oldenburg's third places are predicated on the relationships of regulars in those places (1989). Hetherington (1989) and Hiss (1990) recognize the value of public places for developing community-based and social identities, such as through the practices of people gathering to watch others or take pictures of their friends in front of unique art or other structures. Redfoot (1984), by championing tourists who seek relationship-building opportunities with family and friends above so-called "authentic" historic or entertainment experiences, is clearly in line with such place-based scholars who recognize the importance of situating people in embodied relationships with place and space.

Of critical importance in the development of indicators are the politics of representation in authenticity, particularly in cultural and heritage sites and attractions (Richter, 1999). Even at the community level, sense of place is a contested notion such as where the differing objectives of newcomers versus long-term residents create different meanings for what constitutes authenticity in a town influenced by modernization and change (Fees, 1996). In Aboriginal cultural sites like the Tjapukai Aboriginal Cultural Park, the Brambuk living cultural centre (Spark, 2002) and the Minnumurra Rainforest Centre located in Budaroo National Park, Australia (Staiff et al., 2002), the politics of authenticity are an even more important consideration for it is related directly to the survival and well-being of these groups. As a TACP member said of her people, their cultural park is a way by which the Tjapukai can express an important need: they want the world to know that they are a living culture, not a dead one as some might assume. Having control over their heritage and over the commodification and commercialization of their material and symbolic culture is integral to their ethnicity and identity (see Lanfant *et al.*, 1995; Swain, 2001). The cultivation of "living heritage" through living spaces, places and sites like the ones mentioned above is vital to the contested politics of ethnicity, identity and nationhood in Australia. This dynamically constitutive nature of heritage (both past and living) is a similarly important consideration for other national and public spaces characterized by emergent economies, globalizing cultures and hybrid populations.

As natural and cultural sites continue to be brought in to the global stage of a growing international travel and tourism industry, developing a comprehensive set of objective, sociocultural and experience-based indicators to assess and ensure the sustainability of these global heritages may emerge to become a pressing task. By understanding the philosophical and methodological assumptions being made about authenticity, researchers and practitioners may be able to develop effective frameworks for the study of authenticity (as commenced in Table 1), and for the management of heritage tourism (as illustrated for indicator development in Table 2). Moreover, as Tables 1 and 2 indicate, understanding and managing the "authenticity" of tourist objects, sites, events and experiences involves dealing with the politics of authenticity, i.e., issues of identity, place, space, representation, nationhood, and interpretation. This includes addressing the embodied encounters and meaning-making activities by which cultural objects, places and spaces are negotiated through the situated practices of inhabitants and visitors. By understanding the dynamic relationships between these various elements, it may be possible to develop useful strategies and approaches for monitoring the development, marketing, and protection of local to global cultural heritages. The framework in

Table 1 and examples in Table 2 are intended to assist with the task of constructing multi-dimensional indicators for heritage and cultural tourism management, based on the recognition that these are not three separate dimensions but are integrated through interactive space, embodied time and situated narratives within a local-global, social-political industry of travel and tourism.

References

Berger, P. & Luckmann, T. (1967). *The Social Construction of Reality.* Penguin Books, London.

Bruner, E. (1994). Abraham Lincoln as authentic reproduction: a critique of postmodernism. *American Anthropologist*, 96(2), 397–415.

Cheney, J. (1989). Postmodern environmental ethics: ethics as bioregional narrative. *Environmental Ethics*, Summer, 11, 117–134.

Cohen, E. (1989). Primitive and remote: Hill trekking in Thailand. *Annals of Tourism Research*, 16, 30–61.

Cohen, E. (1988). Authenticity and commodification in tourism. *Annals of Tourism Research*, 15, 371–386.

Crouch, D. (2000). Places around us: embodied lay geographies in leisure and tourism. *Leisure Studies*, 19, 63–76.

Dahles, H. (1998). Redefining Amsterdam as a tourist destination. *Annals of Tourism Research*, 25, 55–69.

Dann, G. (ed) (2002). *The tourist as a metaphor of the social world.* CAB International, Wallingford, UK.

Edensor, T. (1998). *Tourists at the Taj: Performance and Meaning at a Symbolic Site.* Routledge, London.

Engler, M. (1993). Drive-thru history: Theme towns in Iowa. *Landscape*, 32, 8–18.

Fees, C. (1996). Tourism and the politics of authenticity in a North Cotswold town. In T. Selwyn (ed), *The tourist image: Myths and myth making in tourism.* John Wiley & Sons, New York.

Gallagher, W. (1993). *The Power of Place.* Simon & Schuster, New York.

Heidegger, M. (1996). *Being and Time. A translation of Sein und Zeit.* [Translated by Joan Stambaugh.] State University of New York Press, Albany, NY.

Hetherington, A. (1989). Rural tourism development: Finding, preserving and sharing your community's heart and soul. *Pacific Mountain Review*, Fall, 5–8.

Hiss, T. (1990). *The experience of place*. Random House, New York.

Hughes, G. (1995). Authenticity in tourism. *Annals of Tourism Research*, 22, 781–803.

Jamal, T. & Hill, S. (2002). The home and the world; (post)touristic spaces of (in)authenticity? In G. Dann (ed), *The tourist as a metaphor of the social world* (pp. 77–107). CAB International, Wallingford, UK.

Jensen, J. (1998). *Nashville sound: Authenticity, commercialization and country music*. The Country Music Foundation Press and Vanderbilt University Press, Nashville.

Kirshenblatt-Gimblett, B. (1998). *Destination culture: Tourism, museums and heritage*. University of California Press, Berkeley, CA.

Lanfant, M. (1995). International tourism, internationalization and the challenge to identity. In M. Lanfant, J. Allcock & E. Bruner (eds), *International tourism: Identity and change* (pp. 1–43). Sage, London.

Lanfant, M., Allcock, J. & Bruner, E. (eds) (1995). *International tourism: Identity and change. Sage Studies in International Sociology 47*. Sage, London.

Littrell, M., Anderson, L. & Brown, P. (1993). What makes a craft souvenir authentic? *Annals of Tourism Research*, 20, 197–215.

Lowenthal, D. (1998). *The heritage crusade and the spoils of history*. Cambridge University Press, Cambridge, UK.

MacCannell, D. (1976). *The tourist: A new theory of the leisure class*. Schocken Books, New York.

MacCannell, D. (1989). *The tourist: A new theory of the leisure class*. Schocken Books, New York.

Moscardo, G. & Pearce, P. (1986). Historic theme parks: An Australian experience in authenticity. *Annals of Tourism Research*, 13, 467–479.

Oldenburg, R. (1989). *The great good place*. Paragon House, New York.

Redfoot, D. (1984). Touristic authenticity, touristic angst, and modern reality. *Qualitative Sociology*, 7, 291–309.

Richter, L. (1999). The politics of heritage tourism development: Emerging issues for the new millennium.

In D. Pearce & R. Butler (eds), *Contemporary issues in tourism development*. Routledge, London.

Ryden, K. (1993). *Mapping the invisible landscape: Folklore, writing and the sense of place*. The University of Iowa Press, Iowa City.

Saarinen, J. (1998). The social construction of tourist destinations: The process of transformation of the saariselka tourism region in Finnish Lapland. In G. Ringer (ed), *Destinations: Cultural landscapes of tourism*. Routledge, London and New York.

Salamone, F. (1997). Authenticity in tourism: The San Angel Inns. *Annals of Tourism Research*, 24, 305–321.

Sofield, T. (2001). Sustainability and pilgrimage tourism in the Kathmandu Valley of Nepal. In V. Smith & M. Brent (eds), *Hosts and guests revisited: Tourism issues of the 21st century* (pp. 257–274). Cognizant Communication Corporation, New York.

Spark, C. (2002). Brambuk living cultural centre: Indigenous culture and the production of place. *Tourist Studies*, 2(1), 23–42.

Staiff, R., Bushell, R. & Kennedy, P. (2002). Interpretation in national parks: Some critical questions. *Journal of Sustainable Tourism*, 10(2), 97–113.

Stokowski, P. (1990). *Place, meaning and structure in community tourism development: A case study from Central City, Colorado*. Paper presented at the Recreation Trends and Mountain Resort Development Conference, Vail, Co.

Swain, M. B. (2001). Ethnic doll ethics: Tourism research in Southwest China. In V. Smith & M. Brent (eds), Hosts and Guest Revisited: Tourism Issues of the 21st Century (pp. 217–231). Cognizant, New York.

Teo, P. & Yeoh, B. (1997). Remaking local heritage for tourism. *Annals of Tourism Research*, 24, 192–213.

Uriely, N. (1997). Theories of modern and postmodern tourism. *Annals of Tourism Research*, 24, 982–984.

Urry, J. (2000). *Sociology beyond societies: Mobilities for the twenty-first century*. Routledge, London.

Wang, N. (2000). *Tourism and modernity: A sociological analysis*. Pergamon, Amsterdam.

Cultural Landscape Values as a Heritage Tourism Resource

Anna Carr

Introduction

Many natural areas of New Zealand (Aotearoa), particularly national parks, are frequently visited by international and domestic visitors attracted by recreational opportunities and the high quality of the scenic landscapes. Many of these landscape features, primarily mountains, lakes and rivers in natural areas, are of cultural significance to the *tangata whenua*, or local Māori people. *Wahi tapu* are sacred sites of particular importance to Māori and the locations of such areas are often kept secret. Until recently scenic landscapes were dominant features of international tourism marketing campaigns by Tourism New Zealand (TNZ) and various Regional Tourism Organisations (RTOs), with little reference made to cultural values. Increasingly tourism operators and land managers are providing interpretation of the cultural values of such places. This chapter examines how interpretation of cultural landscapes can contribute to the heritage tourism experience, and explores visitor demand for such experiences in New Zealand. The chapter draws on research findings from a study of visitors' experiences of cultural landscapes in the South Island of New Zealand (Carr 2004a, b). Visitors' own perceptions of what constitutes culturally significance sites within New Zealand's landscape are discussed with reference to management considerations for the development of a nature-based cultural heritage tourism experience. Finally, the potential for eco-cultural tourism development is discussed in relation to the findings related to visitor demand for cultural interpretation.

Cultural Landscapes and the Heritage Experience

Tourism researchers have noted a global trend of increasing visitor demand for heritage or cultural tourism experiences (Hall and McArthur 1996; McKercher and du Cros 2002; Smith 2003; Timothy and Boyd 2002). Robinson (1999: 4) suggests that the 'cultural tourist' category possibly applies to some

"50% of the tourism market." McKercher and du Cros (2002: 148–152) identify five different types of cultural tourists ranging from the mass market ('incidental', 'casual' and 'serendipitous' cultural tourists) to niche groups of 'purposeful' or 'sightseeing' cultural tourists. The diversification of indigenous cultural tourism products from 'handcraft, heritage and history' categories, to include a focus on 'habitat' (Smith 1996), has gained momentum with adventure tourism and ecotourism operations, enabling visitors to travel through natural areas with indigenous guides (Ceballos-Lascurain 1987; Butler and Hinch 1996; Hinch 1998) on what can be viewed as 'eco-cultural' experiences.

Such guided interpretation experiences have been regarded as one means of communicating intrinsic links between people and the environment which may 'reveal meanings and relationships' (Tilden 1967: 8). Cultural landscapes are regarded as being human constructions resulting from peoples' relationships to the natural areas within which they live or move. Such landscapes may have significant symbolic meaning for a particular cultural group, or groups, of people (Bourassa 1991; Muir 1999). Internationally, there is increasing acknowledgement of the economic and social significance of cultural and heritage landscapes as tourism resources (Shackley 1998, 2001; Timothy and Boyd 2003). Timothy and Boyd (2003: 9) note that "heritage landscapes traverse a multitude of settings ranging from the natural and pristine to the built-urban and artificial." However, many landscapes of significance to indigenous communities have usually been visited by people who, whilst interested in the scenic or recreational values, may have little awareness of the cultural values for such sites owing to a lack of tangible remains on the landscape. The presence of interpretation, either passive

(for example signage) or active (with guides) can direct visitors' attention to these values. Li (2000: 877) describes one possible outcome of cultural tourism tourist experiences as increasing 'geographical consciousness' through "a discourse of learning that knowledge can be gathered through understanding and collecting differences of 'other'."

The term 'geographical consciousness' has connotations of positive outcomes such as increased awareness of significant local values that may arise from visitors' experiences of 'place', including cultural landscapes. The interpretation of the cultural values of landscapes can serve an educational purpose and provide a heritage experience that is specific to the location in which it occurs (Keelan 1996; Brown 1999; Pfister 2000; Shackley 1998, 2001; Timothy and Boyd 2002). If received positively by visitors, interpretation could assist with sustainability goals through education by increasing visitors' awareness of and respect for cultural values, thus reducing negative visitor impacts (Keelan 1996; Pfister 2000; Staiff et al. 2002; Digance 2003; Hinkson 2003).

Māori Tourism

The 1996 New Zealand Tourism Board (NZTB) International Visitor Survey Findings indicated that 36% of all international visitors to New Zealand are attracted to Māori cultural activities: "the unique culture of the Māori people is a strong and attractive element of our national heritage" (NZTB 1996). Rotorua was, and still is, the destination most associated with Māori by international visitors (Ryan 1997, 1998; Ateljevic and Doorne 2002; Ryan and Pike 2003). The Māori people of Rotorua have a history of tourism involvement extending back to the 1880s and many visitors to the area are attracted by numerous Māori cultural attractions including *hangi*, *kapa haka* (song and dance) performances and existing or recreated traditional villages.

In the mid-1990s, tourism demand for non-commercialized encounters with Māori, away from traditional tourism settings, was predicted to grow, with demand being met by new cultural tourism regions, particularly in the North Island (Cloher 1998; Warren and Taylor 2001). Over the past decade Tourism New Zealand (TNZ), formerly NZTB, has advocated that, alongside natural environments and wilderness areas, there has been an increasing demand for cultural tourism. The 1990s was a period of rapid growth and diversification of the Māori tourism product from traditional cultural based performances based in Rotorua to a wide range of products spanning all sectors of the tourism industry (McIntosh *et al.* 2000; Tourism Strategy Group 2001; Zydaglo *et al.* 2003). Even operations that were not owned, operated or managed by Māori have offered cultural dimensions (usually after extensive consultation with Māori) within the visitor experience. At Te Papa, New Zealand's national museum, guided tours, permanent or short-term displays and an audio visual film, *Blast Back*, introduces visitors to the origins of the country from the Māori perspective, the latter incorporating references to the Creation myth and legend of the Māori god Maui.

Cultural tourism opportunities including operations that enable "learning about Māori mythology" and "tours of a region with a Māori guide" were identified by Van Aalst and Daly's (2002) review of 82 reports and studies concerning cultural tourism in New Zealand. Van Aalst and Daly identified strong demand from cultural tourists with high levels of satisfaction with experiences to various Māori attractions. Other research supports the enduring attraction of Māori culture to international visitors with less demand from domestic visitor markets for traditional Māori tourism products such as cultural performances and marae visits (McIntosh *et al.* 2000; Ateljevic and Doorne 2000; Ryan 2002; Ryan and Pike 2003). At the same time domestic visitors are major segments for some Māori tourism operations (McIntosh *et al.* 2000; Warren and Taylor 2001). Similarly, Pearce and Tan (2004) attribute part of the success of Māori tourism operations in Rotorua to be the "broad appeal by offering a distinctive cultural experience as part of a visit to New Zealand by international visitors, both group and independent" (Pearce and Tan 2004, 232).

The scale of Māori involvement within the tourism sector has been estimated to be over 250 indigenous themed or Māori owned and managed operations nationwide (The Stafford Group 2001; TPK 1998; TNZ 2003a,b). The Indigenous New Zealand website lists 97 Māori tourism products ranging from accommodation and transport to guided walks with a cultural heritage focus (Indigenous New Zealand 2005). TNZ's Three Year Strategic Plan 2003–2006 has one strategic outcome to "Naturally express through the campaign the values of New Zealand's Māori cultural identity" (TNZ 2003a: 3). Many attractions, services and iconic destinations are promoted with images that have accompanying statements about the relationship between Māori and the land. TNZ's promotional activity has recently utilized images of landscape features with cultural significance for Māori, for example Aoraki/Mount Cook, the Moeraki Boulders, Cape Reinga, Milford Sound and Rotorua. Māori involvement with such international tourism promotion has improved, with TNZ employing Māori staff and having Māori members on the governing board.

Since 2004, the Māori Regional Tourism Programme was allocated NZ$1.3 million to assist with the development of thirteen Māori RTOs to support Māori tourism operators throughout the country. Working alongside the Ministry of Tourism, Ministry of Māori Development (Te Puni Kokiri) and TNZ, the Council ensures Māori have a more active role in developing, managing and promoting cultural tourism experiences. At a regional level Māori RTOs such as the Tai Tokerau Tourism Association in Northland are actively promoting the cultural landscape to visitors.

The demand for indigenous cultural heritage in New Zealand is increasingly leading to a number of new nature tourism products providing indigenous perspectives within the format of 'eco-cultural' tourism. Operators are offering new experiences to visitors by integrating cultural experiences within a natural setting. At the local level owner-operators and family-based businesses such as Ulva's Guided Walks (Stewart Island) or Kapiti Alive (Kapiti Island, Wellington) enable visitors to socialise with operators who have ancestral links to landscapes that can be traced through many generations. With respect to cultural landscapes, myths and legends associated with actual locations offer an exotic dimension to contemporary tourists. In the Tai Tokerau (Northland) region two of the main tourist destinations are Te Rerenga Wairua (Cape Reinga), where spirits of Māori depart to the ancestral lands of Hawaii, and Tane Mahuta, New Zealand's largest kauri tree representing Tane, the God of the Forest. Bay of Islands Heritage Tours offers 'Swimming with the Dolphins', an adventure activity where according to the company brochure the tourist is able to hear 'myths and legends relevant to the children of Tangaroa (Māori God of the Sea)'.

Mythology and legends throughout the world link people to their ancestral lands, such narratives forming an important aspect of collective heritage identity and place identity (O'Regan 1990; Prentice 1992; Walker 1992; Uzzell 1996; Prentice and Guerin 1998; Kearsley et al. 1999; Avery 1999; Pfister 2000; Shackley 2001; Timothy and Boyd 2003). Mythology relates, for contemporary Māori, the deeds of their ancestors and explains the traditional view of the formation of the natural world. The association of a myth with a geographical location identifies the spiritual or ancestral significance of a place to the Māori people (Walker 1992). The retelling of a myth provides Māori guides with an opportunity to convey their sense of place (turangawaewae) by informing visitors of their historic, ancestral and spiritual ties with culturally significant areas.

As New Zealand's tourism industry seeks to differentiate itself from competing destinations in the global market there has been acknowledgment that the cultural landscape may offer a truly authentic and unique selling point. A recent Mana magazine article reported George Hickton (Chief Executive of TNZ), commenting on the launch of a nature walk at Te Puia (formerly the New Zealand Māori Arts and Craft Institute in Rotorua), as saying that "The sorts of people Tourism New Zealand is targeting to attract to New Zealand are very interested in Māori culture and are seeking an authentic and genuine exposure to it. Te Puia offers the kind of experience these visitors are looking for" (Mana 2005: 25). Thus, from a commercial perspective, indigenous owned tourism operations providing quality interpretation such as guided walks with a cultural focus are emerging as important contributors to New Zealand's diversifying cultural tourism product.

Non-commercial Interpretation of the Cultural Landscape

The opportunities for visitors to experience Māori cultural values for natural areas or significant landscapes also include formal and informal encounters at non-commercial tourism sites such as interpretive media in national park visitors centres or on-site interpretive panels on walks or tracks. From a management perspective, cultural interpretation has been introduced at natural areas throughout New Zealand for the specific purpose of educating the public and raising visitor awareness of cultural values in each area (Keelan 1996; MacLennan 2000; DOC 2001a, b).

The interpretation of Māori perspectives of the environment is therefore considered a way of strengthening *iwi* (Māori tribe) relationships with traditional resources and historic heritage (O'Regan 1987, 1990; Keelan 1996). Much existing interpretive material tends to provide *iwi* perspectives through the explanation of history, traditional use of natural resources, place names and narration of tribal mythology or legends. The increased use of this *taonga* as subject matter in interpretive material widens the audience from a traditional Māori base to other community members and, consequently, visitors to the areas.

The Department of Conservation (DoC) is the New Zealand government's primary land manager responsible for the protection of natural areas. Other organisations involved in the management of cultural and heritage landscapes of significance to Māori in New Zealand include individual *iwi* organisations;

the New Zealand Historic Places Trust (NZHPT); Nga Whenua Rahui and Nature Heritage Fund; and the Queen Elizabeth the Second National Trust and Office of the Parliamentary Commissioner for the Environment. DoC has been encouraged, through successive policy arising from legislation, to preserve and protect the values held by local Māori using numerous approaches including visitor education or interpretation. Documents such as national park management plans regularly include references to management issues relevant to local *iwi* and *tangata whenua*, including interpretation policies (DOC 2001a, b, 2005). Writing of the need for a Māori dimension in national park interpretation that not only explained about the natural features but also the ancestral links with the land, a *kaumatua* of the Ngāi Tahu *iwi* observed that "above all the tribe has stated its desire to exercise absolute authority in the Māori historical and cultural interpretation of the parks to the public" (O'Regan 1990: 104). DoC has encouraged the active participation of local *iwi* groups in all stages of the interpretation process from initial planning to the actual delivery of the information (Keelan 1996). Since 1987, interpretive material about Māori values and cultural heritage increasingly required *iwi* involvement in the provision of interpretation experiences to maintain the integrity of the culture (O'Regan 1987, 1990; Molloy 1991, 1992; Keelan 1996). At regional offices DoC employs Kaupapa Atawhai managers to inform, liaise and consult with *iwi* to ensure Māori perspectives are considered within DoC policy and management practises. Nevertheless, blank walls have been present at some DoC visitor centres whilst interpretive material awaited consensus from *iwi* representatives as to which aspects of *iwi* heritage (if any) was appropriate for public display (Molloy 1991;

Keelan 1996). In some areas DoC encourages that tourism operators liaise with and integrate local *iwi* values as necessary. Thus both commercial and non-commercial experiences provide visitors with cultural insights into the areas through which they travel.

Visitor Demand for Cultural Landscape Interpretation

Three South Island visitor centres located in areas that are significant to the *tangata whenua* were chosen as sites for research on cultural landscape as a heritage tourism product. Each visitor centre was frequented by international and domestic visitors to the South Island, with estimated annual visitor numbers of approximately 100,000 people. All three sites had interpretive material about the cultural significance of each area to the *tangata whenua*. Ngāi Tahu are the recognised *iwi* of Te Waipounamu, the South Island of New Zealand, their rights being affirmed within the *Ngāi Tahu Settlement Act 1997*. As part of their cultural development policy Ngāi Tahu are very active in management of cultural and heritage resources, in particular the interpretation of such resources (Te Runanga o Ngāi Tahu 2005).

The main study site was the DoC visitor centre located in Aoraki/Mount Cook National Park. Ngāi Tahu have been involved in Aoraki/Mt Cook National Park interpretation delivery with Ngāi Tahu interpreters employed to assist with summer holiday programmes walks and evening talks. The legend of the Māori ancestral god or *tupuna*, Aoraki/Mount Cook, is presented within an audiovisual show for park visitors. The legend is repeated in display panels and a brochure explaining the *iwi* ties to the highest mountain in New Zealand, 'Aoraki/Mount Cook the ancestor of Ngāi Tahu', was pro-

duced by DOC in collaboration with Ngāi Tahu representatives from Arowhenua Rūnanga at the Temuka *marae* (DOC 1999a). An interpretive panel at the Kea Point Track lookout over the Mueller Glacier, a site visited regularly by walkers, recalls another legend explaining the creation of the glaciers and mountain peaks. The second site was the Fiordland National Park DoC visitor centre at Te Anau and the third site was an independent visitor centre at Lake Pukaki near Aoraki/Mt Cook.

Qualitative interviews were conducted with nine *iwi* representatives from Ngāi Tahu, to gain their perspectives of cultural landscape interpretation. Six interviews were conducted with DOC staff regarding management issues at the study sites and 15 visitors were interviewed about their experiences of the cultural values presented in interpretation at the sites. The findings from the interviews contributed to the design of a survey that resulted in 472 eturns. The remainder of this chapter discusses the findings from the research pertaining to visitor expectations of and demand for experiences of cultural landscape in New Zealand.

Research Findings

The majority of respondents (52.1%) were male and the average age of all respondents was between 35 and 44 years old. International visitors ($n = 328$, 69.9%) reflected New Zealand's three main originating regions, with the majority of international visitors being from Australia (16.5%), the United Kingdom (16%) and North America (14%). Respondents were well-educated with 70.5% having had a tertiary education, and 75% held managerial or professional occupations.

Overall, the responses suggested strong support for, or previous experience of, cultural tourism activities, 343 respondents (73%) reporting experiences with other indigenous cultures outside New Zealand. The indigenous cultures encountered most frequently by the respondents, prior to their experiences of Māori culture, were those of Aboriginal Australian ($n = 144$, 41.9%) and Native American Indian/Inuit peoples ($n = 91$, 26.5%).

Respondents were asked whether they had sought out or read information about Māori culture when planning their holiday trip (see Table 1). Only 71 respondents (15%) did not access any information about Māori culture. One hundred and seventy four visitors (37%) had accessed multiple information sources. The media, visitor centres and museums were the most frequently cited sources of information. Brochures and guidebooks were also significant, with the *Lonely Planet* guide being identified by 80 respondents.

Whilst travelling through the country 49% of respondents mentioned that most of the information they encountered about cultural values for the landscape came from their guides, visitor centre/interpreter staff, bus drivers and tour escorts. Most visitors reported the cultural dimensions of landscapes as being incidental to their main purpose for visiting New Zealand; however, Māori culture offered a dimension to the visit that enriched the visitor experience.

Visitor origin was a significant factor in determining the level of interest in learning more about Māori culture. One hundred and seventeen (26%) respondents were 'very interested' and 66 (14%) respondents were 'extremely interested' in future opportunities to experience Māori culture. There was a marked statistical difference between domestic visitors ($n = 144$) and international visitors who were interested in Māori culture when means were compared ($\chi^2 = 13.416$, $df = 4$, $p = .009$). This finding supported previous reports and research indicating strong international interest in Māori culture (NZTB 1996; Te Puni Kokiri 1998; Ryan 2002; Van Aalst and Daly 2002). It lends support to Ryan's observations that the integration of Māori within New Zealand

Table 1 Information Sources About Māori Culture

Information source	Frequency (n)	Percentage (%)
Media – video, TV, Internet, etc.	208	42.0
Visitor Centres	185	39.2
Museums	170	36.0
Brochures	123	26.0
Books/guide books	118	25.0
Friends and relatives	60	12.7
Educational institutions	40	8.50
Travel agents	32	6.80
Other	35	7.0
Total responses	971	–

(Note: Sum to more than 100 percent due to multiple responses)

society has created a situation where "cultural proximity" and "familiarity" between Māori and non-Māori has weakened demand for experiences with Māori tourism attractions by New Zealanders – "European New Zealanders are not drawn to Māori culture as an attraction in the manner that those from Europe and North America are" (Ryan 2002: 952). Reasons behind this are unclear but could be due to lack of travel opportunities, with New Zealand's geographical isolation from other countries, despite both Māori and Pacific Island cultures residing in many New Zealand cities, particularly urban Auckland. Much of New Zealand's tourism promotional material represents Māori as the exotic 'Other', and is seldom representative of contemporary Māori, many of whom live in urban environments and are removed from their traditional landscapes.

The educational aspects of experiencing another culture, related to learning, understanding or broadening knowledge, were strong reasons for 138 (38.5%) of respondents' interest in future experiences of Māori culture. Changing societal factors, for example the impact of globalisation and the increasing multiculturalism of New Zealand, were given as reasons by respondents who were personally interested in cross-cultural understanding. For some visitors there was an acknowledgement that experiencing Māori culture provided an opportunity for personal enrichment and self-reflection about their own lives. One respondent commented that "Everyone 'grows' as a person from learning about and grappling with another culture/belief system whatever it may be."

Respondents were asked to indicate their levels of interest in a range of issues and themes relating to Māori cultural values for the area (see Table 2). There was greater support amongst international visitors for an indigenous perspective of the area than domestic visitors, with the exception of European history where New Zealanders were more interested than international participants. Existing material concerning Māori culture in national park visitor centres often incorporates mythology or legends and this was a theme highly favoured by 35.6% of visitors (mean = 3.02) as was pre-European Māori history.

Spiritual values were of particular interest to several respondents in this study. Such visitors could be described as exhibiting 'New Age' tendencies, and similar traits were exhibited of visitors in the Northern Territory of Australia (Ryan and Huyton 2000: 81). A few respondents commented on what they perceived to be a spiritual connection that indigenous peoples have with nature, in contrast to the materialism of western lifestyles. These reactions hark back to cultural stereotypes of the 'Other' being at one with the natural environment, implying a 'spiritual' dimension could be attained through personal contact with the indigenous lifestyle. As one respondent commented "Indigenous cultures provide a connection to traditional ways of living where there was more of a connection to nature – spiritual world – we need to reconnect with that aspect of life or we are doomed to merely existing – not living."

It was notable that a small sample of 32 respondents reported mixed feelings about opportunities to experience Māori culture, including information about cultural values for landscape, whilst travelling. Sixteen New Zealanders felt that overexposure or bad publicity surrounding the Treaty of Waitangi (New Zealand's founding constitutional document) had resulted in their negative feelings towards Māori. Some respondents perceived that by including the *iwi* perspective of the environment at visitor centres or in on-site

Table 2   Interest in Interpretation Themes

Variable	Intl. Mean	Domestic Mean	Total Sample Mean	χ^2	df	p
Māori Mythology and Legends	3.26	2.59	3.02	16.549	4	0.002
Pre-European Māori History	3.13	2.59	2.94	12.011	4	0.017
Spiritual and Cultural Values	3.12	2.60	2.93	8.664	4	0.070
European History	2.83	3.11	2.92	10.694	4	0.030
Post-European Māori History	2.93	2.66	2.83	7.673	4	0.104
Māori Environmental Issues	2.99	2.43	2.79	13.267	4	0.010
Traditional Māori Land Uses	2.96	2.46	2.79	11.661	4	0.020
Contemporary Māori Land Use	2.70	2.26	2.55	9.776	4	0.044

'1' = not at all interested to '5' = extremely interested.

interpretation, DoC was succumbing to political correctness, for example one visitor commented that "I do not want a foreign culture rammed down my throat...I'll choose what I'm interested in NOT from a manipulating government's decisions."

Several respondents reported feeling disadvantaged by the lack of opportunity to interact with Māori outside commercial environments. 'Stereotyping', 'commercialism', 'superficiality' and the tendency for tourism to sustain certain aspects of what would otherwise be a 'dying' culture' for purely 'economic 'benefits were amongst the observations made by a few of the visitors. These are important issues for the developers and presenters of the culture to the domestic and international visitor markets, indicating that a 'thick skin' is required when dealing with a spectrum of visitors who have diverse feelings towards the cultural heritage tourism experience. Not all visitors seek an authentic experience and are content with the stereotypes portrayed in tourism promotional material. Referring to the American

context, Albers and James (1988: 137) have noted a similar paradox: "When tourists see Navajos working in places such as banks, hospitals, and mining operations, they are no longer identified as 'real' American Indians." Nevertheless the opportunity to experience Māori culture at tourism attractions was valued by some visitors, whilst others sought experiences that were 'deeper', or 'more meaningful', in a non-commercial environment. As one Japanese visitor commented "I've stayed with a Māori family in Ruatoria, East Cape, for three days. I was taught about any Māori cultures, history and the relationship between Māori and the landscape by this family and other citizen." Commercial tourism activities were regarded as a gateway to an introduction to the Māori way of life, enabling some visitors to get 'behind the scenes' and meet Māori people.

Visitors' Concepts of 'Cultural Landscape'

Respondents were asked to report what they considered to be culturally significant sites (see Table 3). The most recurrent references were made to well-known tourism destinations including Rotorua and the Whakarewarewa Māori Arts and Crafts Insitute attraction (now Te Puia); Waitangi (Bay of Islands); Cape Reinga and Tongariro National Park. Rotorua was the area most often associated with Māori. Explanations for cultural significance of the area, according to the visitors, included local legends or myths, history,

and the traditional use of geothermal resources for daily activities such as cooking and bathing.

A high level of awareness about Cape Reinga as the natural area identified with a strong Māori focus was reported, despite this destination being one of the less visited sites identified by respondents. Tane Mahuta (Northland), Waipoua Forest, One Tree Hill/Maungakiekie, Mt Maunganui, Ruatoria, Abel Tasman, Golden Bay, Pupu

Table 3   Visitors' Perceptions of Natural Areas of Significance to Māori

Site	Total Responses (*n*)	Intl (280)	Domestic (127)
Rotorua/Whakarewarewa	170	123	46
Waitangi	87	57	29
Cape Reinga	47	28	19
Tongariro National Park	43	28	15
General mountains, rivers, lakes	43	19	21
Northland (incl. Bay of Islands (13), Tane Mahuta (6), Waipoua Kauri Forest (3), Maungati (1), Ruapekapeka (2).	36	25	10
West Coast (incl. Hokitika (3) Punakaiki (4), Franz Josef (3), Arahura (2))	30	21	9
Canterbury incl. Kaikoura (8), Banks Peninsula (6), Lake Ellesmere (2), Kaiapoi 3, Christchurch (3), Castle Hill (2), Arowhenua (2).	26	8	18
Mt Egmont/Taranaki incl. Parihaka (2)	24	10	13
Auckland area One Tree Hill/Maungakiekie (9), Bastion Point (2), Rangitoto (1), Manukau (1).	18	14	4
Otago incl. Moeraki Boulders (13), Duntroon (2), Otakou (1), Shag Point/Matakaea (1), Otago Peninsula (1)	18	12	6
Aoraki/ Mount Cook	14	8	6
Bay of Plenty incl. Mt Maunganui (4) and Whakatane (2)	18	12	6
Waikato incl. Ngaurawahia (5), Taupiri (1), Kihikihi (1), Lake Ngaroto (1)	12	1	11
Taupo	10	6	4
Milford Sound	10	9	1 (1)

(number of respondents = 407, missing = 65)

Springs, Moeraki Boulders, Punakaiki, Franz Josef and Hokitika were other natural areas mentioned by visitors who had noticed on-site cultural interpretation. Not all of the sites depicted in Table 3 have commercial tourism activities operating from them and some of these sites could provide opportunities for more in-depth cultural interpretation.

Conclusion

Tourism New Zealand has identified the 'ideal' tourist as the 'interactive traveller' who may "seek interaction with local culture, especially Māori culture" in his or her search for "new experiences that involve engagement and interaction and demonstrate respect for natural, social and cultural environment" (TNZ 2003b). This research identified a small but strong niche visitor demand for personalised interpretation that provides cultural perspectives of natural areas and the landscape in New Zealand. In particular, visitors were interested in mythology, legends, stories and history that was specific to particular areas or reflective of the New Zealand cultural identity. Visitors who prefer natural attractions to cultural tourism sites may consider indigenous nature-based tourism operations offering cultural interpretation as an attractive way to experience the cultural landscape. Incorporating indigenous or local community perspectives offers visitors authentic insights into the cultural and natural heritage of the landscape. The different values *iwi* have for landscapes in New Zealand offer the potential for Māori to differentiate their tourism ventures from competitors by offering 'localised' *iwi* perspectives of place to visitors.

Nurturing visitors' understanding of Māori relationships with natural resources may be a management objective for some organisations but it is necessary to keep in mind that this may not be what visitors seek when visiting natural areas. At the same time there is limited evidence to suggest that the provision of interpretation can change visitor behaviour but respondents' recollections of cultural values for the landscape indicated an emerging awareness or understanding of places significant to *tangata whenua* amongst those who did take the time to comprehend any material they were exposed to This awareness may assist the visitors with 'performing' appropriately but the effectiveness of the interpretation would require site and interpretation specific evaluation (Moscardo 1999; Brown 1999).

Ascertaining visitor demand and interest levels whilst developing cultural interpretation could assist with management and respective host communities setting realistic goals for what they hope to achieve with such interpretation. It is recommended that there is monitoring of the effectiveness of any cultural heritage interpretation, particularly in relation to visitor satisfaction. Managers also need to consider whether, despite tourism providing an opportunity for economic development, by commodifying culture Māori are unwittingly placing yet another layer of western 'economic' values on their land.

This chapter has referred to the need for consultation with and consent from Māori and other local community members when heritage tourism is developed to ensure the authenticity and integrity of the culture or cultures concerned are not compromised (O'Regan 1990; Keelan 1996; Brown 1999; Robinson 1999; Pfister 2000; Staiff *et al.* 2002; Digance 2003). Pfister (2000: 122–123) regarded interpretation of indigenous cultures to be an important tourism resource where "the potential incorporation of storytelling into cultural tourism encounters with indigenous communities may be a very effective way to deepen visitors' understanding and appreciation of aboriginal non-material culture." Pfister (2000) identified several relevant issues to be considered when using traditional cultural material for interpretive purposes: trivialisation and simplification of the material; respect for privacy by traditional 'owners'; sacredness of the material; accuracy or authenticity of the material; protocol and the need for users to obtain permission and authority. These issues apply in the New Zealand context where already *iwi* consultation is necessary for any such developments. Furthermore, at the time of writing this chapter, the New Zealand tourism industry is faced with an additional problem with respect to quality interpretation training. There are limited interpretation training providers and, unlike Australia or North America, New Zealand does not yet have a national interpretation association.

In conclusion, it must be remembered that both indigenous and non-indigenous nature tourism operators can provide valued local perspectives for visitors in a personalised manner through offering their own interpretations of the cultural values for the landscape. The inclusion of the cultural heritage dimensions of natural areas has the potential to provide a truly unique experience for visitors travelling through New Zealand. Māori tourism operators offering visitor experiences of cultural landscapes have the advantage of providing an indigenous experience that cannot be found outside of New Zealand.

Glossary

Iwi – a Māori tribal group
 Kaumatua – elder
 Maunga – mountain

Māori – indigenous people of Aotearoa/ New Zealand
 Runanga – assembly; council; decision makers appointed to administer tribal affairs
 Tangata whenua – original inhabitants, people of the land, indigenous people, Māori
 Taonga – things of value, treasured
 Te Waipounamu – the South Island
 Wahi Tapu – sacred place

References

Albers, P.C. and James, W.R. (1988) Travel photography: a methodological approach. *Annals of Tourism Research*, 15: 134–158.

Ateljevic, I. and Doorne, S. (2002) Representing New Zealand: tourism imagery and ideology. *Annals of Tourism Research* 29: 648–667.

Avery, P. (1999) Between myth and history: mythology and legends as tourist attractions. In E. Arola and T. Mikkonen (eds) *Tourism Industry and Education Symposium Proceedings, Reports and* Proceedings, pp. 140–158. Jyväskylä, Finland: Jyväskylä Polytechnic.

Bourassa, S.C. (1991) *The Aesthetics of Landscape*. Belhaven, London.

Brown, T.J. (1999) 'Antecedents of culturally significant tourist behaviour', *Annals of Tourism Research*, 26: 676–700.

Butler, R.W. and Hinch, T.D. (1996) *Tourism and Indigenous Peoples*, International Thomson Business Press, Boston.

Carr, A.M. (2004a) *Interpreting Culture: Visitors' Experiences of Cultural Landscape in New Zealand*. PhD Thesis, Department of Tourism, University of Otago, Dunedin, New Zealand.

Carr, A.M. (2004b) 'Mountain places, cultural spaces – interpretation and sustainable visitor management of culturally significant landscapes: a case study of Aoraki/Mount Cook National Park.' *Journal of Sustainable Tourism*, 12 (5): 432–459.

Ceballos-Lascurain, H. (1987) 'The future of "ecotourism"' *Mexico Journal*: 13–14.

Cloher, D.U. (1998) 'A Sustainable Māori tourism in Northland. New Zealand', in J. Kandampully *Proceedings of New Zealand Tourism and Hospitality Research Conference*, 3rd Biennial conference, Advances in Research, Akaroa, December 1998.

Department of Conservation (1999) *Aoraki/Mt Cook Fact Sheet* Department of Conservation, Canterbury Conservancy, Christchurch.

Department of Conservation (2001a) *Interpretation Strategy, Canterbury Conservancy 1991–2001*, Department of Conservation, Canterbury Conservancy, Christchurch.

Department of Conservation (2001b) *Draft Aoraki/Mt Cook National Park Management Plan*, Department of Conservation, Canterbury Conservancy, Christchurch.

Department of Conservation (2005) *Interpretation Handbook and Standard: Distilling the Essence*, Department of Conservation, Wellington.

Digance, J. (2003) 'Pilgrimage at contested sites' *Annals of Tourism Research* 30(1): 143–159.

Hall, C. M. and S. McArthur (1996) Managing community values: Identity–Place Relations: an Introduction. *Heritage Management in New Zealand and Australia.* C. M. Hall and S. McArthur. Melbourne, Oxford University Press, 180–184.

Hinch, T. (1998) 'Tourists and indigenous hosts: diverging views on their relationship with nature', *Current Issues in Tourism*, 1(1): 120–124.

Hinkson, M. (2003) 'Encounters with Aboriginal sites in metropolitan Sydney: a broadening horizon for cultural tourism', *Journal of Sustainable Tourism*, 11(4): 295–305.

Indigenous New Zealand (2005) http://www.indigenousnewzealand.com Poutama Trust, Wellington (accessed August 2005).

Kearsley, G.W., McIntosh, A.J. and A.M. Carr (1999) 'Māori Myths, Beliefs and Values: products and constraints for New Zealand Tourism', pp. 292–302 in E. Arola and T. Mikkonen *Tourism Industry and Education Symposium Proceedings, Reports and Proceedings Jyvaskyla Polytechnic No 5*, Jyvaskyla Polytechnic, Finland.

Keelan, N. (1996) Māori Heritage: Visitor Management and Interpretation. *Heritage Management in New Zealand and Australia.* C. M. Hall and S. McArthur. Melbourne, Oxford University Press, 195–201.

Li, Y. (2000) Geographical consciousness and tourism experiences. *Annals of Tourism Research* 27, 4: 863–883.

Mana: the Māori news magazine for all New Zealanders (2005) Number 66, October–November: 25.

MacLennan, P. 2000, *Visitor Information as a Management Tool*, Science and Research Internal report 180, Department of Conservation, Wellington.

McIntosh, A.J., Smith, A. and T. Ingram (2000) *Tourist Experiences of Māori Culture in Aotearoa, New Zealand.* Research Paper Number Eight, Centre for Tourism, University of Otago, Dunedin.

McKercher, B. and du Cros, H. (2002) *Cultural Tourism: The Partnership Between Tourism and Cultural Heritage Management*, Haworth Press, Binghamton NY.

Molloy, L. (1991) 'Te Wahipounamu: an approach to the interpretation of World Heritage wilderness', pp. 286–289 in R.S. Tabata, J. Yamashiro and G. Cherem *Proceedings of the Heritage Interpretation International Third Global Congress*, Honolulu, Hawaii.

Molloy, L. (1992) 'Natural heritage interpretation in New Zealand', pp. 15–20 in S. Olsson and R. Saunders *Open to Interpretation 1992, Conference papers of the Inaugural Conference of the Interpretation Australia Association*, Interpretation Australia Association, Australia.

Moscardo, G. (1999) *Making visitors mindful: Principles for creating sustainable visitor experiences through effective communication*, Sagamore Publishing, Champaign.

Muir, R. (1999) *Approaches to Landscape*, MacMillan Press Ltd, London.

New Zealand Tourism Board (1996) *International Visitor Survey.* Wellington, NZTB.

O'Regan, T. (1987) 'The bi-cultural challenge to management', in Croll, W. *Proceedings Centenary Seminar: 100 Years of National Parks in New Zealand, 24–28 August 1987*, Department of Continuing Education, University of Canterbury, Christchurch.

O'Regan, T. (1990) 'Māori control of the Māori heritage', pp. 95–106 in P. Gathercole, and D. Lowenthal *The Politics of the Past*, University Press, Cambridge.

Pearce, D.G. and Tan, R. (2004) Distribution channels for heritage and cultural tourism in New Zealand. *Asia Pacific Journal of Tourism Research*, 9(3): 225–237.

Pfister, R.E. (2000) Mountain culture as a tourism resource: Aboriginal views on the privileges of storytelling. *Tourism and Development in Mountain Regions.* Godde, P.M., Price, M.F. and Zimmerman, F.M. (eds), Wallingford: CAB International, 115–136.

Prentice, R. (1992) 'The Manx National Glens as treasured landscape', *Scottish Geographical Magazine*, 108(2): 119–127.

Prentice, R. and Guerin, S. (1998) 'The romantic walker? A case study of users of iconic Scottish landscape', *Scottish Geographical Magazine*, 114: 180–191.

Robinson, M. (1999) 'Collaboration and cultural consent: refocusing sustainable tourism', *Journal of Sustainable Tourism*, 7(3–4): 379–397.

Ryan, C. (1997) 'Māori and tourism, a relationship of history, constitutions and rites of tourism', *Journal of Sustainable Tourism*, 5(4): 257–278.

Ryan, C. (1998) 'Māori and New Zealand tourism' pp. 229–245 in M. Robinson and P. Boniface *Tourism and Cultural Conflicts*, CABI Publishing, Oxon.

Ryan, C. (2002) 'Tourism and cultural proximity: examples from New Zealand', *Annals of Tourism Research*, 29(4): 952–971.

Ryan C, and Huyton, J. (2000), 'Who is interested in Aboriginal tourism in the Northern Territory, Australia? A cluster analysis', *Journal of Sustainable Tourism*, 8(1): 53–87.

Ryan, C. and Pike, S. (2003) 'Māori-based tourism in Rotorua: perceptions of place by domestic visitors', *Journal of Sustainable Tourism*, 11(4): 307–321.

Shackley, M. (ed.) (1998) *Visitor Management: Case Studies From World Heritage Sites*, Butterworth-Heinemann, Oxford.

Shackley, M. (2001) *Managing Sacred Sites*. London: Continuum.

Smith, M.K. (2003) *Issues in Cultural Tourism Studies*, Routledge, London.

Smith, V. (1996) 'Indigenous Tourism: the 4 Hs', pp. 283–307 in R. Butler and T. Hinch (eds.) *Tourism and Indigenous Peoples*, International Thomson Business Press, London.

Staiff, R., Bushell, R. and Kennedy, P. (2002) 'Interpretation in national parks: some critical questions', *Journal of Sustainable Tourism*, 10(2), 97–113.

Te Puni Kokiri (TPK) (1996) *Sites of Significance*, Ministry of Māori Development (Te Puni Kokiri), Wellington.

Te Puni Kokiri (TPK) (1998) *Māori Tourism Directory*, Ministry of Māori Development Te Puni Kokiri, Wellington.

Te Runanga o Ngāi Tahu (2005) http://www.Ngāitahu.co.nz/RockArt/

The Stafford Group (2001) *He Matai Tapoi* Māori: *A Study of Barriers, Impediments and Opportunities for* Māori *in Tourism*, Ministry of Māori Development and the Office of Tourism and Sport, Wellington.

Tilden, F. (1967) *Interpreting our Heritage*. Chapel Hill, University of North Carolina Press.

Timothy, D.J. and Boyd, S.W. (2003) *Heritage Tourism*. Harlow: Prentice Hall.

Tourism New Zealand (2003a), *Tourism New Zealand 3 Year Strategic Plan 2003–2006*, Tourism New Zealand, Wellington.

Tourism New Zealand (2003b), *New Zealand's Ideal Visitor: the Interactive Traveller*, Tourism New Zealand, Wellington.

Tourism Strategy Group (2001) *New Zealand Tourism Strategy 2010*, Tourism Strategy Group. Wellington.

Uzzell, D. (1996) 'Creating place identity through heritage interpretation', *International Journal of Heritage Studies*, 1(4): 219–228.

Van Aalst, I. and Daly, C. (2002) *International Visitor Satisfaction With Their New Zealand Experience: The Cultural Tourism Product Market – a summary of studies 1990–2001*. Tourism New Zealand, Wellington, New Zealand.

Walker, R. (1992) 'The Relevance of Māori Myth and Tradition', pp. 171–184 in King, M. *Te Ao Hurihuri: Aspects of Māoritanga*, Reed Books, Auckland.

Warren J. A. N. and Taylor C. N. (2001) *Developing Heritage Tourism in New Zealand*, Centre for Research, Evaluation and Social Assessment. Wellington.

Zygadlo, F.K., McIntosh, A., Matunga, H.P., Fairweather, J. and Simmons, D.G. (2003) Māori *Tourism: Concepts, Characteristics and Definition*, Report No. 36, Tourism Research and Educations Centre, Lincoln University, Canterbury.

"The Southern Sound" (Nanyin): Tourism for the Preservation and Development of Traditional Arts

Paul Leung Kin Hang

Introduction

In recent years, there has been a growing concern in investigating the possibility of developing cultural and heritage tourism as a source of revenue (McHone & Rungeling, 1999; McIntosh & Prentice, 1999; Simons, 2000). Heritage, including monuments, folk arts and artifacts, is often commodified as a product for sale (Hughes, 1987; McIntosh & Prentice, 1999; Simons, 2000). There is, however, a gap in the knowledge regarding the capitalization of cultural tourism for social considerations, especially in the preservation of culture (Dann, Nash & Pearce, 1988; Brayley, Var & Sheldon, 1990). While tourism has been criticized for trivializing authenticity and commercializing cultural assets (MacCannell, 1973; Greaves, 1994), it is also noted as a means for preserving and conserving cultural heritage (Cohen, 1988; McIntosh & Prentice, 1999; Timothy & Boyd, 2003). Tourism represents "an indispensable source of financial resources for the preservation and restoration of the heritage that otherwise faces shrinking budgets and

state transfer" (Russo & Van der Borg, 2002, p. 631).

This research paper aims to position culture and traditional arts in a touristic setting and the possibility of capitalizing on them as tourism products. Using *Nanyin* (the Southern Sound) as a case, the study addresses the challenge of balancing commodification and preservation of traditional culture. *Nanyin* is a very traditional story-singing performance in southern China with a history of more than 300 years, but it is now under threat of extinction.

Culture and Tourism

The concept of culture was first defined by Sir Edward Burnett Tylor as a complex set of knowledge, beliefs, arts, law, morals, customs and other capabilities and habits acquired through the membership of a society. Since then, the definition of culture has been proliferated and diversified between behaviors and shared values (Haviland, 1999). Culture, as Haviland (1999) argues, can be defined as an assortment of abstract values, beliefs and perceptions of the world. It prescribes and gives reasons for human behaviours. Members of a community share a common set of cultural traits, which are learned rather than biologically inherited and change gradually over time in response to the environment, especially crises. Although culture can be rather stable over time, it is flexible and ever-changing through the process of borrowing and intervention (Podolefsky & Brown, 2001). Abdurrahman Wahid, former president of Indonesia, in his opening remarks to the International Symposium on Cultural Heritage Conservation in Bali, stressed that in preserving the past we must not deny people's right to find a new heritage as they look to the future and develop a new identity according to modern needs. Cultural expressions are thus not usually confined in a historical setting but should be opened to welcome new ideas, innovative applications and improvisations. Although President Wahid was referring to Bali, this post-modern prospective is inspirational and justified in the pursuit of cultural tourism. This idea of cultural commodification is taken to an extreme when Firat (1995, p. 118) argued that "cultures of all types...that are able to translate their qualities into marketable commodities and spectacles find themselves maintained, experienced and globalizes. Cultures that cannot or do not present themselves in terms of marketable qualities, simulated instances, experiences, and products are finding themselves divested of members... Cultures that cannot succeed in translating some of their qualities into spectacles or commodities seem to vanish only to become museum items." Contrasting this view with those of MacCannell (1973) and Greaves (1994), as mentioned earlier, it is apparently not just a debate between authenticity and

modification but a strategic decision regarding preservation and commodification. It is also a matter of survival of traditional cultures. While there are arguments advocating both extremes, the mainstream literature argues for conservation: a sort of mid-point between the two extremes of the continuum.

Haviland (1999, p. 412) contended that "no known culture is without some form of art." Even items for purely utilitarian purposes are the makers' expression of their culture, which reflects their view of humanity, cosmology, society and religion. Apart from providing pleasure in everyday life, arts have various functions in society. It could be in praise of a god, a vow of love, an expression of happiness or sorrow, an order for the community to follow, a record of history, or an attempt to promote social cohesiveness and solidarity (Haviland, 1999). In other words, every expression has a story behind it. Today, arts embrace a new dimension. They can be commercialized as commodities for tourists and other outsiders to enjoy and consume. The exoticism of ethnic performances, visual illustrations, ceremonies, festivals and music has become an attraction for promoting tourism, and is sometimes measured in terms of tourist arrivals and receipts.

Many nations have identified tourism as a major economic tool and development agent (Richter, 1999; Dieke, 2000). Tourism has also attracted a high level of interest and attention of NGOs and inter-governmental organizations, for instances the UNDP, UNESCO, Oxfam, and the World Bank. Tia Duer, leader of the World Bank's Cultural Assets for Poverty Reduction unit, expressed that the unit had "great interest in working with trade and professional associations and companies in adventure, ecological and cultural tourism to help poor communities develop sustainable tourism, which improves their incomes and conserves their culture and way of life" (World Bank, 2000b). Lately, specialized forms of tourism, including cultural, adventure and nature-based tourism, have received special attention for their potential contribution to the preservation of the natural and cultural environment and to destination economies, and to their lower likelihood of creating negative impacts comparing to traditional mass tourism. In a conference, sponsored by the World Bank's Cultural Assets for Poverty Reduction unit and organized by The Policy Sciences Center, Inc. (PSC), an organization founded at the Yale Law School, examined the link between community-based tourism and poverty. Delegates argued that niche market segments that focus on cultural and ecotourism markets are especially advantageous to culturally or environmentally sensitive areas. These alternative types of travellers, it is argued, "typically spend more and stay longer in a destination than the average tourist, thus generating a higher yield, but with lower impact on the community's life" (World Bank, 2000a), although this assertion has seen some critical debate in recent years.

As noted earlier, tourism has been cited for its ability to preserve and promote culture and arts (Sethna & Richmond, 1978; Sheldon & Var, 1984; Liu, Sheldon & Var, 1987; de Kadt, 1979). It also has the potential threat of over-commercialising cultural products, leading to the loss of inherent cultural value and significance (Murphy, 1985; Cohen, 1988; Browne & Nolan, 1993; Ryan, 1991). Dr. Rosanne Martorella in her letter to the editor of *New York Times* (May 28, 2000) expressed this concern. She wrote, "Government money continues to support arts-related activities because they supposedly boost the economy, and are crucial to cultural tourism. Legitimating the arts and culture solely in these terms dangerously neglects to accept them solely for their aesthetic importance. This is the very reason recent architecture is "Disneyfied" – because it is part of the cultural tourism model, the dogma Mr. Muschamp warns us about. Architecture, as other forms of art and culture, should have no rival for its support." In other words, the current logistics in conservation of cultural heritages might somehow skew towards the market. This might imply that only those arts and culture with high commercial values would receive public resources for their preservation and protection. Although Martorella's concern has to be qualified, it seems reasonable to readdress the issue of conservation and mechanisms for public resource allocations.

Redefining Cultural Tourism – The Quest for Authenticity

Cohen (1988) argued that contemporary literature on cultural tourism development has three basic assumptions. First, tourism leads to a 'commoditization' of culture; second, commoditization destroys authenticity and substitutes it with 'staged authenticity'; and third, staged authenticity thwarts the tourists' genuine desire for authentic experiences. It is, therefore, a debate about authenticity and commoditization. His observation is that the literature is largely scornful towards cultural tourism. Although the literature might have become more neutral in recent years, the concern over authenticity still prevails (McHone & Rungeling, 1999; McIntosh & Prentice, 1999; Simons, 2000; Timothy & Boyd, 2003). The fear still thrives that commodification of cultural assets leads to alterations of, and even destroys, the authenticity of the local cultural products.

Authenticity is a value which emerged with the process of modernization and its impacts on social unity (Cohen, 1988). The quest for authenticity can either turn inward for an *ens realissimum* or outward from the geographical elsewhere (Cohen, 1988). According to MacCannell (1973) modern humans seek authenticity in the inauthentic modern world. This quest is a primary concept and has become a motif of modern tourism (MacCannell, 1973). In other words, tourism seeks to satisfy travelers' quests for a unity between the opposing self and the modern societal institutions. They seek to find pristine, primitive, natural forms of existence in other times and other places, when and where modernization has not yet taken place (MacCannell, 1973). This proposition, however, is in contrast with the post-modern prospective, for instance, the two commentators cited earlier (Wahid and Martorella), who argued that any changes and alterations of the modern world are just as genuine and authentic as their traditional counterparts.

Cohen (1988) further argued that this philosophical construct of authenticity, especially for its application in tourism studies, should consider its sociological counterpart as well. The quest for authenticity, according to Cohen (1988), is subject to the nature of the quest and the person who pursues the quest. Although tourists are not as rigid as ethnologists in assessing authenticity (Nettekoven, 1973; Desai, 1974), they are sophisticated and may not be satisfied with mere entertainment (Goldberg, 1983). The challenge for developing cultural tourism, therefore, is to strike a balance between the contrived modernity and the traditional authenticity. More 'puristic' assertions, including those of Greenwood (1977) and McLeod (1976), damned tourism for the expropriation of culture and invention of tradition. Cohen

(1988), however, argued that authenticity is not a primitive given but a negotiable condition. In other words, it will change over time and when different cultures interact. From a post-modern perspective, tradition is even changing and revolting. Authenticity, therefore, redefines itself with or without tourism.

It is common in the literature for authors to assert that cultural tourism utilizes and brings impacts to traditional cultural environments (e.g. Belisle & Hoy, 1980; Sheldon & Var, 1984; Liu & Var, 1986; Brown, 1993). It is, however, possible for cultural tourism to build on a contrived form of culture that is completely detached from the traditional arena (see Picard, 1996, 1997; Wall, 1995; Wall, Cooper & Wanhill, 1997). That means the 'new' staged authenticity is an improvisation of the traditional culture for touristic purpose. The new arts, performance and presentation should, therefore, be treated with a separate identity rather than as an alternative, a replacement or a threat to the more traditional ones (Picard, 1993, 1996, 1997).

Research Objectives and Methodology

The existing literature on cultural tourism and heritage tourism is dominated by descriptive accounts of tangible artifacts, sites and monuments (Carter, Baxter and Hockings, 2001). With the exception of some recent volumes (e.g. McKercher & du Cros, 2002; Timothy & Boyd, 2003), works on performing arts and intangible heritage, however, is limited.

This exploratory study is designed to identify facilitators and barriers for the development, preservation and conservation of performing arts as cultural tourism attractions. With tourism as the context, factors contributing to the sustainability and/or causing loss of these assets are identified. A single case study with embedded units of analysis was selected as the design of this research project. This case study explores the latest development and the preservation of *Nanyin (the Southern Sound)*; a performing art of China. The study identifies the role of government in conserving and promoting the subject; the perceived attractiveness of the art to the local community; the perceived attractiveness of the performance to the tourists; and other environmental issues that have led to the decline in practice and form of the tradition.

The study used focus group interviews and critical reviews of government policies on culture and arts as major data sources. Informants were selected by their related experience, qualifications or knowledge about the subject, or relevant official position. They included government officials, amateur and professional performers, tutors, event organizers, promoters, publishers and audiences. As requested by the informants, their identities have been disguised.

A Traditional Art: Nanyin

Nanyin, the Southern Sound, is a traditional Chinese musical performance that originates and flourishes in southern China, especially in cities of the Guangdong province, including Hong Kong. Hong Kong was once perceived as the home base for this particular folk art. *Nanyin* is a form of story-singing performance. Its origin can be traced back to the Tong Dynasty (618–907 AD) when monks used songs for promoting Buddhism. Story-singing reached its peak in the Qing Dynasty (1644–1911 AD) when more than 300 forms of story-singing co-existed in China. Story-singing came to Guangdong and evolved into

a new form – *Nanyin*. The height of *Nanyin*'s popularity was between the turn of the twentieth century and the 1950s. All three types of southern sound, including *Laogui Nanyin, Musi Nanyin* and *Wutai Nanyin*, were performed in Hong Kong, especially between the 1920s and early 1960s. *Musi Nanyin* is the most traditional type of *Nanyin*, which was sung by blind fortune-tellers. *Laogui Nanyin* is a specific form sung by prostitutes, and *Wutai Nanyin* is a stage performance done by professionals. This intangible art is in danger of eroding by rapid westernization and modernization of southern Chinese society (Chen, 1999; Li, 2000). *Laogui Nanyin* has vanished, and *Musi Nanyin* can only be heard in a few old recordings. Even the *Wutai Nanyin* as the last and most well preserved form of *Nanyin* is rarely performed today.

Barriers for the Development of Traditional Arts

Some art critics have argued that art forms which cannot advance with the pace of contemporary life would, soon or later, only exist in historical records. To assess the attractiveness of *Nanyin* to the 'modern' audience groups, audio and video recordings were presented to small focus groups of Hong Kong residents and tourists. The initial feedback, in contrast with the prior proposition, suggests that it has potential to be developed as a tourist attraction. The study, therefore, proceeds to identify other factors that might explain the failure to practice the cultural tradition.

Several fundamental threats were identified as causes for the demise of *Nanyin*. Cultural change was identified as the most prominent factor. According to various informants, westernization in Hong Kong over the last century has brought critical impacts on traditional arts. In the past, people had fewer choices for entertainment. Traditional festivals and performances (e.g. Chinese operas and *Nanyin*) were popular leisure activities for Hong Kong. During the colonial period and through rapid trade development, Hong Kong was pushed through a rapid westernization process. The Hong Kong Chinese also became skewed to the west culturally. Chinese art forms have become increasingly seen as inferior and therefore have given way to Western arts and other forms of entertainment. Public interest, attention, and consumption have been diverted from traditional local arts to imported arts (Lo, 2000; Ng & Cheung, 2001).

Driven by the influence of Western culture, changes in the demographic, social and cultural characteristics of the market, such as lifestyle and individual preferences, also have seriously altered the direction of the development of traditional arts. Since an art is a product of culture, it reflects certain values, purposes or preferences in its formation process. As the bases change among members of the community, the market may switch to alternative forms of activities for enjoyment. *Nanyin*, as an example, is an activity that developed in response to the particular market situation and the occasion of consumption. In reviewing recent development, however, it can be seen that most of these backgrounds, which shaped the development of *Nanyin*, have ceased to exist. *Nanyin* performance, therefore, has lost its attractiveness as it has been detached from the values and beliefs of the current world. Relating this situation to the Martorella's letter, it reinforces the necessity of the government to step in to assist in preserving traditional art forms through either financial support or technical assistance to the transformation of product, or both.

Another apparent reason for the demise in *Nanyin* is a lack of successors. Owing to the loss of a substantial and sustainable demand, people are discouraged to learn and to develop a career in *Nanyin* performance. With the exception of a few artists, whose main career is in Chinese opera, few artists are willing to engage in *Nanyin* as a profession. To intensify the situation, there is a lack of an effective documentation mechanism for information on this traditional art, including knowledge, skills and attached cultural values. To rectify the situation, the Culture and Heritage Commission (CHC) in Hong Kong, established in March 2001, proposed in its consultation paper that the government should initiate the recording of the customs and history of Hong Kong in a systematic manner. However, the suggestion did not detail how this would be implemented and whether it would include the documentation of traditional Chinese arts.

The traditional art forms that survived through time have one commonality. They adapted to the changes in audiences' needs and preferences (Lo, 1994; Chen, 1999; Li, 2000). This is important especially for traditional arts to be developed as tourism products. Marketing techniques have been applied to promote business, and gimmicks have been utilized to create public attention. In many traditional Chinese performances, however, masters are just too proud to do so (Chen, 1999). They stand firm in what they perceive as authentic and refused to compromise their art for revenue. As a result, patronage to traditional art performances has shrunk in number (Lo, 1994; Chen, 1999). The lack of earnings for improvement and the intensifying competition broaden the gap between traditional and modern arts wider.

Another possible alternative for preserving art is to capitalize on tourism as a revenue generator. The art sector, as they contended, has difficulties in cultivating the tourism market, given their limited knowledge about tourism. Hence, they are more incline to rely on other sectors. Collaboration between different sectors, however, is easy to advocate but difficult to implement. This can be attributed to the different mandates and interests of the various parties. For the art sector, the art forms themselves are the focus of management practices. Preserving traditions is perceived as their primary responsibility. For tourism, however, art is developed as a tourism product because it can be explicitly consumed by tourists when it satisfies their needs and wants. Performances, for example, have to be developed into a form preferred by tourists. This might imply alterations in form, duration, and style that are perceived as elements not to be altered. Therefore, the denial from the art sector, sometimes, is a great hurdle for developing any art form for tourism. For governments, supports are public resource allocation on a zero-sum bases. The achievement of a delicate balance between commodification and conservation thus necessitates careful management strategies.

The government's policies are seriously criticized by various informants for being too narrow-minded and too market-driven and commercialised, which they see as detrimental to the preservation of traditional art forms. The Hong Kong Government's participation, as informants asserted, rather than assisting in preservation, hinders conservation and jeopardizes the subject's sustainability. Government policies on arts development and resource allocation mechanisms have an impact on the loss of *Nanyin*. Using the direction provided by a CHC consultation paper as an example, CHC promotes what it calls the community-based mode of development and also suggested that the culture and art sector should operate according to the rules of the market. In other words, if a performance can sell more tickets, it is entitled to more government support, whereas those forms of arts that are not financially self-sustainable would be difficult to secure governmental resources for despite how aesthetically important they might be. Although it would be unfair to conclude that the failure of traditional arts is caused by government policies, it seems sensible to argue that the government's decision has a part to play in the failure of the preservation of such art forms.

As suggested by the informants, the lack of mediators, which included performers, venues and materials, alone or in combination have had detrimental impacts on traditional arts too. Rapid urbanization, in many cases, has detached the traditional arts from the natural setting. *Nanyin* used to be performed in tea houses, temples, and brothels. As these venues and occasions became less popular, the performance of *Nanyin* followed suit. Some informants further argued that *Nanyin* could have lost its cultural proximity and practicality as a form of entertainment as the lifestyle of the inhabitants changed. For example, the lyrics of many *Nanyin* pieces featured a traditional religious celebration of July 7. This event, however, is rarely celebrated nowadays, creating a gap between the historic stories and the modern daily lives of audiences.

Some respondents also argued that education, as an indirect factor, has a long-term influence on the maintenance of traditional culture and arts. The colonial status of Hong Kong not only affected the lifestyle of Hong Kong residents, it also had a significant bearing on the focus of education. The use of English as the main teaching medium as well as the inclination of school curriculum towards western culture ran the danger of creating a loss and appreciation of traditional Chinese culture. Moreover, the emphasis on students' cognitive growth by studying more traditional academic subjects (e.g. mathematics and science) also hindered the development of students' aesthetics, creativity and expressive abilities. Arts education was usually taken up as a pastime or hobby with significant devaluation in the education system. Is this a coincidence or the result of a causal relationship? It seems reasonable to argue for the potential relationship.

Conclusions

In developing traditional arts as a tourism product, several general conclusions emerge from this analysis. First, the potential of traditional and folk arts to be developed as tourism products is largely determined by the product design. The original form of art being the core product should be augmented by presentation and add-on services to make it more consumable and able to enhance consumers' level of satisfaction. Alterations are sometimes necessary to enhance tourists' appreciation of a living art form. For example, the normal length of a *Nanyin* piece is more than 15 minutes, which might be too long for tourists who do not speak the language.

The government, as a funding agent, provider of performing venues, and promoter of traditional art forms, has a stake in the preservation and conservation of cultural expressions and should contribute to these aspects of heritage conservation. The traditional market-oriented approach cannot serve the purpose of preserving endangered

cultures. A new resource allocation mechanism, which addresses the needs of particular art forms, should be adopted.

Relying solely on government subvention and tactical assistance is not viable in Hong Kong. The non-profit and private sectors, as well as the local community, therefore, must fill in the gaps and rectify the deficiencies. Once again, this requires the collaboration of the various sectors and stakeholders for a common mission.

Regarding the market for *Nanyin*, respondents suggested cultural tourists from western societies, overseas Chinese and mainland Chinese are the most obvious potential consumers. As mentioned earlier, however, the product needs to be re-designed in a way that will deliver the ultimate satisfaction level and provide an enjoyable experience for the public. The design of the total experience should pay attention to the selection of venue, the offering of interpretation and guided presentations, and the constructed ambiance.

Finally, preservation and commoditization need not be mutually exclusive strategies. There could be separate sets of products, meaning an altered tourist product can be developed to the specific market to generate revenue for the preservation of more traditional forms of performance.

References

Belisle, F. & Hoy, D. (1980). The Perceived Impact of Tourism by Residents. *Annals of Tourism Research*, 7(1), 83–101.

Brayley, R., Var, T. & Sheldon, P. (1990). Perceived influence of tourism on social issues, *Annals of Tourism Research*, 17(2), 285–289.

Brown, T. J. (1999). Antecedents of Culturally Significant Tourist behavior. *Annals of Tourism Research*, 26(3), 676–700.

Browne, R. J. & Nolan, M. L. (1993). Western Indian reservation tourism development, *Annals of Tourism Research*, 16(3), 360–376.

Carter, R. W., Baxter, G. S. & Hockings, M. (2001). Resource Management in Tourism Research: A New Direction? *Journal of Sustainable Tourism*, 9(4), 265–280.

Chen, S. (1999). *Xianggang Yue ju dao lun*. Hong Kong: Chinese University Press.

Cohen, E. (1988). Authenticity and Commoditization in Tourism. *Annals of Tourism Research*, 15, 371–386.

Dann, G., Nash, D. & Pearce, P. (1988). Methodology in tourism research. *Annals of Tourism Research*, 15(1), 1–28.

De Kadt, E. (1979). *Tourism: Passport to development? Perspectives on the social and cultural effects of tourism in developing countries.* New York: Oxford University Press.

Desai, A. V. (1974). Tourism – Economic Possibilities and Policies. In *Tourism in Fiji*, 1–12. Suva: University of the South Pacific.

Dieke, P. U. C. (ed) (2000). *The Political Economy of Tourism Development in Africa.* New York: Cognizant Communication Corporation.

Firat, A. F. (1995). Consumer Culture or Culture Consumed? In J. A. Costa & G. J. Bamossy (eds), *Marketing in a Multicultural World: Ethnicity, Nationalism, and Cultural Identity* (pp. 105–125). Thousand Oaks, CA: Sage.

Goldberg, A. (1983). Identity and Experience in Haitian Voodoo Shows. *Annals of Tourism Research*, 10(4), 479–495.

Greaves, T. (1994). *Intellectual Property Rights for Indigenous Peoples: A Sourcebook, Society for Applied Anthropology.* Oklahoma City: Society for Applied Anthropology.

Greenwood, D. J. (1977). Culture by the Pound: An Anthropological Perspective on Tourism as Cultural Commoditization. In V. L. Smith (ed), *Hosts and Guests* (pp. 129–139). Philadelphia: University of Pennsylvania Press.

Haviland, W. (1999). *Cultural Anthropology*, 9th ed., Forth Worth, TX: Harcourt Brace.

Hughes, H. L. (1987). Culture as a tourist resource – a theoretical consideration. *Tourism Management*, 8(3), 205–216.

Li, K. S. (2000). *Xianggang Daisui Nanyin.* Hong Kong, Step Forward Multimedia.

Liu, J. & Var, T. (1986). Resident Attitudes toward Tourism Impacts in Hawaii. *Annals of Tourism Research*, 13(2), 193–214.

Liu, J., Sheldon, P. & Var, T. 1987. A Cross-National Approach to Determining Resident Perceptions of the Impact of Tourism on the Environment. *Annals of Tourism Research*, 14(1), 17–37.

Lo, J. (1994). Yue *qu ge tan hua cang sang*. Hong Kong: Joint Publishing.

Lo, J. (2000). *Yue qu ge tan hua cang sang*, 2nd Ed. Hong Kong: Joint Publishing.

MacCannell, D. (1973). Staged Authenticity: Arrangements of Social Space in Tourist Settings, *American Journal of Popular Culture*, 15(1), 157–165.

McKercher, B. & du Cros, H. (2002). *Cultural Tourism: The Partnership Between Tourism and Cultural Heritage Management.* New York: The Haworth Press.

McLeod, M. D. (1976). Limitations of the Genuine. *African Art*, 9(3), 31, 48–51.

Nettekoven, L. (1973). Touristen sind eben keine Volkerkundler. *Auslandskurier*, 3, 28–29.

Ng, C. H. & Cheung, C. W. (2001). *Reading Hong Kong Popular Cultures: 1970-2000.* Hong Kong: Oxford University Press.

Picard, M. (1993). Cultural Tourism in Bali: National Integration and Regional Differentiation. In M. Hitchcock, V. King & M. Parnwell (eds) *Tourism in South-East Asia* (pp. 71–98). London and New York: Routledge.

Picard, M. (1996). Dance and Drama in Bali: The Making of an Indonesian Art Form. In A. H. Vickers (ed), *Being Modern in Bali*, New Haven: Yale University.

Picard, M. & Wood, R. (1997). *Tourism, Ethnicity, and the State in Asian and Pacific Societies.* Honolulu: University of Hawaii Press.

Podolefsky, A. & Brown, P. J. (2001). *Applying Cultural Anthropology: An Introductory Reader.* Mountain View, CA: Mayfield.

Ryan, C. (1991). Tourism and marketing: a symbiotic relationship?, *Tourism Management*, 12(2): 101–111.

Richter, L. K. (1999). After political turmoil: The lessons of rebuilding tourism in three Asian Countries. *Journal of Travel Research*, 38(1), 41–45.

Martorella, R. (2000). Cultural Tourism. [Letter to the Editor] *New York Times*, 28 May, p. 2.

Russo, A. P. & van der Borg, J. (2002). Planning Considerations for Cultural Tourism: A Case Study of Four European Cities, *Tourism Management*, 23, 631–637.

Sethna, R. & Richmond, B. (1978). U.S. Virgin Islanders' perceptions of tourism. *Journal of Travel Research* 17(1), 30–31.

Sheldon, P. & Var, T. (1984). Resident Attitudes to Tourism in North Wales. *Tourism Management*, 5(1), 40–48.

Timothy, D. J. & Boyd, S. W. (2003). *Heritage Tourism.* Harlow: Prentice Hall.

Wall, G. (1995). Quality management in urban tourism. *Annals of Tourism Research*, 22(4), 939–940.

Wall, G., Cooper, C. & Wanhill, S. (1997). *Tourism Development: Environmental and Community Issues.* Chichester & New York: Wiley.

World Bank (2000a). Indonesian President Wahid opens International Symposium on Cultural Heritage Conservation in Bali. M2 Presswire; Coventry; Jul 14, 2000.

World Bank (2000b). World Bank examines links between community-based tourism and poverty. M2 Presswire; Coventry; Jun 5, 2000.

Heritage Sites as Tourism Assets for Asian Pacific Destinations: Insights from Ancient European Tourism

Eric Laws and Grace Wen Pan

Introduction

Most guide books and travel videos of Asian and Pacific destinations emphasise the attractions of local culture, heritage and festivals to visitors. In most destinations, a feature of the tourist experience is a spectacular dance or even a feast staged commercially for their entertainment, but reflecting more or less accurately a traditional celebration. The Hawaiian Hula dance and the pig roast are enjoyed by almost every visitor to the Islands.

Despite the long history of human interest in older cultures and heritage, few authors have directly addressed the topic. A search of journal articles published between 1996 and early 1999 identified only one study (Sofield & Li, 1998a) which sought to take advantage of ancient insights into tourism. Consistently limited research has been conducted on heritage tourism management in Asian destinations. As Casson noted in the preface to his book, *Travel in the ancient world* "(This) is the first full-scale treatment, in any

language, of travel in the ancient world." In the preface to the second edition, he added the sentence "It is still the first and only treatment, for the twenty years that have elapsed since it came out have produced no other" (Casson, 1994: Preface). His text highlights the interest which inhabitants of the ancient world took in older cultures, he discusses the events they experienced in their journeys, and he reviews the ways in which early tourism was organised. Of particular relevance to this paper, he provides examples of the early commercialisation of heritage sites, and identifies a range of problems for the custodians of those sites and for heritage site visitors which many contemporary managers will recognise as continuing to present challenges.

The problems and approaches to heritage tourism management relevant to contemporary tourism which Casson discusses are:

- motivations for heritage tourism visits
- definitions of heritage tourism
- protecting and managing heritage sites

- authenticity
- heritage site interpretation
- heritage site access
- the value of heritage tourism.

In this paper, a brief example from Casson's work is given for each topic, which is then reviewed in the light of contemporary heritage tourism studies.

The growing interest in managing heritage sites for tourism has produced a considerable body of recent research, and in addition to the discussion of ancient insights, two further issues are noted: the modern approach to visitor satisfaction management and management recognition of the concerns and interests of wider stakeholders. This paper also reviews the development of heritage tourism in Asian destinations, such as Myanmar, Singapore, Hong Kong and China. It seems that some of the problems and approaches to heritage tourism management discussed by Casson also occurred in these regions.

Motivations for Heritage Tourism Visits

Casson (1994) has identified the first signs of tourism as occurring in Egypt around 1500 BC. It began there rather than in Mesopotamia because of the quality of the Nile valley building stone which the Pharaohs used to construct their grandiose tombs and temples as early as 2700 BC. As a result, Egyptians of later ages found themselves living in a veritable museum, surrounded by structures of hoary antiquity. In the great days of the New Kingdom, from 1600 to 1200 BC, when Thutmose and Akhenaton and Ramses and other such renowned figures held the throne, the step pyramid ... at Sakkarah, the Sphinx at Gizeh, and the like, were already over a thousand years old...On their walls, we find

messages left by people who had made a special trip to see these impressive witnesses to the might of their past... 'Hadnakhte, scribe of the treasury', reads one such message dated 1224 BC, on the wall of a chapel connected with Djoser's pyramid, '.... came to make an excursion and amuse himself on the west of Memphis, together with his brother, Panakhti, scribe of the Vizier' (Casson, 1994: 32).

At a recent international conference, agreement was reported on "the need for heritage providers to focus more directly on the consumer of heritage. In particular, an understanding of visitor needs, motivations, experiences and benefits gained were asserted as the essential way forward for heritage tourism" (Frochot & Beeho, 1997: 272).

Research indicates that contemporary heritage visitors are motivated by a combination of relaxation and educational interests (Davis, 1994; Timothy & Boyd, 2003). Moscardo (1996) has also noted that most heritage visitors wish to learn about the site, but while many seek to be educated, a majority want merely to be informed. However, Chinese domestic travel to local cultural and historical places has been considered a voluntary cultural decision related to Chinese ideology as a pilgrimage to these sites (Sofield & Li, 1998b). For example, there is a Chinese saying, "He who has never been to the Great Wall is not a true man." Hence, many domestic Chinese tourists would like to visit the Great Wall to prove that they are "true men"! In the other case in Singapore, Singaporeans' interests in local heritage sites contribute to the outcome of the social and cultural evolution in Singapore that Singaporeans themselves would like rediscover their roots (Chang, 1999).

Jansen-Verbeke (1997) distinguished three main sub groupings of cultural tourists: intentional, that is those who are culturally motivated; opportunistic or culturally inspired; and non-intentional visitors to cultural sites, the culturally attracted. However, many tourists do not participate in the heritage or cultural activities of the regions they visit. One study concluded that the main reason visitors do not include cultural attractions on their tour itinerary is lack of awareness of them (Ralston & Kelly, 1996). A survey of why people did not visit museums identified six criteria which influence the choice of (other) leisure activities, summarised in Table 1.

Definitions of Heritage Tourism

A basic contemporary definition of heritage tourism, developed by the National Trust for Historic Preservation (cited in Richards, 1997), is travelling to historic and cultural attractions to learn about the past in an interesting and enjoyable way. The World Tourism Organisation (1992) defines heritage tourism as "an immersion in the natural history, human heritage, arts, philosophy and institutions of another region or country." Yale (1991: 21) notes that "the fashionable concept of heritage tourism really means

Table 1 FACTORS INFLUENCING THE CHOICE OF LEISURE ACTIVITY

- being with other people
- doing something worthwhile
- feeling at ease
- experiencing new challenges
- the opportunity to learn
- active participation

(based on Hood, 1983).

little more than tourism centred on what we have inherited, which can mean anything from historic buildings to art works, to beautiful scenery."

Casson (1994: 229–230) notes that this variety also characterised heritage tourism in classical times.

At the end of the summer of 167 BC, Aemilius Paulus, commander in chief of the Roman army, was in Northern Greece resting on his laurels as victor in a bitter struggle against Macedon. The historian Livy recounts that "he decided upon a tour of Greece, to see those things which, through their fame or reputation, had been magnified by hearsay into more than what the eye beholds ... he travelled across Thessaly to Delphi ... then to the temple of Zeus Trophonius ... to Chalsis to see the Euripus and Euboea, ... the gathering point for the thousand ships of Agamemnon's fleet and the site of the temple of Artemis, where the King of Kings sought a fair wind for Troy by sacrificing his daughter on the goddess' altar."

Brown (1998) has reviewed the Heritage Tourism National Study in the USA, which investigated travellers' definitions of "heritage tourism", compared the definitions of the public with those of tourism professionals, and tested whether activities and specific places were described as heritage attractions. Half the respondents were unable to supply an unaided definition of heritage tourism. Perhaps more significantly, as Table 2 indicates, tourism professionals differed from the public in defining which activities and sites are heritage tourism. Heritage tourism is supposed to play a dual role in attracting visitors to a certain destination while fulfilling the social, cultural and recreational aspirations of locals, although this dual role is not always successful (Chang, 1999).

Table 2   Industry and Public Definitions of Heritage Tourism

Which of the following are heritage tourism?	% answering each question positively	
	Heritage tourism managers	Public
History museum	93	82
Colonial Williamsburg	100	81
Historical district of a town	87	78
American Indian reservation	87	77
Family reunion	0	58
Driving along scenic byways	33	46
Watching 4th July fireworks	7	45
Buying locally produced craft	53	40
Shopping for antiques	0	23
Shopping in Mall of America	0	12
Casino gambling at Indian reservation	0	9
Shopping at outlet malls	0	12

Source: after Brown (1998).

Protecting and Managing Heritage Sites

Heritage sites around the world are targets for malicious or thoughtless attack and can provide rich pickings for unscrupulous visitors. Casson (1994: 33) discussed an example of graffiti, written some time in the thirteenth century BC in Djoser's pyramid complex, which records that "it was done in the view of the whole body of the 'School of ... the Nine' – in other words, a school for scribes conducting a visit *en masse*, like the groups of school children we see today making the rounds of sites."

The need for site protection in ancient times is reinforced by another quotation.

There was no question that temples had to be kept locked, for they were robbed as ruthlessly as churches today. At Rome, thieves made off with a hoard of gold stored in the temple of Jupiter ... the sword of Caesar that was kept in the temple of Mars the Avenger, even the helmet from the statue of Mars there. The situation got so bad at times that the Roman authorities made the guardians of temples with particularly valuable pieces responsible for them with their life (Casson, 1994: 271).

The Manila Declaration on World Tourism emphasises that the primary responsibilities of States is "protecting and enhancing the tourism resources which are part of mankind's heritage" (UNEP, 1988). The Chief Inspector of Historic Buildings, Historic Scotland, concurred with the need to protect heritage sites. "The combination of tourism and heritage in the absence of proper integrated heritage and tourism plans is, inevitably, unsuccessful. This is evident when we examine destruction rates for monuments generally and is even more obvious when the scale of destruction by tourists of monuments and sites and the negative impacts of tourism on cultures is examined" (Mullane, 1994: 79).

Recent literature on heritage tourism development in Asia illustrates that the government authorities play a critical role in protecting and managing heritage sites in China (Sofield & Li, 1998b), Singapore (Chang, 1999), Myanmar (Miksic, 2002) and Hong Kong (Henderson, 2001). Sofield and Li (1998b) provide a classic example of how the changes of the development of policy in China impact the destiny of heritage sites. China is a country with a long history. A unifying theme for China is a destination of "culture and the traditions of heritage tourism and pilgrimage" (Sofield & Li, 1998b: 362). However, during the cultural revolution period (1966–1976), under the policy of rejecting the cultural past as a whole in replacement with a new Chinese socialist culture by the Chinese Communist Party, massive destructions and damages of China's rich and varied built heritage sites occurred. For example, Xi'an was "the supreme metropolis of the medieval world, unrivalled by Baghdad and surpassing Rome" (Brown, 1991 in Sofield and Li, 1998b). However, the heritage sites in Xi'an, such as the world famous Terra Cotta Warriors and Buddhist temples were severely damaged or even destroyed during the Cultural Revolution. Only with the introduction of Deng Xiaoping's "open door" policy and reaffirmation of China's heritage as a valuable resource, did restoration of heritage sites begin. In the meantime, the Heritage Conservation Act 1982 was activated to strengthen the conservation and protection of China's heritage to carry out scientific research and to promote patriotic and revolutionary education for local Chinese (China Travel News, 2003). The restoration of cultural and heritage sites, such as the Great Wall and the Forbidden City, have been undertaken in China under Deng's regime (Sofield & Li, 1998b).

Authenticity

Visitors to heritage sites often expect to be entertained. Casson (1994: 272–273) discussed several sites which provided ancient visitors with some form of diversion. He notes the scepticism of Strabo, the Roman historian, when describing the two colossal statues (still standing) near the Valley of the Kings, one of which had already been damaged in an earthquake and subsequently became famed for "talking".

It is believed that once a day, a noise like a blow of no great force is produced by the part of the statue remaining on the throne and base. I myself was present (along with the Governor of Egypt), and, an hour after sunrise, I heard the sound – whether it came from the base of the statute or was made deliberately by one of the people ... I cannot say.

Presenting heritage sites to visitors in appealing ways is a matter of importance to modern managers. "Interpretation involves making information available and interesting to visitors before, during, and after their visits" (Miksic, 2002: 90). In selecting, presenting and interpreting an area's heritage to tourists, the objective is usually to attract and please visitors. Hewison (1987) referred to the "manufacturing" approach of the heritage industry, criticising the narrow commercial perspectives which result in a shallow, consumerist appreciation of complex matters. The distortion results from two main factors: the need to present the past in visually exciting ways to be successful in a commercial sense and to be selective in what is chosen for presentation. He cited the Jorvik entre in York, which represents the area's Viking era by employing interesting technology in the forms of lighting, people movers and smells and sounds evocative of the era, but with no authenticity. As a result, although the tourist's experience is enjoyable, the issues of the time, and the complex realities of daily life tend to be trivialised. However, Sofield and Li (1998b) pinpoint that the natural cultural and heritage sites in China are often incorporated with man-made features from antiquity like gardens and temples to illustrate that these places are also the product of thousands of years of intelligence and hard work by Chinese people. Tiger Hill in Suzhou, China, is a typical example of this combination with an ancient tomb where Emperor Wu (500 BC) was buried and surrounded by gardens (Sofield & Li, 1998b). Some sites in China are presented combined with natural and man-made features. This urges the need for tour guides' appropriate explanations of these sites. More discussions on this matter will be carried out in the following section.

A distinct identity for a heritage site has become a goal for the interpretation in heritage sites in Myanmar (Miksic, 2002), Hong Kong (Henderson, 2001) and Singapore (Chang, 1999). Miksic (2002) states that the heritage and cultural asset must be properly understood with respect to how the resource is to be interpreted to the public before it can be marketed. When Miksic (2002) tried to interpret ancient cities in Myanmar, comprehensive research was conducted by examining other research projects previously conducted elsewhere in Southeast Asia. Previous projects show that it is important to identify the feature of these ancient cities whether they are restricted to cultural and ritual activities or have a much wider range of activities than religion and ritual prior to marketing these cities.

This identification would affect the essential mode of interpretation for the main sites in Myanmar (Miksic, 2002).

Richter (1997) has discussed a popular tourist attraction in Hawaii, the Polynesian Cultural Centre, where exhibits and performances depict the cultural groups of the South Pacific, showing traditional dwellings, dances and crafts. "There is some attention to accuracy in terms of the cultures presented, but the performers – from the Mormon college – may or may not be from the group they are depicting. Fijians and Tongans may be doing Samoan dances. The individuals are merely acting. Does it matter? ... The more interesting question is "who gets what?" Are the performers properly paid for their labour? Who controls what is presented? ... Do the visitors get an appreciation of South Pacific cultures or a sense of superiority over these societies? We do not know." (Richter, 1997: 96).

Despite the appeal of exotic cultures and histories, one of the characteristics of the tourism industry has been a marked tendency to commoditise products, experiences and even destinations (Laws & Cooper, 1998). Williams and Shaw (1992) cite Britton's (1991) view that commodification of place occurs in one of two ways: by controlling access to a site so that a rent can be collected from visitors, or by commodification of other aspects of the visit, either essential tourist services such as hotels and restaurants, or the site-markers which tourists purchase there to take home. Jansen-Verbeke (1997: 2) has noted that "convergency on the demand side and standardisation of products on the supply side fit well into the current views on and the practice of economies of scale. This also explains why the option of diversification and divergency in tourist product development, with an emphasis on uniqueness and cultural identity of resources, places and people is regarded as the more risky option. . . . However, there are clear signs that gradually the awareness of the competitive advantages by communicating the cultural identity of a place and the uniqueness of tourist products in a global market grows." Richards (1996), has also detected a convergence of cultural tourism development and marketing policies in Europe. He found an explanation in "the changing relationship between cultural consumption and production," and growing competition for "the consumption power of the service class . . . and . . . the mobile consumer" (Richards, 1996: 311–312).

Heritage Site Interpretation

Many heritage sites and cultural traditions are complex and difficult to appreciate fully without expert guidance.

(Heroditus) inevitably depended upon Greek speaking guides. When he went through temples, he was shown about . . . by priests . . . The conversations must have been carried on through his guide or an interpreter. Some of the mistakes he makes may be because he had no way of verifying what these told him . . . . Certain statues he was shown had no hands and given some esoteric explanation of their absence; "it was nonsense," he remarks, 'even I could see that the hands had fallen off through age (Casson, 1994: 105–106).

Western and oriental cultural differences may lead Westerners not appreciating some of the heritage sites in an ancient oriental country, such as China. Sofield and Li (1998a) provide an example of poetic stanzas which were carved into the rock hundreds years ago highlighted in red and blue paint in China. This may be regarded as a form of graffiti, but for Chinese, the poems enhance the

cultural significance of the site. Hence, the different interpretations of the heritage sites urge the mission for Chinese tour guides providing appropriate explanations from cultural perspectives so that tourists would appreciate the beauty of the heritage sites.

Tour guides play a critical role in interpreting and conveying the cultural and heritage site to visitors. A case study of Putuo Mountain in China, the ancient Holy Land of Buddhism around Avalokitesvara, indicates that the cultural heritage religious tourism development in that area is highly dependant on the quality of Chinese tour guides when they explain the richness of the true meaning of Buddhism to visitors (Li *et al.*, 2000). They go on to recommend providing appropriate and specific training for local tour guides.

Although visitors may benefit from an informed commentary, an appropriate style must be used. As Daskalakis (1984) explains,

the sociological-anthropological interpretation of the leavings of a people leads us to knowledge of the human thought and behaviour of certain societies and enriches our historical knowledge to the extent of allowing us to "exercise control" over the answers of the society in which we live and its reactions to the same problems.

He contrasts the scientific and touristic styles of heritage interpretation.

The scientific interpretation gives (the tourist) more data than he really needs while the popular interpretation gives him less ... a well defined and synoptic description of the artefact's characteristics, always in relation to its quality as a tourist attraction ... made in such a way as to simplify without detracting from the substance or from the value of the artefact ... presenting the necessary historical and technical data which form its identity, underlie its uniqueness and its originality and give positive help to the listener ... in understanding the value of the monument and in making a personal, cultural assessment (of) its social and cultural importance and the social influences ... that are revealed in it (Daskalakis, 1984: 27–28).

Pelaggi (1996) and Timothy (1997) consider that the tourist's individual experience of the site is what determines his/her notion of its authenticity. Similarly, Teo and Yeoh (1997: 199) cite Ashworth and Tunbridge (1990), saying that "while authenticity derives from the intrinsic aesthetic or historic value of an object/place for its sake, heritage derives its meaning from the user." A further point can be added. The personal understanding gained from a heritage site visit is mediated by educational and social factors. Brown (1997: 85) has studied the ways in which adults help children to appreciate museum visits. "Helpers can make a wide range of contributions to children's learning ... (they) should be provided with information ... about the range of responses they might make." Brown has identified four positive types of interaction:

- watching; detached/close surveillance
- interpreting; receptive behaviours with the helper
- supporting; encouragement or help
- participating; initiating or sharing in the activity.

Bennet (1988) has noted the problematic gap between heritage professionals and consumers with regard to perceptions and evaluations of heritage products. She discussed interactive technology as one way of adapting the product, allowing visitors to choose freely the media they can best relate to.

Heritage Site Access

Many heritage sites are in quite remote locations, and travellers in ancient times, as now, require road maps and advice about accommodation and other en route facilities.

Anyone using the cursus publicus (Roman roads) had to know exactly where the various inns and hostels belonging to it were located. Handlists called itineraria were available, which detailed for a given route the stopping places along it and how far each was from the next. ... A copy made in the Middle Ages of one of these has survived, the so called Tabula Peutingeriana. Done on an elongated piece of parchment that is no more than thirteen inches wide but over twenty-two feet long, it presents a map of the Roman Empire as if seen through a trick mirror ... (It provides) just about the same information we find on a modern automobile map: lines showing routes; names of cities, towns, and other stopping places; numbers indicating the distance in Roman miles between them. In addition, and most interesting, alongside many of the names there stands a little coloured picture symbol. These serve the same purpose as the surprisingly similar symbols used in the guide Michelin or other modern guide books, to show at a quick glance the nature of the facilities available for spending a night (Casson, 1994: 186–187).

Ashworth and Tunbridge (1990) noted three requirements for successful heritage cities: attractive and well preserved buildings from a range of periods; the buildings should be used for purposes which are appropriate to encourage visitors; and their historical significance is enhanced through association with a major event or person. Two further requirements can be identified for heritage sites in general. Access is a crucial factor in the commercialisation of heritage sites. Many interesting sites are located in remote and sometimes dangerous places, in jungles, deserts, or areas suffering from war or civil strife, thus inhibiting their tourist development. Secondly, Mallam (1989) has pointed out that making heritage resources available for visitor enjoyment is an economic activity; the site has to be made safe to visit, equipped with signing and interpretation to assist visitors in understanding its significance, provided with ancillary services such as car and coach parking, all weather access roads and internal footpaths, and catering and toilet facilities. To achieve this level of development a site requires capital investment, staffing and management. It is therefore usually fenced, and paybooths are installed in order to collect entrance fees to defray the costs of its operation, and also to contribute to its further development for visitor enjoyment and as a site of scientific interest. This point in the development of a heritage site is often controversial, as it represents recognition of

the maintenance, development and management of the public property which forms a substantial component of the attraction for tourists (natural heritage, cultural heritage, the ambience of a historic town etc.), and which is considered a "free good" in economic terms, i.e. one which is not taken into account in evaluating the impact of tourism and its costs (Grant *et al.*, 1998: 101).

The Value of Heritage Tourism

From the earliest times, the economic benefits to residents of a heritage site in their locality have been apparent.

Art stood high on the tourist's agenda. Paulus' visit to Phidias' statue of Zeus at Olympia turned out to be one of the high points of his tour ... (The statue) competed with Praxitiles Aphrodite for the distinction of being the most famed work of art of the ancient world. (It) was in Cnidus. and a wealthy king once offered to pay off the city's entire public debt in exchange for it. The Cnidians turned him down (because) the statue ... attracted droves of tourists to the island yearly (Casson, 1994: 230–236).

The contemporary commercialisation of the heritage and culture of a place can be justified on three economic grounds, it is a driver of economic regeneration, it funds site preservation and development, and it may be less damaging than alternative uses, or neglect. Moreover, the heritage of a place is part of the cultural stock of the community, and a number of issues arise from this perspective. Seale (1996: 487) discussed the significance of local perspectives in developing Canadian heritage sites, and commented,

the essence of the area is based not upon an obvious amalgam of natural and cultural values ... Rather, it rests upon the varying perceptions of two widely differing cultures in their responses to and valuations of the same area of land ... First, heritage professionals involved in the identification, planning, development and operation of site must accept an all encompassing definition of historical/ cultural heritage. Second, because a culture's e.g., aboriginal perspective, of historic and cultural significance are of great importance in the selection of the heritage resource, the people in question must be meaningfully involved in the entire process.

The Virginia Tourist Corporation (1997) found that people with an interest in that State's rich heritage tended to stay longer and to spend more per day than other visitors, visiting more sites, cities and towns, and undertaking more activities. The economic value of contemporary heritage tourism has been confirmed by other studies. "There is a core economic reason ... for the burgeoning of cultural and heritage tourism internationally. That is that it deepens the tourism product, lengthens the tourism season and attracts the more discerning and higher income, higher spending tourists" (Aylward, 1994: 105). He described how a partnership of private country houses including hunting lodges and great ancestral homes was formed under the banner of "Hidden Ireland." "These heritage houses otherwise represent a financial millstone for their owners ... the 'Hidden Ireland' group has created a source of income compatible with the original design of the houses ... the intimate scale (for staying guests and private dinners) ... enables visitors to acquire an understanding and appreciation of Irish culture" (Aylward, 1994: 107).

Souvenirs also provide a source of income from visitors to heritage sites.

Having visited a spot ... the tourist had one thing left to do: find an appropriate souvenir ... the religious minded Roman lady touring in Egypt brought back a container of Nile water to use in the service of Isis ... The amateur art lover came home from Athens with a replica in miniature of the great statue of Athena by Phidias ... The wealthy did not content themselves with miniatures, they order full-scale reproductions ... When St Paul came to Ephesus he had some uneasy moments because a certain Denetrius, a silversmith who specialised in 'silver temples of Artemus' called upon his fellow artesans to protest at the way Christianity was hurting their business (Casson, 1994: 285–287).

The wider economic impacts of tourism on destinations are well documented. Of particular relevance here, it has been noted that tourists' interest in local crafts causes changes to the destination area's retailing sector, including the introduction of new styles of service and special stock lines to suit visitors' tastes. Souvenirs often displace traditional resident-oriented products (Swain, 1989). Cohen (1993) has commented that when these tourist-purchased products undergo heterogenisation there is a need for financial and technical support, raising the issue of what forms of souvenir business organisation to support. Richter (1997) discusses the example of Ute pottery. These American Indian native peoples had a long tradition of decorative textiles, but recently they learnt pottery skills from an outsider and set up a shop factory in 1986. Ute pottery now features in speciality catalogues; Richter points out that it is authentic, but the tradition is only a dozen years old!

Further Discussion

Ashworth (1993) has commented on the evolution of modern heritage management from its initial preservation concerns to its contemporary commercialisation as a tourist commodity. This raises issues regarding the relationships between conservers of heritage products, the local authorities using heritage as part of their development strategies and the tourism industry. Preservation is often seen as the paramount responsibility of all heritage managers, but other priorities are evident in the literature. Ralston and Kelly (1996) identified five objectives of concern to most managers of heritage and cultural sites:

- focus on authenticity and quality
- preservation of resources
- make sites come alive
- find the fit between community and heritage tourism
- collaborate with tourism managers.

The discussion so far has noted that many matters of concern to heritage site managers and visitors in the ancient world are still relevant. However, contemporary heritage tourism literature indicates that managers are more concerned than previously with two general issues: visitor satisfaction and the reduction of any negative impacts of tourist activity on host communities and their cultures. Effective visitor management strategies are therefore a key responsibility of contemporary heritage managers.

Visitor Satisfaction

Increasingly, managers of heritage sites are developing strategies to influence their visitors' experiences through the design and resourcing of the visit (Laws, 1998; 2004; Leaske & Yoeman, 1999; Masberg & Silverman, 1996). Laws (1998) has discussed the importance of historic buildings as tourism assets throughout Europe, noting the attractiveness to tourists of their imposing, solid appearance, and fortifications whose original purpose was usually to keep unwanted visitors out. However, the structure of their interiors, with narrow, dark staircases, and complex corridors, also present difficulties to tourists. Although the contemporary managers of a historic building operate within the physical constraints of its structure, usually heavily protected by conservation rules (Suddards, 1982), they are able to influence their visitors' experiences through the design and resourcing of the visit strategy (Gummesson, 1988; King & Garey, 1997). It has been suggested that heritage sites should adopt a "visitor ethic": "It is important in trying to cater, or 'care' for the visitor, that every step along the way is considered as part of a strategy or *visitor management plan*. Each element is important and a lack of caring, whether it be

in the signing, car parking, quality of catering, or the cleanliness of the toilets, can destroy the overall visitor experience" (Parkin *et al.*, 1989: 110, *original italics*).

The quality of the service experience for each visitor is affected by interactions with staff, but this takes place in the context of the physical setting and the managerial concepts underlying the visit (Hollins & Hollins, 1991). In most historic buildings, visitors are either accompanied by a guide, or encounter custodians located in each major exhibit area. Service management theory recognises the importance of encounters between staff and clients (Bowen & Schneider, 1985). In castles, these points of contact are important in providing visitors with information to help them enjoy their visit, but also ensure that every visitor follows the predetermined sequence through the building's internal spaces and exhibits. Tourists also come into contact with staff at catering and retail outlets, and when participating in any of the activities which form an increasing feature of visits to historic buildings and their grounds, including displays of traditional skills such as archery or falconry, or crafts, and attending musical or other performances. The significance for service sector managers of these contact points is that they are "moments of truth" (Carlzon, 1987; Normann, 1991) in which the customer judges the quality of his or her experience.

Stakeholder Interests

The second issue for heritage site managers is to control the local effects of tourism by implementing policies designed to gain the most benefit while minimising any harmful consequences which result from tourist activity. In particular, the consequences for other stakeholders, including local residents and businesses, need to be made explicit if tourism is to be sustainable as the basis for continuing economic and cultural development in heritage areas such as Europe's historic walled cities where the pressure from tourist numbers and their behaviour is sometimes detrimental to locals.

The process begins with a clear analysis of the specific issues and characteristics in a particular destination as a basis for a coherent, systematic view of the various policies to resolve them. Each heritage site has to identify local problems and develop its own management response, based on local circumstances. However, many do not have sufficient resources to implement effective tourism management policies, as was noted in a recent study of Canterbury.

It will always be necessary to balance the demands of visitor management with the legitimate claims of the local area on local authority discretionary spending. Increasingly, an emphasis on partnership working means that more and more communities will be turning to national funding mechanisms and the commercial sector to help fund their efforts to manage positively the impacts of tourism at the local level (Le Pelley & Laws, 1998: 92).

Conclusion

This paper has drawn attention to some aspects of a rather neglected study of tourism in ancient times by Casson (1994), and in particular it has discussed the insights provided by Casson into contemporary heritage tourism management. These include an understanding that interest in heritage tourism is perhaps as old as civilisation, and that it encompasses a wide range of motivations and types of attraction. Visitation caused problems for site security in ancient times and provided opportunities for local employment and profit, although sometimes resulting in the embellishment of factual explanations of the site. While travel opportunities and horizons were more restricted in ancient times, the issues of access and traveller information remain as important constraints for contemporary travellers.

Cultural and heritage tourism, if properly managed, can provide benefits to all related parties: cultural and historical assets can be preserved, protected and repaired with funds obtained from visitors, and authentic and educational experiences can be provided to tourists (Miksic, 2002). Although management of visitor satisfaction and the impacts of tourism appear to be modern concerns, many of the issues which confront contemporary managers and heritage tourists would be recognised by our predecessors from as long ago as three and a half millennia. Yet relatively little is known about how these issues were managed differently from the present. It would be at least interesting if one stream of research in the future could be focused on learning more about the ancient and recent history of the industry. The little evidence that has been published suggests that this could become a rich source of insights for the further development of heritage tourism. As stated before, limited research has been conducted in Asian regions, although many countries in Asia have been embodied with rich and massive cultural heritage sites. More research therefore needs to be conducted in these regions. Problems and issues that occurred in European countries may be an alert or a good lesson for heritage tourism management in Asia and Pacific regions.

References

Ashworth, G. (1993). Culture and Tourism: Conflict or Symbiosis in Europe? In W. Pompl & P. Lowry (eds), *Tourism in Europe, Structures and Developments* (pp. 13–35). CAB International, Wallingford.

Ashworth, G. & Tunbridge, J. (1990). *The Tourist Historic City*. Belhaven, London.

Aylward, A. (1994). *The Appeal of Heritage Tourism: The Quality of Yesteryear*. WTO, Madrid.

Bennet, T. (1988). Museums and the People. In R. Lumley (ed), *The Museum Time Machine, Putting Cultures On Display* (pp. 63–85). Routledge, London.

Bowen, D. E. & Schneider, B. (1985). Boundary Spanning Role Employees and the Service Encounter: Some Guidelines For Management and Research. In J. A. Czepiel, M. Soloman & C. Surprenant (eds), *The Service Encounter, Managing Employee/Customer Interaction In Service Business*. Lexington Books, Boston.

Britton, S. (1991). Tourism, Capital and Place: Towards a Critical Geography of Tourism. *Environment and Planning, D: Society and Space*, 9, 451–478.

Brown, M. (1998). Defining Heritage Tourism: Implications for Marketing and Impact assessment. Discussion paper presented at the annual TTRA conference, Fort Worth, Texas.

Brown, A. (1997). Helpers, Children, and Hands Oo Exhibits. *Museum Management and Curatorship*, 6(1), 80–90.

Casson, L. (1994). *Travel in the Ancient World*. Johns Hopkins University Press, Baltimore.

Carlzon, J. (1987). *Moments of Truth*. Harper and Row, New York.

China Travel News (2003). Heritage Conservation Act 1982 (in Chinese).

Chang, T. C. (1999). Local Uniqueness in the Global Village: Heritage Tourism in Singapore. *Professional Geographer*, 51(1), 91–103.

Daskalakis, G. (1984). Tourism and Architectural Heritage – Cultural aspects. *Proceedings of the 34th AIEST Conference, Prague*, pp. 23–36.

Davis, S. (1994) *A Strategic Analysis of the Market Potential For Museums and Art Galleries in the UK*. Museum and Galleries Commission, London.

Frochot, I. and Beeho, A. (1997). The Future for Heritage Tourism, conference report. *Progress in Tourism and Hospitality Research*, 3(4): 271–272.

Grant, M., Human, B. & Le Pelley, B. (1998). Who pays for the free lunch? Destination management and the 'free good' factor? *Insights*, 9, 95–101.

Gummesson, E. (1988). Service Quality and Product Quality Combined. *Review of Business*, 9(3), 134–156.

Henderson, J. (2001). Heritage, Identity and Tourism in Hong Kong. *International Journal of Heritage Studies*, 7(3), 219–236.

Hewison, R. (1987). *The Heritage Industry: Britain in a Climate of Decline*. Methuen, London.

Hollins, G. & Hollins, B. (1991). *Total Design, Managing The Design Process In The Service Sector*, Pitman, London.

Hood, M. (1983). Staying Away: Why People Choose Not to Visit Museums. *Museum News*, 61(4), 50–57.

Jansen-Verbeke, M. (1997). Developing Cultural tourism in Historical Cities, The Local Challenge in a Global Market. Discussion paper at the International Academy for Tourism Studies Conference, Melaka.

King, C. & Garey, J. (1997). Relational quality in service encounters. *International Journal of Hospitality Management*, 16(1), 39–63.

Laws, E. (2004). *Improving Tourism Services*. Thomson Learning, London (in press).

Laws, E. (1998). Conceptualising visitor satisfaction management in heritage settings: An exploratory blueprinting analysis of Leeds Castle, Kent. *Tourism Management*, 19(6), 545–554.

Laws, E. & Cooper, C. (1998). Inclusive tours and commodification: the marketing constraints for mass market resorts. *Journal of Vacation Marketing*, 4(4), 337–352.

Leaske, A. & Yeoman, I. (eds) (1999). *Heritage Visitor Attractions: An Operations Management Perspective*. Cassell, London.

Le Pelley, B. & Laws, E. (1998). A Stakeholder-Benefits Approach to Tourism Management in a Historic City Centre: The Canterbury City Centre Initiative. In E. Laws, W. Faulkner & G. Moscardo (eds), *Embracing and Managing Change in Tourism: International Case Studies* (pp. 70–94). Routledge, London.

Li, J., Zhang, X., Fang, G., Li, J., Zhang, X. & Fang, G. (2000). How to Develop the Tourist Trade at Putuoshan. *Journal of Zhejiang Forestry College*, 17(4), 398–403.

Mallam, M. (1989). Can Heritage Charities be Profitable? In D. Uzzell (ed), *Heritage Interpretation: The Natural and Built Environment* (pp. 44–50). Belhaven, London.

Masberg, B. & Silverman, L. (1996). Visitor Experiences at Heritage Sites, A Phenomenological Approach. *Journal of Travel Research*, 34(4), 20–25.

Miksic, J. N. (2002). Early Burmese Urbanization: Research and Conservation. *Asian Perspective*, 40(1), 88–107.

Moscardo, G. (1996). Mindful Visitors, Heritage and Tourism. *Annals of Tourism Research*, 23(2), 376–397.

Mullane, F. (1994). Heritage Interpretation, Ideology and Tourism. In P. Breathnach (ed), *Irish Tourism Development*, Geographical Society of Ireland, Special Publication No 9 (pp. 79–86). Maynooth, County Kildare.

Normann, R. (1991). *Service Management: Strategy and Leadership In Service Businesses*. Wiley, Chichester.

Parkin, I., Middleton, P. & Beswick, V. (1989). Managing The Town and City for Visitors and Local People. In D. Uzzell (ed), *Heritage Interpretation*, Volume 2 (pp. 108–114). Belhaven Press, London.

Pelaggi, M. (1996). National heritage and global tourism in Thailand. *Annals of Tourism Research*, 23(2), 432–443.

Ralston, L. & Kelly, K. (1996). A model for the evaluation of potential Utah heritage tourism destinations. Proceedings of the annual TTRA Conference, Las Vegas, 339–343.

Richards, G. (1996). European Cultural Tourism, Trends and Future Prospects. In G. Richards (ed), *Cultural tourism in Europe* (pp. 311–333). CAB International, Wallingford.

Richards, S. (1997). *National Heritage Tourism Forum, Review and Summary*. Ohio Division of Travel and Tourism, Cleveland, Ohio.

Richter, L. (1997). The Politics of Heritage Tourism. Paper presented at the *International Conference on Tourism Development: Issues for a New Agenda*, Melaka.

Seale, R. (1996). A Perspective From Canada On Heritage And Tourism. *Annals of Tourism Research*, 24(3), 484–488.

Sofield, T. & Li, F. (1998a). Historical Methodology and Sustainability: An 800 Year Old Festival From China. *Journal of Sustainable Tourism*, 6(4), 267–292.

Sofield, T. & Li, F. (1998b). Tourism Development and Cultural Policies in China. *Annals of Tourism Research*, 25(2), 362–392.

Suddards, R. (1982) *Listed buildings: the law and practice*. Sweet and Maxwell, London.

Swain, M. (1989). Gender roles in indigenous tourism: Kuna Mola, Yuna Yala and Cultural survival. In V. Smith (ed), *Hosts and Guests, The Anthropology of Tourism* 2nd edn. University of Pennsylvania Press, Philadelphia.

Teo, P. & Yeoh, B. (1997). Remaking local heritage for tourism. *Annals of Tourism Research*, 24(1), 192–208.

Timothy, D. J. (1997). Tourism and the personal heritage experience, *Annals of Tourism Research*, 24(3), 751–754.

Timothy, D. J. & Boyd, S. W. (2003). *Heritage Tourism*. Prentice Hall, Harlow.

UNEP (1988) *Sustainable tourism development, Industry and Environment*. United Nations Environmental Program, Geneva.

Virginia Tourism Corporation (1997). *Heritage Tourism National omnibus Study*. Virginia Tourism Corporation, Norfolk, Virginia.

Williams, A. & Shaw, G. (1992). Tourism Research, a Perspective. *American Behavioural Scientist*, 36(2), 133–143.

World Tourism Organisation (1992). Guidelines: Development of National Parks and Protected Areas for Tourism. World Tourism Organisation, Madrid.

Yale, P. (1991). *From Tourist Attraction to Heritage Tourism*. Elm Publications, Huntingdon.

40 Sheds and 40 Kilometers: Agricultural Sheds as Heritage Tourism Opportunities

Ros Derrett and Justin St Vincent Welch

Introduction

This chapter reports on a project that was designed to identify a distinctive series of iconic farm buildings along a section of the Pacific Highway in northern New South Wales (NSW), Australia, and establishes the potential for developing a tourist route to promote these buildings to visitors and residents. In part, the project focuses on how farm buildings, and specifically those known as sheds, can be identified as representing a portion of the rural heritage that is often seen by urban dwellers as representing the spirit of the Australian outback. This aspect of rural architecture was specifically selected because it represents the agrarian economy on which rural settlements were built.

The project also explored how cultural mapping processes can inform appropriate development and delivery of cultural tourism experiences for the host community and the visitor. While few of the agricultural sheds identified in the project are individually of high heritage value, as a collection of sheds and in the particular landscape they are

located in, they provide an opportunity to recognize, interpret and manage a significant cultural resource.

The study area, located along a 40 km stretch of highway between Grafton (south) and Maclean (to the north) in the Northern Rivers region of NSW, the Clarence area, is a densely settled farming district that exhibits a diversity of rural landscapes. The agricultural sheds represent the region's rural and agrarian past. Built out of a diverse range of material, including predominantly rough sawn hardwood and corrugated iron, as well as brick, block, fibro, sawn timber and wire mesh, the sheds are a link to the formal regional identity derived largely from past rural pursuits. In part, they represent a shift from dairying, sugar cane and horticulture to contemporary uses including the incorporation of rural properties into the growing urbanized landscapes providing dormitory settlements for nearby towns such as Maclean and Grafton.

The project documented over 40 farm buildings through photography, drawing, storytelling and design dimensions and was underpinned by research on the history of the buildings, interviews with property owners and extensive recording of oral histories by district settlers describing their experiences in primary production. The project was also aimed at developing interpretive material for touring exhibitions and hardcopy material for numerous individuals and groups.

This exercise identified the appeal to visitors of the densely settled diverse agricultural area. Residents and outside visitors regard the landscape of this region as authentic Australiana, just as Canadians and Americans regard their rural heritage as true Canadiana and Americana (Hopkins 1998; Timothy 2005). The humble 'rude' shed is the built element that links human activities to the landscape. Domestic dwellings, while significant, have a different appeal and do not represent the region's rural economy in the same manner as the sheds that are the focus of this project.

From another perspective the structures featured in this research reflect the broader notion of immigrants and settlers. Waves of migration shaped the rural landscape, and echoes of these waves can be seen in the sheds being considered here. These sheds and their associative representations of historic Australiana also provide a passive 'drive by' experience for contemporary urban visitors to the region. To establish greater interaction between landholders and visitors considerable heritage product development of this nature is seen as a salient need in this region.

Cultural Tourism

The culture of the region is no longer the exclusive domain of the residents. It is now, more than ever, shared with visitors. This does, however, raise the risk of confusing what belongs to 'culture' and what belongs to 'tourism'. The notion of place being affected by tourism development (Hall and Jenkins, 1995) is under scrutiny in the Clarence area. The tension demonstrated by how history is organized, interpreted and valued in tourism settings and how it can transform the cultural and historical life of host communities can be observed. The process of cultural mapping can be used to investigate the historical values, interests and aspirations of a discrete group of people in their landscape. By doing so, a cultural tourism product, if desired, can be generated. The expectations of host and guest are thus transformed. By creating cultural tourism products the sense of place for both host and guest is altered.

Within the context of heritage as a tourism product lies the notion that at any cultural site there are multiple meanings constructed by different groups of people who claim an association with the site. Boyd *et al.* (1996: 125) describe this interest or association as cognitive ownership. This ownership is an inherent cognitive quality, derived from the activity of knowing the site. In the case of the sheds, not only do the local long-term residents and owners make this claim but also, it appears, newcomers and drive-by visitors express some resonance with the site as an expression of an historic culture of which they have some generational experience. So as Boyd *et al.* suggest, to manage the heritage resource satisfactorily so as to maximize its success, an acceptance of the multiplicity and connectedness of socially constructed meanings needs to take place. In the context of the sheds, this may mean that appropriate management structures are installed to minimize the pressures associated with conservation, and at the same time provide access to those cognitive owners for whom the sheds have particular meaning.

Definitions of culture include the relationship of people to their past – familiar, communal and societal; their built and natural heritage, their spirituality, rituals and ceremonies; their art form practices and celebrations; political evolution and lifestyle choices. Cultural tourism as a distinctive sector of mainstream tourism is attractive to regional communities. The opportunity to ground the visitor experience in the daily life of destination communities provides considerable management and marketing challenges for stakeholders, including local government, state agencies, specific community cultural groups (like museums and historical societies) and landholders as they come to terms with the attendant increased visitation.

A criterion based upon *what* is visited (monuments and artistic events) is being replaced by one that deals with *how* they are visited (Wood, 1992). This shift reflects a move from cultural tourism being represented as a way of protecting monuments *from* tourists, *'whereas now we tend to speak of using cultural tourism's educative role to teach people to respect them and its economic power to nurture them'* (Wood, 1992:4). This contextual framework is central to definitions represented in the literature.

Cultural assets in Australia are defined by the Australian Heritage Commission Act 1975 as consisting of "those places, being components of the natural environment of Australia, or the cultural environment of Australia, that have aesthetic, historic, scientific or social significance or other special value for future generations as well as for the present community" (cited in Brokensha and Guldberg, 1992: 67).

"Cultural tourism involves customised excursions into other cultures and places to learn about their people, lifestyle, heritage and arts in an informed way that genuinely represents those cultures and their historical contexts" (Craik, 1995: 6). Cultural tourism has to do with the human environment. This is where culture signifies a whole range of human creations, customs, historic structures and activities. Cultural tourism offers a special dynamic of its own. It allows linkages with substantial elements of the human condition, the joys and hopes, not only for travellers (tourism visitor/guest) but also for host communities. It means enrichment, offers opportunities for reflection for locals and tourists and can improve the quality of life of both parties. It also encourages cultural exposure in a wider context and can be a cause for celebration.

Cultural tourism is also about the ways of a place; essentially people would be cultural tourists to do what locals do. They wish to experience the authentic bits of life of the destination community and want to go home with a story. This storytelling element has been central to travel since time immemorial; thus, culture and tourism are not strangers to one another, and it is not a new phenomenon. The collaborative nature of cultural tourism is in fact the content of tourism. The sheds project described here allowed for contact with local social historians, and stories from settlers contributed to an oral history that could be included in tourism promotional material.

Like other tourism products, culture can act as a catalyst for broader cultural development (McKercher and du Cros 2002; Richards 1996; Timothy and Boyd 2003). It can provide increased employment and training opportunities in labor-intensive industries such as the arts, heritage, conservation and tourism. Culture-based tourism can also generate pride in communities' built and natural environments and can initiate infrastructure and amenity development for destination communities. Moreover this form of tourism can encourage partnerships and packages in a commercial sense through tours, conventions, events and meetings, and encourage partnerships between the public and private sector. Finally, in common with all types of tourism, cultural tourism can extend visitors' length of stay and increase income for a wider cross-section of the community.

Cultural tourists generally require an experience, an authentic, hands-on, peace and quiet, interactive exchange, skills development, spiritual, responsible, safe and unique type of experience. The marketing of such a cultural experience can be challenging though it offers opportunities for partnerships with other specialised tourism providers and technologies. The Internet allows the sharing of information, and the making of effective entrepreneurial connections between existing or new tourism providers.

Cultural Mapping

The marketing of the cultural heritage as a tourism product requires considerable knowledge and information about the cultural resources and assets contained within a community. The assessment of the tangible aspects of a community's past is relatively straightforward. This entails the identification of museums, galleries, distinctive landmarks, landscapes and industries. It is, however, the intangibles associated with community culture, the how and why we do and have done things around here that gives identity and resonance to that culture.

Documenting and assessing the diversity of knowledge a community has of itself is termed cultural mapping. It is a process that provides an understanding "of how people are experiencing their place and culture" (Grogan and Mercer, 1995: 74). The process of cultural mapping is generally needs driven from within a community and can serve as a community building tool by alleviating unemployment, and developing tourism and other creative cultural and social activities. Cultural mapping defines a community in terms of its diverse socio-cultural and economic values; it records, preserves and allows development of those values in new and creative ways.

These views introduce the issue of interpretation of the values expressed within the cultural mapping exercise. This is in relation to the collection of buildings as an expression of a cultural tourism product. Fundamental to this product is the notion of the shed as the linkage between human endeavor and landscape. It is this linkage, combined with long held local traditions and activities, that create within a community its sense of place. Upitis (cited in Uzzell, 1989:154) suggests that it is more than simply a 'physical location'. This sense, developed over time, is an expression of attitude and personality at a community level. It draws on the success and adversity experienced by the community and so develops as a sense of local identity.

So the interpretation of values that will accurately reflect the sense of place, of which the sheds are a major element, needs to be carefully considered from the perspective of a sensitivity to cultural ownership and the imposition of intellectual and personal values held by the interpreter. To undervalue cultural ownership and local interests is to miss out on the full support and good will of the community, thereby diminishing the richness and effectiveness of the interpretation program. Brokensha and Guldberg (1992: 172) concur with this notion and suggest that "local people are a huge but largely under-utilized cultural resource." Indeed a tourism product based on the interpretation of a community's local heritage environment, complete with the diverse and special characteristics, is as Binks (cited in Uzzell, 1989:193) remarks, "(much more) likely to be self-sustaining long after the fashion for a more ephemeral tourist activity has passed."

The 40 Sheds and 40 Kilometres Heritage Tourism Project engaged in a cultural mapping exercise by developing an educational program that identified and documented a collection of farm buildings. The project further interpreted the buildings using photo-documentation and interpretation derived from the reminiscences of community members who had either owned, worked with or grew up on the farms of the lower Clarence River. Several other methods were also used, as noted below, as part of this exercise.

Project Objectives and Methodology

The project's objectives required that research be conducted into the background and history of a distinctive series of aging farm buildings. The research was limited to the buildings' social and industrial context at a local level and did not attempt to define or assess the buildings formally in terms of their technical and aesthetic significance. This process may be seen as the first step in the production of a formal statement of significance and relates directly to the initial stage of the NSW Heritage Management System, that of an investigation of significance.

The research undertaken involved both primary and secondary data gathering. Primary research took several forms including consultation with the relevant heritage committees. The purpose of this consultation was twofold: to determine if any previous studies had taken place relating to the sheds and to establish if the committees possessed and were willing to share any useful information.

Information and comments were solicited from the public at large using a discrete public relations campaign that alerted the public, through the electronic and print media, to the existence of the project and its research requirements. This approach provided the public with the opportunity to access directly the researcher through a face-to-face meeting and provided opportunities for future contact. Further to this, the researcher was able to gauge the level of awareness and interest in the subject with respect to the issues of preservation and local identity.

Interviews were conducted with key personnel who were reputed to have a keen interest in the subject or who had some specialist knowledge of the subject. Most mature communities will more than likely have individuals who are the self-appointed social historians of that community. In this situation it was essential to locate these individuals and gain their cooperation to provide an overall view of the subject from a local perspective and to give an indication of long standing family ownership, as well as current ownership. This was important when approaching historical societies and the individual owners themselves.

Interviews conducted with past and present property owners provided a more precise and intimate overview of the sheds and the landscape. Information received from key persons about elderly community members who have specialist knowledge and experience of the subjects was helpful. Contact with these individuals, who were in some cases residents of retirement homes, was made easier with a referral or introduction from a familiar source. These individuals must be regarded as a highly valuable source of information, particularly in terms of producing an oral history associated with the subject. This issue should perhaps be regarded with some urgency given that some individuals are of advanced years.

Oral history was also extensively used. In the following transcript a local resident recalls his knowledge of a number of sheds as the researcher drove him along a short stretch of highway. The project collected a number of transcripts of this nature and collectively they were used to develop a history of the sheds.

Oral history excerpts from a drive with Don McPhee, a local resident

The trip started at South Grafton and the speedo was zeroed at the Jacaranda Motel. The left hand side of the road was said to be the northside and right was the south.

2.6 kms – South side, Want's old barn. This structure featured in Jolliffs 'Salt Bush Bill'

3.2 kms – North side, at the Swan Creek Bridge, Want's farm and home. Originally Smalls homestead, allegedly the place where Water Hyacinth was first introduced to the Clarence River as the result of disposing of an unwanted potted specimen.

Diversion off the highway to the south to view very large shed that had previously been the show pavilion at Ullmarra Showground, this is on Bert McKay's farm originally Charlie Watkins' farm at Swan Creek. '*He gave the game away after 19 floods in 23 years and a nervous breakdown!*"

9.1 kms – Sam Watkins farm. Dairy and bails, barn and home that has a separate kitchen. This is a very good collection of buildings all in reasonable order and very representative of the era. The house is of particular interest as it is of a particular style with high pitched roof and separate kitchen (Ken Watkins' uncle).

10.5 kms – Northside. Doug Miller's barn and Hayshed. The hay shed was built from materials from the Ramournie Meatworks at the Orara River west of Grafton and transported to Ullmarra by bullock team.

2.1 kms north of Ulmarra – North side. A hybrid barn, the original structure having vertical sawn timber and in the standard configuration. Butted up to this structure is an addition that has horizontal weatherboards. This is the remains of a cottage which was transported to the site and used to create additional space for the storage of paspalum grass seed.

2.5 kms – North side. Charlie Blanch's farm. Interesting collection, Hay shed and attached feed stalls, bails and a separate dairy that makes this collection pre in-house separator. The old open ended barn though modified somewhat was originally a sugar mill and has a small split slab shed nearby that has the remains of a brick tank sunk in the ground that was used to collect and store the molasses.

3.2 kms – North side. Ken Bultitude's farm. Old barn was for corn and gear, old rusty roofed shed is the cow shed with the dairy and bails and the house facing towards the river, this is because in the early days the main road ran between the house and the river. South side, a smooth skin concrete silo used for storing silage usually corn chop, plaque on the wall facing the road reads: '*Erected for the Grafton Dairy Co. through NCSN Co. Fodder Conservation Scheme. No 3 11.2.33 Builder Willis and Garlon, Maroubra Sydney.*'

Another silo can be seen on the river bank about opposite Doughety's Tea Tree plantation close to South Grafton. This one is No.2.

4.4 kms – South side. Old brick school house complete with teacher's residence and brick outhouse. This was called the Lower School and was at times referred to as the 'Wesleyan School'. It had a class of 52 children in its first year of operation. The teacher at that time was Mr William Hattersley. There is also an underground water tank, complete with domed roof also constucted from brick, circa 1882. "Avondale" homestead has been moved to a site just behind the school by the RTA.

6.0 kms – South side. John Staples' farm, old barn and former school building from Grafton High School. This was the Music Room.

9 kms – North side. Very old house now missing its verandah. Small garage nearby. House is distinctive because of the high pitched roof and vertical timber cladding. This property is subdivided into residential blocks because this was once the village of Cowper.

Secondary research material was based on searches of the archives of historical societies at Maclean and Grafton. Generally the information gathered from these sources related to the regional history and activities associated with the agricultural nature of the subject, though not specific to individual buildings or properties. Information of this kind may well have been found within the documentation relating to particular proprietor families. Another source of agricultural activity relating to the buildings was found in the records of the various agricultural show societies.

Project Outputs

The exercise revealed an array of comments related to the buildings. Some representative feelings and attitudes include:

- There was a sense of reverence expressed for the past as many of the sheds are regarded as direct links to the pioneering families of the area.
- They (the buildings) appeared to epitomize the lost sense of social cohesiveness in this

agricultural setting. Clearly, they symbolized a time of relative prosperity and importance in a largely agrarian society.
- From the community at large, who had no direct connection to the buildings, came a sense of value that was related to the buildings as representing authentic links to the past and to a somewhat less complicated world.

When asked what image could be assigned to symbolize this locality, most people thought that the local farming landscape and the river were the two most representative. It was interesting to note that most of the older people referred to the river that transects the study area as a source of benefit despite the ever-present threat of flood. It was often referred to as 'the road in the old days'. Many of the old homesteads were orientated towards the river much as a house faces the street. The highway on the other hand was referred to as a disruptive influence, having various realignments that caused inconvenient subdivisions of farms and ever increasing traffic, which inevitably made many properties unmanageable as dairy farms. The road was viewed as one of the main contributing elements to irreversible change, both from the perspective of altering farming activities away from the traditional and delivering a new and unfamiliar population to the locality.

An important part of the project was the presentation of the findings in formats that could be communicated to local residents to alert them about the significance of rural sheds and gain their support for preserving the sheds. The most significant outcome was the identification of 40 representative sheds over a 40 kilometer stretch of highway and the use of these sheds in a range of exhibitions based on photos and accompanying interpretation. An award winning photographer was engaged to photograph the sheds and an exhibition of black and white photographs was held between February 28 and April 8, 2001, at the Grafton Regional Art Gallery. Over 1500 visitors saw the exhibition, a substantial number of which had never been to the Gallery before, but as regional residents they were interested in seeing 'their' sheds. Two images were purchased for the Gallery's permanent collection. The exhibition later showed at the Southern Cross University Art Museum in Lismore for wider coverage.

To develop the tourism potential of the 40 sheds identified as having some heritage worth, a drive route map was designed and distributed through several tourism information centers operated by the Clarence Valley Tourist Association. The simple driving tour guide was popular with visitors and formed the basis of later promotional material. The research was also used to produce a calendar to celebrate the people and places in the focus area. These were distributed to local government, tourism outlets, museums and community outlets to indicate that there are numerous options for further print documentation.

Another activity organized as part of the project was a bus trip from Grafton Gallery to Maclean with local residents who came to hear experts talk about the research. More stories were gleaned from residents who were familiar with the history of the area and incorporated in the final documentation.

The cultural mapping exercise benefited from considerable media attention. Radio and print media demonstrated an interest in this aspect of rural heritage. A comprehensive report has been compiled of heritage tourism product development ideas generated by university students during a field trip and intensive primary and secondary research (Special Interest Tourism, 2000). Guest speakers and visits to sites, museums, galleries and tourism offices underpinned the work undertaken by the students.

Local government, heritage advisers, architects, independent investors, the Nature Tourism Taskforce and the NR Regional Cultural Tourism Organisation and the Director of the Grafton Regional Gallery were all active participants in the process working closely with the project manager and the researcher.

Observations

The public appeal for community input served as a tool to gather information and also to create awareness of the project and its potential outcomes. In the first instance this strategy did not yield the richness of anecdote or remembrance that was hoped for. A few useful contacts were made, which may have even created some defensive reaction amongst some of the shed owners because of their preconceived view of heritage listing. Most property owners expressed some concern at the prospect of the possibility of their buildings being listed even though they also professed an interest in the conservation of the structures that they regarded as being representative of a more significant time. The strategy did, however, succeed in creating considerable awareness of, and interest in, the project across a wide section of the community.

The informal interviews on the other hand were very successful as a research tool, considering the requirement for a degree of assessment of the social significance attached to these buildings by the local community. The level of significance would be difficult to determine without allowing for personal interpretation by members of the community. The interview also allowed for clarification of the project's position on the issue of inclusion into the NSW Heritage Database. Cross-referencing of stories was also made possible by interviewing different people about the same subject. This also provided opportunities for referral to new contacts and sources of information. An additional advantage of this form of primary research was the opportunity to compile a reference list of knowledgeable and helpful individuals that may be used as a resource for future studies and assessments.

Opportunities Identified

While not funded in this project, the opportunities identified may be of interest in future research of this nature. While all formal project objectives were achieved, numerous opportunities were identified during its development and completion. These included:

- the need for an assessment of the heritage significance of the built landscape for inclusion in the NSW Heritage database;
- opportunities to apply for funds to sponsor the Sheds Photographic Exhibition and Texts to other regional towns;

- the development of riverside heritage interpretation at designated picnic spots;
- the opportunity to create detailed heritage inventories of the sheds for other regional areas;
- opportunities to compile a register for filmmakers (a substantial cultural sector on the northern rivers) who regularly seek authentic rural locations for film productions;
- use Geographical Information System (GIS) to document the location and scale of these buildings;
- compile oral histories in conjunction with local museums and historical societies;
- develop community festivals or specific 'shed' events; develop appropriate signage (and interpretation) to identify significant sheds whose owners are happy to allow public access;
- preparation of a detailed map locating each of the sheds;
- development of a scenic drive to include the established Squatters Rest Museum (at Tucabia). The Pacific Highway route is a possibility for enterprising tour operators;
- conducting workshops for property owners along the route to establish interest in a heritage tourism route. Some owners have expressed interest in knowing more about how to realise the potential of their buildings;
- developing a tourism agency managed survey of visitors' 'favourite shed';
- developing further collateral including postcards, a book of the images and text supplied by recognized authorities in landscape architecture, heritage management and tourism and other merchandising.

Discussion and Conclusion

This project allowed a series of indicative processes to establish the value the public places on a heritage environment of agricultural buildings and established how the local people felt about the sheds as a tangible representation of their culture. This was a significant aspect of the response by interviewees to this project. They considered that this element of their culture could soon be lost as the structures were replaced or demolished. They felt increasing pressure either to share their heritage with visitors, abandon the sheds to decay or adapt them for alternative agricultural purposes. The sheds are on the brink of disappearing from the landscape; in fact during the project some actually did. This twilight zone of absorbing heritage into a tourism framework highlights the issues of commodification to people unfamiliar with mainstream tourism. The research recognised the importance of the lifestyle and landscape choices residents have made over time and how these can be teased out for storytelling, documenting change in a landscape and challenges to land use.

Buildings such as the sheds identified in this project are an integral part of cultural heritage. Even though contemporary visitors have no personal involvement with the buildings in the past or present, they seem comfortable in the belief that this heritage landscape should be available to them and others. Mackay (1993:211) suggests this rather romanticised and unrealistic view stems from the notion that the Australian bush has strong symbolic value; it reminds contemporary Australians of the early explorers and pioneers through whom Australians live their heritage. Though Australia is one of the world's most urbanized societies, the nostalgia derived from belonging to the bush is pursued by those escaping the stresses of life in the twenty-first century city.

The appeal of the nostalgic sentiment of visitors may be at odds with property owners who are obliged to secure, maintain and develop the sheds and whose personal commitment to heritage is negligible. Dilemmas of this nature arise when visitors express the desire for all these building to be preserved. Landowners come under pressure to preserve something that could now cost time, money and other resources to maintain. Yet, while realizing that the sheds represents a rich and dynamic past, the shed owners are nevertheless constrained by the current economic climate.

With people wanting to do what locals do, or at least see what locals used to do, those associated with the desire to use the sheds as a tourism product must encourage a commitment from landholders. Such agreements are required to ensure that everyone understands the mutual benefits from this unique tourism resource. Destination communities need to be well informed and an association with experienced distributors of tourism product needs to be established. They will then introduce the most effective tourism products to their networks. Understanding markets like the 'grey nomads' (defined in Australia as active retired travellers) who tour by car and are ready to hear a story, and the recently introduced term WHOPPIES (wealthy, healthy, older people) may be appropriate. Grey nomads have a particular interest in this type of experience because they have the time and desire to reflect on such a potent symbol of their cultural heritage.

Perhaps most important in this study is the realization that elements of the ordinary cultural landscape, that of a place's agrarian and peasant past, have social and tourism value and should not be ignored in sole favor of historic places associated with the wealthy elites. The uniqueness of a series of sheds (in any condition) in a discrete location is identified as extremely marketable. Tourism could provide the framework for some landholders on the Pacific Highway between Grafton and

Maclean to conserve the sheds. The age and condition of some sheds make them attractive to the drive tourism market. While few sheds are individually of high heritage value, as a collection of sheds and the particular rural landscape in which they are located, they provide an opportunity to recognise, interpret and manage a significant cultural resource which in turn allows the conservation of property for its inclusion in an effective cultural tourism experience.

Acknowledgement

The project partners included the Northern Rivers Cultural Tourism Organisation, the NSW Heritage Office, Maclean, Pristine Waters and Grafton Councils, Southern Cross University's School of Tourism and Hospitality Management, Grafton Regional Art Gallery and Break of Day Investments.

References

Boyd, B., Cotter, M., O'Connor, W., Sattler, D. (1996) Cognitive Ownership of Heritage Places: Social Construction and Cultural Heritage Management. *Tempus*, 6: 123–140.

Carman, K. and Keith, K. (1994) *Community Consultation Techniques: Purposes, Processes and Pitfalls*. Brisbane: Department of Primary Industries.

Commonwealth of Australia (1995) *Mapping Culture: A Guide for Cultural and Economic Development in Communities*. Canberra: Department of Communications and the Arts.

Earthlines Consortium (1999) *Best Practice in Park Interpretation and education*. Victoria: Department of Natural Resources & Environment.

Brokensha, P. and Guldberg, H. (1992) *Cultural Tourism in Australia: A Report on Cultural Tourism*. Canberra: Australian Government Publication Service.

Craik, J. (1995) Are there cultural limits to tourism? *Journal of Sustainable Tourism*, 3(2): 87–98.

Grogan, D., Mercer, C., and Enwright, D. (1995) *The Cultural Planning Handbook: An Essential Australian Guide*. St Leonards, NSW: Allen & Unwin.

Hall, C.M. (1994) *Tourism and Politics: Policy, Power and Place*. Chichester: Wiley.

Hall, C.M. and Jenkins, J.M. (1995) *Tourism and Public Policy*. London: Routledge.

Hall, C.M. and McArthur S. (eds) (1993) *Heritage Management in New Zealand and Australia: Visitor Management, Interpretation and Marketing*. Melbourne: Oxford University Press.

Hopkins, J. (1998) Signs of the post-rural: marketing myths of a symbolic countryside. *Geografiska Annaler B: Human Geography*, 80(2): 65–81.

Leask, A. and Yeoman, I. (eds) (1999) *Heritage Visitor Attractions: An Operations Management Perspective*. London: Cassell.

Lips, K.E. (1990) Newsletter, National Committee on Cultural Tourism, Canada, p. 4.

Mackay, H. (1993) *Reinventing Australia: The Mind and Mood of Australia in the 90s*. Sydney: Angus and Robertson.

McKercher, B. and du Cros, H. (2002) *Cultural Tourism: The Partnership between Tourism and Cultural Heritage Management*. New York: Haworth.

Prentice, R., Davies, A., and Beeho, A. (1997) Seeking Generic Motivations for Visiting and Not Visiting Museums and Like Cultural Attractions. *Museum Management and Curatorship*, 16(1): 45–70.

Richards, G. (1996) Production and consumption of European cultural tourism. *Annals of Tourism Research*, 23: 261–283.

Shackley, M. (1994) When is the past? Authenticity and the commoditisation of heritage. *Tourism Management*, 15: 396–397.

Timothy, D.J. (2005) Rural tourism business: a North American overview. In D. Hall, I. Kirkpatrick, and M. Mitchell (eds) *Rural Tourism and Sustainable Business*, pp. 41–62. Clevedon: Channel View.

Timothy, D.J. and Boyd, S.W. (2003) *Heritage Tourism*. London: Prentice Hall.

Tourism New South Wales (1999) *Attractions Development Strategy for regional* New South Wales. Sydney: TNSW.

Uzzell, D. (ed.) (1989) *Heritage Interpretation: The Natural and Built Environment*, Volume 1. London: Belhaven.

Wood, C. (1993) *Package Tourism and New Tourism Compared*. Proceedings of the National Conference, Community Culture and Tourism, July 1993, Melbourne, p. 11.

Implications of Sporadic Tourism Growth: Extrapolation from the Case of Boracay Island, The Philippines

R.W. (Bill) Carter

Introduction

Butler (1980) and others (e.g. Lundberg, 1980; de Albuquerque & McElroy, 1992) have described the growth progression of a tourist destination (Figure 1). These models identify that growth phases are associated with changes in the physical, environmental and social aspects of the destination, which ultimately lead to a reduction in attractiveness of the destination to specific markets. Commonly used indicators of growth are visitor numbers, physical development (e.g. number of tourist facilities or services) (Debbage, 1990) and economic indicators (Haywood, 1986; Nicholson, 1997). All such indicators fall within a paradigm of economic growth (Nelson et al., 1993).

Cooper (1994) suggests that the life cycle concept provides the "seeds of a generalized theory of tourism" and often it is contended that the models are useful tools for tourism planning (Hinch & Butler, 1988; Johnson et al., 1992; Walsh, 1992; Teo, 1994; Wilkinson, 1987). However, Mercer (1991) proposes that they simply have value as heuristic or explaining devices, and Choy (1992) finds that their best use is as a "diagnostic tool after the fact". Nevertheless, in some case studies, direct application has been difficult because of:

- operational and application complexities (Agarwal, 1997; Haywood, 1986; Strapp, 1988; Weaver, 1990);
- difficulties in identifying causal relationships (Harrison, 1995; Meyer-Arendt, 1985); and
- difficulties in determining the phases and the turning points or transitions (Haywood, 1986; Cooper & Jackson, 1989; Agarwal, 1997).

Such difficulties may stem in part from a misinterpretation of the nature of tourism growth. Rather than being a smooth curve, growth may occur in sporadic increments with important implications for resources,

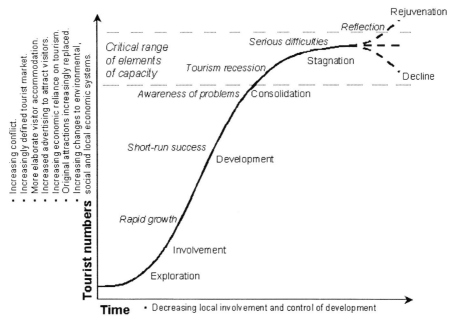

Figure 1   Butler Model of Tourism Growth, Overlain by Lundberg's Phases (in italics) (modified from Butler, 1980).

host communities and cultural changes, and hence planning and management. This paper seeks to explore the nature of tourism growth and the implications of the growth pattern on destinations, especially the environmental and cultural dimensions. Using analyses of the growth pattern of tourism at Boracay Island in The Philippines, and aligning this with reported environmental and social changes (e.g. Trousdale, 1997a, b, c, 1999), the paper proposes a clarification of the destination life cycle model of Butler and others.

The Case of Boracay Island, The Philippines

Boracay is a 9.7 km² dumbbell shaped island, about 7 km long and 1 km wide at its narrowest point. It is 300 km south of Manila and 20 minutes by boat from the adjacent island of

Panay, in the municipality of Malay, Aklan Province, The Philippines. The island communities (*barangays*) of Yapak, Balabag and Manoc-Manoc support about 12000 local residents who, in the past, gained their livelihood through copra plantations and fishing, but now are dependent on tourism (see Trousdale, 1999). The primary tourist assets are a 4 km protected white coral-sand beach (Long or White Beach), clear water and the resultant marine focused activities.

Tourism commenced in the mid 1970s with small accommodations but grew rapidly in the 80s and 90s with television promotion (c1984) and the arrival of SCUBA diving and expanded accommodation. Around the mid-1990s, with almost all of the primary assets developed, consideration of the future began by government and the private sector. In 1997, the first 4–5 star resort was opened on the southern point of the island, around the same time that the Department of Environment and Natural Resources announced that White Beach was polluted with coliform bacteria.

Today, about 100 "traditional" style marine vessels, with their shallow draft and double out-rigging, anchor off the beach or are involved in ferrying goods, guests and workers from Caticlan on Panay Island, or taking dive trips around the island. The coconut palm lined foreshore hides the development immediately out of sight from the ocean. There are over 220 accommodation places (2200 rooms in 1998) ranging from 4–5 star to half star cottages, over 60 restaurants (excluding accommodation related facilities), and numerous wayside tourist retail stores and shops (see NSCB, 2002). Almost all items for sale are imported. Behind the foreshore accommodation, a narrow, shop-lined road is alive with motorbikes and bicycles. Additional international resorts are planned, and the Philippines Government has recently completed construction of an international standard golf course with associated resort accommodation in the northern centre of the island. Golf courses now cover 10% of the island (Tenenbaum, 2000). Accommodation and restaurants reflect a western tradition in name and food offered. Most serve traditional Filipino meals but dominated by French, Italian, Germanic, Indian and Thai cuisine. A casino proposal exists, but is attracting local resistance.

Government overtly regulates tourism facilities and services to effect quality service (see Trousdale, 1999). Organization for guest transfer is of a high standard and with a minimum of fuss. Mains power, a reliable water supply, and a modern sewage treatment system are being provided. At White Beach, the bamboo walled and thatched cottage accommodation of local architectural vernacular style is being replaced with more expensive Spanish style concrete and tile forms. The shift is rapidly towards a more up-market type of facility and service.

Boracay's Tourism Growth Cycle

Growth of tourism at Boracay superficially appears to have followed Butler's cycle with tourist arrivals, although exhibiting considerable seasonal fluctuation (Figures 2 and 3), including a significant decline in tourist arrivals, which continued through to 1999, following the 1997 pollution announcement and with the Asian economic crisis (see Table 1). In 2003, the SARS crisis resulted in a 25% decline in visitor arrivals. Nevertheless, an exponential function applied to the annual arrival data gives an R^2 value of 0.9383, suggesting that the growth of tourism has indeed followed Butler's model.

Aggressive marketing to free independent travellers from Europe and then tour groups, especially the Korean, Japanese and German markets, rapidly followed initial small-scale tourism targeting adventure tourists. This marketing was highly successful, with services to bring visitors to the island well planned. However, infrastructure planning appears to have fallen behind market growth. Boracay's growth appears to plateau in the early 1990s and again in the late 1990s (Figure 2 and Table 1), but continues with private investment largely within the existing tourist centre of White Beach (see Trousdale, 1999). Towards the end of the 20th century, the destination attracted US$43 m and 8000 domestic and international visitors each month (CUI, 1997). Growth has again occurred with the new millennium. While Boracay's popularity as a tourist destination has greatly contributed to its economic growth, rapid and unplanned development on the island to meet the demands of its increasing number of

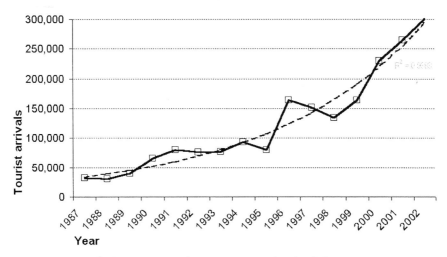

Figure 2 Annual Tourist Arrivals to Boracay Island, Philippines (1987–2002).

visitors has resulted in environmental degradation (CUI, 1997). At the end of the millennium, to avoid stagnation and address degradation, the Island entered a phase of rejuvenation based on government-funded investment (suggested as stagnation by Trousdale, 1999). Table 1 summarizes these events with an attempt to apply Butler's growth cycle phases to the exponential trend line of visitor arrivals (see Figure 2).

Despite the high degree of fit of the exponential trend line to the visitor arrival data (Figure 2), events presented in bold in Table 1 suggest that Boracay may have reached a stag-

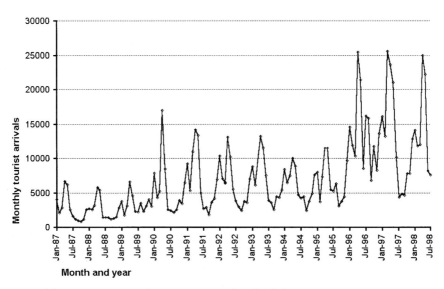

Figure 3 Monthly Tourist Arrivals to Boracay Island, Philippines (1987–1997) (note: monthly data not available post 1998).

Table 1   Boracay Island's Phases of Tourism Growth (Adapted From Butler, 1980, Based on Trousdale, 1997a, b, c, 1999)

Indicator	Phase		
	Exploration Pre 1970–early 1990s	Involvement Early 1990s–mid 1990s	Development Mid 1990s – present
Visitor numbers	Few	Increasing	Market shaped by advertising. Rapid increase in visitor numbers.
Community response	Fascination, minimal conflict.	Positive, providing facilities and services.	Positive but increasing concern over loss of control and impacts. **Polarization with support by those involved with tourism but objection by others.**
Travel arrangements	Individual.	Locally arranged with some special interest tours.	Group tours sold off-shore. Mass tourism increases.
Visit pattern	Irregular.	Seasonal pattern beginning.	Seasonality marked with continuity.
Local facility use	High.	High.	Increasingly reduced, often viewed as objects or commodified.
Tourist facilities	Minimal or absent.	Some tourist-only.	Local and external investment. **Tourist-only facilities, often contrasts with the local architecture.**
Interaction with local community	High.	High	Reducing as migrant labour increases. Employees only or through performances.
Natural environment impacts	Low.	Low, activity maritime focused. However, all well samples in 1993 contain faecal coliforms.	Increasing, visitors explore island in numbers. **Increased water quality decline.**

(continued)

Table 1 Continued

Indicator	Phase		
	Exploration Pre 1970–early 1990s	Involvement Early 1990s–mid 1990s	Development Mid 1990s – present
Physical and social impacts	Low.	Low but altered "income" base for some; 50% of 207 households sampled do not have a toilet.	Obvious to older community members, including loss of cultural identity. **Waterborne diseases account for 10 leading illnesses in 1995. Child prostitution reported (ILO, 2000).**
Attractions	Natural environment and existing cultural expressions.	Natural and cultural features, especially SCUBA diving.	Modified natural plus dining and bars. Managed natural and cultural environment, including some not directly related to attractions of the exploration phase (e.g. casino proposal).
Key events and indicators.	Fewer than 5000 visitors per year pre 1970s; 30000 by 1987. Diving market.	Visitors increasing to 100000 per year by 1996. Backpacker market.	Visitors increase to 200000 by 2000, 300000 by 2003. Mass tourism market. Dip in 1997–98 due to Asian financial crisis (Ibajay, 1999). **Master Planning undertaken.**
	Little competition for primary attractions.	Initial market moves elsewhere, replaced by new market.	White Beach reaches social carrying capacity for existing market, but **acceptable to altered market.**

(continued)

Table 1 Continued

Indicator	Phase		
	Exploration Pre 1970–early 1990s	Involvement Early 1990s–mid 1990s	Development Mid 1990s – present
	Visitor numbers within natural capacity of the land.	Exploitation of natural systems assimilative capacity.	Concern for water quality, sewage and solid waste management results in **infrastructure development at end of millennium.**
	Small-scale development and local investment.	Investment by nationals.	10% of resorts (211) fail to install 3-chamber septic tanks (Militante, 1997). **Investment by overseas interests. Traditional architectural vernacular replaced with brick and tile. Major infrastructure development completed (OTI, 2003).**
	Island natural resources depleted by previous land use	Use of principal attractions within resource capacity	Expansion of resources desirable but not available. **Construction of built attractions** (golf course)
	Tourism supplements traditional income.	Rapid shift to local dependence on tourism.	Outside labour introduced. **Specialist expertise introduced including aliens. Increased foreign investment.**
	Market focuses on activity in natural and cultural context	Market focuses on natural and cultural values	**Market prefers higher standard – natural and cultural values provide the setting only.** SARS results in 25% decline in visitors in 2003.

nation phase in the late 1990s and is currently in a rejuvenation and a new growth phase.

The Underlying Trends in Visitor Arrivals

If the visitor arrival data are seasonally adjusted (by estimating "average" month effect with ANOVA, then subtracting month effects from the monthly data), a stepped pattern of growth becomes evident. If the masking effect of variation is removed (applying a log transformation to the data), then a distinctly episodic trend in growth is clear (Figures 4 and 5). These transformations indicate that Boracay has undergone two cycles and is currently in its third cycle of tourism growth (see Butler, 1980).

Associated with this episodic growth in tourist arrivals, is an apparent change in the type of tourist accommodations available to visitors. The number of accredited tourist establishments is characterized by an increasing number of resort establishments and a decreasing number of small-scale accommodation facilities and restaurants (Figure 6). From an investment perspective, it is likely that local investors have more opportunity to hold greater equity in small-scale facilities than resorts. Indeed, Goodwin (2000) reports that 25% of the island has been bought by outsiders with limited infrastructure benefits to residents. Consequently, the likely trend is leakage of profits from the Island (see Trousdale, 1999).

These data and analyses strongly support a sporadic incremental model of tourist growth and suggest that investment profiles, as well as predicted and reported impacts on local environments and communities, may result from these changes (see Trousdale, 1997a, b, c). In addition, the growth in tourist arrivals and efforts to maintain growth

through developing new facilities is at the cost of natural environment qualities and crowding of the principal attraction (White Beach) (Trousdale, 1999).

The probable result of the Boracay development process is that:

- the currently utilised assets/attractions are at capacity (at least social carrying capacity, based on crowding) (see Trousdale, 1997b, c);
- past market segments have or are being usurped and now seek new destinations (see Trousdale, 1997a, 1999);
- existing market demand can not be accommodated through accessing additional natural resources because they have been degraded, although restoration of degraded forest resources remains a long term option;
- promotion, marketing and development have altered the market towards one that is less appreciative of or dependent on the natural and cultural values of the destination (see Trousdale, 1999), and now seek built attractions;
- the local community is in imminent danger of losing control of and access to their island resources (Trousdale, 1999);
- the ability of the local community to determine its tourist future has been reduced through economic dependency and development-based growth (although Trousdale (1999) highlights the role of governance in this process);
- growth options are limited only to the style of rebirth, which will increasingly focus on built attractions, within an exceptional maritime setting.

Such concerns led to the development of a partnership between the Philippines Department of Tourism and the Canadian Urban Institute in 1996 (The Canada-Philippines

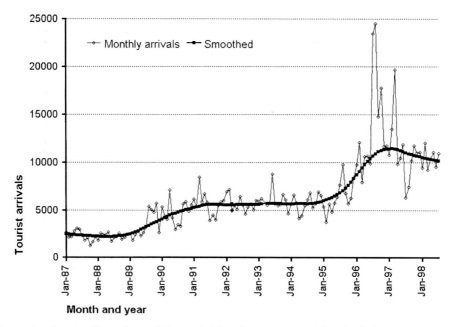

Figure 4   Seasonally Adjusted Growth Trend at Boracay Island, Philippines to 1998.

Cooperative Program on Sustainable Development for Boracay Island), which has emphasised a community-based and participatory approach to local development.

However, of importance to this paper is the direct influence of the pattern of growth and the processes that resulted in observed outcomes, interpreted as environmental degra-

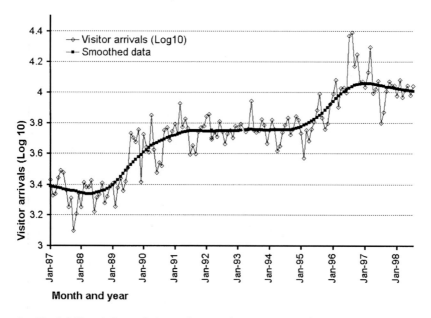

Figure 5   Variability Adjusted Growth Trend at Boracay Island, Philippines to 1998.

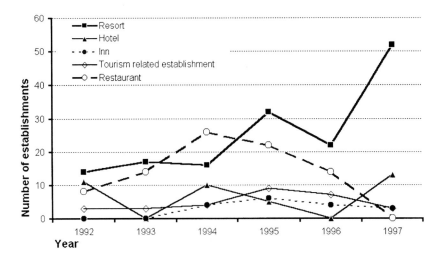

Figure 6   Accredited Tourist Accommodation Trends in the Boracay Island Tourist Region.

dation and community disempowerment (see Trousdale, 1999).

Clarifying the Models of Tourism Growth

In contrast with the findings of others (Weaver, 1990; di Benedetto & Bojanic, 1993; Juelg, 1993; Oppermann, 1996), and superficially indicated by visitor arrival trends (Figure 2), tourism growth at Boracay does not follow a smooth S-shaped or asymptotic curve. Rather, growth (change) occurs in steps, with visitor numbers reflecting episodic physical development of facilities and infrastructure, which increase more rapidly with each step. Alternatively, demand has given impetus to additional facility provision (Figure 7). What has led the change at Boracay is unclear and, if the pattern is not unique to Boracay, then it will probably vary between destinations (supply or demand driven). What is significant is that the change is sporadically incremental or episodic.

Of particular moment here are the social and environmental changes that often accompany tourism growth (WTO, 1993; Archer & Cooper, 1994; Ioannides, 1995; Mieczkowski, 1995; Bleasdale & Tapsell, 1996). Particularly for indigenous communities, tourism and infrastructure developments are often associated with a decline in cultural integrity and diminution of environmental quality (Dearden, 1989; Eber, 1992; McKercher, 1993). These changes are depicted notionally (they might also be episodic in particular circumstances) as a reverse asymptotic curve (broken line) in Figure 7. That is,

Tourism growth

$= f$(visitor numbers, physical development,

wealth generation, market forces,

marketing, etc); but

Environmental integrity

$= f(1/\text{tourism growth})$; and

Cultural integrity $= f(1/\text{tourism growth})$

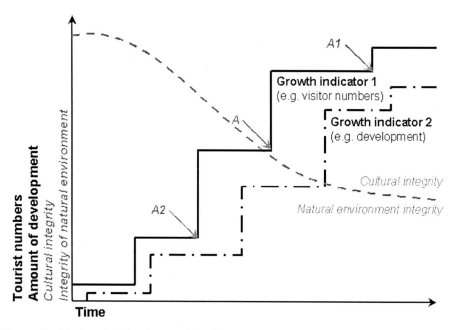

Figure 7 Notional Episodic Model of Tourism Growth and Some Consequences.

(see Jafari, 1983; Smith, 1989; Craik, 1991; Mason, 1996).

While the y-axis scales for the parameters indicated are obviously different, conceptually, points A, A1 and A2 are highly significant. If the integrity of the natural environment line "crosses" the tourist numbers episodic growth line towards point A1, then the natural environment is resistant (and/or resilient). In this case, the need for pro-active management of natural resources is likely to be relatively small. The same applies to the cultural integrity of a host community. This situation gives considerable flexibility for management. Alternatively, if the lines cross towards point A2, then the environment is highly susceptible to change related to growth (e.g. visitor numbers). To sustain valued environmental qualities, management of both visitors and the natural system is required.

For tourism planning, understanding the sensitivity to change of the natural environment and host community culture is vital. This especially applies under the episodic growth model, because growth (e.g. large changes in visitor numbers) can occur rapidly. The effects on natural and cultural integrity and social structure can be especially dramatic, as shown at Boracay. Management is rarely in place to identify and respond to the related threat of change in environmental or cultural integrity, which is often perceived as decline in quality. For environmental quality, decline can be relatively easily identified and quantified, with technological solutions or management responses available to address decline. This is the case at Boracay, where, after some delay, government action addressed the issues of water pollution and other infrastructure problems. However, these actions may have facilitated the rapid rejuvenation and growth experienced with the new millennium. However, for host community culture, decline is perceptual and best considered simply as change. The management issue is one of who is in control of the nature, direction and rate of change. For both environmental degradation and cultural change, management must be prepared for the possible changes that growth can bring. As experienced at Boracay, this is particularly difficult if growth is episodic.

Response Options to Growth

As a tourist destination grows, there are three planning and management options:

- to re-establish the *status quo*;
- to renew and expand existing facilities, services and image; or

- to enter a phase of rebirth, where the essential elements of the 'attraction' are altered.

Boracay appears to be rapidly adopting the latter approach, with considerable community concern (Trousdale, 1999). Table 2 presents some implications of adopting each option. It is important to realize that these options apply at the individual facility or service level as well as at the destination level.

Typically, these options are considered incrementally (if at all) and in an *ad hoc* fashion as management perceptions of need and markets change. However, the option of re-establishment is rarely given much consideration when economic indices of growth are the principal data source. In addition, those who make decisions that bring about change in a destination rarely identify the pro-

Table 2   Options for Tourism Areas and Facilities Throughout Life-Cycle Phases

Option	Action	Image	Market
Re-establish	Replace existing facilities and services with more modern equivalents, including some site hardening.	Maintain existing image and niche.	Maintain existing market.
Renew	Replace and enhance existing facilities and services with upgraded equivalents, extended and new facilities and services, including significant site hardening.	Maintain existing image but present as a reinvigorated and dynamic tourism destination.	Maintain existing market and incrementally expand to include new market segments (usually up-marketing).
Rebirth	Substitute existing facilities and services with new products, associated with renewal action.	Develop a new image for the destination.	Target new markets (often more up-market).

blems or broader outcomes that eventuate, nor do they accept responsibility or made accountable for the consequences (see Volkman, 1990 for an Indonesian example and Trousdale, 1999 for the Boracay response). Lozano (1998) laments that at Boracay entrepreneurs show no concern for environmental and cultural degradation. They continue to dictate development trends and the emerging character of the island and island tourism, as well as the decline in the inherent nature of the island. Market forces and marketing eventually create a tourism product and image that is often unplanned and frequently at odds with that initially envisaged. Such events and decision-making power arrangements imply a high degree of inevitability about destination and tourism growth: an implication inherent in the models of growth and the cause of concern in discussions of growth and the practicability of the models for planning (Cooper & Jackson, 1989; Martin & Uysal, 1990; Getz, 1992; Trousdale, 1999).

An inference is that tourism growth can be likened to the laws of thermo-dynamics. A destination expands and develops as energy is added, but ultimately decays. Revitalization is needed. Agarwal (1997) contends that regeneration is an on-going process, resorts must continually re-orient and rejuvenate their product to keep apace with competing destinations and constant market changes. To continue growth, increasing levels of energy need to be applied for the tourist product to change:

- to maintain a dynamic equilibrium that sustains viability (re-establish),
- to metamorphose into a related form (renew), or
- to evolve into a different and, what is often considered to be, a more competitive and better-adapted product (rebirth).

Unless options are considered at each incremental step of the life cycle, as destinations approach the end of a rapid growth phase, rebirth becomes the only option. This includes acceptance of the implication that the renewed/rebirthed product will have to compete with other destinations offering similar experiences (offering the same or better product at less relative cost). Ironically, the industry then requires the development of new product to service the market that has been usurped: a market that seeks to maintain environmental and cultural integrity. Failure to consider the range of options in an iterative way with each incremental step makes the ultimate outcome inevitable in the manner reflected at Boracay, in the models of tourism growth, and attitudes held widely within the industry.

When a built (contrived) environment is the basis of a tourist destination, the choice of option is of little concern beyond viability and economic considerations. However, when cultural or natural assets are integral to the destination's attraction and image, the choice can be debilitating and ultimately detrimental to the image and future of the destination. The assets provided by natural or cultural resources (including the culture of the host community) are renewable but destructible resources with limits of acceptable change (Lundberg, 1980; Trousdale, 1999). These need to be conserved to maintain the competitiveness of the destination over longer periods.

The Tourism Asset, Community and Market Dynamic

Planners, faced with the options for the future of destinations, often give emphasis to facilities. In their absence, "developers" naturally focus on commercial product development. Often forgotten are the primary attractions, the tourism assets, of a destination. These may include natural areas and the culture of the host community. These elements of the tourism equation also alter with growth and may be in need of reinvigoration and growth to match the changing circumstances. Alternatively, they may need rest, recuperation, conservation and even protection.

As exemplified at Boracay, the primary attraction often becomes degraded, certainly physically in the absence of pro-active resource management, but also in a contextual sense. A natural environment may retain its natural integrity in a physical sense, yet the level and style of tourist development may alter the perception of integrity. This may be at the heart of the wilderness and resort debate, which usually focuses on physical impacts of a proposal, rather than "appropriateness" and cumulative effects. Examples are common throughout the world, but clearly reflected in Australia by objections to tourism development in the Hinchinbrook area of north Queensland and, less recently, tourism development on Fraser Island. At Boracay, Trousdale (1999) highlights the effect of incrementalism and accumulation, and the perception of impact by tourists (43% "happy" with changes) and the host community (50% happy with changes, with 82% identifying a need for limits to growth).

Associated with changes to the primary attractions are those of the host community (Sharpley, 1994). At worst, communities go through a process of objection, resistance, accedence, adoption, acceptance and integration (c.f. Doxey, 1975). Notwithstanding concerns for the issue of loss of cultural identity, with indigenous cultures there is often rapid acceptance and integration of tourism into the economy and often a shift to economic and social dependence on tourism. This is reflected at Boracay, where Trousdale (1999) reports community acceptance of the benefits of tourism despite serious concern for the process of planning and management and inequitable distribution of costs and benefits. This process of "acceptance" is associated with increasing levels of desensitising to changes brought by tourism. Poor levels of service, poorly maintained facilities, pollution and *ad-hoc* changes are not so much accepted, but become tolerated by the eye attuned to incrementalism. For the market, however, such shifts in quality may be stark, discordant and unacceptable. These dynamic elements of a tourism destination can be envisaged as in Figure 8.

Figure 8   Elements of a Tourism Destination.

Assets are usually finite (cultural resources, landscape features) with quality principally depending on the integrity of the asset. It is possible for communities to maintain their integrity and gain social and economic benefits at a rate that is sustainable and controllable (c.f. Keesing & Strathern, 1998), but as advocated by Trousdale (1999) for Boracay, this requires processes for community empowerment. In any case, the appropriate community development rate may be slower than the rate of change of tourism growth (at Boracay a tripling of visitor arrivals in 7 years). The reverse of these options is also possible. Rather than the assets and host community having to change, markets can grow or change to ones that are more, or less exploitative and impacting on the primary assets and host community. This option, suggests a long-term future for a destination that is in dynamic equilibrium, where the host community, the market and product change in an interacting fashion without diminution of the principal assets – a process of mutual adjustment (Lindblom, 1965) where sustaining viability is the objective in contrast with growth *per se*.

In balance, three conditions should be satisfied to ensure the sustainability of the destination:

- the quality and integrity of the primary tourist assets must be conserved and sustained (no nett change) and possibly enhanced;
- the community must continue to receive benefits and additional socio-economic gains (positive, manageable and sustainable change); and
- the market, through facilities, services and interaction with the primary assets, must continue to gain satisfaction (positive, managed and sustainable change).

Similarly, the conditions necessary to allow for integrated short-term growth are:

1. the host community is able to manage and accommodate changes; and
2. assets have sufficient capacity to absorb use by the market (an extensive resource and low visitor numbers); or
3. additional assets can be found and used to accommodate increased demand (increased resource and the same visitor numbers); or
4. markets can be managed to be less impacting on and more supportive of the assets (same resources and protective behaviour).

For Boracay, it appears that, at least until 1996, point 1 was not facilitated; points 2 and 3 were not physically possible on the island without significant restoration work; and point 4 remains to be attempted, with development trends possibly making this approach increasingly difficult.

The Impact of Incremental and Episodic Growth

As an incremental change (usually facilities) occurs in a destination, there is an associated change in the attracted market. This may take the form of a change in the number of visitors or the profile of the market, as reflected in the study of de Albuquerque and McElroy (1992) and at Boracay, where attracted visitors are increasingly dominated by Korean and Japanese tourists (DOT, 1997). If the change in market type is towards a more asset-appreciative and protective one, then balance can be maintained. If the shift is towards a more exploitative market or an increase in numbers, then assets and attractions are likely to change. This change may be expressed as degradation, or associated with management action that alters the experience of the asset (e.g. formalized walking tracks or barriers to cultural sites) (see Carter & Grimwade, 1997).

For the host community, diminished natural resources may be involved. Clearly, the host community will be required to accept (through sharing) reduced access to resources for recreation or exploitative use (see Trousdale, 1999 for community concern for this issue at Boracay). However, tourism activity may also affect traditional land use practices and economies. Initially, these disbenefits might be considered offset by an increase in economic gains from the altered market, or greater community involvement in tourism. However, if traditional practices are associated with the natural resource, then a loss in cultural integrity inevitably follows. These changes are presented in Figure 9.

An incremental change in a destination, for example expanded facilities and services, will lead to expansion of capacity to attract a target market. As incrementalism continues, the initial socio-economic benefits to the local community can decline, for example through incremental acculturation, loss of access to traditional resources and displacement with imported labour. Equally, the original tourism assets of the destination (e.g. environmental features) can erode as they are slowly replaced by altered and constructed forms of attractions, alienating traditional resources from local community use. Ultimately, the change in destination character leads to an unsatisfactory experience for the original market and a new one, which is oblivious of the past and accepting of the changes, slowly dominates the old in terms of numbers and in demand for the altered experience.

These incremental changes, in the absence of global economic influences, occur throughout the life cycle of a destination and, in terms of Butler's model, bring the destination into a phase of imminent decline. At this point, the original tourist-attracting asset is so degraded or altered, the attracted market has so changed, the host community has so altered and the product presented so differently, that rebirth is the only option. Options for sustaining viability have been reduced.

Ultimately, no resource or asset is infinite, no market can grow indefinitely without loss of client satisfaction, and no community can continually absorb change without major shifts in social structure. For a tourism destination approaching senescence, major changes are required, or the reaffirmation of the tourism vision or dedication to sustainable management without growth (measured in numbers). The state of dynamic equilibrium, with manageable growth if necessary, must be found.

Figure 9 Effect of Episodic Growth on the Market, Asset and Community Dynamic.

Economic Benefits to the Host Community

Considering the economic impacts of tourism on host communities at a local level further illustrates this process. The often-attributed benefit of economic growth to host communities (DeKadt, 1979; Moore & Carter, 1993; Picard, 1993) is persuasive for local people, but growth can ultimately result in a nett disbenefit to host communities, especially in small island destinations with a small local population. While initial changes in the economic profile experienced by a host community are often welcomed, unplanned movement through the destination life cycle frequently leads to increasing community dissatisfaction (see Tooman, 1997; Trousdale, 1999).

During Butler's "exploration" and "involvement" phases of the destination life cycle, local community economic benefits stem from the number of community members directly involved in tourism activities, local investment and profit, and employment in associated tourism industries such as construction and tourism support services.

As the growth of the destination proceeds through the "development" phase, economic benefits to the local community continues through employment in construction etc., but local investment is increasingly replaced by investment and profit taking by outsiders (see Shah, 2003). In addition, the absence of a large local workforce means that labour is increasingly imported with leakage of the financial input away from the local community. Ultimately, nett economic benefit to the local community declines, unless government investment in local community infrastructure increases through reinvestment of funds received through taxation, for example, of the non-locals who are benefiting from tourism success.

As the destination enters the "consolidation" and "stagnation" phases, investment reduces/ceases, employment in construction reduces dramatically and outflows increase as external investors increasingly draw profit. Unless the destination is capable of moving to one of Butler's "rejuvenation" scenarios, the local community faces unemployment, unless skill upgrading has been achieved (unlikely in a sporadic growth scenario), and a probable social cost through the unemployment and rapidly diminishing economic balance. In these cases, with growth, nett economic benefit to local communities actually declines, even though nett benefit to a region/state may significantly increase. This situation seems to be the case at Boracay, where Trousdale (1999) reports considerable community concern for tourism growth based on these scenarios.

However, nett community economic disbenefit can occur also during the development phase, stemming from the episodic nature of tourism growth. This particularly applies where the land and other resources (e.g. water) are finite, as in island destinations. If outside capital initiates episodic change, the nett benefit to local communities will be less than if local investment is applied. The gains are presumed to lie in rapid community development. However, an insidious side effect can occur. During the "development" phase, with episodic growth, "consolidation" is often involved. The option to "renew" or "rebirth" a facility is often associated with upgrading and amalgamation of premises: the situation occurring at Boracay. Apart from the external investment that upgrading attracts, it is often associated with importing specialist workers. In addition, consolidation can mean a nett reduction in employment. Two small businesses that merge often result in fewer employees, especially at the low-skilled level. Again, these are concerns expressed by the local community at Boracay and reported by Trousdale (1999). This has considerable implications for developing nations and local communities with low skill levels and a high dependency on tourism.

Conclusions

The analysis of tourist arrival figures presented here, which indicate sporadic episodic growth, with the subsequent discussion, tend to reflect and explain, at least in part, outcomes at Boracay reported by Trousdale (1997a, b, c, 1999). Trousdale (1999) proposes the importance of effective community-based governance (or its absence) in both the change process brought by tourism and action to address unacceptable change. However, this paper proposes that the lack of preparedness for rapid sporadic growth has been an underlying factor in the nature and extent of environmental and social impacts at Boracay.

While the life cycle concept never was meant for use as a forecasting tool (Wilkinson, 1996), there remains an urgent need for such tools. Butler (1980) postulates that public and private sector agencies appear to believe in the eternal life of tourist areas as they rarely, if ever, refer to the anticipated life span of a tourist area or its attractions in tourism planning (also reported by Trousdale (1999) at Boracay). He emphasizes that not all tourist areas experience the stages of the model as clearly as others do, and identifies the need for a change in the attitude of planners, developers and managers of tourist areas.

One attitude that needs to change is that relating to planning being a one-off or irregular event, invoked only when problems or impacts become obvious and pressing. There is a need to shift the emphasis from outcomes or product and place it on process for managing change and the empowerment of host communities (Smith, 1989; Carter & Davie, 1995; Trousdale, 1999). Planning needs to be

iterative, constantly reviewing the vision and objectives with every macro or micro change proposed. It is the episodic nature of change, in growth or decay, that passes unnoticed that leads to Butler's implied dilemma of decline or rejuvenation and its associated environmental, financial and social costs. The process of decision-making needs to be what Lindblom calls partisan mutual adjustment, shifting from manipulated to adaptive adjustment (Lindblom, 1965) towards a long-term vision.

Indicators of tourism growth also need expansion beyond superficial indicators such as visitor numbers and gross economic activity. More detailed analysis of data is needed to determine who gains from increased tourism income as well as who loses. In addition, growth should not be determined without subtracting costs. Bleasdale and Tapsell (1996) and Tooman (1997) use indicators of social welfare to address this. Welfare needs to be considered with respect to clients and host communities as well as the principal assets of the destination.

Part of the solution to a change in planning attitude lies in empowering the host community (Hall, 1994) to determine their tourism future rather than entrepreneurs or remote governments: a position strongly advocated by Trousdale (1999) for Boracay. It then becomes the planner's role to clarify community aspirations, to communicate options and consequences of their choices and then reflect decisions in appropriate actions. Growth *per se* is not the principal concern. Rather, it is rapid sporadic growth that creates circumstances that challenge local communities and threatens the tourist product. Responsible management in this case may mean positive action to slow the tourism growth cycle (stretching the S-curve). As the S is stretched, episodic growth becomes less significant because communities have time to adjust, operators have time to develop the product and achieve viability, and management has time to respond to impacts.

Finally, the dynamic relationship between tourist destination assets, the market and the host community, and its effect on the tourist product needs greater consideration. The currently perceived ultimate outcome for a tourist destination (to rejuvenate or accept decline) may prove fallacious. Economic growth to meet community aspirations may not necessitate continuous expansion of facilities and visitor numbers (renewal or rebirth). Rather, this growth scenario could be replaced with predetermined facility levels for targeted niche and specialized markets willing to pay a premium for a unique product that includes and relies on the protection of valued resources of the destination (re-establish). This requires a redefinition of competition from doing the same at less cost to consumers, slashing prices and grabbing market share, to value-adding with an emphasis on quality. In effect, this is almost the antithesis of competing. Inherent in this scenario is the need for resource assessment rather than resource inventory, with emphasis placed on values and significance of resources and clearly enunciating to whom the resources are valued and significant and why (Carter & Bramley, 2002). By itself, this change in planning perspective would necessitate greater consideration of the dynamic relationship between the tourist product and the market, tourist assets and host community.

Acknowledgments

I gratefully acknowledge the assistance of the Philippines Department of Tourism for providing visitor data for Boracay Island and Allan Lisle for his help in analysing these data. Special thanks go to Marc Hockings who acted as a crucial sounding board for the ideas presented in this paper. He, with Dr Jim Davie and Professor Bob Beeton from the University of Queensland, Dr. Dallen Timothy of Arizona State University and Robert Basiuk of the Sarawak Tourism Board provided valued encouragement and review comments on draft manuscripts.

References

Agarwal, S. (1997). The resort cycle and seaside tourism: an assessment of its applicability and validity. *Tourism Management*, 18, 65–73.

Archer, B. & Cooper, C. (1994). The Positive and Negative Impacts of Tourism. In W. Theobald (ed), *Global Tourism the Next Decade* (pp. 73–91). Oxford: Butterworth-Heinemann.

Bleasdale, S. & Tapsell, S. (1996). Saharan Tourism: Arabian Nights or Tourist 'Daze'? The Social-Cultural and Environmental Impacts of Tourism in Southern Tunisia. In M. Robinson, N. Evans & P. Callaghan (eds), *Tourism and Culture: Towards the 21st Century, Conference Proceedings*, Vol. Tourism and Cultural Change (pp. 25–48). Sunderland, UK: (The Centre for Travel & Tourism in association with Business Education Publishers Ltd.)

Butler, R. W. (1980). The Concept of a Tourist Area Cycle of Evolution: Implications for Management of Resources. *Canadian Geographer*, 24, 5–16.

Carter, R. W. & Bramley, R. (2002). Defining Heritage Values and Significance for Improved Resource Management: an application to Australian tourism. *International Journal of Heritage Studies*, 8, 175–199.

Carter, R. W. & Davie, J. D. (1995). Culture and Tourism in the Asia Pacific Region. In H. Richins, J. Richardson and A. Crabtree (eds), *Ecotourism and Nature Based Tourism: Taking the Next Steps. Proceedings of the Ecotourism Association of Australia National Conference* (pp. 67–72). Alice Springs, Northern Territory: Commonwealth Department of Tourism.

Carter, R. W. & Grimwade, G. (1997). Balancing use and preservation in cultural heritage management. *International Journal of Heritage Studies*, 3, 5–53.

Choy, D. J. L. (1992). Life Cycle Models of Pacific Island Destinations. *Journal of Travel Research*, 30, 26–31.

Cooper, C. P. (1994). The destination life cycle: an update. In A. V. Seaton (ed), *Tourism: The State of the Art* (pp. 340–346). Chichester: John Wiley & Sons.

Cooper, C. and Jackson, S. (1989). Destination Life-Cycle: the Isle of Man case Study. *Annals of Tourism Research*, 16, 377–398.

Craik, J. (1991) Social Impacts and Cultural Commodification. In J. Craik (ed) *Resorting to Tourism: Cultural Policies for Tourism: Culture Policies for Tourist Development in Australia* (pp. 79–106). Allen & Unwin Pty Ltd, Sydney.

CUI (1997). *Tenth Interim Report for the period: July 1 to September 30 1997*. International Programs Office, International Assistance Program on Strategic Urban Management, Canadian Urban Institute (CUI).

de Albuquerque, K. & McElroy, J. L. (1992). Caribbean Small-island Tourism Styles and Sustainable Strategies. *Environmental Management*, 16, 619–632.

Dearden, P. (1989). Tourism in Developing Societies: Some Observations on Trekking in the Highlands of North Thailand. *World Leisure and Recreation*, 31, 40–47.

Debbage, K. (1990). Oligopoly and the Resort Cycle in the Bahamas. *Annals of Tourism Research*, 17, 513–527.

DeKadt, E. (1979). *Tourism: Passport to Development?* New York: Oxford University Press.

di Benedetto, C. A. & Bojanic, D. C. (1993). Tourism Area Life Cycle Extensions. *Annals of Tourism Research*, 20, 557–570.

DOT (1997). *Summary Report on Tourist Arrivals*. Boracay, Manilla: Philippines Department of Tourism (DOT).

Doxey, G. (1975). A causation theory of visitor-resident irritants: methodology and research inferences. In *Proceedings of the Travel Research Association Sixth Conference*, San Diego (pp. 195–198).

Eber, S. (1992). Tourism and UNCED. *Contours Bangkok*, 5, 13–17.

Getz, D. (1992). Tourism planning and destination life cycle. *Annals of Tourism Research*, 19, 752–770.

Goodwin, H. (2000) Pro-poor Tourism: Opportunities for Sustainable Local Development. *D & C Development Cooperation*, 5, 12–14.

Hall, C. M. (1994). *Tourism and Politics: Policy, Power, and Place*. Chichester, UK: Wiley.

Harrison, D. (1995). Development of tourism in Swaziland. *Annals of Tourism Research*, 22, 135–156.

Haywood, K. M. (1986). Can the tourist-area life cycle be made operational? *Tourism Management*, 7, 154–167.

Hinch, T. & Butler, R. (1988). The rejuvenation of a tourism centre: Port Stanley, Ontario, *Ontario Geography*, 32, 29–52.

Ibajay (1999). *Banner year for Aklam's Tourism*. Aklam News Archives, Ibajay Home Page, http//:www.geosites.com/Tokyo/Pagoda/3129/latenews.html/, visited June 2003.

ILO (2000). *At Your Service: Combating Child Labour in the Tourism Industry*. National Union of Workers in the Hotel Restaurant and Allied Industries; International Labour Organization (ILO), http//:www.childprotection.org.ph/monthlyfeatures/je2k2a.rtf, visited June 2003.

Ioannides, D. (1995). Planning for International Tourism in Less Developed Countries: Towards Sustainability? *Journal of Planning Literature*, 9, 235–254.

Jafari, J. (1983) Understanding the Structure of Tourism. In E. C. Nebel (ed) *Tourism and Culture: A Comparative Perspective* (pp. 65–84). University of New Orleans: New Orleans.

Johnson, P., Thomas, B. & Cooper, C. (1992). The life cycle concept and tourism. In P. Johnson & B. Thomas (eds), *Choice and demand in tourism* (pp. 145–160). London: Mansell Publishing.

Juelg, F. (1993). Tourism product life cycles in the central Eastern Alps: a case study of Heiligenblut on the Grossglockner. *Tourism Recreation Research*, 18, 20–26.

Keesing, R. M. & Strathern, A. J. (1998). *Cultural Anthropology: A Contemporary Perspective*. Fort Worth: Harcourt Brace & Company.

Lindblom, C. E. (1965). *The Intelligence of Democracy: Decision Making through Mutual Adjustment*, New York: The Free Press.

Lozano, J.R.B. (1998). Boom and Bust in Boracay. *Fieldnotes*. Philippine Association for Intercultural Development Inc., http//:www.humanrights.uchicago.edu/joeylozano/joey09.html, visited June 2003.

Lundberg, D. E. (1980). *The Tourist Business*. Boston, Mass: Cahners Books.

Martin, B. & Uysal, M. (1990). An Examination of the Relationship between Carrying Capacity and the Tourism Life-Cycle: Management and Policy Implications. *Journal of Environmental Management*, 31, 327–333.

Mason, G. (1996) Manufactured Myths: Packaging the Exotic for Visitor Consumption. In M. Robinson, N. Evans and P. Callaghan (eds) *Tourism and Culture: Towards the 21st Century*, Conference Proceedings, Vol. *Tourism and Culture: Image, Identity and Marketing* (pp. 121–135) The Centre for Travel & Tourism in association with Business Education Publishers Ltd, Sunderland.

McKercher, B. (1993). Some fundamental truths about tourism: understanding tourism's social and environmental impacts. *Journal of Sustainable Tourism*, 1, 6–16.

Mercer, D. (1991). *A Question of Balance – Natural Resources Conflict Issues in Australia*. Sydney: The Federation Press.

Meyer Arendt, K. J. (1985). The Grand Isle, Louisiana resort cycle. *Annals of Tourism Research*, 12, 449–465.

Mieczkowski, Z. (1995). *Environmental Issues of Tourism and Recreation*. Lanham, MD: University Press of America.

Militante, G. (1997). Boracay's safe waters fail to lure tourists. TTG Asia October 10–16, http//:www.ttg.com.sg/current/archive/1997/1010-16/br101997100.1htm/, visited June 2003.

Moore, S. & Carter, B. (1993). Ecotourism in the 21st century. *Tourism Management*, 14, 123–130.

Nelson, J. G., Butler, R. & Wall, G. (1993). *Tourism and Sustainable Development: Monitoring, Planning, Managing*. Heritage Resource Centre Joint Publication No 1. Canada: University of Waterloo.

Nicholson, T. (1997). Tourism Development and Community: four Philippine case studies in Boracay, Samal, Mariduque and Davao. Quezon City: VSO Philippines.

NSCB (2002). *Boracay: One of the world's finest beaches*. National Statistical Coordination Board, Republic of the Philippines, http://www.nscb.go v.ph/ru6/boracay.htm, visited June 2003.

Oppermann, M. (1996). The changing market place in Asian outbound tourism: implications for hospitality marketing and management. *Tourism Recreation Research*, 21, 53–62.

OTI (2003). *Boracay tourist arrivals reaches all time high*. Office of Tourism Information (OTI) media released 3 June 2003.

Picard, M. (1993). 'Cultural tourism' in Bali: National integration and regional differentiation. In M. Hitchcock, V. T. King, & M. J. G. Parnwell (eds), *Tourism in South-East Asia* (pp. 71–98). New York: Routledge.

Shah, K. (2000). *Tourism, the poor and other stakeholders. Asian Experience*. London: ODI Fair Trade in Tourism.

Sharpley, R. (1994). The tourist-host relationship. In R. Sharpley (ed), *Tourism, tourists and society*. Huntingdon, UK: Elm Publications.

Smith, V. L. (1989). *Hosts and guests. The anthropology of tourism*. Philadelphia: University of Pennsylvania Press.

Strapp, J. D. (1988). The resort cycle and second homes. *Annals of Tourism Research*, 15, 504–516.

Tenenbaum, D. J. (2000). *Trampling Paradise: Dream Vacation – Environmental Nightmare?* Environmental Health Perspectives, 5, 108.

Teo, P. (1994). Assessing socio-cultural impacts: the case of Singapore. *Tourism Management*, 15, 126–136.

Tooman, L. A. (1997). Applications of the life-cycle model in tourism. *Annals of Tourism Research*, 24, 214–234.

Trousdale, W. J. (1997a). *Is it Too Late For Boracay? The Tourist's Perspective, Results and Analysis of the May 17 1997 DOT Tourist Survey*. Report for the Philippines Department of Tourism and The Canadian Urban Institute, Toronto.

Trousdale, W. J. (1997b). *Zero Waste Management: Towards a Sustainable Future: Assessment and Action Plan*. Report for the Philippines Department of Tourism and The Canadian Urban Institute, Toronto.

Trousdale, W. J. (1997c). *Carrying Capacity Considerations: The Need for Managing Change in a Unique Tourism Destination, Boracay Island*. Report for the Philippines Department of Tourism and The Canadian Urban Institute, Toronto.

Trousdale, W. J. (1999). Governance in Context, Boracay Island, Philippines. *Annals of Tourism Research*, 26, 840–867.

Volkman, T. A. (1990). Visions and revisions: Toraja culture and the tourist gaze. *American Ethnologist*, 17, 91–110.

Walsh, D. J. (1992). The evolution of the Disneyland environs. *Tourism Recreation Research*, 17, 33–47.

Weaver, D. B. (1990). Grand Cayman island and the resort cycle concept. *Journal of Travel Research*, 29, 9–15.

Wilkinson, P. F. (1987) Tourism in small island nations: a fragile dependence, *Leisure Studies*, 6, 127–146.

WTO (1993). *Sustainable Tourism Development: Guide for Local Planners*. Madrid, Spain World Tourism Organization (WTO).

Part Two

Impacts of Tourism on Culture and Heritage

Heritage Tourism in Japan

A Synthesis and Comment

Malcolm J. M. Cooper, Masakatsu Ogata and Jeremy S. Eades

Overview – Cultural and Heritage Tourism in Japanese Life

The stereotype of the Japanese as having little time or desire outside of work to appreciate even their own culture has been thoroughly debunked in recent years (Cole, 1992; Havens, 1994; Clammer, 1997; Linhart and Frühstuck, 1998; Hendry and Raveri, 2002; Ritchie, 2003). A more realistic picture of a culture with a long tradition of conserving its heritage even while it has gone through similar transitions to the post-modern world as other developed nations is now emerging in the literature (Ritchie, 2003). There is increasing recognition that any observable differences between Japan and other countries are not of kind but of degree. As a result, the importance of religious pilgrimage, restoration of historical monuments, conservation of ceramic and artistic traditions, and an increasing interest in war and peace, are now recognised in the Japanese heritage tourism tradition as much as in European, Middle Eastern or Australasian traditions. This

Chapter will examine parts of that tradition and attempt to build a rounded picture of modern Japanese heritage tourism.

It is also necessary to place this discourse firmly within the post-modern paradigm (Appadurai and Breckenridge, 1988; Urry, 1990; Ivy, 1995; Raz, 1999; Hendry, 2000; Hollinshead, 2002; Ryan, 2002), especially its emerging emphasis on 'glocalisation' (Robertson, 1995; Yamashita, 2003a), because Japan is arguably a modern world economic superpower and if understanding of the totality of heritage tourism as it is currently expressed in the Japanese context is desired, globalisation combined with localisation of culture has to be taken into account. The historical traditions that are Japan's also include an attempt to make sense of the opening up of Japan to Western influence at the end of the EDO period (1615–1868), and after the Meiji Restoration (1868). This is expressed in many ways, but in none so important to present-day *domestic* tourism as Tokyo Disneyland and the other theme parks depicting Western influences and cultures.

Previously dismissed as being just borrowings of western cultural forms (the 'global'), they are now seen as being very firmly stamped with Japanese indigenous forms (the 'local'), and it is this amalgam that informs present day heritage tourism in Japan just as much as other more traditional forms of heritage.

Nevertheless, Japanese historical forms of tourism do have a great similarity to other countries' experience of tourism precursors. During the EDO period, for example, while travel for pleasure was strictly restricted, it was for special purposes (merchant, official duties, visits to the Grand Shrine at Ise, and others), on the agreement of each Feudal Clan office. Equally, while the 'work-ethic' appears dominant during this period, it is manifestly obvious that this was to some degree at least balanced by the concepts of *asobi* (play, pleasure, fun), of *tanoshimi* (delight, happiness, pleasure), and of *kaiko* (nostalgia) (Linhart and Frühstuck, 1998). Thus, even before the introduction of the 5-day working week the available evidence shows that attendance at theatres (*Kabuki*), *Eiga* (movies), opera, and importantly for the present discussion *naniwabushi* or *rokyoku* (stirring historical tales with *samisen* music), shrines and temples was commonplace. Not only did the population travel to such centrally important shrines as Ise, but also local shrines offered *matsuri* (festivals) and *ennichi* (the local deity's day of worship) as reinforcers of important cultural heritage traditions (Ashkenazi, 1993; Plutschow, 1996).

In this it is also possible to recognise a sound tradition of rural heritage items and urban-based tourist visitation, as is common in the rest of the world. Japanese regional heritage variations are the catalyst for a considerable amount of domestic tourism as well as international tourism, and encompass historical icons like Kyoto, Nara and Ise, along with many castles of the Edo and earlier periods. The southern Island of Kyushu, for example, contains many references to Japan's past and its relationship with Korea, as it was a gateway to the rest of Asia in earlier eras. Another is *Sengoku-jidai* in southern central Honshu, a recreated village of an age of chronic civil war (1467–1568). Considerable numbers of tourists visit such sites in the course of a year (Hendry, 2000), although in the case of the replica villages it is problematical whether the attraction is not the high-tech nature of the displays (audio-animatronics) rather than the actual history (which may in fact be mythologicised).

From the perspective of the Japanese heritage tourist, though, it has been suggested that travelling within Japan may not be all that different than travelling abroad in terms of the 'exoticism' of the experience (Hendry, 2000, 148). Japanese historical parks and other items of heritage are then seen as fitting easily into the post-modern urban tourist 'bubble' experience, especially when the substitution of the *theme park* already mentioned for trips abroad is taken into account. This consideration will be more fully discussed later in this chapter.

In addition, it should also be noted that Japanese tourists may well go overseas for reasons other than to observe other cultures at first hand, or for the sun, sea, sand experience offered to them by the likes of Australia (Yamashita, 2003b). There is the question of their curiosity (or lack of it) in relation to *Japanese* overseas heritage (Korea, China, Southeast Asia, and the Pacific), even though data on this is difficult to obtain (Mok and Lam, 2000; You and O'Leary, 2000). While there is information on an increasing trend of Japanese tourists to want to experience overseas cultural heritage (Australian Tourist Commission, 2002), little is known about their propensity to visit their own heritage of the Pacific War battlefields for example (but see Buruma, 1994). Equally, the nature of the common heritage of Japan and Korea as it impacts specifically on *heritage tourism* is yet to be fully explored.

What the Chapter is About

Is Japanese heritage tourism different to, more or less developed than, or is it very similar to that of other developed nations? This chapter is about analysing available evidence from a number of sources in an attempt to track down heritage tourism in Japan, both in a theoretical and an empirical sense. It thus attempts to provide a framework for the examination of heritage tourism in Japan, and a springboard for further research.

Cultural Tourism in Theory and Practices

Before the Japanese experience can be effectively described, however, it is necessary to briefly look at cultural tourism in its wider theoretical context, to provide the necessary grounding for the subsequent discussion of Japanese forms. In recent years, cultural tourism and its subset, heritage tourism, has taken on a similar iconic status to that of eco-tourism (Hitchcock *et al.*, 1993; Graburn, 1997; Sofield, 2000, amongst many others). The debate about the effects of tourism on cultures and cultural heritage has swung back and forth between the beneficial and the negative (Sofield, 2000, 46–49). Increasingly, attention has moved from the 'tourism is destructive of the environment (including the cultural environment)' approach towards an approach that recognises that it no longer makes sense to conceive of tourism as a force external to contemporary societies, impacting them from the outside (Picard and Wood, 1997). In other words, indigenous cultures are not static, waiting for an external impulse to become active, nor are they incapable of absorbing and using such impulses when they occur. Indeed, the Japanese experience after the end of World War II would indicate the truth of the latter statement very strongly (e.g. Treat, 1996; Martinez, 1998).

As Sofield notes, when culture is conceived of as a static entity, lacking internal dynamics of change, the actions, motivations and values of the indigenous local community members may be ignored (Sofield, 2000, 50). As a result it has been the tendency in much academic writing on the effects of tourism on cultures, even within the authenticity debate, to see external influences not as a sign of creativity but as evidence of 'neo-colonialism', of cultural degradation through touristic hegemony (Hitchcock *et al.*, 1993, 9). However, to survive a culture must be adaptable. This involves both continuity and change (Harrison, 1996), and is particularly evident in the Japanese context. Where it occurs in any strength tourism, both international and domestic, is of course involved in this process of change, but its impacts are often secondary to the evolutionary process. Harrison thus goes on to warn that academic observers should not impose their own judgements about what is right and good for cultures under their gaze.

There is no doubt that tourism has played a major role in the imaging and re-creation, or even creation, of national identities and cultures in Asia and elsewhere, including Japan (Yamashita, 2003b). While a thorough exposition is outside the scope of this chapter, the examples of Singapore (creation of a national culture, e.g. Tong and Lian, 2003), and Thailand (reinforcement of culture, e.g. Ganjanapan, 2003) are but two of the well documented examples of the use of culture to boost tourism and accommodate its impacts. Before such directed use of tourism is criticised, however, the argument put forward by Hollinshead should at least be noted. In a thoughtful exposition of power and truth in the discourse of history and heritage in relation to tourism, Hollinshead (2002, 176–181) makes the very pertinent point that 'when the history of a place is presented to tourists or the heritage of a people is otherwise projected afar, *choices* (author's italics) have to be made about what ought to be exhibited'. The representation of culture and heritage that tourists experience is therefore always going to be a presentation of local choice and even bias that will be mixed up with previously borrowed cultural forms and political requirements. In fact, a review of the contemporary literature on history and heritage reveals that historical truth is a problematic concept (Hollinshead, 2002) anyway.

Thus, the prevailing view of potentially disastrous cultural impact from tourism (as typified by much of the literature dealing with international tourists) and static recipient cultures cannot now be considered as appropriate in the analysis of the impact of heritage tourism (Yamashita, 2003b, Chapter 1). In explicitly recognising that local culture is dynamic, that tourism can be a force for positive change as well as a potential problem, and that the theoretical relationship between culture and tourism is by no means settled satisfactorily but is much more robust and pertinent than previously, this chapter can now proceed to explore the antecedents of Japanese cultural heritage tourism in a useful contribution to these debates.

But before doing so, another factor must also be taken into account. Whereas other cultures may insist upon physical authenticity in the representation of their cultural artefacts (Cooper and Asplet, 1999), the Japanese have a view of cultural property that incorporates important elements of intangibility (Hendry, 2000). Resulting from this, it is perfectly possible that a good replica will be more highly prized for display than a 'real' but not very well preserved original, unless the site or object in question has been declared a national treasure or an important cultural asset (legal protection and preservation regulations come into play in this situation). Tourists looking for physical remnants of earlier epochs may well find the actual sites less well cared for and/or interpreted than a replica. In the Japanese heritage context it is considered much more important to preserve the *form* of an object than the actual object itself.

The Historical Roots of Japanese Heritage and Heritage Tourism

Japan has a very long cultural heritage. Its varied beginnings can be traced back to Neolithic times (Barnes, 1993, Chapter 7), where a mixture of immigrants from the areas that were to become Siberia, China, Korea, or the Polynesian Islands resulted in the Jomon culture (began *circa* 12,000 years Before Present). The characteristic pottery of this period is one of the earliest ceramic traditions developed by human beings. The historical period proper began with the Yayoi of around 500BC, and encompassed many of the forms found in other parts of the world. From that time forward it is possible to trace burial mound traditions, early nation building, infusions of Korean and Chinese culture, feudalism, the rise of an imperial family and imperialism, rival religious traditions (Buddhism and Shintoism), distinctive ceramic, artistic and architectural traditions, and military rule, all of which have left an impression in at least the cultural landscape, if not always in the physical. As a consequence there are many facets of Japanese culture that continue to inform present day society, and the desire of the Japanese to retain and/ or develop them for the future is just as strong as in other cultures.

In terms of a cultural heritage tradition underlying early forms of tourism that have been recognised elsewhere (Hall and Page, 2001), traditional Japanese agrarian society made a distinction between normal working time (*ke*) and special time, which included sacred time (*hare*) devoted to festivals and similar activities. *Hare* time comes closest to present day concepts of leisure, and the festivals involved heritage tourism (Linhart and Frühstuck, 1998), at least in its broadest definition (Graburn, 1997). By the end of the Edo period (1615–1868), and uninfluenced by European pressure, this had developed into a desire for more days of rest and entertainment, and *travel* (Furukawa, 1986). By contrast, in the cities there had always been more time for leisure, festivals, and travelling. While other forms of social activity may have been tightly constrained by a rigid social structure prior to the Meiji period, religion provided the required excuse for travelling for both the urban and rural masses, and thus their involvement in early domestic tourism.

In recent years the Edo-period pilgrimage has been recognised as a forerunner of modern-day Japanese tourism (Linhart and Frühstuck, 1998), although its associated features such as visiting *onsen* (spas) and other features of interest may mean more that a 'lifetime' experience was actually the drawcard, rather than the pilgrimage per se (Linhart and Frühstuck, 1998). To accommodate pilgrimages and official transport and communication, the Shogunate laid out a nation-wide system of highways radiating from Edo,

and esignated post-stations on the roads to serve the needs of travellers. Formanek (1998) notes that the increased mobility of lay people during this period, and many of the characteristics of the pilgrimage itself, account for some of the main characteristics of modern domestic tourism; specifically, the *oshi* (lay priests) who toured the countryside promoting and arranging the pilgrimages (travel agents), the practice of *omiyage* (souvenirs for those back home), an increasing tendency to recreation rather than the religious aspects of the trip, group travel, and the tendency to only seek out sites of national importance. All these characteristics are mirrored in present day Japanese domestic and international tourism, although of course the passage of time has modified and continues to modify them.

The historical texts of the Edo period reveal an increasing trend for the religious aspects to be purely nominal (Formanek, 1998, 168). The religious aspect is now seen to have served as a pretext to circumvent the restrictions on mobility otherwise enforced by the authorities. This has also passed over into modern usage, in that trips for pleasure are often characterised as serving a higher purpose than just fun – for example the *kenshu ryoko* (study tours), and *shotai ryoko* (invited journey).

In 1853 Japan's self-imposed international isolation of the Edo period was essentially terminated by the arrival of an American fleet known as the 'Black Ships' and other foreign vessels. The Meiji, or imperial, restoration that eventually resulted (Gluck, 1985; Jansen, 1995) ushered in a period of rapid economic growth reflected in industrialisation and military adventures overseas, but also in the growth of domestic tourism. The Second World War and the Occupation which followed led to another period of rapid social change, and the associated economic revival was accompanied by the growth of mass tourism outwards from the Japanese home islands (Yamashita, 2003b), and within them, a new interest in Japan's long history.

Japanese cultural heritage is thus a fusion of indigenous, Korean and Chinese motifs and experiences, with a recent overlay of western cultural forms and usages. While it is now accepted that there is historical continuity in much of the domestic heritage tourism based on these traditions, it must be stressed that the present-day 'nostalgic' confirmation of the Japanese cultural landscape that results probably evokes very different feelings to those experienced by the first travellers (Formanek, 1998, 186; cf. Ivy, 1995; Yamashita, 2003b, Chapter 11). Because tourism in Japan is mainly internally generated, with comparatively few foreign tourists, there have until recently been very few attempts to 'sell' local culture to international visitors directly (Hendry, 2000, 15 and Chapter 4 – guide books such as *Lonely Planet* being an obvious exception), though of course they are at liberty to experience it if they happen to stumble across it.

Current Themes in Japanese Heritage Tourism

Local Culture

In the two decades 1980 to 2000 the domestic tourism market in Japan grew exponentially, in line with the trend to more leisure time in the society as a whole (Harada, 1994). By the end of this period, domestic tourism had grown to over 300 million trips per year by more than 60 million tourists. As part of this trend, the revival of traditional local festivals (*matsuri*) and cherry-blossom viewing, and

the development of a vast range of theme parks, was added to visits to health spas and pilgrimages during the 1990s (Raz, 1999). Examples of local heritage-oriented *tema-paku* (theme parks) include Edo Village in Nikko, Meiji Village (near Nagoya), and the previously mentioned Sengoku-jidai (Ise), with its Ninja training house and high-tech civil wars museum.

In discussing the theme park as an aspect of the growth of domestic heritage tourism, Raz (1999) reinforces the earlier point that it is more important in Japan to be able to preserve the *form* of culture rather than its physical expression in the landscape. He notes that, as a result, the native culture as represented in these parks takes on the dimensions of a theme, produced by the Japanese for their own consumption (Raz 1999, 154) and makes no claim to be physically authentic. However, this does not mean the result is a *fake*, it means that the Japanese domestic tourist is not necessarily concerned with MacCannell's quest for authenticity (MacCannell, 1976) or the commodification of culture (Cohen, 1988), even of their own, if the theme park retains the essential elements of the *form* of the cultural period represented.

In the same way, the form of the present-day pilgrimages to major national shrines such as Ise includes many of the same features as in earlier times without perhaps religion being as central as formerly, and remains an important part of Japanese heritage tourism. However, in addition to the famous temples and shrines, often now found in expanding urban areas, there is a growing focus on old farm houses and the like as part of the various *furusato* (re-attachment to rural traditions through reviving visitation) campaigns since the 1970's. These campaigns were designed to persuade urban dwellers to travel into the countryside (Graburn, 1998) to 'rediscover' Japan. Originally built upon the idea that urban dwellers should maintain a direct connection with their rural places of origin (kikyo, the annual pilgrimage home), the furusato have evolved into a generalised tradition of cultural preservation through active interest in rural pursuits as the direct links for most people with the countryside were sundered by the passage of time.

As a result of the particular way the Japanese tourist is likely to view historical sites, the maintenance of the strictly historical fabric (built form) in Japan has achieved much less prominence than in other countries. The continual rebuilding over many centuries of shrines such as Ise, for example, preserves the form but means that the shrine itself is built of modern materials every 20 years or so. The posited direct relationship between materials and preservation of cultural heritage that underlies much of western town planning's attempts to preserve heritage in countries like the United Kingdom or Australia has very little relevance here. While there is an increasing attempt to preserve many of the feudal era castles, for example, the original stones, artefacts and other materials may only be observable in the attached museums, and even then these may be replicas in modern materials. Nevertheless, the importance of the feudal and other periods for Japanese cultural heritage *is* being recognised in contemporary heritage tourism through these developments (Ehrentraut, 1995).

Equally, the modern domestic tourist's interest in ceramic and artistic traditions and the historical use of natural environments (and foods) is actively being stimulated as part of the preservation of Japanese cultural heritage. Managed nature has in fact become very much a part of cultural 'tradition' and therefore of heritage tourism (Graburn,

1998), as has the new lease of life experienced by pottery villages (Moeran, 1997, 1998).

One modern form of cultural heritage tourism that is not particularly obvious though in the modern domestic Japanese heritage tradition is World War II sites. The impact of World War II and Japan's brief control of a number of countries in Southeast Asia and the Pacific rates little mention in the popular press (there is a large academic literature), despite there still being a sizeable group of ex-service people from that time within the ranks of potential international tourists from Japan. While there are memorials to individuals and to particular groups, these tend also to be more localised and sparse on the Japanese mainland than is the case in the Western tradition. The exceptions to this are the national monuments describing and remembering Hiroshima and Nagasaki.

As a consequence there appears to be little Japanese battlefield tourism such as occurs with Gallipoli (ANZAC, Turkish tradition), North Africa, Normandy (German, American and British), Northern France (all combatants of WWI), Guam (American). It is however doubtful that Korea, Malaysia, the Philippines, Indonesia and China, the major areas of the Asian part of the WWII conflict, would be particularly interested in publicising or even tolerating explicit battlefield tourism by large numbers of Japanese tourists.

The Incorporation of Foreign Cultures into Heritage Tourism Within Japan

The final major factor in the development of Japanese heritage tourism to be covered in this Chapter is that of the impact of foreign cultural traditions. In the process of industrialisation since the second half of the Nineteenth Century, endogenous leisure activities coexisted with an increasing input of Western cultural forms. Promoted by contact with the outside world, especially during the early to middle 20th Century, changing forms of entertainment (the development of a Japanese national theatre) and sports, and the development of summer vacation resorts, contributed much to the changes in domestic tourism that subsequently occurred.

The outcome of greatest interest to the theme of the present chapter is that of the emulation of foreign cultures through the construction of 'foreign country villages' or *Gaikoku Mura*. From the 1980s, in the form of the *gaikoku mura*, leisure parks in Japan have developed into a phenomenon that has important socio-economic ramifications as well as resulting in a sophisticated service industry (Linhart and Frühstuck, 1998, 237). This development appears to have been a side effect of the *Law for Development of Comprehensive Resort Areas, 1987*, which resulted in massive government investment in local tourism projects such as resorts (the provision of 100 million yen for every hometown project (1988) program), but also reflects a fascination with Western cultural heritage, albeit in a strangely sanitised way (Raz, 1999, 153).

The 1987 Act was directed towards the promotion of the effective use of leisure time, the stimulation of domestic tourism demand, and private sector investment in resort projects. Prior to this, private resort development saw the construction in 1983 (with an addition in 2001, Disney Sea) of Tokyo Disneyland (TDL), by far the most successful theme park and celebrating its 20th year of operation in 2003. In its first 10 years TDL saw 125 million visitors (309 million by 2002), and currently welcomes 25 million visitors a year, a number in aggregate about the same as that to all other theme parks throughout the

country, and equal to that enjoyed by the original Disneyland. TDL attracts most of its visitors (98.6%) from domestic sources, with more than 66% coming from the Tokyo Metropolitan Area, and employs about 12,000 people.

Going abroad at home is the result of the construction of this and many other detailed and accurate representations of selected destinations, led by Huis Ten Bosch (a representation of Holland, on Kyushu), Universal Studios (Osaka), Space World (Kyushu), Canadian World (Hokkaido), Parque Espana (Honshu), Tobu World Square and Russian Village (Honshu), and Swiss Village (Tohoku). These resorts effectively mean that Japanese tourists can make visits to foreign countries without a passport or language ability, long journeys are avoided and it is not necessary to change money to buy souvenirs of the country visited (Raz, 1999; Hendry, 2000).

Replicas and reconstructions of buildings and furniture are offered; imported experts perform music and crafts; and there is food, drink and *omiyage* from the country in question, often advertised as exclusive to that particular park. In some cases, more than one country is featured in a particular park. On the south-central island of Shikoku, one such park offers a trip through a Thai temple, past a first-century Nepalese temple, into a Chinese restaurant complex, to a Bhutanese building, and out into a middle-eastern bazaar complete with Islamic domes. In all cases the parks try to create a space that will induce visitors to feel that they have actually entered the foreign country concerned.

In a more recent development, within a day's journey from Tokyo, another park opens with an English neighbourhood, then a replica steam train ride to a Canadian section, but returns to the entrance through a formal Japanese garden and a row of houses from the Japanese countryside, each accommodating a specific local craft. The 'Rainbow Village', or *Njinosato*, introduces the idea that heritage tourism as encapsulated by the theme parks can and should include representations of Japanese culture alongside the foreign.

How then to interpret these parks in the context of Japanese heritage tourism? That they are obviously important to domestic tourism is seen by their patronage (although this interest did not stopped the likes of Huis Ten Bosch entering receivership in 2002–2003), but do they represent 'westernisation' of Japan's cultural tourism, or should their classification be specifically Japanese despite the importation of foreign terms to describe them (Hendry, 2000, 7)? There are clearly many western models that influenced the Japanese theme park builders (Disneyland is an obvious example), and most of the gaikoku mura were built after the construction of Tokyo Disneyland. Equally, Sovereign Hill in Australia or the present function of Versailles in France may have provided suitable models. However, this does not necessarily mean that they should be interpreted solely as indications of the globalising influence of Western culture, even in the case of Tokyo Disneyland.

Tobin (1992) suggests that while it is tempting to see the playing out of familiar western social, economic and political theory in such examples of Japanese consumption, this not entirely appropriate. In the contemporary theoretical discourse on cultural tourism referred to earlier in this Chapter, these parks could be represented as a postmodern pastiche of replicas and simulations made possible by reconstructions and modern electronics, and devoid of contact either with their country of origin or Japan's cultural heritage. However, this would miss the point made earlier about the way in which the Japanese actually view heritage, or in other words 'form should not be confused with content, nor should we fail to recognise that apparently similar forms can carry quite dissimilar meaning' (King, 1990, quoted in Hendry, 2000, 11). Hendry prefers the view that, in Japan the foreign culture theme parks and their hybrid alternatives perform the role of being cultural interpretations from a Japanese point of view, and are thus not reflections solely of the globalising or westernising tendency evoked by other writers. In fact, it appears that Japan has simply incorporated much of the wider world into its own identity, and thus feels justified in displaying the cultures portrayed in the gaikoku mura as examples of its own heritage (Hendry, 1997; Raz, 1999), although Notoji (1993) argues that TDL at least has no cultural overtones for the younger generation, but is simply a gigantic amusement and consumption space.

Conclusions: The Patterns of Japanese Heritage Tourism

The preservation of culture in Japan and therefore the heritage tourism associated with it can be seen as a total social phenomenon (Ohnuki-Tierney, 2000), incorporating multiple dimensions in similar ways to that of other nations. Physical remnants and documentary evidence vie with religious, economic, political and symbolic interpretations of heritage, and the resultant distinctly Japanese whole is what makes up the background and context for this form of domestic tourism (and indeed any heritage tourism that Japanese overseas travellers or domestic tourists in the theme parks are involved in).

We would therefore conclude, in answer to the question posited at the beginning of this chapter – is Japanese heritage tourism different to, more or less developed than, or is it very similar to that of other developed nations? – that Japanese heritage tourism has had a very similar development to that of other countries, with some very interesting differences as outlined, and that it has a very strong future in Japan. It is noticeable that the theme parks have shifted from the satisfaction of a desire for entertainment towards a use of leisure time that informs and stimulates (self-improvement), and that the re-establishment of local festivals and museums proceeds strongly. That this development of Japanese heritage tourism may have had or now has overtones of globalisation and foreign cultural imperialism is however seen as more positive than negative by the Japanese tourist and in fact, as this chapter has shown, somewhat paradoxically provides strength to the preservation of the total culture that is the heritage of the Japanese nation as a whole through the locally grounded process of glocalisation. The *Japanese* give meaning to their heritage, including that of its interactions, forced or otherwise, with the outside world.

References

Ashkenazi, M. 1993 *Matsuri: Festivals of a Japanese Town*, Honolulu: University of Hawaii Press.

Appadurai, A. and Breckenridge, C. 1988 Why Public Culture? *Public Culture* 1 (1), 5–9.

Barnes, G. 1993 *The Rise of Civilization in East Asia: The Archaeology of China, Korea and Japan*, London: Thames & Hudson.

Buruma, I. 1994 *The Wages of Guilt: Memories of War in Germany and Japan*, New York: Farrar, Straus & Giroux.

Clammer, J. 1997 *Contemporary Urban Japan: A Sociology of Consumption*, Oxford: Blackwell.

Cohen, E. 1988 Authenticity and Commoditisation in Tourism, *Annals of Tourism Research*, 15, 371–386.

Cole, R. E. 1992 Work and Leisure in Japan, *California Management Review*, 34 (3), 52–63.

Cooper, M. J. and Asplet, M. 1999 An assessment of the appeal to tourists of cultural designs in Australasian fashion apparel — The question of Authenticity', *Tourism Management*, Vol 21 (3), 307–312.

Ehrentraut, A. 1995 Cultural Nationalism, Corporate Interests and the Production of Architectural Heritage in Japan, *CRSA/RCSA*, 32(2), 215–242.

Formanek, S. 1998 Pilgrimage in the Edo period, in S. Linhart & S. Frühstuck (eds), *The Culture of Japan as seen through its Leisure*, New York: SUNY, 165–193.

Furukawa, S. 1986 *Mura no asobibi: Kyujitsu to wakamonogumi no shakai-shi*, Tokyo: Heibonsha sensho 99.

Ganajanapan, A. 2003 Globalization and the dynamics of culture in Thailand, in S. Yamashita and J. S. Eades (eds), *Globalization in Southeast Asia Local, National and Transnational Perspectives*, Oxford: Berghahn, 126–141.

Gluck, C. 1985 *Japan's Modern Myths: Ideology in the Late Meiji Period*, Princeton NJ: Princeton University Press.

Graburn, N. H. H. 1997 Tourism and Cultural Development in East Asia, in S. Yamashita, K. Din and J. S. Eades (eds), *Tourism and Cultural Development in Asia and Oceania*, Selangor: Penerbit Universiti Kebangsaan Malaysia, 194–214.

Hall, C. M. and Page, S. (eds) 2000 *Tourism in South and Southeast Asia*, Oxford: Butterworth Heinemann.

Harada, M. 1994 Towards a Renaissance of Leisure in Japan, *Leisure Studies*, 13 (4), 277–287.

Harrison, D. 1996 Sustainability and Tourism: reflections from a muddy pool, in L. Briguglio, B. Archer, J. Jafari, and G. Wall (eds), *Sustainable Tourism in Islands and Small State: Issues and Policies*, London: Pinter, 69–89.

Havens, T. 1994 *Architects of Affluence*, Cambridge Mass.: Harvard Council on East Asian Studies.

Hendry, J. 1997 The Whole World as Heritage: Foreign Country Theme Parks in Japan, in W. Nuryanti (ed), *Tourism and Heritage Parks in Japan*, Yogyakarta: Gadjah Mada University Press.

Hendry, J. 2000 *The Orient Strikes Back: A Global View of Cultural Display*, Oxford: Berg.

Hendry, J. and M. Raveri (eds) 2002 *Japan at Play: The Ludic and the Logic of Power*, London: Routledge.

Hitchcock, M., King, V, and Parnwell, M. (eds) 1993 *Tourism in South-East Asia*, London: Routledge.

Hollinshead, K. 2002 Playing with the past: Heritage tourism under the tyrannies of postmodern discourse, in C. Ryan (ed) *The Tourist Experience*, London: Continuum.

Ivy, M. 1995 *Discourses of the Vanishing: Modernity, Phantasm, Japan*, Chicago: University of Chicago Press.

Jansen, M. ed. 1995 *The Emergence of Meiji Japan*, Cambridge: Cambridge University Press.

Linhart, S. and Frühstuck, S. (eds) 1998 *The Culture of Japan as seen through its Leisure*, New York: SUNY.

MacCannell, D. 1975. *The Tourist: A New Theory of the Leisure Class*. New York: Schocken.

Martinez, D. P. (ed) 1998 *The Worlds of Japanese Popular Culture: Gender, Shifting Boundaries and Global Cultures*, Cambridge: Cambridge University Press.

Moeran, B. 1997 *Folk Art Potters of Japan*, Richmond, Surrey: Curzon.

Moeran, B. 1998 *In a Far Valley*, Tokyo: Kodansha International.

Mok, C and Lam, T. 2000 Travel-Related Behaviour of Japanese Leisure Tourists: A Review and Discussion, in K. S. Chon, T. Inagaki, and T Ohashi (eds), *Japanese Tourists: Socio-Economic, Marketing and Psychological Analysis*, New York: The Haworth Hospitality Press.

Notoji, M. 1993 *Dizuniirando to-iu seichi*, Tokyo: Iwanami Shoten.

Ohnuki-Tierney, 2000 Cherry Blossoms and their viewing, in S. Linhart and S. Frühstuck (eds), *The Culture of Japan as seen through its Leisure*, New York: SUNY, 213–236.

Picard, M. and Wood, R. (eds) 1997 *Tourism, Ethnicity, and the State in Asian and Pacific Societies*, Honolulu: University of Hawaii Press.

Plutschow, H. 1996 *Matsuri: The Festivals of Japan*, Richmond, Surrey: Japan Library.

Raz, A. E. 1999 *Riding the Black Ship*, Cambridge: Harvard University Press.

Ritchie, D. 2003 *The Image Factory: Fads & Fashions in Japan*, London: Reaktion Books.

Robertson, R. 1995 Glocalization: time-space, and homogeneity-heterogeneity, in M. Featherstone (ed), *Global Modernities*, London: Sage, 25–44.

Ryan, C. (ed) 2002 *The Tourist Experience*, London: Continuum.

Sofield, T. 2000 Rethinking and reconceptualizing social and cultural issues in Southeast and South Asian tourism development, in Hall, C. M. and Page, S. (eds) 2000 *Tourism in South and Southeast Asia*, Oxford: Butterworth Heinemann.

Tong, C. K. and Lian, K. F. 2003 Cultural knowledge, nation states and the limits of globalisation in Southeast Asia, in S. Yamashita and J. S. Eades (eds), *Globalization in Southeast Asia Local, National and Transnational Perspectives*, Oxford: Berghahn, 42–61.

Treat, J. W. (ed) 1996 *Contemporary Japan and Popular Culture*, Richmond, Surrey: Curzon.

Tobin, J. J. 1992 *Remade In Japan: Everyday Life And Consumer Tastes In A Changing Society*, New Haven: Yale University Press.

Urry, J. 1990 *The Tourist Gaze: Leisure and Travel in Contemporary Societies*, London: Sage.

Yamashita, S. 2003a Introduction: 'Glocalizing' Southeast Asia, in S. Yamashita and J. S. Eades (eds), *Globalization in Southeast Asia Local, National and Transnational Perspectives*, Oxford: Berghahn, 1–17.

Yamashita, S. 2003b *Bali and Beyond: Explorations in the Anthropology of Tourism*, Oxford: Berghahn.

You, X. and O'Leary, T. 2000 Age and Cohort Effects: An Examination of Older Japanese Travellers, in K. S. Chon, T. Inagaki, and T. Ohashi (eds), *Japanese Tourists: Socio-Economic, Marketing and Psychological Analysis*, New York: The Haworth Hospitality Press.

Sharing the Heritage of Kodiak Island with Tourists: Views from the Hosts

Christine A. Vogt, Angela Kah, Chang Huh and Sarah Leonard

Introduction

The growing heritage preservation movement has helped residents of many communities around the world recognize, embrace, and share their stories about their place to outsiders or tourists (National Trust for Historic Preservation, 2001a, 2001b). Heritage can range from a building that once housed significant people or events to the natural environment, which provides food, scenery, and history to residents (Millar, 1989). Communities that practice tourism management and marketing, including positioning themselves as a place where tourists are invited and experiences are managed, may find that local history and identity can be difficult to protect with growing numbers of visitors. Some places have developed very thoughtfully and thus have attempted to provide authentic representations of the past. Other places have taken a more commercialized route and are "playing to the camera" to meet the expectations of a broader tourist profile (Wrobel & Long, 2001).

Broadly speaking, tourism development is often the "agent" in the switch from manufacturing (and commodity industries in the United States) to services industries, including the more recent information and experience industry evolution. Heritage tourism may be more palatable to communities than other forms of tourism since it is viewed as being more organic and from inside the community. This paper presents research on a place known for its wilderness heritage: Kodiak Island, Alaska. Heritage preservation, conservation and tourism efforts are examined through the perspectives of residents, businesses, and local stakeholders' using Millar's (1989) conservation and tourism framework and Larkham's (1995) three phases of heritage: preservation, conservation and exploitation. Further, Millar's (1989) framing of heritage conservation and heritage tourism is employed to identify transitional patterns in infrastructure, the importance of tourism and other industries, and attitudes toward tourism development.

Literature Review

Heritage Tourism

Heritage preservation and conservation is an established scientific and practiced field that has responded to the responsibilities that have been placed upon one generation to the next to save history and traditions (Herbert, 1995). More recently, heritage and tourism professionals have gained a greater understanding of shared interests between preservationists and tourism managers, despite their different intentions and end goals. Often heritage preservation and conservation calls for limited human access because of delicate conditions and an emphasis on minimized impacts or potential changes, while tourism professionals often set goals of large numbers of visitors to gain positive economic impact. Larkham (1995) identified three main aspects of heritage in the context of planning and conservation as follows: 1) "preservation" involves the maintenance in mostly unchanged form, of sites of major historical significance; 2) "conservation" takes in the restoration undertaken to bring old buildings and sites into suitable modern figure; and 3) "exploitation" recognizes the value of heritage sites and encompasses the development of existing sites. It may be that all three levels of heritage are needed to maintain the heritage subject existence for future generations.

Millar (1989) argues heritage tourism can be multi-purpose, addressing: 1) heritage as an attraction to draw tourists, 2) community identity for residents, 3) formal and informal education for youth and adults, and 4) economic regeneration for downtown redevelopment and attraction of new enterprises. All these community-based outcomes are not necessarily contradictory to what preservationists stand for; however, preservationists are generally not willing to destroy authentic heritage subject matter or allow for interpretation in an inauthentic manner. For heritage to be "staged" in a real setting, residents, businesses and other organizations must be willing to accept tourists in their everyday

lives and space or choose to not accept tourists and tourism (Doxey, 1976).

One way of managing resident dislike of tourists is to offer contrived heritage attractions that are placed in a special area where tourists are encouraged to visit and residents to stay away. Access to a site, either an entire destination or a special place in a destination, is a critical element in drawing tourists to an area (Gunn & Var, 2002). Not all visitors have time and money resources to visit a distant or difficult site to reach and instead become satisfied just being "near" a place or consuming contrived or commodified versions of a true heritage place. As Miossec (1977) suggested, destinations undergo transformations where attraction and transportation development occurs in stages which impacts both visitor behavior and attitudes of tourism managers and the host population. Time becomes an important factor to monitor evidence of heritage exploitation that may begin to change quality of life for residents and the integrity of the heritage subject matter (Howe *et al.*, 1997). Butler's (1980) destination life cycle has been frequently applied to help determine where a destination is operating on a birth to decline visitation curve. As Butler and more recently Getz (1992) suggest, research accompanied by tourism policy can help communities achieve desired benefits from tourism or improve on unacceptable costs.

The level of benefits from heritage tourism may differ according to the nature of inherited pasts. Some places are naturally important in local and national history because of past events or former residents. Other places offer something so unique that draws residents and tourists to see and experience a phenomenon. Despite the subject matter of the inherited past, successful heritage management often includes investments in conservation policy, long-term planning, commitments to heritage tourism, and partnerships involving public and private sectors (Boyd, 2002). Examining heritage efforts over time is also important, as "heritage" by its very essence is time dependent. Millar (1989) argues for heritage continuity from the past to the present and future with a goal of attaining better conservation and visitor experiences, concurrently. As many have argued, long-term planning and management are needed to endure the tensions between preservation and tourism interests.

Resources to fund only heritage preservation efforts may not exist, thus the full spectrum of heritage from preservation and exploitation may be necessary from an economic perspective. Larkham (1995) presents that tourism may provide resources that preservation needs; that is, tourism income often allows for the maintenance of areas or buildings and staffing when other funding is absent. The growing trend of focusing on tourism as local economic diversification and as a means to rally heritage preservation and conservation is a phenomenon that calls for increased awareness by communities and researchers who search for answers on the appropriate balance of the different treatments of heritage, and the necessary stakeholders and process to achieve balance.

Role and Importance of Hosts in Heritage Destinations

As with any tourism encounter or vacation, the roles of hosts and guests are central to the nature of the experience (Smith, 1989). Heritage tourism is no exception and the role of host may be more amplified given that heritage means "from the birth or roots of the people." Boyd (2002) calls for partnerships comprised of hosts, guests and managers to ensure heritage tourism is sustainable. Partnerships need to work toward planning and management roles, but should also be respected at the field sites when hosts and guests encounter each other. Often the focus of tourism research is on the guest or visitor, but recently the role of residents is becoming more noticed as integral to the vacation experience and industry. Lankford and Howard (1994) developed a tourism impact scale to detect opinions held by resident who live in destination areas. Their research showed that residents' attitudes are quite diverse depending on how tourism personally impacted their own lives. Those who work in the industry tend to be more accepting of and positive toward tourism. Those whose personal lifestyle may have changed in a negative way (i.e. crowding at their favorite recreation site) tend to be less positive. Madrigal (1993) found that residents who were economically dependent on tourism held stronger positive feelings about tourism. Residents' negative perceptions of tourism were less tied to economic dependency and instead was more a function of the level of tourism development in a community (more development, stronger negative attitudes). King and his colleagues (1993) reported residents of an area in Fiji, most of whom worked in the tourism industry, recognized "the good and the bad" impacts brought on by tourism. Economic benefits were desirable and residents felt social costs were brought on by outsiders to their homeland, including drug addition, organized and individual crime, and alcoholism. In a study of seven rural communities in Arizona, Andereck and Vogt (2000) showed that support for tourism product development options varied greatly across communities. Their results point to the need to consider residents' opinions and desires for tourism development programs, as they should be tailored to meet the needs of the residents who live and work in a community.

Another example of understanding the role of residents in the tourism planning and development process is studying how engagement of residents leads to relationships in a community. Huang and Stewart (1996) studied a sample of residents in a community, some were associated with tourism and others were not. They found that tourism, particularly in a rural community with strong German heritage, encouraged conformity to an ideal image of the community and this shared image was a source of bonding amongst residents. Original residents were found to need time to adjust to increasing community diversity (with new residents and tourists) and new residents learned how to fit into their new community. Tourism, particularly heritage-based tourism, has the potential to facilitate community sharing and learning for residents of all types.

Focus of this Paper

This paper examines a place with significant heritage assets that potentially could see a dramatic change and increase in tourist visitation in the near future. Historically, many communities and places in Alaska are very difficult to visit because of weather challenges and a lack of adequate and consistent transportation. In the last 50 years, modern transportation forms (e.g. trains, planes, highways, boats, ferries, cruise ships) have enabled tourists to visit places once deemed the "past frontier" of the United States. Similar to many of the island features outlined by Swarbrooke (1999), Kodiak Island and nearby village areas can be expensive and sometimes difficult to reach compared to other Alaska communities on the road system. The cruise ship

industry has created a strong and growing market for the Island Passage of Canada and Alaska, as well as inland destinations such as Denali National Park. Coastal towns such as Skagway and Juneau host thousands of disembarking cruise ship passengers primarily in the summer. Alaska's visitors are drawn to the heritage of the state, which includes pristine natural scenery and frontier-like lifestyles. Most cruise ship passengers experience Alaskan communities in half-day doses that may include a trip to a remote area such as a glacier or wildlife refuge. Often these side trips cost hundreds of dollars and are extra expenses incurred above the base cruise ship package. Other passengers may choose to disembark and spend their day walking around the port area. Seasonal businesses, primarily for tourists, exist to provide an experience for visitors and economic benefits to the local community. As tourism has changed and grown dramatically in some coastal Alaska communities, Kodiak Island has intentionally kept the number of cruise ships per year below ten.

To understand better the dynamics of a tourism-dependent community, primarily based on the heritage of the Alaskan lifestyle, we have studied the current relevance and future prospects of tourism, from residents' and businesses' perspectives. Millar's (1989) framing of heritage conservation and heritage tourism is employed to identify distinctive community assets, transitional patterns in infrastructure, the importance of tourism and other industries, and attitudes toward different levels of tourism development. Specifically, the following research questions were examined using four mail questionnaire-generated data sets and transcriptions from a focus group held with stakeholders representing heritage conservation and tourism interests. Longitudinal data sets of randomly selected resident samples in 1995 and 2001, and census business samples from the same years were used. Focus group data were generated shortly following the 2001 surveys.

1. What is the heritage that residents are willing to share with tourists?
2. Is a destination's heritage likely to be the top rated "assets" of a destination and community?
3. Following Millar's (1989) framing, is there evidence of heritage continuity from past, current, and future? Is there evidence of heritage consistency from residents' or businesses/organizations' perspective?
4. How do residents and businesses rate the current and future states of heritage using Larkham's (1995) heritage continuum of preservation to exploitation?
5. Can heritage conservation and heritage tourism co-exist? What are signs of co-existence?

Study Site

Kodiak Island is in the Gulf of Alaska in the southwest portion of the state of Alaska. Kodiak is the second largest island in the United States, behind the Big Island of Hawaii. The population is under 20,000 residents. Many people work in the commercial fishing industry with the port being one of the country's largest. King crab is one of the fish commodities from the sea, and on land, the island is known for the Kodiak brown bear of which there are several thousand. In recent years, Kodiak Island has seen some industry and livelihood shifts. Drastic changes (e.g., yields) in the commercial fishing industry have forced the communities to broaden their economic base.

Tourism has become one of the industries to create jobs and greater economic diversity. Walmart, the quintessential big box retailer, opened a store in 2000, which has caused downtown merchants to begin a revitalization program aimed at tourists, as well as attracting local residents to buy locally. Kodiak Island is also receiving requests to be a port-of-call for cruise ships. In the last eight to ten years, five to ten cruise ships have embarked at Kodiak's port each year. These ships have been more specialty ships (smaller boats of hundreds of passengers, not thousands of passengers like the sizes of ships along the Island Passage). Requests have been made in recent years to Kodiak officials to allow for larger and more frequent ships to visit the island. Thus far, the requests by cruise companies have been turned down.

Methods

The role of local residents and businesses in any form of community planning is central. In communities that identify themselves as tourism destinations, local residents and businesses most often play a central role in local policies that guide and regulate land use, transportation access, and taxation. Tourism researchers have long recognized the importance of studying these host groups to understand the support for tourism activities in a community (Allen et al., 1993; Allen et al., 1988; Andereck & Vogt, 2000; Getz, 1992; Huang & Stewart, 1996; Lankford, 1994; Lankford & Howard, 1993; Long et al., 1990; Madrigal, 1993). Sometimes these studies seek to understand the dynamics of tourism comparing residents and tourists (Teo & Huang, 1995) or businesses and tourists (Vogt & Fesenmaier, 1995). Many of these mentioned studies feature a series of questions, often measured with a five-point agreement scale, that assess attitudes held toward tourism activity in their community or region. While many studies include several communities (e.g., Allen *et al.* studies included 20 Colorado communities, Andereck and Vogt included 7 Arizona communities), very few researchers have replicated studies in the same community to understand consistency and continuity amongst community hosts or stakeholders.

Our research employs a longitudinal survey design to study two host groups, both who live and work in Kodiak Island Borough, Alaska (USA). We were only involved in the more recent study efforts conducted in 2001. However, the procedures followed for studying the host groups, residents and businesses, were fairly similar in nature and attempted to follow, yet improve upon, procedures used in the earlier study of 1995. For the resident and business studies in 2001, a questionnaire was mailed to almost a census or complete population. Detail procedures are described for residents and businesses separately.

Resident Sample

A four-page mail questionnaire was designed by a team of university researchers, the executive director of the local convention and visitors bureau, and an executive director of a statewide tourism and recreation association. The content of the questions administered in 2001 closely match the questionnaire used in 1995. A one-page personalized letter was mailed to a sample of Borough residents in early November 2001 that came very close to including every household in the Borough. A total of 2,349 households were mailed a letter, questionnaire, and a business reply envelope. As shown in Table 1, only in

the City of Kodiak was a systematic sample used where every third household was randomly selected to receive the mail questionnaire. An incentive was used to reward the first respondent as well as a randomly selected additional respondent. The incentive was $100 for the first received survey and a single drawing from those surveys received by the deadline to win $50. A week after the original mailing, a reminder postcard was mailed to everyone in the sample as either a thank you or as a reminder to complete the survey. Letters and postcards were mailed by a mail firm, which followed the sampling procedures provided by the researchers. The list included homeowners and renters and was deemed to be as up-to-date as possible. However, after a few weeks, approximately 500 envelopes that were mailed to residential households were undeliverable. In mid-December, 2001, this group of addresses was remailed a letter and questionnaire to "occupant at this address" in an attempt to gain a response. Very few of these questionnaires were returned completed. In addition to the mailing procedures, several publicity efforts were used to market the research study. News releases were mailed (and published by) the local newspaper The Kodiak Daily Mirror. The destination's convention and visitors bureau executive director, spoke on a radio show promoting the study and asked residents and businesses to complete the survey. A final response rate of 16.4 percent or 385 completed questionnaires was achieved which is lower than most tourism studies receive, however significantly higher than the rate of 10.6 percent achieved in 1995. Resources were not available to complete a second mailing; however, non-response bias was evaluated by comparing the demographic profile of respondents to the 2000 Census

Table 1   Sampling Frame for 2001 and 1995 Resident and Business Surveys

	2001		1995	
	Residents	Businesses	Residents	Businesses
Population (households/ businesses)	4,424	537	Not provided	178 (est.)
Sample	2,349	537	1,882	178
Respondents	385	118	200	46
Response rate	16.4%	22.0%	10.6%	25.8%
Sampling procedure				
City of Kodiak (including Coast Guard Base, Service District One)	1 out of 3 households	All	1 out of 5 households	All
All other areas (Kodiak Island Borough)	All	All	All	All

data for the Borough. Respondents were found to be slightly more educated than the general population.

Business Sample

An eight-page business questionnaire was designed at the same time the resident survey was designed. Similar to the resident study, questions in the 2001 instrument targeting business owners or managers paralleled those asked in 1995. A one-page personalized letter, questionnaire, and business reply envelope were mailed in November 2001 to all businesses on the Kodiak Chamber of Commerce member list and the Visitor's Bureau list (removing duplicates). A non-member list was also provided by the Chamber and Visitor's Bureau and included in the sampling frame. In total, 537 business surveys were mailed to the main contact at the business/

organization (e.g. President, owner, community affairs) with no mail returned as undeliverable (Table 1). Similar to the resident survey, an incentive was provided to the first respondent and a randomly picked additional business. A reminder postcard was mailed a week after the original mailing as a thank you or a reminder. A final response rate of 22.0 percent or 118 complete questionnaires was achieved which is slightly lower than in 1995; however, the sample size for the 2001 study was increased significantly and was more diverse than the 1995 sample (537 names versus 178).

Measurement

To answer the research questions, data were drawn from primarily the resident and business questionnaires that were administered in 1995 and 2001. Heritage was self-defined by residents (research question #1) in the responses of two open-ended questions. Respondents were asked to describe the top reasons people visit Kodiak Island Borough and the words or phrases that best describe "the image of your community that you would like visitors to have when they leave." The responses provided were coded and summarized to provide a description of activities, places and ethos of the community that they were willing to share with tourists. To address research question #2, community assets were evaluated by residents and businesses using a four-point scale ranging from "1" equaling an excellent rating to "4" equaling a poor rating. Residents and businesses rated 17 items that covered community services, tourism infrastructure, and heritage/cultural and environmental assets. Comparisons were made between the 1995 and 2001 data on this community asset scale to test continuity in views of heritage, tourism, and community quality change (research question #3). Consistency was examined by comparing residents' and businesses' views of heritage, tourism and community quality change. The assessment of hosts' attitudes toward heritage used five-point agreement statements, which personified Larkham's three phases of heritage (preservation, conservation, and exploitation) (research question #4). The final research question (#5) examined heritage conservation and tourism exploitation co-existing and was addressed by using data collected during stakeholder meetings held with agencies and organizations directly involved in heritage and tourism activities.

Findings

The first research question established the heritage Kodiak Island residents identify with and are willing to share with tourists. One way this was examined was by asking residents why tourists come to visit the island. Residents believe tourists come to the borough primarily for hunting and fishing (40% of responses). The next most common reason for visiting is to view the scenic beauty of the area (17% of responses). Visiting friends or relatives (11%), outdoor activities (hiking, camping, kayaking) (5%), business transactions (7%), wildlife viewing (7%) and an assortment of other reasons (13%) were offered. Businesses were asked a similar question but with close-ended responses. The businesses responses were very similar to residents' response on the reasons or attractors that bring tourists to the Island. Many business owners replied tourists come seeking a wilderness experience, however this was not something mentioned by residents in their provided response.

Another way to examine residents' perceptions of heritage was asking residents to express the image they would like visitors to have of their island. The most frequently mentioned images or adjectives were beauty, spectacular and picturesque (grouped as natural beauty), quaint, friendly and safe (grouped as social environment), and fishing and working village (grouped as economy). It is based on the findings from this first research question that "heritage" was considered as a core element of the community that encompassed natural beauty, residents as hosts (friendly and helpful to tourists), historical buildings and sites, cultural attractions, recreation (particularly outdoor), and community festivals and events.

The second research question examined how a destination's heritage is rated as a community asset. Six community asset categories were considered as representative of heritage and the other categories were considered as general community assets or infrastructure. As a group, heritage assets were more highly rated by residents than items in "other assets." The top rating by residents was for natural beauty with nearly a perfect score (mean = 1.1), followed by friendly and helpful people/residents (mean = 1.6) (Table 2). On average, cultural attractions, recreation and festivals received between "good" and "fair" ratings. For those assets not considered to be heritage in nature, the weakest rated ones were restaurants and dining, retail, transportation, and the condition of roads on the island.

The third research question examined whether there is evidence of: (1) heritage continuity from the past, current times, and future perspective, and (2) heritage consistency from residents' and businesses' perspectives. Continuity was defined as similar or improved conditions of the heritage assets. As shown in Figure 1, heritage assets were rated by business and resident respondents as either not changing or improving slightly from the mid 1990s to 2001. Natural beauty was rated at the highest level of excellence during this time period. Festivals and events improved the most over the 6-year time period. Smaller rating improvements were made for friendly and helpful people (hosts), historical buildings, cultural attractions, and recreation and entertainment. Heritage consistency was measured by similar ratings held by residents and businesses at a point in time. As shown

Table 2   Resident's Rating of Kodiak Borough Community Assets in 2001 (n = 385)

Assets of Kodiak Borough	Mean[a]	Standard Deviation
Heritage Assets		
Natural beauty	1.1	0.5
Friendly and helpful people	1.6	0.8
Historical buildings and sites	2.1	0.8
Cultural attractions	2.4	0.8
Recreation and entertainment	2.4	0.9
Festivals and events	2.5	0.8
Other Assets		
Environmental quality (air, water, land)	1.5	0.7
Police and fire protection	2.0	0.7
Education (K-12)	2.2	0.7
Lodging facilities	2.4	0.7
Visitor services	2.4	0.8
Education (college, technical)	2.4	0.8
Restaurants and dining facilities	2.8	0.8
Retail/shopping	2.8	0.7
Transportation options/access	2.9	0.8
Roads (condition of)	3.1	0.7

[a]Scale equals "1" as excellent, "2" as good, "3" as fair and "4" as poor.

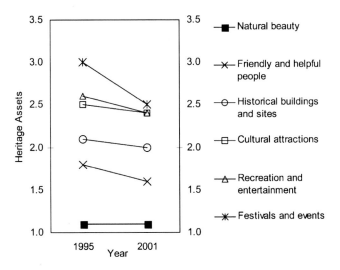

Scale equals "1" as excellent, "2" as good, "3" as fair and "4" as poor.

Figure 1 Heritage Asset Continuity by Resident and Business Respondents in 1995 and 2001.

in Table 3, residents and businesses held similar evaluations of heritage assets in Kodiak Island with the exception of natural beauty, friendly hosts, and recreation and entertainment in recent years. On these few items where evaluations were slightly different, businesses tended to rate the heritage assets more positively than residents.

The fourth research questions assessed residents' and businesses' attitudes toward the

Table 3 Heritage Consistency Between Business (n = 118) and Resident (n = 385) Respondent Groups

	1995		2001	
	Mean[a]		Mean[a]	
Heritage Assets	Business	Resident	Business	Resident
Natural beauty	1.1	1.1	1.0*	1.2
Friendly and helpful people	1.7	1.8	1.4*	1.6
Historical buildings and sites	2.1	2.1	2.0	2.1
Cultural attractions	2.4	2.6	2.0	2.4
Recreation and entertainment	2.6	2.6	2.2*	2.4
Festivals and events	2.9	3.0	2.4	2.5

[a]Scale equals "1" as excellent, "2" as good, "3" as fair and "4" as poor.
*Significant at the $p < .01$ level in 2001 between business and resident respondent groups.

128   C. A. Vogt et al.

three levels of heritage defined earlier in the literature section of this paper (Larkham, 1995). The first level is preservation representing possibly the strong standards for limited usage and keeping nature or culture similar to its original state. The second level is conservation, which represents standards that allow for modest visitation levels with limited environmental and social impact. The final level is exploitation representing heavy, possibly uncontrolled, visitation levels with little regard to environmental and social impact. Residents and businesses were provided with some of the same questions, however businesses were asked a few additional conservation and exploitation questions. As shown in Table 4, Kodiak Island residents held the strongest levels of agreement over preservation

efforts for both wildlife and natural areas (mean = 2.0), and historical buildings and cultural sites (mean = 2.3). The next highest agreement was on conservation efforts to allow, but limit cruise ships (mean = 2.4), and grow the tourism industry with resource protection in mind (mean = 2.8). The least agreed upon heritage strategy was exploitation by allowing Kodiak Island to be an emerging international destination (mean = 3.0). Residents tended to agree that tourists at the current time are not a burden on community services (mean = 3.8). Businesses exhibited a similar pattern to residents' attitudes with preservation and conservation efforts being most supported and exploitation the least supported (Table 5). Businesses expressed strong agreement that the growth of the

Table 4   Residents' Perspectives Toward Tourism in 2001 (n = 385)

Attitude Statements	Mean[a]	Standard Deviation
Preservation		
I believe preservation of wildlife and natural areas on public lands contributes to a sustainable economy.	2.0	1.0
The development of the Borough's tourism industry will benefit local projects such as the preservation and restoration of historical building and cultural sites.	2.3	1.0
Conservation		
I'd like to see cruise ships with less than 1,000 passengers make occasional visits (once a week or less) to the Borough.	2.4	1.2
Increased protection of natural resources will result from the growth of the tourism industry.	2.8	1.1
Exploitation		
The Borough will emerge as an international tourist/visitor destination within the next five years.	3.0	1.1
Tourists are a burden on a community's services.	3.8	1.1

[a]Mean scored based on a 5-point scale where "1" equals strongly agree, "2" equals agree, "3" equals neutral, "4" equals disagree, and "5" equals strongly disagree.

Table 5   Businesses' Perspective Toward Tourism in 2001 (N = 118)

Attitude Statements	Mean[a]	Standard Deviation
Preservation		
I believe preservation of wildlife and natural areas on public lands contributes to a sustainable economy.	1.8	0.8
I believe natural characteristics and cultural heritage contribute to my quality of life in the Borough.	1.9	0.9
Conservation		
Growth of the tourism industry should be planned and managed to minimize any negative impact on the local community and environment.	1.7	0.7
I believe the tourism industry can play an important role in building a sustainable economy.	1.7	0.7
I feel the natural or wilderness areas are an important part of the success of my business or product.	1.9	1.1
Use of popular areas in the Borough should be managed (limiting permits, regulation, guidelines, etc), if needed to sustain residents' quality of life.	2.1	1.0
I would like to see cruise ships with less than 1,000 passengers make occasional visits (once a week or less) to the Borough.	2.3	1.0
Exploitation		
Local government should build a convention center to attract meeting business during the fall, winter and spring.	2.5	1.2
I would like to see large cruise ships coming to the Borough on a regular basis.	2.5	1.2
Current tourism promotional efforts for the Borough as a visitor are sufficient.	3.0	1.0

[a]Mean scored based on a 5-point scale where "1" equals strongly agree, "2" equals agree, "3" equals neutral, "4" equals disagree, and "5" equals strongly disagree.

tourism industry should be planned and managed to minimize any negative impact on the local community and environment (mean = 1.7) and that tourism should play an important role in building a sustainable economy (mean = 1.7).

The final research question draws on stakeholder discussions occurring in Kodiak Island Borough. The resident and business surveys discussed were part of a community-level effort to guide tourism growth in a variety of socio-economic and ecological landscapes in the state of Alaska (Alaska Wilderness Recreation & Tourism Association, 2001). One of the community examples is Kodiak Island, which represents an island/coastal community that is highly dependent on commercial fishing and harvesting and seafood processing, historically and currently. Tourism is a newer and growing industry on Kodiak Island. While tourists are likely to be interested in coastal sites, scenery and activities, tourists can also add increased demand for and impacts on interior resources. Toward understanding future demand levels and potential impacts, stakeholder meetings were held to discuss heritage conservation (representing preservation and conservation) and heritage tourism (representing exploitation and conservation). One stakeholder meeting was comprised of supply-side representatives including representatives from the local chamber of commerce, convention and visitors bureau, national wildlife refuge located on the island, local state park, local Audubon (birding) society, local government planners, and Native tribes. It is within the comments shared in this meeting that signs of co-existence are evident. First, the construction of the stakeholder group represents that heritage conservation and heritage tourism interests are at least willing to meet and possibly work together. Next, comments from participants shed light on the possible balance to be found in heritage conservation and tourism. Comments from a bush pilot and the Native representative suggest that tourism is positive and needed for economic growth; however, it should be based on wilderness values and tourism planning efforts. The two public land managers (from refuge and state park) recognized the need to provide outdoor recreation and wilderness experiences to residents of the island and tourists, although both agencies manage thousands of acres that allow for preservation and very limited backcountry uses. Representatives from the Audubon society shared that they will monitor tourism's impacts on the environment and community

and assure that they are minimized. The society also has a popular hiking program that it would like to turn into a commercial venture. In each set of comments these tourism representatives showed signs of heritage conservation and tourism coexisting. These same stakeholders discussed strengths and weaknesses of tourism on the island. Emerging strengths were that the tourism industry currently has infrastructure and a tourism service system, which is relatively undeveloped (not over commercialized), the cultural heritage of the island is rich and unique, and the natural environment allows for outdoor recreation and wildlife viewing and consumption. These strengths will appear to guide Kodiak Island's heritage efforts.

Conclusion and Discussion

Kodiak Island residents and businesses identify with their heritage as a means of creating an image for their community and island. Their heritage includes the wilderness setting, the fishing industry and the hospitality of residents living on an island in the most northern US state. Heritage assets were found to be distinctive for residents and businesses and the findings suggest that these community assets had not declined in quality over the past six years. Heritage continuity over time and heritage consistency across the two host groups was evident on Kodiak Island. The most recent measure of residents' and businesses' attitudes (in 2001) suggest that preservation efforts are most important to the wellbeing of the residents and sustainability of the ecosystem. The greatest disagreement was voiced for tourism growth that suggests large number of visitors at one time (i.e. large cruise ships, conventions). Evidence was also seen for current levels of heritage exploitation and preservation efforts coexisting. Numerous projects are currently underway (e.g. Mainstreet program), which suggests residents and businesses are supportive and willing to work toward heritage sustainability. Based on feedback from presentations and reporting of the findings of this research in the community, as well as ground truthing with community leaders, the findings from the resident and business surveys appear to represent the views held within the community. Importantly, garnering host or stakeholder opinions involves and empowers more individuals in the community and tourism planning processes.

As heritage tourism becomes more demanded by travelers and a means for existing destinations to sustain their tourism industry and for preservationists to engage and gain support from a more diverse group of interested citizens, the need for understanding the processes associated with heritage efforts are needed. Research on tourists (e.g. Kerstetter, Confer & Graefe, 2001), partnerships (e.g. Timothy, 1999) and residents (this article; Ap & Crompton, 1993) are needed to display the successes and challenges communities face in preserving their heritage and also sharing it with outsiders. Ap & Crompton (1993) suggest a continuum of strategies (i.e. embrace, tolerate, adjust, withdraw) with attitudinal and behavioral signs that aid communities in understanding where in a destination life cycle they might be currently operating or be facing in the future. The interaction between tourists and hosts frequently needs consideration to determine the "health" of the tourism industry. In the case of Kodiak Island, tourists have traditionally visited for a week or more to experience Alaska's wild lands and its people. Modern-day tourism brings a new traveler group via cruise lines that may dock for a few hours or perhaps a day and have few interactions with hosts. This study suggests the residents of Kodiak Island at this time were more supportive of tourism planning and marketing that follows tradition and yields consistency between hosts and continuity over time.

This research also intended to show that tourism planning and marketing could work toward some level of diversified heritage consumption. As shown in this paper, heritage efforts can range between preservation, conservation and exploitation. The Borough of Kodiak Island is not unlike many other communities and destinations in the Pacific Rim that with increased accessibility, more and new types of tourists will visit. McKercher & du Cros (2002) segment tourists by the importance of culture/heritage tourism in the decision to visit a place and the experience sought (deep versus shallow). In the past, the residents and businesses of the Kodiak Island Borough have hosted and targeted primarily deep, purposeful heritage visitors who desire the Alaskan experience. New forms of tourists are a contrast. The cruise industry or other forms of itinerary-driven vacations bring many visitors for a short period of time. In Kodiak Island's case, much of the heritage of the place is deep in the interior of the island. Great potential exists for small business tour operators to provide half-day excursions that could explore selected heritage sites and natural resources. These tourists and their experiences, however, are more different from the traditional tourists who stay for several days or weeks. Additionally, there are the cruise tourists who disembark and choose to "stay near the harbor" or in town. Their heritage experience is quite different from the aforementioned tourist types. Importantly, residents and local businesses have the opportunity, through their expressions and involvement, to shape their own heritage and the heritage that is shared with others. This examination of Kodiak Island shows early, but strong efforts in community-based heritage tourism planning, which recognizes the delicate balance between heritage preservation and conservation and full-fledged tourism exploitation.

References

Alaska Wilderness Recreation & Tourism Association (2001). Guiding Alaska Tourism: Strategies for Success. Anchorage: AWRTA.

Allen, L. R., Long, P. T., Perdue, R. R. & Kieselbach, S. (1988). The impact of tourism development on residents' perceptions of community life. *Journal of Travel Research*, 27(1), 16–21.

Allen, L. R., Hafer, H. R., Long, P. T. & Perdue, R. R. (1993). Rural residents' attitudes toward recreation and tourism development. *Journal of Travel Research*, 31(4), 27–33.

Andereck, K. L. & Vogt, C. A. (2000). The relationship between residents' attitudes toward tourism and tourism development options. *Journal of Travel Research*, 39(1), 27–36.

Ap, J. & Crompton, J. L. (1993). Residents' strategies for responding to tourism impacts. *Journal of Travel Research*, 32(1), 47–50.

Boyd, S. (2002). Cultural and heritage tourism in Canada: Opportunities, principles and challenges. *Tourism and Hospitality Research*, 3(3), 211–233.

Butler, R. (1980). The concept of a tourist area cycle of evolution: Implications for management of resources. *Canadian Geographer*, 24, 5–12.

Doxey, G. (1976). When enough's enough: The natives are restless in Old Niagara. *Heritage Canada*, 2(2), 26–27.

Getz, D. (1992). Tourism planning and destination life cycle. *Annals of Tourism Research*, 19, 752–770.

Gunn, C. & Var, T. (2002). *Tourism Planning*, 4th edn. Taylor & Francis, New York.

Herbert, D. T. (1995). Heritage, Tourism, and Society. Mansell, London.

Howe, J., McMahon, E. & Propst, L. (1997). Balancing Nature and Commerce in Gateway Communities. Island Press, Washington, DC.

Huang, Y. H. & Stewart, W. P. (1996). Rural tourism development: Shifting basis of community solidarity. *Journal of Travel Research*, 34(4), 26–31.

Kerstetter, D. L., Confer, J. J. & Graefe, A. R. (2001). An exploration of the specialization concept within the context of heritage tourism. *Journal of Travel Research*, 39(3), 267–274.

King, B., Pizam, A. & Milman, A. (1993). Social impacts of tourism: Host perceptions. *Annals of Tourism Research*, 20, 650–665.

Lankford, S. V. (1994). Attitudes and perceptions toward tourism and rural regional development. *Journal of Travel Research*, 32(3), 35–43.

Lankford, S. V. & Howard, D. R. (1994). Developing a tourism impact attitude scale. *Annals of Tourism Research*, 21, 121–139.

Larkham, P. J. (1995). Heritage as planned and conserved. *Heritage, Tourism, and Society* (pp. 85–116). Mansell, London.

Long, P. T. Perdue, R. R. & Allen, L. (1990). Rural resident tourism perceptions and attitudes by community level of tourism. *Journal of Travel Research*, 28(3), 3–9.

Madrigal, R. (1993). A tale of tourism in two cities. *Annals of Tourism Research*, 20, 336–353.

McKercher, B. & du Cros, H. (2002). *Cultural Tourism: The Partnership between Tourism and Cultural Heritage Management*. The Haworth Hospitality Press, New York.

Millar, S. (1989). Heritage management for heritage tourism. *Tourism Management*, March, 9–14.

Miossec, J. M. (1977). Un modele de l'espace touristique. *L'Espace Geographique*, 6(1), 41–48.

National Trust for Historic Preservation (2001a). *Stories Across America: Opportunities for Rural Tourism*. National Trust for Historic Preservation, Washington, DC.

National Trust for Historic Preservation (2001b). *Share Your Heritage: Cultural Heritage Tourism Success Stores*. National Trust for Historic Preservation, Washington, DC.

Smith, V. (ed) (1989). *Hosts and Guests: The Anthology of Tourism*, 2nd edn. The University of Pennsylvania Press, Philadelphia.

Swarbrooke, J. (1999). *Sustainable Tourism Management*. CABI Publishing, Wallingford.

Teo, P. & Huang, S. (1995). Tourism and heritage conservation in Signapore. *Annals of Tourism Research*, 22, 589–615.

Timothy, D. J. (1999). Cross-border partnership in tourism resource management: International parks along the US-Canada border. *Journal of Sustainable Tourism*, 7(3/4), 182–205.

Vogt, C. & Fesenmaier, D. (1995). Tourists and retailers' perceptions of services: A confirmatory factor analysis of multiple groups. *Annals of Tourism Research*, 22, 763–780.

Wrobel, D. M. & Long, P. (2001). *Seeing and Being Seen*. University Press of Kansas, Kansas.

Managing Cultural Change and Tourism: A Review and Perspective

R. W. Carter and R. J. S. Beeton

Introduction

The impacts of tourism on indigenous peoples have been reported by McKean (1982), Volkman (1990), Picard (1993) and McArthy (1994), with some attempts at modelling the phenomenon (e.g. White, 1974; Doxey, 1975; Smith, 1977; Kariel and Kariel, 1982; Getz 1983; Graburn, 1984; Jafari, 1987). In some areas, economic and cultural benefits to the host community are identified (de Kadt, 1979; Belisle and Hoy, 1980; Jordon, 1980; Silver, 1992; Picard, 1993), including enhancement and revitalisation of local cultures (Jafari, 1992; Grahn, 1991; Bleasdale and Tapsell, 1996). The cultural revitalisation argument is based on the premise that societies find niches through tourism that help build group solidarity, pride in traditions and strengthened identity (Rabibhadana, 1992). This in turn benefits tourists, tourism promoters, and national cultures (Klieger, 1990).

Dogan (1989) has pointed out that impacts, both positive and negative, have varied between localities and with the type of tourism. The reactions of indigenous hosts have been diverse, ranging from an active resistance to passive adoption of Western culture. At times, local culture is treated as a 'commodity', as influential Western societies interact with less affluent hosts (Rabibhadana, 1992). Alternatively, interactions may be detached and primarily economic, rather than social (Esman, 1984). In other circumstances, visitor influx, seasonality and opportunistic investment in real estate that radically affects local land values may indirectly influence destination communities (Craik, 1991).

In the early stages of tourism, and with limited experience, indigenous communities face the dilemma that tourism often relies on culture and may threaten it (Picard, 1993). Once the tourism option is selected, risk of customer dissatisfaction and economic insecurity 'force' the less-affluent culture to continue to service tourism needs. This suggests that the incentives in tourism are persuasive (Ascher, 1985) and may be imposed on local communities that have little power (and knowledge) to manage their future. In the colonial or imperialistic situation, the needs of local communities are often secondary to national and international goals of development. For the tourist industry to survive, one or both cultures must bend — usually the one with least power (Nunez, 1963; Crick, 1988; Nash 1989). This creates pressure for acculturation in the direction of the society of the tourist.

Smith (1989) argued that cultural impact is minimal where the flow of visitors is small and sporadic, while increasing tourist numbers may compromise the cultural heritage of host communities (see also Jafari, 1983; Craik, 1991; Mason, 1996). To preserve cultural resources and enhance the economic base, local communities must decide whether to control or restrict tourism to preserve their cultural integrity, or encourage tourism as a desirable economic goal and restructure their culture to absorb it (Smith, 1989; Rabibhadana, 1992).

Boorstin (1964) and Urry (1990) argued that tourist demand is a strong influence, with tourist attractions (best) serving their purpose when they are reduced to 'pseudo-events'. While there may be a trend away from this situation, it has been proposed that many tourists realise that there are no 'authentic' experiences and actually enjoy the trivial nature of cultural presentations because they match the holiday environment (Feifer, 1985). Holidays spell 'freedom', which possibly explains the tourist acceptance of the inauthentic (Krippendorf, 1987), with tourists being more interested in their own culture rather than that of the destination community (Crick, 1988). Such perspectives add pressure to change traditional tourist arts and cultural expressions (Graburn, 1984).

While tourists might be satisfied with modified cultural presentations, it is unclear whether the presenters are satisfied beyond the economic rewards, and their awareness of how modifications to cultural expressions are influencing broader socio-cultural dynamics. It is also unclear why tourism appears to benefit some indigenous societies and not others (Craik, 1991). Tourism is an agent of culture change in indigenous communities (Smith, 1989a). However, cultures continually change with or without tourism (Keesing and Strathern, 1998). A significant issue is whether indigenous communities retain control of their cultural heritage under tourism (Nash, 1989; Bleasdale and Tapsell, 1996). This means the amount, the direction and the rate of change, and the degree of power communities have over these changes.

The effect of tourism on cultures has generally been discussed in two broad areas: acculturation and modernisation (descriptive), and imperialism and commodification (moralistic and ethical). Acculturation theory proposes that when two cultures interact they increasingly become like each other through a process of borrowing. The nature of the contact, the profiles of the contact personnel, and the level of socio-cultural integration and population sizes result in asymmetrical borrowing of cultural expressions (Nunez and Lett, 1989). One effect of acculturation is modernisation. Tourists often complain how modern things are in contemporary indigenous communities (Dagnal-Myron, 1990). Writing on the impact of tourism in northern Thailand, Cohen (1979) noted that tourism promotes an attractive, marketable image of a locality, giving visitors certain expectations. However, he proposed that the introduction of tourism changes the locality, removing its physical appearance from the promoted tourist image. Van den Berghe and Keys (1984) argue that all tourism is based on 'exoticism'. As such, ethnic tourism is self-defeating in that it makes natives less exotic and become 'tourees', modifying their behaviour to suit tourist demand for 'pseudo-authenticity'. Such interpretive discussions give little attention to the dynamic role or response of host communities to the tourism perturbation.

In contemporary Western society, everything can be bought and sold. It can be treated as a commodity (Watson and Kopachevsky, 1994). When a culture attracts visitors to a destination, the culture itself can become a commodity (Hitchcock and King, 2003; Kirtsoglu and Theodossopoulos, 2004; Nunez, 1977). This is of no apparent concern to indigenous people when they accept payment to perform for tourists. However, of concern is when tourists treat cultural activities, and even the people themselves, as the 'attraction' without their consent or benefit (MacCannell, 1976; Greenwood, 1989). Commodification occurs at all levels in tourism. Tourism planners may treat cultural resources as 'objects' to be exploited (Ascher, 1985). Commodification can also take the form of names or artefacts taken from indigenous culture for tourist ventures. Important questions are not asked about what is being 'borrowed'. At times, the names and artefacts displayed are sacred, and not meant for public display.

Bleasdale and Tapsell (1996) identified four tourism-related forces that affect social and environmental change: the nature of the host society at the local and national levels; the nature of the tourist industry; features of the economy; and geographic features (see also Pearce, 1989; Swarbrooke, 1996). Craik (1991) added the privatisation of public land as a major factor in changing attitudes to tourists and tourism (see also Mathieson and Wall, 1982; de Kadt, 1979).

With or without tourism, the culture of people and communities is dynamic. Thus, culture change is not the prime concern, except from a reduced tourist experience perspective. The suggested real threat lies in the erosion of the power of communities to control the boundaries of tourism (Smith 1989a; Carter and Davie, 1995). The implied model is that if communities retain control, indigenous culture will be less influenced by the tourist's culture and impacts on cultural resources will be reduced. The converse is that, if control is not in the hands of local communities, outsiders will increasingly dictate the nature and extent of tourism products and their consequences.

Research into the social and cultural effects of tourism, as well as models to assist planning and aid in decision-making, remains poorly developed. In addition, why tourism benefits some indigenous societies and not others is poorly explained, as are the processes behind the varied impacts of tourism. This paper explores the concept of cultural change. It borrows across disciplines to construct a model that is useful for the informed management of tourism impacts on local community culture.

Cultural Change and Tourism

The absence of distinctive tourism theory has been noted by many tourism scholars (Jafari, 1983; 1990; Cohen, 1984; Rogozinski, 1985; Przeclawski, 1987; Jovicic, 1988; Dann *et al.*, 1988; Comic, 1989; Witt *et al.*, 1991; Pearce, 1993; Pearce and Butler, 1993). This lack of theory particularly applies to tourist–host interactions. The literature on culture and tourism is biased towards descriptive essays of cultural expressions and impacts brought to a community by tourism (Getz, 1986; Dann *et al.*, 1988; Carter *et al.*, 2001). Where tourist–host interactions are considered within a theoretical framework, a constructivist paradigm predominates. Relative deprivation theory has been used to explain acculturation (Stouffer *et al.*, 1949; Merton, 1957; Runciman, 1966; Seaton, 1996) and 'demonstration effects' (Mathieson and Wall, 1982; Murphy, 1985; Pearce, 1989; McIntosh and Goeldner, 1990). Seaton (1996) further proposed that if an individual or host community perceives it is deprived through tourism, and the differences cannot be absorbed within the community's social or moral value system, then there is strong incentive to forego traditional practice in favour of alternative activities to improve well-being. Therefore, the traditions predictably at risk are those that are most valued by tourists. It can be inferred that unless strong cultural factors are in place to resist change, perceived deprivation will encourage host communities to adopt commercial practices that may have links to other cultural expressions.

Similarly, social exchange theory relates to the exchange of resources (material, social or psychological) between individuals or groups when interacting (Emerson, 1972), the underlying assumption being that people seek to maximise the rewards and minimise the costs experienced (Madrigal, 1993). Ap (1992) proposed a social exchange-based model for application to tourism host–guest interactions when explaining residents' perceptions of tourism. With reference to Cohen and Bradford (1990), Ap also introduced the issue of power in determining the balance in exchange outcomes. Ap further demonstrated the usefulness of the theory for predicting social exchange and likely attitudinal outcomes, but the model only indirectly deals with cultural change processes that might be associated with social exchange. The social exchange process model explains the exchange but does not define the change. However, in reapplying Ap's model to cultural change processes it assumes that:

- change in traditions are observable and hence able to be evaluated;
- owners of the cultural tradition are in a (power) position to withdraw, adapt or substitute a cultural tradition as an item of trade; and
- either the cultural traditions being traded (changed) are not linked to others, or
- the links between the traded cultural tradition and others are known, and hence a 'rational' choice, including consideration of flow-on effects, is possible.

It is unlikely that all of these assumptions will be valid in a specific case. Hence, while the adaptation of social exchange theory might suggest further avenues for research and clarification of a change in cultural expression, its immediate application is difficult.

Pearce *et al.* (1996) assert the usefulness of the social representation concept to understand a community's response to tourism. Here, social representations are concepts and explanations originating through an individual's life experience and communication with others (Moscovici, 1981). This is similar to Craik's (1952) concept of mental models and Kelly's (1955) personal construct theory. Pearce *et al.* (1996) and Dougherty *et al.* (1992) claim that social representations will vary according to the level of involvement that a group has with a topic, event or object. Direct experience then provides a possible force for change, subject to the level of individual influence (Moscovici, 1981). Hence, social representations are also behaviourally prescriptive (Moscovici, 1981), predisposing individuals to seek conformity with the social representation. Social representations also influence perception and influence how experiences are interpreted, and hence the response (Pearce *et al.*, 1996).

The process of creation and communication defines a social/cultural change mechanism, however it only implies the pathway for change. Dann (1992) addresses this in a social representations-based model by including individual action and outcomes. Although Dann's (1992) work is in education, it can be applied to tourism if social representation is replaced by 'cultural knowledge', and 'actions and outcomes' with 'expressions of culture'. In this context, an individual's cultural knowledge regulates the individual's expression of culture, and expression (i.e. regularity and importance) modifies knowledge (Figure 1). The individual's expression of culture is also regulated by group knowledge and expression, that is, cultural knowledge that requires group practice and a specific stimulus, or is held by a particular individual of the group. Equally, the expression of an individual's cultural knowledge has consequences for group

knowledge. The loss of a person with extensive knowledge of traditional medicine, or their failure to practise or pass on the tradition, would affect the group's collective cultural knowledge, and thus its expression. However, expression or practise of group knowledge reinforces individual cultural knowledge. Again, an individual's cultural knowledge and power within the group can influence group behaviour and ultimately cultural expression. If a village chief in Papua New Guinea embraces a Western religion, then it is probable that his personal influence will alter the expression of cultural elements relating to animistic beliefs through direct social control, or propagation or propaganda (Moscovici, 1992). In this context, tourism is a change agent acting at the individual level and influencing expression of cultural knowledge personally, collectively and outside the group (Figure 1).

While anthropology theory adequately explains cultural evolution at a macro scale, and accounts for the development of similar

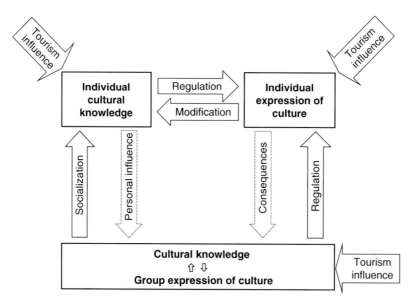

Figure 1   Cultural Expressions and the Influence of Tourism (Modified from Dann, 1992).

cultural expressions in disparate communities, it is silent at the micro level in explaining change in response to a perturbation such as tourism. Social-psychology theory and analyses applied to host–tourist interactions provide a framework for inquiry and planning because they provide an explanation of social change processes. Notwithstanding the merits of these theories to the development of individual cultural expressions and change, their applicability to tourism-induced change and management of change is limited, because tourism trades directly in cultural expressions, exerting immediate direct and indirect pressure on a culture to change. In an attempt to facilitate the integration of these perspectives into tourism planning and management, and their pragmatic needs, we propose a framework for considering cultural change precipitated by tourist–host interactions.

Culture Change, the Individual and the Community

Culture change depends on the robustness of the culture and the degree of impact (Craik, 1991). It may be reflected in the changes to the various cultural resources and expressions that are peculiar to a community (Goodenough, 1963; Steward, 1979). As proposed by Goodenough (1963), particular traditions in a community relate to:

- the number of individuals who have knowledge of each tradition;
- the standards and perceptions in each individual's version of these traditions and how they should fit into the culture of the community; and
- the knowledge and perceptions of the traditions of outside cultures.

Goodenough (1981) presented these concepts mathematically:

$$P_1 = (p_1{:}a_1, b_1, \ldots n_1)$$
$$+ (K_1, L_1, M_1, \ldots N_1)$$
$$+ (x_1) \ldots \qquad \text{(equation 1)}$$

In this equation, P_1 is an individual whose personal culture consists of:

- their distinctive version of the community culture (p_1), which is the result of their knowledge, understanding, expression etc. of cultural traditions a to n, plus
- their working knowledge of an external culture K to the extent of K_1, L_1 etc; plus
- personal views and understandings that can be attributed to no other, x_1.

A culture (C) then is the sum of the individual cultures of community members:

$$C = P_1 + P_2 + P_3 + \ldots P_n \text{ or } \Sigma(P_{1-n}) \ldots$$
$$\text{(equation 2)}$$

Goodenough's (1981) conceptualisation of a community's culture included the idea that people differ in the number of traditions in which they are competent. That is, there are some traditions and cultural expressions (a to n) that are common to all individuals, with others that are known only to subgroups of the community (e.g. gender related), and others known only to one or a few individuals (e.g. knowledge of traditional healing). Thus, these latter individuals may be key cultural resource people.

The loss or change of a tradition may be for reasons such as:

- individuals who are competent in it do not pass on their knowledge;

- individuals who are not competent in it do not want the knowledge, having found new methods (e.g. modernisation); or
- a choice is consciously made to vary a tradition within the culture (acculturation).

Such change processes may be institutional or imperialistic. However, society members choose new and different ways of thinking and acting that seem suitable for their purposes. Such changes occur at every level of cultural organisation, from the substitution of one element for another within a value system, to the substitution of one complete tradition for another.

The relationship between members of a community and their personal cultures (P_{1-n}) can bestow resistance and resilience, or what Craik (1991) calls robustness, to the community's culture (ΣP_{1-n}). Individual cultural relationships vary in strength relating to cultural knowledge and interdependence, as well as direct dependence on the culture for individual well-being. The interrelationships are similar to a food web. Figure 2 shows

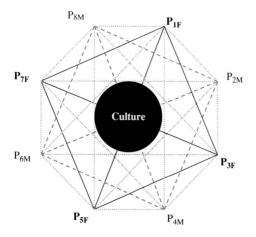

Figure 2   Inter-Relationships Between Community Members.

the notional relationships between members P_1 to P_8 of a community modelled by Goodenough (1981). The diagram is necessarily schematic: obviously, the web is multidimensional. For the purposes of this discussion, individuals on the community level are designated as F (female) and M (male). While gender is often a determinant in the functioning and roles within a culture, other demographic characteristics may be equally important. Embodied in these individuals is their cultural knowledge.

In all communities, individual members have different relationships with other members; some relationships will be close and strong (as between husband and wife) or distant and weak. Equally, some members hold information or a status vital to the functioning and integrity of the culture. Thickened lines (Figure 3) represent the strength of these relationships. For the purpose of illustration, the members of the community are presented as four couples. Couple P_{1F} and P_{2M} have a status that results in many strong relationships. For example, they could be the parents, or the chief and head woman of the community. Equally, they might be essential community members because of their cultural knowledge (e.g. traditional medicine). Broken lines indicate relationships bounded by some important trait, nominally indicated in the diagram as gender.

By way of contrast, couple P_{5F} and P_{6M} has weak relationships with others in the community. For example, they might be living away from the community. Consequently, both their reinforcement of relationships and their practice of cultural expressions may be rare events. The distance from the core of cultural traits (represented by a solid circle) to the individual represents this relationship. In the diagram, the longer the line, the greater the practice of cultural expressions. Thus, the

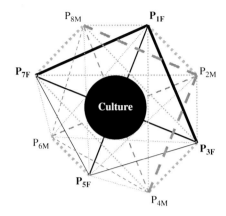

Relationships	Cultural link Strong Medium Weak
Female - male	
Female - female	
Male - male	

Figure 3 Strength of Relationships Between Community Members.

sum of the product between length and width of relationship lines indicates the relative importance of individuals P_{1F} and P_{2M} to the structure of the community. By way of contrast, individuals P_{5F} and P_{6M} exhibit a nett shorter and less robust series of links.

From a cultural impact perspective, loss of individual P_{1F} from the community or failure to contribute their special knowledge would result in a significant breaking of cultural links. This would be compounded by the loss of individual P_{2M} (Figure 4).

The combined loss of cultural knowledge, the nett reduction in links and the strength of those links means that the culture, as a whole, is weakened and less resistant and resilient to change. Further, it is likely that absence of reinforcement of cultural traits by these key individuals would act synergistically on other members of the community (because of the strength of the links), resulting in a general weakening of all links and possibly a significant loss in cultural knowledge of individuals.

By way of contrast, loss of community members P_{5F} and P_{6M} and their cultural knowledge and contribution to the community is of less nett significance (Figure 5).

While the application of Goodenough's (1981) model may explain the process of permanent cultural change within a community, the problem remains to unravel the complex web of relationships if prediction is to be achieved. In the model presented, it would be possible to measure, emically, the number and strength of relationships that exist within a small community, with sufficient cross-referencing to verify individual

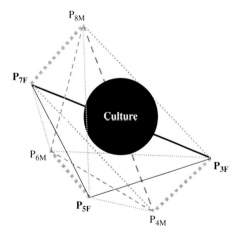

Figure 4 Loss of Cultural Rigor Through the Loss of Two Key Community Members (P_{1F} and P_{2M}).

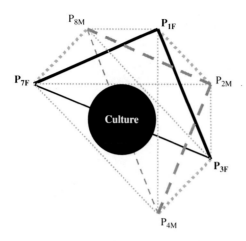

Figure 5 Minimal Loss of Cultural Rigor through the Loss of Two Non-Key Community Members (P_{5F} and P_{6M}).

determinations. In this way, key cultural resource individuals could be determined. However, the process would be intrusive on the community and necessarily slow. Therefore, change may well occur before key cultural resource individuals are identified and remedial action to manage change implemented.

In reviewing models of cultural development and change, we are left with the view that while socio-cultural frameworks provide useful explanations of the cultural change process, they lack reliable predictive power. This is essential for tourism planning and negative impact minimisation, and for the more pragmatic purpose of managing the change process. For this reason, it is proposed that understanding the change process itself and its dimensions may be more useful for tourism planning and practical management.

Change and Perturbations

If the management of change is considered in a problem-solving context, then the problem solver is seeking to:

- establish if the problem is reversible (solvable), capable of being arrested or slowed;
- determine if the problem will, if left alone, get worse;
- if the problem is going to get worse, then determine the pattern of change; and
- identify the point at which the problem becomes effectively irreversible (unsolvable).

Four change scenarios are considered. In Figure 6, the change is reversible. That is, change and impact occurs in a linear fashion and is fully reversible. For a culture in this case, integrity has not diminished and cultural resources in the form of expressions, traditional knowledge and resource people remain intact. This is never the case in the real world; however, the model proposes that in some circumstances, change is acceptable because it is reversible.

An example (though not absolutely faithful to the model) of this type of change process lies in the hunting preferences of some near traditional communities in Papua New

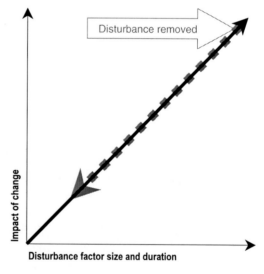

Figure 6 Simple Linear Change and Response.

Guinea. Under the influence of severe food shortage, community members use modern weapons for hunting. Once food supply is not limiting, the community reverts to traditional hunting methods with no apparent long-term change in the traditional practice. The reversion to less-efficient hunting practice appears to be related to maintaining traditional social relationships (Carter, 2000).

In Figure 7, the system is less resilient, and relaxation of the disturbance does not lead to full recovery. If applied to a cultural system, some integrity is lost and the culture cannot return to its undisturbed state, because cultural resources have been lost.

This change scenario is exemplified by most cultural interactions. As a specific example, outsiders might challenge the values of a traditional village community. While behaviours return to 'normal' once the visitors leave, the village may consciously change community behaviour to minimise future impact of such experiences. In this case, while the shift in

community structure might be relatively small, the change may be permanent (see Carter 2000).

In Figure 8, the rate of change increases exponentially beyond a certain level of disturbance, a point beyond which the change is irreversible. Often there is no clear indication when the response accelerates. In situations such as this, the relaxation pattern can vary depending on the point where relaxation is applied. From the cultural impact perspective, reversibility is impossible, significant change has occurred and cultural resources lost. The issue becomes determining how far into the change process a culture has progressed and the likelihood that removing (or managing) the perturbation will return cultural integrity to an acceptable state.

This situation is exemplified in many Papua New Guinea communities by the loss of the traditional men's ceremonial long house. Traditionally, the long house is the centre for much cultural ritual with associated objects. Its removal, through the influence of Western

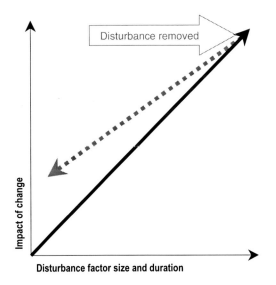

Figure 7   Linear Change with Offset Linear Response.

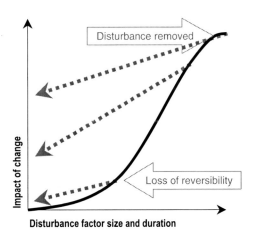

Figure 8   Accelerated Change to a Point Where the Impact Reaches an Asymptote with Offset Linear Response.

value systems, means that many cultural expressions are no longer practised. Failure to practise traditions associated with the long house means that young community members no longer have the detail of these ceremonies or the meaning behind associated objects. Failure to practise the multiple traditions and communicate their essential elements means that even if a long house is restored, the complex of cultural resources necessary to reinvigorate the tradition might no longer exist.

Figure 9 presents a management scenario where irreversible change has occurred and two options exist requiring the input of resources. As an example, in some communities in Papua New Guinea relatively few cultural resources (knowledge in particular) have been lost. Documenting cultural traditions could at least 'preserve' cultural knowledge (Figure 9, trajectory 1). Reversion towards a traditional lifestyle (Figure 9, trajectory 2) would involve a cost to the community that would probably be unacceptable, that is forgoing the benefits of economic growth.

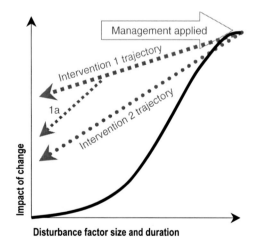

Figure 9 Accelerated Change and Management Applied with a Linear Response.

However, tourism could assist the reversibility of the change, through fostering practice of specific cultural expressions. That is, payment for continuing to maintain cultural traditions (Figure 9, trajectory 1a).

Perhaps a more explicit example of the relevance of this model to change can be found when comparing 'near traditional' communities with those whose traditional lands are centred near a major city (e.g. Port Moresby). In dollar terms, it would be easier to restore knowledge of more traditional cultural resources and expressions to the 'near traditional' community than their fellow metropolitan nationals. In this case, if maintenance of cultural integrity is desirable for all cultures, there is clearly a moral dilemma. With limited resources, is ease of reversing the impact of change a deciding factor for determining effort or should equity considerations dominate? In these cases, internal and external communities must clearly decide the cost-benefits of attempting to recapture a semblance of the past culture. Trajectory 2 (Figure 9) may achieve a higher level of return to the condition before the disturbance was applied, but may cost considerably more to do so. Apart from economic considerations, the issue is again one of what is acceptable and desirable, especially to the people of the culture involved. These are socio-political decisions, certainly relevant but not of immediate concern, save to the extent of defining the change and the likelihood of returning cultural resources to an acceptable level.

This approach to management when applied to culture may appear brutally pragmatic and unsympathetic to individuals within a culture undergoing change. Tourism–culture interactions are, however, not subtle or sensitive. Similarly, the response cannot afford to be gentle when time is of the essence. Clearly, the preferred scenarios are represented by Figures 6 and 7 or, in the case of Figure 8, to arrest the disturbance before or near the point of irreversibility and immediately apply remedial action. Alternatively, the option exists to acknowledge that change is inevitable (Bee, 1974) and to manage the dimensions of the change process. Of course, this will be more effective if applied before the change occurs or as quickly as possible. Two options exist:

- to manage the intensity of the disturbance, by altering its magnitude and duration; or
- to manage the impact, by altering the character of the elements affected; making them more resistant and resilient to the perturbation.

Managing the Tourism Perturbation

Tourism is clearly an agent of change. To manage change requires either managing the intensity of the change-causing agent or to manage effects through buffering the change.

Generally,

$$I = MD \ldots \qquad \text{(equation 3)}$$

where intensity (I) is the product of magnitude (M) and duration (D).

In the case of tourism:

$$M \, (Magnitude) = f_1[sQ + k_{sQ}] \ldots$$
$$\text{(equation 4)}$$

where s is a numerical indicator of the size of tourism activity (e.g. the number of tourists), Q is the type or 'quality' of tourism (Smith, 1989), and k is a variable inherently related to tourist activity and intensity. That is, it is an s by Q matrix (Figure 10).

	Q^1	Q^2	Q^3	...	Q^n
s^1	$k_s1_{Q^1}$	$k_s1_{Q^2}$	$k_s1_{Q^3}$	...	$k_s1_{Q^n}$
s^2	$k_s2_{Q^1}$	$k_s2_{Q^2}$	$k_s2_{Q^3}$	...	$k_s2_{Q^n}$
s^3	$k_s3_{Q^1}$	$k_s3_{Q^2}$	$k_s3_{Q^3}$	...	$k_s3_{Q^n}$
...	...	...	...	...	...
s^n	$k_{s^n}{}_{Q^1}$	$k_{s^n}{}_{Q^2}$	$k_{s^n}{}_{Q^3}$	...	$k_{s^n}{}_Q$

Figure 10 Derivation of the Variable Specifically Related to Tourism Activity. s is the 'Size' of Tourism Activity and Q is the Type or Qualities of Tourism.

Craik (1991) considers, with other factors, that the nature of impacts depends on the ratio of tourists to residents, the kind of tourism and whether tourism is the main industry. That is, s is a ratio rather than an absolute indication of size, and k includes the relative size of tourism in relation to other income generating activities within a community. By including k, it is suggested that tourism affects change (Δ) irrespective of the number of tourists (s) and its type (P), and will have a different effects (Δ) to other economic activities.

Duration (D) cannot be considered simply as the length of time since the first arrival of tourism. Rather, it involves consideration of seasonal variation and its sporadic nature. Therefore:

$$D \, (Duration) = f_2\left[\left(\sum_0^T A\right)\left(\sum_0^t a\right)\right]$$
$$\text{(equation 5)}$$

where ΣA is the combined length of time (A, 0 to time T) a community is exposed to or is associated with tourism, and Σa is the intervening exposure-free or non-association time (a, 0 to time t). Thus, the intensity of exposure (I) of a community to the change causing effects of tourism can be managed by manipulating either magnitude (*M*) or duration (*D*), or the elements of these variables:

$$I\ (Intensity) = \left(f_1\left[sQ + k_{sQ}\right]\right)$$

$$\left(f_2\left[\left(\sum_0^T\right)\left(\sum_0^t a\right)\right]\right)$$

(equation 6)

Magnitude of tourism activity can be managed through manipulating:

(a) the numerical size of tourism (*s*) (e.g. tourist numbers); and/or

(b) the type of tourism activity and development form (*Q*) (e.g. the pre-education of visitors or the nature of infrastructure provided).

The duration of tourism effects can be managed through manipulating:

(a) the contact time with a community (*A*); or

(b) the intervening contact-free time (*a*).

This is the conventional approach to managing tourism, where:

• tourist numbers are constrained by bed numbers (e.g. Port Douglas, Australia, where town planning has capped bed numbers) or, indirectly, by the number of inbound flights (e.g. Solomon Islands);

• tourist type is constrained by development limitations and minimum standards; and

• tourist zones are established effectively limiting exposure time of the host community to tourists by space (e.g. Bali, see Wall and Dibnah, 1992; Martopo and Mitchell, 1995; Picard, 1996).

While management of each of these variables has been used in tourism plans, it has rarely been used as a proactive method for limiting cultural change. In most such cases, only the type of tourism element (*Q*) can be managed in the long term. This is because managing the other variables is anathema to tourism growth. The economic viability of tourism tends to rely on regular arrival of visitors because overhead and 're-start-up' costs make managing sporadic arrivals inefficient in terms of costs, staff resourcing and community time management. Further, in the early stages of tourism development, duration variation (equation 5) is common, with operators striving to regularise tourist arrivals and diversify the range of product available. This understandable behaviour is the opposite of niche marketing that is often suggested as the basis for ecotourism, responsible tourism, and sustainable tourism, established the conditions for entry to the tourist destination life cycle of Butler (1980). Also, the adoption of a zoning strategy to manage tourism rapidly generates issues of equity of opportunity to gain the economic benefits of tourism. The type of tourism (*Q*) preferred is equally difficult to manage. The conundrum is that both investors and tourists resist regulation through product characteristics. However, altering tourist expectations of visit experiences and informing them of appropriate cultural behaviours has the potential to alter tourist type (*Q*) effectively and hence product type. This management approach is yet to be attempted in any meaningful and co-ordinated way, either by well-targeted marketing or with pre-visit education campaigns. The current dominant marketing-led approach is to attract the broadest range of tourist types possible. Typically, these strategies target multiple niches.

Therefore, long-term management of the type of tourism, and other elements of perturbation intensity, involves strategic planning decisions and/or increased awareness of visitors of their potential impact. Hence, increasing potential impact awareness of decision-makers and tourists would be a strategic action to affect magnitude. In this sense, a descriptive model of the effects of tourist interactions with host communities could be used to explain the process of change and how one action (a change) can have flow-on effects to a culture.

Managing the Effects of Tourism Activity

Apart from the effects of tourism intensity, Craik (1991) considers that tourism impact depends on the demographics of the local community and the level of involvement in the industry. In the context of the change models presented, she is implying that it is possible to manage the affected elements of tourism perturbations: the host community. That is:

$$\Delta\,(Change\ or\ impact) = f_3[I(Ei_Q)]$$

(equation 7)

where I is the intensity of perturbation, E is the demographic character of the host community, and i is the level of host community involvement in tourism product delivery (type Q), or, by substitution,

$$\Delta\,(Change\ or\ impact) = f_3\Big\{(f_1[sQ + k_sQ])$$

$$\Big(f_2\Big[\Big(\sum_0^T A\Big)\Big(\sum_0^t a\Big)\Big]\Big)\big(Ei_Q\big)\Big\}$$

(equation 8)

As already indicated, managing the intensity of tourism perturbation on host communities has limitations given the usual desire of com-

munities to maximise the economic benefits from tourism. This is usually interpreted as maximising tourist numbers. Thus, managing the intensity (I) of the tourism perturbation through tools such as regulation and zoning is difficult and likely to ultimately fail. That is, progression through Butler's (1980) tourism destination life cycle is almost inevitable if these tools of management are those only applied. However, managing impact or change itself provides some room to manoeuvre. Like the intensity (I) component of the impact equation (5), the level of involvement of host communities in tourism (i_Q) is equally difficult to manage in the long term, although licensing of operators is the usual mechanism applied in an attempt to do this. However, changing the demographic character (E) of the host community is possible, but again, rarely considered in tourism planning in a pro-active way.

Where improved human well-being is a goal for embarking on tourism, this management option is really the only, or at least, the most realistic option, given the usual expectations of host communities of tourism. Changing the demographic character of the host community does not mean altering elements such as numbers, age, marital status and religion, but rather demographic factors such as education level and awareness of tourism impacts. This involves preparing the culture (host community) for the disturbance. Principally, this is an educational activity, but incorporates planning for the acceptable level of change, with that level determined by members of the culture. That is, the demographic variable is closely aligned with empowerment, which includes elements of knowledge and decision-making power or influence. In this case, an understanding of the internal and external host cultural dynamics and tourist interactions is essential.

Models to improve understanding of tourism–cultural impacts would be useful to alert host communities to the threat tourism presents on destination cultures. If forearmed with awareness, normal (and traditional) social processes for decision-making can be invoked to respond to change effects. Decisions to manage tourism, using mechanisms to regulate intensity, can be applied to delay rapid change and maintain impact within the zone of complete reversibility. With knowledge (and time) social adjustment processes will 'naturally' occur, making the community more resistant to tourism impacts, or at least enable host community members to determine their tourism destinies.

The assumption that host communities can be appropriately informed of the consequences of tourism and thus empowered to make sagacious decisions is largely untested. Host communities usually embark on the tourism development cycle in ignorance and respond as each crisis arises. That is, often host communities embark on tourism development both ignorant and not empowered to respond to the socio-cultural challenges tourism brings.

Resistance and Resilience of Culture to Change: A Rationale for Empowerment

To this point, this discussion of tourism and cultural change has largely adopted an etic perspective, treating the host community as passive recipients of strategies to manage tourism. This is a mistake commonly made in tourism planning, which in itself may commodify host communities. Cultures and communities are dynamic (Bee, 1974) and responsive to perturbations. They adapt and can be resistant to change either because of their inherent character or because of societal determinations in response to change forces.

Ecologists imply resistance and use resilience when referring to natural communities or natural resources (Holling *et al.*, 1995), that is, a resource's inherent ability to absorb the effects of a perturbation without irreparably destroying its integrity (resistance), as well as its ability to return to its previous state after a change occurs (resilience) (Berkes and Folke, 1998). Resilience is a measure of the relative ease of revival usually expressed in terms of the biological community's inherent natural regenerative capacity (temporal) or under the influence of a manipulative restoration program (temporal and resource dependent). Fundamental to resilience is the need for the physical elements of the natural system to be in place (i.e. the substrate, the biota and the gene pool) as well as the ecological processes that enable re-establishment (e.g. soil fertility, temperature and water regimes and pathways).

These concepts are the foundation of the impact assessment and management tools used in natural systems management known as 'limits to acceptable change' (LAC) (Stanley *et al.*, 1985). The LAC concept assumes that natural systems can withstand perturbation to a definable point beyond which the system shifts from an existing state to another (Holling *et al.*, 1998). The LAC is the (often-subjective) point where a human community values one species assemblage and structure ahead of another and can distinguish the difference. Alternatively, it is the (objective) point where the potential of the ecological community to return to its previous state:

- has been removed;
- will take an exceedingly long time to recover; or
- will require an excessive level of human intervention.

The concepts of resistance, resilience and limits to acceptable change are equally relevant to cultural systems and cultural resources (Figure 11).

In Figure 11 situation **a,** the culture is able to resist the influence of the tourism perturbation. It retains its inherent integrity. In situation **b,** the tourism perturbation has resulted in changes in the culture, but it retains its essential elements and is considered acceptable or even desirable. The non-shaded area and the extended shaded area of the 'original' shape (**a**), representing the culture, indicate the changes caused by tourism. The non-shaded area represents loss of cultural traditions and interactions, while the extended area represents new or adopted traditions gained through tourism interaction. If these changes are acceptable, then the non-shaded area represents change that is within the

culture's inherent ability to retain its integrity, as perceived by the community and/or tourists. Equally, the extended shaded area represents adopted traditions that are within the community's aspirations and remain acceptable to visiting tourists. That is, the change in cultural traditions and expressions are not sufficiently dramatic to be unacceptable to either the destination community or tourists.

In situation **c,** the tourist influence has been removed. If the culture is to be resilient, there will need to exist (persist) 'all' the cultural resources that existed before the perturbation occurred. This is rarely the case after intensive and extensive cultural interaction. However, the degree of resilience depends on the desire of the community to maintain elements of its pre-change condition, the extent of loss of cultural resources, and the level of empowerment

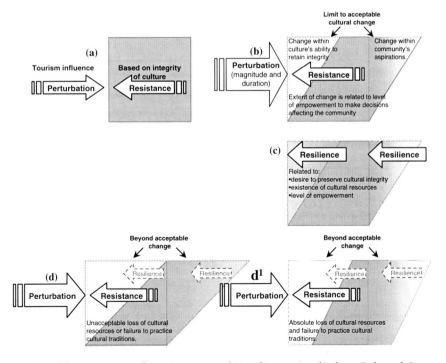

Figure 11   The Concept of Resistance and Resilience Applied to Cultural Systems.

given to effect traditional cultural re-creation or revitalisation. Empowerment includes the ability to make decisions and the persistence of resources (material, ideational and informational) for application to effect resilience (element E of equation 7). Of course, it is possible that change has been so great that many cultural resources have been lost and the culture has moved beyond its capacity to return to an acceptable state. Such situations reflect the change model given in Figures 8 and 11, situations $\mathbf{d}^1$ and $\mathbf{d}^2$, with resultant implications for management and the application of management resources.

Resistance as an indicator defines the limits of cultural resource change if the culture is to remaining functionally viable. As such, resistance defines the limits of resilience. The more people in a community with knowledge of a cultural practice, the greater is the chance of its continuance (Goodenough, 1981). Cultural resources and expressions, and hence cultural integrity, are increasingly 'buffered' against loss as more people have knowledge of them and the internal relationships of the culture and expression of cultural traditions (C). However, resistance is also related to the level of power (E) a community has over its future. (E) measures the community's ability to respond to the magnitude of change and control the rate of change that some external or internal change force (I) might effect. That is,

$$R \ (Resistance \ to \ perturbation) = f_4[ICE]$$
(equation 9)

Resilience of a culture is dependent on the amount of change that has occurred, community desire to return to the pre-existing state and the level of empowerment to effect restorative change. That is,

$$r \ (Resilience \ to \ perturbation) = f_5[|\Delta C|E]$$
(equation 10)

Like natural systems, the resilience of a cultural requires the presence of all cultural resources, including traditions and expressions of the culture. This is a necessary precondition to the restorative process. However, unlike natural systems, cultures have discretion. A choice exists, be it overt or covert, on what is acceptable or desirable in terms of the changes to culture. These decisions result in substitution, discarding or maintaining cultural elements.

It follows that the ultimate change in a culture or impact from a perturbation (Δ) depends on the combination of the culture's inherent resistance and resilience to the perturbation. That is,

$$\Delta(Change \ or \ impact) = f_6[R, r]$$
(equation 11)

or

$$\Delta(Change \ or \ impact) = f_6\{(f_4[ICE]), (f_5[|\Delta C|E])\}$$
(equation 12)

Keesing and Strathern (1998) argue that ethnic communities know that there are limits to the ways in which a cultural resource can change yet remain functionally viable, indicating a measure of its resistance. Cultural traditions also differ in their resilience. Once diminished, a resilient tradition is capable of revival, while non-resilient cultural resources and traditions are effectively non-renewable. Continuity is generally enhanced in situations where the community has control of the pressures on their culture

(Nash, 1989). Therefore, while the intensity of tourism has the potential to effect change in a culture, ultimately it is the internalities of the culture and the level of empowerment of the community to resist and restore change that determine actual change and hence impact.

Conclusion

Management of the type of tourism (Q), and other elements of perturbation intensity (equation 6), involves strategic planning decisions and/or increased awareness of visitors of their potential impact. Hence, increasing the awareness of the potential impacts of decision-makers and tourists would be a strategic action to manage the intensity of tourism disturbance through manipulating tourism type (Q).

Cultural change is dynamic and continuous. Rituals and art forms associated with a particular region change as the people within the region adapt. This adaptation follows individuals' choice of direction, learning new skills and interacting with outside cultures. The forms that cultural expressions take would be free, in the past, to fluctuate while being internally regulated. Ultimately new cultural form depends on how many individuals use particular cultural expressions and the acceptance by the community of the changed forms. However, tourism trades in culture and exerts direct pressure on cultural expressions (cultural resources) to change, as well as exerting pressure on individuals (also cultural resources) to change. The former is a somewhat peculiar characteristic of tourism while the latter is simply part of the 'normal' cultural change process, embraced by the term acculturation, but with tourism being, potentially, a particularly intense acculturation force.

Where $f_6[R, r] < f_3[I(Ei_Q)]$ (equation 13), the intensity of tourism may be particularly high and thus pervasive, creating cultural instability and change. Where $f_6[R, r] \Longleftrightarrow f_3[I(Ei_Q)]$ (equation 14) there is a steady state, though it may be in dynamic equilibrium. The implication for tourism management, then, is to seek to activate internal socio-cultural dynamics to provide resistance and resilience. At the same time, care must be taken to protect (retain), at least in the short term, the full suite of cultural resources so that host communities can choose which to retain, substitute or discard.

The concern of ethical tourism management is not simply about culture being altered. Of importance is that cultural expression should remain free to alter as the owners of the culture see fit. This rationale applies equally to arts and crafts and to ceremonies and rituals. That is, local communities must retain control over their cultural resources if these are to be preserved and retain their value and meaning. In terms of equation 7, $\Delta(Change\ or\ impact) = f_3[I(Ei_Q)]$, the management focus should be on the (Ei_Q) term of the change rather than on the intensity (I), as is usually the case. In terms of equation 14, $f_6[R, r] \Longleftrightarrow f_3[I(Ei_Q)]$, management needs to focus on activating resistance and resilience within communities so the conscious, acceptable and timely internal adjustments can be made or cultural institutions used to buffer the perturbation. Inherent in these management approaches is the primacy of the cultural characteristics of the community (E), with the level of real empowerment to control change or make adjustments being the significant dimension.

The benefits of tourism are all too obvious to developing communities and equally influential on all communities embarking on tourism development. Interventions that include community education are needed to ensure the community knows how to maximise these benefits and to ensure equitable distribution of benefits (and costs). However, what is less obvious and readily understood are the impacts, especially the potential changes to cultural mores and expressions. Cultural dynamics are complex and largely esoteric, yet cultural expressions, the tradable items of a culture, are tangible. Understanding how tourism trades in these commodities and affects them and related expressions, empowers a community to make more considered and knowledgeable decisions regarding their tourism–culture future. A community could decide to regulate the intensity of tourism perturbation or respond with modified social structures to buffer tourism effects.

The inherent principles of this discussion are reflected in the Bali, Indonesia, experience, often presented as successful cultural tourism (Bell, 1992; Picard, 1993). While tourism planners attempted to minimise cultural impact through managing the intensity of the tourism perturbation by separating tourism from the community (Wall and Dibnah, 1992; Picard and Lanfant, 1995), it was ultimately the resistance shown, and power exercised, by religious and social institutions that established the acceptable balance in the tourism–culture dynamic. Initial planning did not have programs of community education that not only reinvigorated cultural expressions for tourist 'sale' (which did exist) but also enriched Balinese culture to act as a buffer to the change process. Perhaps fortuitously, Balinese religious social and general cultural institutions were able to respond to the incremental and episodic nature of tourism growth before significant cultural changes had occurred. Balinese culture itself responded to regulate its own changes as well as the nature of tourism.

Overall, a model was proposed that elucidates the elements that contribute to a change in cultural expressions. We conclude that the only enduring way to address such change is through empowering the community to shape such change while, in the short term, minimising the loss of cultural resources so that time is available for communities to express their power over change forces of tourism. This will involve greater clarification of the change process, the links between cultural expressions targeted by tourism and their collective importance to maintaining cultural integrity.

References

Ap, J. (1992) Residents' perceptions on tourism impacts. *Annals of Tourism Research* 19, 665–90.

Ascher, F. (1985) *Tourism transnational corporations and cultural identities*. Paris, UNESCO.

Barnett, H.G. (1953) *Innovation: The Basics of Cultural Change*. New York, McGraw-Hill Book Company Inc.

Bee, R. (1974) *Patterns and Processes*. New York The Free press.

Belisle, F.J. and Hoy, D. (1980) The perceived impact of tourism by residents: a case study in Santa Marta. *Annals of Tourism Research* 7, 83–101.

Bell, C.A. (1992) Bali: how to maintain a fragile resort. *Cornell Hotel and Restaurant Administration Quarterly* 33, 28–31.

Berkes, F. and Folke, C. (1998) Linking social and ecological systems for resilience and sustainability. In F. Berkes, C. Folke and J. Colding, J. (eds) *Linking Social and Ecological Systems* (pp.1–25). Cambridge, Cambridge University Press.

Bleasdale, S. and Tapsell, S. (1996) Saharan Tourism: Arabian Nights or Tourist 'Daze'? The Social-Cultural and Environmental Impacts of Tourism in Southern Tunisia. In M. Robinson, N. Evans and P. Callaghan (eds) *Tourism and Culture: Towards the 21st Century, Conference Proceedings*, Vol. Tourism and Cultural Change (pp.25–48). Sunderland, The Centre for Travel & Tourism in association with Business Education Publishers Ltd.

Boorstin, D. (1964) *The Image: A Guide to Pseudo Events in America*. New York, Harper.

Butler, R.W. (1980) The Concept of a Tourist Area Cycle of Evolution: Implications for Management of Resources. *Canadian Geographer* 24, 5–16.

Carter, R.W. (2000) *Cultural Change and Tourism: Towards a Prognostic Model*. PhD thesis, Brisbane, The University of Queensland.

Carter, R.W., Baxter, G.S. and Hockings, M. (2001) Resource Management in Tourism Research: New Direction. *Journal of Sustainable Tourism* 9(4):265–80.

Carter, R.W. and Davie, J.D. (1995) (Eco)Tourism in the Asia Pacific Region. In H. Richins, J. Richardson and A. Crabtree (eds) *Taking the Next Steps: Ecotourism Association of Australia 1995 Conference Proceedings* (pp. 67–72). Alice Springs, Commonwealth Department of Tourism.

Chagnon, N.A. and Hames, R.B. (1979) Protein Deficiency and Tribal Warfare in Amizonia: New Data. *Science* 203, 910–3.

Cohen, A.R. and Bradford, D.L. (1990) *Influence Without Authority*. New York, John Wiley.

Cohen, E. (1979) Rethinking the Sociology of Tourism, *Annals of Tourism Research* 6, 18–35.

Cohen, E. (1984) The Sociology of Tourism: Approaches, Issues and Findings. *Annual Review of Sociology* 10, 373–92.

Comic, D.K. (1989) Tourism as a subject of philosophical reflection. *Revue de Tourisme* 44, 6–13.

Craik, J. (1991) Social Impacts and cultural commodification. In J. Craik (ed) *Resorting to Tourism: Cultural Policies for Tourist Development in Australia* (pp. 79–106). North Sydney, Allen & Unwin Pty Ltd.

Craik, K.J.W. (1952) *The Nature of Explanation*. Cambridge, Cambridge University Press.

Crick, M. (1988) Sun, Sex, Sights and Servility: Representations of International Tourism in the Social Sciences. Melbourne, University of Melbourne.

Dagnal-Myron, C. (1990) Where are your moccasins? A guide for tourists. *Cultural Survival Quarterly* 14, 38–41.

Dann, G., Nash, D. and Pearce, P. (1988) Methodology in Tourism Research. *Annals of Tourism Research* 15, 1–28.

Dann, H. (1992) Subjective Theories and Their Social Foundation in Education. In M. von Cranach, W. Doise and G. Mugny (eds) *Social Representations and the Social Basis of Knowledge* (pp. 161–8). Lewiston, Hogrefe and Huber.

de Kadt, E. (1979) *Tourism- Passport to Development: Perspective on the Social and Cultural Effects of Tourism in Developing Countries*. New York, Oxford University Press.

Dogan, H.Z. (1989) Forms of adjustment. Sociocultural impacts of tourism. *Annals of Tourism Research* 16, 216–36.

Dougherty, K.C., Eisenhart, M. and Webley, P. (1992) The Role of Social Representations and National Identities in the Development of Territorial Knowledge: A Study of Political Socialization in Argentina and England. *American Educational Research Journal* 29, 809–35.

Doxey, G. (1975) A causation theory of visitor-resident irritants: methodology and research inferences. In *Proceedings of the Travel Research Association Sixth Conference* (pp. 195–8) San Diego, Travel Research Association.

Duveen, G. and Lloyd, B. (1993) An Ethnographic Approach to Social Representations. In, G.M. Breakwell and D.V. Canter (eds) *Empirical Approaches to Social Representations* (pp. 90–109). Oxford, Clarendon Press.

Emerson, R. (1972) Exchange Theory. Part 1: A Psychological Basis for Social Exchange. In J. Berger, M. Zelditch and B. Anderson (eds) *Sociological Theories in Progress* (pp. 38–87). New York, Houghton-Mifflin.

Esman, M.R. (1984) Tourism as ethnic preservation: the Cajuns of Louisiana, *Annals of Tourism Research* 11, 451–67.

Feifer, M. (1985) *Going Places*. London, Macmillan.

Geertz, C. (1973) *The Interpretation of Cultures*. New York, Basic Books.

Getz, D. (1983) Tourism, community organisation and the social multiplier. In *Leisure Tourism and Social Change, Congress Proceedings of the International Geographical Union Commission of the Geography of Tourism and Leisure*, Vol. 2 (pp. 4.1.1–15). Edinburgh, International Geographical Union.

Getz, D. (1986) Models in tourism planning. Towards integration of theory and practice. *Tourism Management* 7, 21–32.

Goodenough, W.H. (1963) *Cooperation in Change*. New York, Russell Sage Foundation.

Goodenough, W.H. (1981) *Culture, Language and Society*.Menlo Park, California, Benjamin Cummings Publishing Company Inc.

Graburn, N. (1984) The Evolution of Tourist Arts. *Annals of Tourism Research* 11, 393–419.

Grahn, P. (1991) Using tourism to protect existing culture: A project in Swedish Lapland. *Leisure Studies* 10, 33–47.

Greenwood, D.J. (1989) Culture by the pound: an anthropological perspective on tourism as cultural commoditization. In V.L. Smith (ed) *Hosts and guests. The anthropology of tourism* (pp. 171–85). Philadelphia, University of Pennsylvania Press.

Harner, M. (1977) The Ecological Basis for Aztec Sacrifice. *Ethnology* 4, 117–35.

Harris, M. (1968) *The Rise of Cultural Theory.* New York, Thomas Y. Crowell Company.

Harris, M. (1975) *Culture, People, Nature: An Introduction to General Anthropology.* New York, Harper & Row.

Harris, M. (1979) *Cultural Materialism: The Struggle for a Science of Culture.* New York, Harper & Row.

Hitchcock, M. and King, V.T. (2003) Discourses with the past: tourism and heritage in South–East Asia. *Indonesia and the Malay World*, 31: 3–15.

Holling, C.S., Berkes, F. and Folke, C. (1998) Science, sustainability and resource management. In F. Berkes, C. Folke and J. Colding (eds) *Linking Social and Ecological Systems* (pp. 342–62). Cambridge, Cambridge University Press.

Holling, C.S., Schindler, D.W., Walker, B.W. and Roughgarden, J. (1995) Biodiversity in the functioning of ecosystems: An ecological synthesis. In C. Perrings, K.G. Maler, C. Folke, C.S. Holling and B.O. Jansson (eds) *Biodiversity Loss: Economic and Ecological Issues* (pp. 44–83). Cambridge, Cambridge University Press.

Jafari, J. (1983) Understanding the Structure of Tourism. In E.C. Nebel (ed) *Tourism and Culture: A Comparative Perespective* (pp. 65–84). New Orleans, University of New Orleans.

Jafari, J. (1987) Tourism models: the sociocultural aspects. *Tourism Management* 8, 151–9.

Jafari, J. (1990) Research and Scholarship: The Basis of Tourism Education. *Journal of Tourism Studies* 1, 33–41.

Jafari, J. (1992) Cultural Tourism in Regional Development. *Annals of Tourism Research* 19, 576–7.

Jordan, J.W. (1980) The summer people and the natives: some effects of tourism in a Vermont vacation village. *Annals of Tourism Research* 7, 34–55.

Jovicic, Z. (1988) A plea for tourismological theory and methodology. *Revue de Tourisme* 43, 2–5.

Kariel, H. and Kariel, P. (1982) Socio-cultural impacts of tourism: an example from the Austrian alps. *Geografiska Annaler* 64, 1–16.

Keesing, R. (1976) *Cultural Anthropology.* New York, Holt Rhinehart and Winston.

Keesing, R.M. and Strathern, A.J. (1998) *Cultural Anthropology: A Contemporary Perspective.* Fort Worth, Harcourt Brace & Company.

Kelly, G.A. (1955) *The Psychology of Personal Constructs (Volumes I and II).* New York, Norton.

Kirtsoglu, E. and Theodossopoulos, D. (2004) They are taking our culture away: tourism and culture commodification in the Garifuna community of Roatan. *Critique of Anthropology*, 24(2): 135–157.

Klieger, P.C. (1990) Close Encounters "Intimate" Tourism in Tibet. *Cultural Survival Quarterly* 14, 38–41.

Krippendorf, J. (1987) *The holiday makers: understanding the impact of leisure and travel.* London, William Heinemann.

Lett, J. (1987) *The human enterprise: A critical introduction to anthropological theory.* Boulder, Colorado, Westview Press.

Levi-Strauss, C. (1963) *Structural Anthropology.* New York, Basic Books.

Lindenbaum, S. (1972) Sorcerers, Ghosts, and Polluting Women: An Analysis of Religious Belief and Population Control. *Ethnology* 11, 241–53.

MacCannell, D. (1976) *The Tourist, A New Theory of the Leisure Class.* New York, Schocken Books.

Madrigal, R. (1993) A tale of tourism in two cities. *Annals of Tourism Research* 20, 336–53.

Martopo, S. and Mitchell, B. (eds.) (1995) *Bali: balancing environment, economy and culture*, Waterloo, Canada, University of Waterloo.

Mason, G. (1996) Manufactured Myths: Packaging the Exotic for Visitor Consumption. In M. Robinson, N. Evans and P. Callaghan (eds) *Tourism and Culture: Towards the 21st Century, Conference Proceedings*, Vol. Tourism and Culture: Image, Identity and Marketing (pp. 121–35). Sunderland, The Centre for Travel & Tourism in association with Business Education Publishers Ltd.

Mathieson, A. and Wall, G. (1982) *Tourism: Economic and Social Impacts.* London, Longman Press.

Mayhew, L.H. (1968) Society. In *International Encyclopedia of the Social Sciences*, Vol. 14, (pp. 577–86) New York, Macmillan.

McArthur, M. (1974) Pigs for the Ancestors: A Review Article. *Oceania* 45, 87–123.

McArthur, M. (1977) Nutritional Research in Melanesia: A Second Look at the Tsembaga. In T.P. Bayliss-Smith and R.G. Feachem (eds) *Subsistence and Survival: Rural Ecology in the Pacific* (pp. 91–128). New York, Academic Press.

McArthy, J. (1994) *Are Sweet Dreams Made of This? Tourism in Bali and Eastern Indonesia*, Northcote, Victoria.

McIntosh, R.W. and Goeldner, C.R. (1990) *Tourism: Principles, Practices, Philosophies.* New York, John Wiley & Sons Inc.

McKean, P. (1982) Tourists and Balinese. *Cultural Survival Quarterly* 6, 32–3.

Mead, M. (1928) *Coming of Age in Samoa*. New York, McMillan Morrow.

Merton, R.K. (1957) *Social theory and social structure*. Glencoe, Illinois, Free Press.

Moscovici, S. (1981) On Social Representations. In J.P. Forgas (ed) *Social Cognition: Perspectives on Everyday Understanding* (181–209) London, Academic Press.

Moscovici, S. (1992) The Psychology of Scientific Myths. In M. von Cranach, W. Doise and G. Mugny (eds) *Social Representations and the Social Basis of Knowledge* (pp. 3–9) Lewiston, Hogrefe and Huber.

Murphy, P.E. (1985) *Tourism: A community approach*. New York, Methuen.

Nash, D. (1989) Tourism as a Form of Imperialism. In V.L. Smith (ed) *Hosts and Guests: The Anthropology of Tourism* (pp. 36–52). Philadelphia, University of Pennsylvania Press.

Nunez, T. and Lett, J. (1989) Touristic Studies in Anthropological Perspective (epilogue by James Lett). In V.L. Smith (ed) *Hosts and Guests: The Anthropology of Tourism* (pp. 265–74). Philadelphia, University of Pennsylvania Press.

Nunez, T.A. (1963) Tourism, tradition and acculturation: Weekendismo in a Mexican village. *Ethnology* 2, 347–52.

Nunez, T.A. (1977) Touristic Studies in Anthropological Perspective. In V.L. Smith (ed) *Hosts and Guests: The Anthropology of Tourism* (pp. 207–16). Philadelphia, University of Pennsylvania Press.

Pearce, D.G. (1989) *Tourism Development*. Harlow, England, Longman Scientific and Technical.

Pearce, D.G. and Butler, R.W. (eds.) (1993) *Tourism Research: Critiques and Challenges*, London, Routledge.

Pearce, P.L. (1993) Defining Tourism Study as a Specialism: A Justification and Implications. *TEOROS International* 1, 25–32.

Pearce, P.L., Moscardo, G. and Ross, G.F. (1996) *Tourism Community Relationships*, Oxford, Pergamon.

Picard, M. (1993) Cultural tourism in Bali. In M. Hitchcock, V.T. King and M.J.G. Parnwell (eds) *Tourism in South-East Asia*. New York, Routledge.

Picard, M. (1996) *Bali: Cultural Tourism and Touristic Culture*. Singapore, Archipelago Press.

Picard, M. and Lanfant, M.F. (1995) Cultural heritage and tourist capital: cultural tourism in Bali. In M.F. Lanfant, J.B. Allcock and E.M. Bruner (eds) *International tourism: identity and change* (pp. 45–66). Thousand Oaks, Sage Publications.

Przeclawski, K. (1987) Tourism and its role in contemporary society. *Problemy Turystyki* 10, 96–102.

Rabibhadana, A. (1992) Tourism and culture: Bang-Fai Festival in Esan. In *The 1992 year-end conference: Thailand's economic Structure: towards balanced development? December 12–13, 1992, Chon Buri, Thailand* (pp. 32) Bangkok, Thailand, Thailand Development Research Institute (TDRI).

Rappaport, R.A. (1967) Ritual Regulation of Environmental RelationsAmong a New Guinea People. *Ethnology* 6, 17–30.

Rappaport, R.A. (1968) *Pigs for the Ancestors: Ritual in the Ecology of a New Guinea People*, New Haven, Conn, Yale University Press.

Rappaport, R.A. (1971) Nature, Culture and Ecological Anthropology. In H. Shapiro (ed) *Man, Culture and Society* (pp. 237–67). London, Oxford University Press.

Rogozinski, K. (1985) Tourism as a subject of research and integration of sciences. *Problemy Turystyki* 4, 7–19.

Runciman, W.G. (1966) *Relative deprivation and social justice*. London, Routledge and Kegan Paul.

Salisbury, R.F. (1975) Non-Equilibrium Models in New Guinea Ecology: Possibilities of Cultural Extrapolation. *Anthropologica* 17, 127–47.

Seaton, G. (1996) Tourism and Relative Deprivation: The Counter- Revolutionary Pressures of Tourism in Cuba. In M. Robinson, N. Evans and P. Callaghan (eds) *Tourism and Culture: Towards the 21st Century, Conference Proceedings*, Vol. Tourism and Culture: Image, Identity and Marketing (pp. 197–216). Sunderland, The Centre for Travel & Tourism in association with Business Education Publishers Ltd.

Sharp, L. (1990) Steel Axes for Stone-Age Australians. In J.P. Spradley and D.W. McCurdy (eds) *Conformity & Conflict: Readings in Cultural Anthropology* (pp. 410–24). Glenview, Illinois, Scott, Foresman, Little, Brown Higher Education.

Silver, I. (1992) Truth and Travel. *Cultural Survival Quarterly* Spring 1992, 54–9.

Smith, V.L. (ed) (1977) *Hosts and Guests, The Anthropology of Tourism*. Philadelphia, University of Pennsylvania Press.

Smith, V.L. (1989a) Eskimo tourism: micro-models and marginal men. In V.L. Smith (ed) *Hosts and guests. The anthropology of tourism* (pp. 55–82). Philadelphia, University of Pennsylvania Press.

Smith, V.L. (ed) (1989b) *Hosts and guests. The anthropology of tourism*. Philadelphia University of Pennsylvania Press.

Stankey, G.H., Cole, D.N., Lucas, R.C., Petersen, M.E. and Frissell, S.S. (1985) *The Limits of Acceptable Change (LAC) system for wilderness planning*. Ogden, Utah, USDA Forest Service, Intermountain Research Station.

Steward, J.H. (1979) *Theory of Culture Change: the methodology of multilinear evolution*. Urbana, University of Illinois Press.

Stocking, G.W. (1966) Franz Boas and the Culture Concept in Historical Perspective. *American Anthropologist* 68, 867–82.

Stouffer, S.A., Suchman, E.A., DeVinney, L.C., Star, S.A. and Williams, R.M. (1949) *The American Soldier: Adjustment during army life*. New York, John Wiley.

Swarbrooke, J. (1996) Culture, Tourism, and Sustainability of Rural Areas in Europe. InM. Robinson, N. Evans and P. Callaghan (eds) *Tourism and Culture: Towards the 21st Century, Conference Proceedings*, Vol. Managing Cultural Resources for the Tourist (pp. 447–70). Sunderland, The Centre for Travel & Tourism in association with Business Education Publishers Ltd.

Urry, J. (1990) *The Tourist Gaze: Leisure and travel in Contemporary Societies*. London, Sage Publications.

van den Berghe, P.L. and Keyes, C. (1984) Introduction: Tourism and Re-created Ethnicity. *Annals of Tourism Research* 11, 343–52.

Volkman, T.A. (1990) Visions and revisions: Toraja culture and the tourist gaze. *American Ethnologist* 17, 91–110.

Wall, G. and Dibnah, S. (1992) The changing status of tourism in Bali, Indonesia. *Progress in Tourism, Recreation and Hospitality Management* 4, 120–30.

Watson, G.L. and Kopachevsky, J.P. (1994) Interpretations of tourism as commodity. *Annals of Tourism Research* 21, 643–60.

White, P. (1974) The social impact of tourism on host communities: a study of language change in Switzerland.Oxford, School of Geography, Oxford University, UK.

Williams, R. (1981) The Analysis of Culture. In T. Bennett, G. Martin, C. Mercer and J. Woollacott (eds) *Culture, Ideology and Social Process* (pp. 43–52). London, Batsford Academic and Educational and The Open University Press.

Witt, S., Brooke, M. and Buckley, P. (1991) *The Management of International Tourism*. London, Unwin Hyman.

Rethinking Maori Tourism

Alison J. McIntosh, Frania Kanara Zygadlo and Hirini Matunga

Introduction

While the Maori people of New Zealand have had a long history of involvement in the tourism industry, recent public policy and economic development initiatives in New Zealand have brought issues of Maori tourism development to the fore. For example, the He matai tapoi Maori (Closing the Gaps in Tourism) initiative (Stafford Group *et al.*, 2000, 2001) and the recent release of the New Zealand Tourism Strategy 2010 have sought to increase the involvement of Maori, and benefits to Maori from tourism. In addition, there has been an increase in the number of published studies of Maori tourism, including the history and impacts of Maori involvement in tourism (Hall *et al.*, 1993; Hall, 1996; Ryan, 1997; Ryan & Crotts, 1997; Ryan, 1999), strategies for achieving sustainable Maori development (Hinch *et al.*, 1999; McIntosh *et al.*, 2002), issues of authenticity (Tahana & Oppermann, 1998; Asplet & Cooper, 2000; Taylor, 2001), Maori business development (Page *et al.*, 1999; Barnett, 2001) and visitors' perspectives of Maori tourism (McIntosh, 2004). Although the terms "Maori tourism", "Maori tourism business" and "Maori tourism product" are widely applied and often used interchangeably in the literature, as well as within the tourism industry in New Zealand, there appears to be a lack of an agreed or recognised working definition of Maori tourism. As Poharama *et al.* (1998, p. 43) have noted, "The tourism industry does not appear to have a standard definition or frame of reference for what actually constitutes or qualifies as a Maori cultural tourist attraction". The search for a conceptual clarification of Maori tourism is the aim of the present paper.

The lack of an appropriate recognised definition has resulted in a lack of information, in particular, on the level of Maori participation in the New Zealand tourism industry. As such, there is a paucity of research data on Maori tourism and Maori tourism businesses to guide Maori tourism development (Stafford Group *et al.*, 2000). For example, Statistics New Zealand has not specifically collected information on Maori businesses other than Census and Household Labour Force survey data on Maori self-employment (Te Puni Kokiri, 2000). This is partly due to the lack of a suitable "Maori identifier" on the enterprise and industry surveys carried out by Statistics New Zealand. There is thus a lack of existing data that specifically deal with Maori tourism businesses (their existence, ownership levels, levels of Maori employment or client base). Without this information, it is difficult to match market opportunities with local Maori expertise and skills or investment in plant and infrastructure, and thus, identify or plan for increased participation by Maori in the tourism sector (Stafford Group *et al.*, 2000).

The lack of an agreed definition of Maori tourism is perhaps a result of the conceptual difficulty in defining a Maori tourism business and product. The concept encompasses different elements, including, "Maori culture and identity", "tourism", "business" and "product". This renders statistical measurement for economic development purposes difficult. The wide range of different criteria used to define Maori tourism also contributes to the lack of an agreed definition. Often, these different criteria reflect the different policy issues or agendas of various organisations, groups or individuals. Thus, different perspectives elicit different definitions, depending on whom you ask. For example, Chan *et al.* (2002, p. 3) have described how, "A tourist would regard all tourist experiences associated with the Maori culture to be Maori tourism. People involved in Maori development would consider it encompassing all Maori involved in the tourism industry through business ownership and employment. Tourism marketing people or operators would base it on the nature of the products they provide to tourists". Diversity in the criteria used to define Maori tourism as published in the tourism literature is also evident.

Defining Maori Tourism – A Synthesis of Literature

Three main themes emerge from a review of published definitions of Maori and indigenous tourism. First is a focus on *control* of the business. Second is a focus on the nature of the tourism *product*. Thirdly, more recent studies emphasise a focus on unique cultural *values*. It can be argued that the first two themes provide quantitative dimensions of Maori tourism. This potentially reflects a general understanding of Maori tourism as Maori *involvement* in the tourism sector. However, the latter theme suggests a potential move towards capturing the more qualitative cultural dimensions of Maori tourism that potentially enable Maori to define Maori tourism in terms of their own values-based criteria. However, the latter values-based approach has not been a feature of the existing published studies of Maori tourism.

To date, Butler and Hinch (1996) have provided perhaps the most comprehensive framework for defining indigenous tourism. They describe indigenous tourism as, "Tourism activity in which indigenous people are directly involved either through control and/or by having their culture serve as the essence of the attraction" (p. 9). As such, issues of control and culture become important and these can be plotted on axes for definitional purposes (see Butler & Hinch, 1996, p. 9). The issue of control in tourism development is particularly significant, as whoever has control can usually determine such critical factors as the scale, speed and nature of the development. Control can reflect differing degrees of indigenous involvement or influence on the development – from total control (ownership and management), to no control. It can reflect different roles, including indigenous involvement as employees, advisory board members or formal partners in the development process. As such, issues of indigenous ownership and control have been advocated as prerequisites in the achievement of sustainable ethnic or indigenous tourism (see Sofield, 1993).

In Butler and Hinch's (1996) definition, culture is also important in terms of assessing the nature of the cultural product. That is, the extent to which the tourist attraction or product is based on an indigenous theme. However, where the indigenous theme is absent in the tourist attraction or product, or where it is not controlled by indigenous people, this is classified as non-indigenous tourism. It is not clear, however, whether employment of indigenous people, for example, is considered a low degree of control or cultural theme. If this is the case, then Butler and Hinch's definition would potentially exclude indigenous people employed in mainstream tourism, for example, indigenous staff employed in a non-indigenous owned tourism business such as indigenous tour guides working for a non-indigenous organised tour company. As such, there remains a lack of clarity in the criteria used to define the involvement of indigenous people in tourism.

There is also a lack of clarity among the published definitions of Maori tourism. Building on Butler and Hinch (1996), many definitions of Maori tourism advocate that the level of Maori ownership and control of the business (see Keelan, 1996; Ingram, 1997; Barnett, 2001; Stafford Group *et al.*, 2001), or, the nature of the product (see A.M.T.F., 1996; Ingram, 1997; Barnett, 2001) are critical to Maori tourism. In this way, Maori tourism must at least directly *involve* Maori people, either in the control of the business or in the delivery of the product. For example, Ingram (1997, p. 2) has defined Maori tourism as, "Tourism products that utilize cultural, historical, heritage or natural resources that are uniquely Maori with substantial Maori ownership and control of the business".

However, there appears no consistency from existing published definitions as to what *level* of control or involvement in a business constitutes Maori tourism, nor what *extent* of cultural content in the tourism product is required. For example, the Aotearoa Maori

Tourism Federation has defined a Maori tourism product as, "An opportunity provided within the composite tourist product for the tourist to have contact with Maori culture" (A.M.T.F., 1996). In this way, tourists' contact with culture or the Maori tourism product is inclusive of Maori people or representations of Maori culture as the product. For example, contact with Maori culture could be either a specific cultural product that is provided for tourists, although not necessarily authentic, or it could be a conversation with a Maori owner of a camping ground about the history of the area (Barnett, 1997). In contrast, the definition discussed by Stafford Group *et al.* (2001, p. 48) is more limiting, defining a Maori tourism business as, "Where the tourism product offered focuses on Maori history", or, "Where there is a focus on Maori product and lifestyle".

There is a further lack of clarity with regard to the extent of ownership of a business. For instance, some definitions advocate that substantial (more than 50%) ownership of a business by Maori is required (for example, Ingram, 1997; Barnett, 2001), whereas other definitions adopt a self-identified approach whereby a business is identified as Maori if, "the owners and operators believe it to be so" (Stafford Group *et al.*, 2001, p. 48). This latter approach raises an interesting point. That is, that no definition published to date has been based on collective Maori self-determined criteria, or self-identification. This would result in criteria unique to Maori.

In particular, recent published studies of Maori tourism have proposed Maori values as important defining criteria. Whilst not aiming to define Maori tourism, these studies have sought to explore the sustainable management of Maori businesses. In particular, these studies have argued that a sustainable Maori tourism business must internally incorporate indigenous perspectives and values, and hence, sustain the integrity of Maori culture by providing benefits back to Maori communities and their culture (see J.H.M.R.C., 1998; Poharama et al., 1998; Hinch et al., 1999; Tahana et al., 2000; Zygadlo et al., 2001). This conclusion is reinforced in studies of indigenous tourism development more generally, whereby no single model for development emerges. Instead, strategies for sustainable development must be culture-specific because, "While indigenous people throughout the world share many of the same challenges, and although certain traditions and values may be similar, they do not share the same culture" (Butler and Hinch, 1996, p. 13). This paper therefore advocates that a culturally relevant definition of Maori tourism is essential for sustainable self-determined Maori tourism development. To this end, the paper seeks to identify and describe the common values that characterise or define Maori tourism, as identified by Maori.

This paper, in effect, argues that a distinction needs to be made between two forms of Maori tourism, namely general Maori participation or involvement in tourism and values-based Maori tourism. The first has sought to measure Maori participation in the tourism industry, whereas the second seeks to describe *how* Maori are involved in tourism. If a conceptual clarification of the latter form of Maori tourism is to be sought, there is a need to rethink existing definitions of Maori tourism in a manner that is culturally acceptable to, and defined by, Maori. This is particularly important for not only providing a consistent measurement of Maori economic development and a values-based definition that is culturally acceptable, but also for achieving sustainable self-determined development; in effect, "*Maori-centred* tourism". Maori-centred tourism is crucial if tourism

with Maori values and ideals is to be developed and supported. Thus, defining Maori tourism from a values-based perspective has important policy implications for Maori tourism in New Zealand, especially as the current public policy focus on business and economic development is *incompatible* with holistic or integrated approaches of sustainable development and with Maori self-determined development. In particular, "Maori approaches to development do not recognise clear sectoral demarcations between social, cultural and economic areas" (Loomis, 1999, p. 11). From this perspective, there are also potential issues applicable to indigenous tourism development elsewhere.

"Maori-Centred Tourism": Integrating Maori Values into Tourism Development

The achievement of Maori self-determined development has been widely debated in the development studies literature. For example, studies such as those by Durie (2000, 2002) and Henare (1999) have advocated the incorporation of Maori cultural values and practices into commercial development. As a basis for revitalising traditional institutions and culture as a basis for development, these studies have adopted Kaupapa Maori development models that provide sets of values for potentially defining a Maori-centred business (see for example, Durie, 2002). In this way, the business is run so that it is culturally and socially sustainable as it is essentially non-western in nature (J.H.M.R.C., 1999).

Kaupapa Maori development is a unique Maori approach to sustainable development. It aims to protect and develop Maori social and cultural capital in development. This is achieved by basing development on traditional cultural or customary values. For example, recent Maori intellectual efforts have attempted to identify concepts and principles contained in oral history, myths, whakatauki (proverbs) and waiata (song) that could provide essential components of an alternative Maori model of development and well-being (Loomis, 1999). Kaupapa Maori development significantly embodies the essence of Maori self-determined development. Durie (2000, p. 13) has argued that the overriding aim of Maori development is that it is, "About the development of Maori people as Maori". This is more than Maori participating fully in society, it is about, "Being Maori and being part of te ao Maori, the Maori world". "Maori want to retain their distinct identity that comes from a unique heritage, common journeys, a familiar environment, and a set of shared aspirations" (Ibid). This is reflected in the approach of Kaupapa Maori development in that, "The richness of their retained values, customs and institutions ... are more rather than less relevant as they explore avenues toward more holistic, self determined development" (Loomis, 1999, p. 17). As such, the identification of important cultural values means that Maori retain the ownership and control of their cultural identity and property rights (Hinch *et al.*, 1999). In this way, commercial development meets Maori social and cultural expectations and requirements (J.H.M.R.C., 1997).

Cultural values can be expressed as moral principles, beliefs or standards held by Maori to guide their behaviour, or, as desired states of existence worth striving for (or outcomes). Durie (2002), for example, has suggested that the interaction of both these dimensions provides a framework for a Maori business ethic, or provides distinctive defining characteristics of a Maori-centred business. Therefore, Kaupapa Maori approaches to development

focus on, "Processes, relationships and people's selfhood as on so-called outcomes" (Durie, 2002, p. 17). The critical factor is that Kaupapa Maori development emphasises the *internal* control of these processes, principles and outcomes. Of course, the process of identifying values rests with an individual Maori-centred business. Furthermore, these values will differ due to the diversity of Maori society. However, a review of Maori development studies reveals commonalities that characterise Maori-centred business as a distinctive activity, thereby making business uniquely Maori. For example, *kohahitanga* (Maori unity), *tino rangatiratanga* (self-determination), *whanaungatanga* (belonging), *kaitiakitanga* (guardianship), *wairuatanga* (spirituality) and *manaakitanga* (warm hospitality) are Maori values, among others, that have been identified as central elements of Maori self-determined commercial development (see Henare, 1999; J.H.M.R.C., 1998; Maaka & Fleras, 2000). Indeed, Tahana *et al.* (2000) have noted that the nature of some emerging Maori businesses is distinctive as they are being developed and managed on a cooperative basis, thereby demonstrating both business success, while sustaining Maori values (Tahana *et al.*, 2000, p. 79). In contrast, other Maori businesses operate as a strictly mainstream or western business model (J.H.M.R.C., 1999, p. 79).

Of particular interest is whether these values are also determining dimensions of Maori-centred tourism. Such an approach has relevance to defining a Maori-centred tourism business based on values culturally acceptable to Maori and as defined by Maori. However, despite its perceived importance for achieving sustainable self-determined Maori tourism development, this approach has not readily been considered in the published tourism literature to date. Therefore, the aim of the present study was to identify and describe the common values of Maori-centred tourism as defined by Maori, to essentially rethink existing approaches to defining Maori tourism.

Study Method

The study sought to provide a values-based definition of Maori tourism as defined by Maori. Specifically, the study sought to identify and describe the common values that characterise or define "Maori-centred tourism". To provide a specific Maori perspective, a Kaupapa Maori research approach was deemed appropriate. Essentially, "Kaupapa Maori is derived from different epistemological and metaphysical foundations and it is these which give Kaupapa Maori research its distinctiveness from Western philosophies" (Nepe, 1999 in Smith, 1999, p. 187). Defining Maori tourism within a Maori epistemology is therefore concerned with "*re*framing". Indeed, Smith (1999, p. 153) has advocated that *re*framing occurs where, "Indigenous peoples resist being boxed and labelled according to categories which do not fit". As such, defining Maori tourism according to a culturally relevant perspective overcomes the risk of it being defined within a *pakeha* (non-Maori New Zealander) worldview that "does not fit".

Whilst culturally appropriate research methods have been discussed in the tourism literature (see Berno, 1996), they have not readily been used in the empirical application of tourism research. In the present study, a Kaupapa Maori research approach was expressed in several ways. The assumption of the paper is based on making a "positive difference for the researched" (Smith, 1999, p. 191). Consistent with Smith (1999), the *whanau* (extended family) principle, an important aspect of Kaupapa Maori appro-

aches, was used in the study at a practical level to structure the gathering of the information. This involved incorporating Maori and non-Maori people to be part of what has been referred to as the "research *whanau* of interest" (Bishop, 1994 in Smith, 1999, p. 185). Specifically, Maori staff from national-level organisations involved in the tourism industry (for example, Tourism New Zealand, Creative New Zealand, the Department of Conservation and Te Puni Kokiri, Ministry of Maori Development), individual representatives from eight out of the ten Maori regional tourism organisations in New Zealand and Maori staff from prominent Maori tourist attractions in New Zealand contributed information to the study by participating in in-depth interviews.

In addition, non-Maori people who have written about Maori tourism or indigenous tourism and non-Maori people who hold a responsibility or role with Maori in the tourism industry were also included in the "research whanau of interest". The latter were represented through information gained from in-depth interviews with staff from, for example, the New Zealand Tourism Industry Association, Tourism New Zealand, regional tourism organisations, as well as academics involved in Maori tourism research. It is at the level of "distributing tasks" and "incorporating people with particular expertise" (Smith, 1999, p. 191) that involving non-Maori in the "whanau research group" is justified. In particular, the involvement of non-Maori assists in bringing significant issues to Maori from their particular role(s) in the tourism industry. Therefore, the people (Maori and non-Maori) interviewed to define Maori tourism were selected because of their different roles in the tourism industry and their different perspectives. Maori-centred tourism was thus defined from a supply perspective, bringing together Maori and non-Maori views on values appropriate to characterising Maori tourism business. It should also be noted that the research team involved both Maori and non-Maori researchers. This is a method supported by McIntosh *et al.* (2002) in order that different perspectives can be given to data analysis and interpretation. Furthermore, consistent with a Kaupapa Maori research approach, data analysis was also carried by the "research whanau of interest" to ensure credible content analysis and validation of important values.

The in-depth interviews were conducted between December 2001 and September 2002 and were conducted according to Kaupapa Maori research practices of *kanohi ki te kanohi* (face to face). A Kaupapa Maori research method employing storytelling or oral narrative was applied in the interviews with Maori. This is the preferred mode of communication of some Maori. For instance, "As a research tool, storytelling is a culturally appropriate way of 'representing the diversities of truth' in which the storyteller rather than the researcher retain control" (Bishop, 1996 in Smith, 1999, p. 144). The interview questions were thus structured in an open way to allow for storytelling. While it was not a cultural issue to use storytelling for non-Maori respondents, it was also employed with positive results. Importantly, the interviews elicited the benefits gained from qualitative interviewing (see Patton, 1990). The two main questions posed to Maori and non-Maori respondents were: What is your understanding, or, how do you define Maori tourism? What is the purpose or use of this definition?

Analysis of the data involved the identification of common responses by the research team. The *whanau* (extended family) concept also involves accountability to those providing information

(Bishop, 1994, in Smith, 1999, p. 185). Therefore, the research data were reported back to each interviewee. The data were checked by each participant for accuracy and additional comments were recorded. Furthermore, following final analysis of the data, the research findings and conclusions (that is, the list of values and a diagram of a *koru* (spiral) of values) were sent to the Maori regional tourism organisations for comment and validation.

However, some limitations of the present research must be noted. In particular, the in-depth interviews were restricted to individual representatives who may not portray the full diversity and depth of understanding of Maori involvement in tourism. In this sense, the defining values elicited from the research findings do not represent an exhaustive list, nor are they set in concrete. The present study provides one attempt at rethinking the definition of Maori tourism and is subject to further evaluation and review by Maori. Furthermore, to define Maori tourism from a values-based perspective, an assumption has been made that Maori identity and society is not static but is dynamic and changing. Therefore, Maori identity cannot be assumed to be an expression of traditional values. "The relevance of traditional values is not the same for all Maori, nor can it be assumed that all Maori wish to define their ethnic identity according to classical constructs" (Durie *et al.*, 1995, p. 464). Important, however, is the need to define Maori tourism in an inclusive way that seeks to overcome the risk of assuming a stereotype "Maori identity".

Values as Defining Characteristics of Maori-Centred Tourism

Analysis of the in-depth interviews with Maori and non-Maori in the "research *whanau* of interest" revealed considerable support for conceptualising and expressing Maori tourism as a values-based activity that is based on traditional Maori values. For example, one interviewee from a Maori regional tourism organisation described Maori tourism as being, "More than the person being Maori. There needs to be interaction with those things and values that are Maori and cultural elements that are relevant to Maori society". Similarly, another respondent described how, "spiritual value is a key factor defining Maori tourism, which is different from Maori just doing tourism". Research by the J.H.M.R.C. (1998, p. 255), has similarly observed that "Maori tourism" might well be epistemologically different from "Maori doing tourism" (J.H.M.R.C., 1998). This sentiment is also reflected in the various models of commercial development reportedly adopted by Maori. According to one respondent interviewed from a prominent Maori tourist attraction, "There is a very big difference between Maori businesses that incorporate Maori values and those that primarily focus on profits and efficiency".

Reasons for respondents' support for defining Maori tourism as a values-based activity related to protecting and developing Maori culture and identity to "avoid further misappropriation and misrepresentation of the Maori culture in tourism". These issues are identified in the published Maori tourism literature (see for example, Stafford Group *et al.* 2001). For example, Poharama *et al.* (1998) described the problem where Maori have, "Shared a strong commitment to keeping their cultural heritage intact", but "these aspirations have not been formalised by being incorporated into the tourist 'package' itself" (Poharama *et al.*, 1998, p. 42). Pere (1982 in Tahana and Mariu, undated, p. 5) has coined this situation "com-

mercialising culture". As such, it is concluded that there should be a move to "culturalise commerce", that is, a move towards sustaining culture. There is thus "The need for strong leadership and advocacy within Maori of how culture can be deployed for commercial gain and protected for future generations" (Tahana *et al.*, 2000, p. 78). This advocates a process of Maori self-determination in tourism development.

Applying a Kaupapa Maori research approach, the characteristics of a values-based, or Maori-centred, tourism were revealed. Framing Maori-centred tourism within a Kaupapa Maori approach provided a Maori perspective of Maori tourism. Thus, while the information may not be new, framing it in a culturally relevant perspective is. The approach revealed a number of commonly expressed Maori values (see Table 1). The values revealed were: *nga matatini Maori* (Maori diversity), *kotahitanga* (unity, solidarity), *tino rangatiratanga* (self-determination), *whanaungatanga* (relationship, kinship), *kaitiakitanga* (guardianship), *manaakitanga* (warm hospitality), *wairuatanga* (state of being spiritual), *tuhono* (principle of alignment), *puawaitanga* (principle of best outcomes) and *purotu* (principle of transparency). Each value is expressed as a principle and as an outcome. Some relate specifically to do with the business, while others relate to the activity, and some apply to both. In this way, an important factor to note is that respondents viewed Maori-centred tourism as a conceptualisation based on *whakapapa* (cultural identity, genealogy). That is, that it, "deliberately revolves around Maori people, Maori assets and Maori priorities" (Durie, 2002, p. 6). As expressed by one respondent, it is a view of Maori tourism that captures, "what drives them", or, "describes where they are coming from".

Table 1   VALUES OF MAORI-CENTRED TOURISM AS IDENTIFIED BY RESPONDENTS

Value	Principles	Outcomes
Wairuatanga (state of being spiritual) *Wharaungatanga* (relationship, kinship)	• expressing the spiritual element in the product • making a contribution to Maori self-determined tourism development • fostering a whanau (family) work environment • being part of a Maori tourism network	• recognition and protection of spiritual values • economic, social and cultural sustainability • cultural pride of staff • sense of belonging and support
Nga matatini Maori (Maori diversity)	• belonging to traditional and/or non-traditional Maori tourism organisations • representing the diversity of Maori culture in the Maori tourism product • acknowledging that Maori tourism development is tribally and regionally specific allowing for different types of Maori tourism development strategy	• recognition of diverse Maori structures • a more reflective portrayal of Maori culture in the product • recognition of tribal and regional diversity in Maori tourism • acknowledgement of the different social/commercial realities of Maori tourism development
Kaitiakitanga (guardianship)	• carrying out responsibilities of kaitiakitanga – guardianship and wise care of the environment • acknowledging Maori close affinity to the environment	• environmentally sustainable tourism development • development of products that protect and promote Maori close relationship with nature
Manaakitanga (warm hospitality)	• fostering sharing of knowledge and beliefs being hospitable with tourists	• recognition of Maori way of interaction with visitors
Tino rangatiratanga (self-determination)	• controlling the process of tourism development (i.e., the decision making process) • controlling commercial/economic independence • controlling the representation of Maori culture in tourism • asserting Treaty of Waitangi rights for ownership of resources for tourism development	• ownership of the business (or partnerships with non-Maori) and management • self-determined tourism development • protection of cultural integrity of the tourism product • determination of authenticity of Maori tourism product • expression of "constitutional ownership" under the Treaty of Waitangi
Kotahitanga (unity, solidarity)	• establishing cooperative relationships and strategic alliances with other Maori in tourism	• enhanced tourism business opportunities • sense of unity and cooperation with other Maori involved in tourism
Tuhono (principle of alignment)	• aligning the economic, social, cultural and environmental goals of the business	• integrated, sustainable development
Purotu (principle of transparency)	• addressing both Maori and non-Maori accountabilities and responsibilities	• western and Maori cultural business practices
Puawaitanga (principle of best outcomes)	• using indicators/guidelines that measure the social, economic, cultural and environmental aspects of the tourism business	• integrated measurement of the "best possible outcome" of the business

Significantly, respondents reported that the values identified should not be perceived as a rigid set of rules. They cannot be "treated as concrete absolutes as this falls into the trap of essentialising Maori and Maori culture" (Zygadlo *et al.*, 2001, p. 19). Instead, they constitute guidelines to be maintained. "This recognises the distinctiveness of Maori culture but at the same time acknowledges that Maori culture is fluid and evolves within the context of socio-economic influences" (Ibid).

It was also felt by the majority of respondents that Maori-centred tourism should not be conceptualised as "just a simple list of values"; rather there exists dynamic relationships between the values. Symbolically, therefore, Maori-centred tourism can be represented as "a *koru* (spiral) of values" (see Figure 1). The figure was supported by the majority of respondents (with some changes incorporated in to the design). The concept of a *koru* (spiral) signifies that values for sustainable Maori development are not seen in isolation, nor do they represent a hierar-chy of values. Each value in the *koru* (spiral) has "its own unique nature, life and form, yet each is part of a continuum with an identifiable core. Like a fern's frond an inner core is revealed as it unfolds" (Henare, 1999, p. 52). Each value is also an essence of "growth" as represented by the *koru* shape. This "illustrates that we must understand the parts to understand the whole, as they are all integrated, interconnected and interdependent, both with each other and clusters of other values significant to Maori" (Henare, 1999, p. 52).

Whilst the dynamic and interrelated nature of the values identified by respondents must be taken into account, each value is discussed individually below as an important characteristic in shaping Maori tourism as a values-based activity of expressed importance to Maori.

Wairuatanga (State of Being Spiritual)

Wairuatanga is the spiritual dimension of Maori values. As described under the value

Figure 1   Maori-Centred Tourism–Koru (Spiral) of Values.

of *kaitiakitanga* (guardianship), *whakapapa* (genealogy) "incorporates a spiritual dimension reaching back to the beginning of time and explaining humankind's relationship with the universe, earth and matter, both inanimate and animate" (Keelan, 1991 in Keelan, 1996, p. 197). The importance of spirituality is perpetuated in the creation of myths, art, waiata (song) and demonstrates the indivisibility of Maori people from their environment (Keelan, 1996).

Wairuatanga was identified by respondents as an essential part of Maori tourism. As one respondent stated, "*Wairua* (spirituality) provides guidelines for Maori tourism unique to Maori". One respondent from a regional Maori tourism organisation commented that, "it is the expression of spiritual values in relation to Maori identity to the land, sea and sky that makes Maori tourism distinct. Explaining the spiritual side to visitors makes the product genuine rather than mass produced". In other words, "cultural interpretation to visitors based on genuine Maori values enables visitors to experience the spirit (*wairua*) of living Maori culture" (Zeppel, 1997). As such, communicating the spiritual or emotional experience was reported as essential in protecting the cultural integrity of the tourism product. This is a finding supported by Hinch *et al.* (1999, p. 6) who have concluded that not only is the cultural dimension important, but also "the perspective of actually getting insight into the way Maori view their natural environment and the spirituality that Maori have with their *taonga* (valued resources)". As such, an important characteristic of Maori tourism, for Maori, appears to be the expression of spiritual significance in tourism development that protects the spiritual values of the people in the area.

Whanaungatanga (Relationship, Kinship)

Whanaungatanga is an organisational principle, a way of structuring and maintaining social relations within the *whanau* (extended family), (Smith, 1999). It provides a support structure which has inbuilt responsibilities and obligations. This creates a sense of "belonging and solidarity" (Henare, 1999, p. 48). The notion of *whanaungatanga* is expressed as contributing to Maori development, being part of a Maori network and creating a *whanau* environment in the business.

The majority of Maori respondents interviewed as part of the study reported that being part of a Maori network characterises, for them, Maori tourism development. For instance, some Maori tourism operators are part of a Maori network through Maori tourism regional organisations that support Maori tourism businesses in their role. Similarly, Tahana *et al.* (2000) have noted that the involvement of *kaumatua* (Maori elders) and other *hapu* (Maori sub-tribe) members in an advisory capacity has enhanced the development of some Maori tourism businesses. Furthermore, *marae* (Maori community) or *whanau* (extended family) based tourism development was strongly supported by participants in a study by the James Henare Maori Tourism Research Centre (J.H.M.R.C., 1997). However, not all Maori tourism development is supported by traditional Maori structures. For example, organizations that embrace the urban *whanau* are also important.

As such, one respondent from a prominent Maori tourism attraction commented that, "nurturing staff in a *whanau* (extended family) working environment is an important strategy for Maori tourism". "Empowering staff to make their own decisions consistent with Maori values contributes to this *whanau* work environment". It was further reported that making a deliberate contribution to Maori development also characterises *whanaungatanga* (relationship or kinship). This reflects a strong sense of belonging. As one respondent from a regional tourism organisation commented, "There is natural commitment [among Maori] to tribal or *whanau* based development". In particular, this was reflected in the comments given by respondents from the Maori regional tourism organisations. "Maori tourism entails *whanaungatanga*; supporting the development of *hapu* (Maori sub-tribe), *whanau* (extended family) and *iwi* (tribe) by helping their own people to build up opportunities in tourism". "Maori development is an issue economically, socially and culturally. This takes place at a personal, community, *hapu* level".

As such, a goal reported by many respondents from the Maori regional tourism organisations and Maori tourism operators associations involved providing support for *whanau* and *hapu* tourism initiatives. Essentially, to "assist and empower their *hapu* or *whanau* based tourism businesses to become economically sustainable by providing information, promoting their products and providing business development and planning. This is about the self-determination of *whanau, hapu* and *iwi* in political, social, cultural and economic development". These comments reflect the expressed desire for a sustainable self-determined Maori tourism development model that is "supportive of Maori social systems and productive of a sustainable economic base for their communities, thereby promoting their overall development aspirations which included improved employment opportunities and living standards" (J.H.M.R.C., 1998, p. 708).

Nga Matatini Maori (Maori Diversity)

Nga Matatini Maori is the principle of Maori diversity. "Maori are organised into a variety of traditional and non-traditional bodies, each of which is legitimate in its own right and deserves protection of its integrity" (Maaka & Fleras, 2000, p. 101). Therefore, in tourism development it is important to acknowledge and allow for the complex diversity within Maori society, this includes differences between *iwi* (Maori tribes) and non-traditional organisations as well as differences within *iwi*.

The majority of respondents commented that the representation of Maori culture in tourism must reflect the diversity of Maori identity, essentially "to avoid misrepresenting Maori as a homogenous group" (Zygadlo *et al.*, 2001, p. 10). For example, there are different Maori regional tourism organisations representing the different Maori *iwi* (tribes) in New Zealand. Some regional tourism organisations are *iwi*-based. Other organisations are regionally based and incorporate several or more *iwi* in their *rohe* (territory or area). Respondents also commented on the need to diversify the nature of Maori tourism product and described how, for example, "The existing Maori tourism product needs to be more reflective of the culture itself or more accurate in terms of who we are"; "A diversified Maori tourism product which carries authenticity and integrity is needed"; "There is a need to look at the whole diversity of the Maori tourism product and how to break down the stereotypes of Maori tourism as entertainment. The visitor is aware of the Rotorua experience but this is rather restrictive and limiting if this is the only perception of Maori tourism".

Strategies to promote a diversified culture reported by respondents included Maori tourism products that, "give a portrayal of a 'lived' perspective of Maori culture rather than a staged performance", such as a Maori perspective of a marine wildlife viewing experience (see Hinch *et al.*, 1999). Furthermore, respondents emphasised the need to provide tourists with "a deeper level of interaction" as part of providing an alternative to the staged experience. One respondent from a prominent Maori tourist attraction described how, "We want to provide an authentic learning experience, through which we learn too by interacting with our guests". Examples of these experiences included "guided tours of *pa* (fortified village) sites, old fishing grounds, trails, hunting areas and small rural *marae* (Maori community)".

Nga Matatini Maori (Maori diversity) was also stated by respondents to be reflected in the different types of development strategies for Maori tourism. Indeed, Mahuta (1987, p. 5) has provided a description of some of the different types of models for Maori tourism development. A defining characteristic of these models, among other criteria, is the retention of Maori values and perceptions. The models reflect three types of development. The first, *custodial developments*, involves small-scale developments where the resource is the land held in Maori ownership and provides training and employment opportunities for the local *marae* (Maori community) groups and owners. The second model, *dependant developments* largely involves strategies for joint ventures, for example, the overseas marketing of Maori-owned tourist enterprises carried out by non-Maori companies. The third model, *spontaneous developments* involves keeping the development in Maori control, with each area defining for itself the unique qualities of the resources of each particular area or group. Adopting a mix of these models has been termed the

pluralistic model of commercial integration (J.H.M.R.C., 1997). Some respondents described their application of these models. For example, one respondent from *Ngai Tahu* (South Island Maori tribe) described how the tribe had adopted this pluralistic model as a commercial strategy.

Nga Matatini Maori was also considered by respondents to characterise the different *iwi* (tribe), *hapu* (sub-tribe) or *whanau* (extended family) expressions or interpretations of *tikanga* (meaning or custom) in tourism. For example, one respondent described how, "different *hapu* express *mannakitanga* (hospitality) in different ways, whereby some may *hongi* (press noses) while others may provide a formal *powhiri* (opening welcome ceremony). To emphasise these differences, respondents referred to expressions of "*hapu* tourism" versus "*iwi* tourism". Thus, each *iwi* or *hapu* may provide "a blueprint for policies and procedures for how to do their *iwi* tourism". This is about each *iwi* or *hapu* "restoring and reclaiming their own way of doing things". Accordingly, this reported diversity means that Maori-centred tourism should be considered spatially and/or tribally specific.

Kaitiakitanga (Guardianship)

Kaitiakitanga is defined as the "responsibilities and *kaupapa* (plan), passed down from the ancestors, for *tangata whenua* (Maori people) to take care of the places, natural resources and other *taonga* (valued resources) in their *rohe* (area), and the *mauri* (physical life force) of those places, resources and *taonga* (valued resources)" (Parliamentary Commissioner for the Environment, 1997, p. 132). *Taonga* are the tangible and intangible valued resources of Maori culture, including nature, its resources and the spiritual bond with the natural environment. Therefore, the concept of *kaitiakitanga* involves guardianship of treasured resources and includes aspects of wise care and management such that these resources can be passed on intact to future generations (Tahana *et al.*, 2000).

An important implication of *kaitiakitanga* (guardianship) is that tourism development must not compromise the role of *kaitiaki* (*iwi* (tribe), *hapu* (sub-tribe) and *whanau* (extended family) responsibilities) in caring for the natural environment. As such, for Maori tourism development, the underlying attitudes of Maori towards the environment can affect the manner in which tourism development occurs (Hall *et al.*, 1993). One respondent described how *kaitiakitanga* provides a "philosophical guideline for how we interact with the natural resources in the particular area of the tourism activities. Tourism development must be environmentally sensitive or environmentally responsible". Maori respondents therefore perceived environmental integrity as a central component of sustainable Maori tourism.

From a wider perspective, *kaitikitanga* is grounded, for Maori, in a world view in which humans and nature are not separate entities but related parts of a unified whole" (Roberts *et al.*, 1995, p. 16). This is founded on Maori philosophy whereby *wairuatanga* (state of being spiritual) refers to the spiritual dimension of Maori relationship with the environment. Indeed, Maori affinity with nature was reported by many of the respondents interviewed as an important dimension of Maori tourism. For example, one respondent from a Maori tourism organisation described how, to him, Maori tourism involved, "Sharing an element of our relationship to the land (based on the relationship of *Te Papa* and *Rangi*) with the tourists". In this way, "A tourism product that expresses

this spiritual attachment to the environment allows for Maori tourism that is based on and promotes our *kaitiaki* roles and responsibilities". One further respondent commented that, "A failure to recognise this unique Maori sense of place would seem to be one of the more important factors that has contributed to current issues in Maori tourism related to marketing, product development and environmental impacts". As such, conceptualising Maori tourism in relation to acknowledging the value of *kaitiakitanga* involves environmental stewardship and acknowledgement in product development of Maori close affinity to the natural environment.

Manaakitanga (Warm Hospitality)

Manaakitanga is about the respect given to *manuhuri* (visitors). "Maori notions of hospitality (*manaakitanga*) meant that visitors were accorded a warm welcome" (Ryan, 1997, p. 260). As such, *manaakitanga* is seen as one key element for the way Maori should engage themselves with tourists (Zygadlo *et al.*, 2001).

All of the Maori respondents interviewed reported the value of *manaakitanga* as a central characteristic of Maori tourism. Important therefore to a values-based Maori tourism is the affirmation of the Maori way of hosting and welcoming visitors. This can be summarised in the words of one respondent; "Being Maori means sharing knowledge, hospitality, beliefs and well being and that ultimately is what Maori tourism is". As such, the nature of Maori tourism as a values-based activity is the sharing of core principles and beliefs, hospitality and caring. Indeed, the fostering of practices of *manaakitanga* by Maori staff at prominent Maori tourist attractions in New Zealand has been reported as part of the essence of successful and sustainable Maori tourism (see Hinch *et al.*, 1999).

Tino Rangatiratanga (Self-Determination)

The concept of *tino rangatiratanga* is about the self-determination of Maori. "The right of Maori to have control over their resources, culture, social and economic well-being" (Zygadlo *et al.*, 2001, p. 23). Integral to *tino rangatiratanga* is therefore the issue of control.

Control has been identified as a key issue in tourism for Maori (see for example, Keelan, 1996; Barnett, 1997; Hall, 1996). In terms of *tino rangatiratanga*, respondents identified the need for Maori tourism whereby Maori exert control over their culture and property rights, have business ownership and management responsibilities and, more generally, gain "constitutional ownership" (Ryan, 1997, p. 266) under the rights of New Zealand's Treaty of Waitangi. In terms of control over culture, one respondent described how this "means Maori control over the tourism product". "The definition and use of Maori culture in the tourism industry must be firmly in responsible Maori hands". This ensures, for example, control over authenticity (Hinch *et al.*, 1999). For Maori, authenticity is simply defined as having the right to control access to their heritage (Barnett, 1996 in Ryan & Crotts, 1997).

At a personal level, respondents described *tino rangatiratanga* (self-determination) as "the right to define yourself, who you are, what is important to you and therefore what is authentic". Comments made by Maori respondents included, "It is therefore, the right to express our own personal identity as Maori and it is this which gives our own unique cultural dimension to the tourism product"; "A Maori home stay owner or bus

tour guide who talks about stories about their attachment to the land is providing a Maori cultural dimension to the tourism experience in a way that expresses their identity"; "This allows Maori to present themselves how they would like to present themselves and not compromising their cultural identity". Providing an authentic experience to visitors was reported by one respondent to involve "safeguards", "such as consultations with *kaumatua* (tribal elders) and maintaining appropriate protocol among visitors". This is supported in research by Hinch *et al.* (1999, p. 5) whereby Maori tourist attractions place the *marae* (Maori community) as the central focus of "who they are and what they are about" in terms of the visitor experience.

Consultation may also involve the broader Maori community about permission to exhibit *taonga* (valued resources), the use of *iwi* (Maori tribe) images or stories in promotional material and modifications to cultural protocol. Providing employees who work directly with visitors with a sense of cultural ownership and control is also part of ensuring an "authentic product" (see Hinch *et al.*, 1999). As such, one respondent commented on how "cultural ownership of the product allows Maori to use their cultural identity in tourism to promote Maori culture; to promote Maori ways of doing things".

In terms of control relating to business management and ownership, comments made by respondents advocated the need in the tourism sector for Maori "to be financially independent and make our own decisions and to have pride"; "it means being economically sustainable". This was expressed through the need to heighten business ownership among Maori, "as this gives Maori control over the development process". However, it has been noted that

Maori also recognise the need for investment partners even while seeking retention of control (Ryan, 1997). For example, Maori are pursuing approaches of partnership and cooperation with non-Maori in tourism (Ryan, 1997; Ryan & Crotts, 1997). Further comments made by respondents included, "Maori management of the tourism business is also an important aspect of control over the decision making in the business"; "If *whanau* (extended family) and *hapu* (sub-tribe) have a say in all decision making then tourism development is beneficial, otherwise it is exploitative".

The Treaty of Waitangi includes legal recognition of Maori tribal sovereignty, land ownership and rightful use of natural resources. Thus, Maori ownership of land and culture under the Treaty of Waitangi is about Maori claiming "constitutional ownership" (Ryan, 1997, p. 266). Maori tourism is thus, "intimately related with the overall restoration of rights under the Treaty of Waitangi" (Keelan, 1993 in Hall 1996, p. 172). Therefore, a Maori tourism business operates in a socio-political context where the meaning of *rangatiratanga* is a part of a process of a constitutional partnership with *pakeha* (non-Maori New Zealander) (Ryan, 1997). This was reflected in the comments made by respondents. In particular, it was reinforced that, "*iwi* (tribal) involvement in tourism development must be seen in relation to their political role in driving for an *iwi–crown* partnership". As such, "Maori tourism is also related to rights of Article 2 of the Treaty of Waitangi and the right to self-determined development".

structures, there remains a cohesive core based on a shared sense of belonging and common destiny" (Maaka & Fleras, 2000, p. 102). *Kotahitanga* also means "establishing relationships or alliances between Maori organisations and groups" (Durie, 2002, p. 9). In this way, it is seen that business opportunities will be enhanced as alliances can foster a spirit of cooperation rather than fragmentation of effort. In sum, *kotahitanga* "recognizes linkages and reinforces them through cooperation" (J.H.M.R.C., 1997, p. 179).

A majority of respondents from the Maori regional tourism organisations interviewed in the study commented on the importance of the Maori regional tourism organisations for developing useful networks for Maori in tourism. They also expressed the need to strengthen their national Maori tourism relationships in addressing common issues. It was also felt by a majority of respondents that forming relationships also means Maori operators clustering their products and services with other Maori tourism operators. For example, one respondent described how, "several *marae* (Maori community) stays in an area may link up together or a *marae* stay may link up with guided bush tours". An expression of *kotahitanga* (unity or solidarity) as Maori being part of a network was also felt to be interrelated and reinforce the value of *whanaungatanga* (relationship, kinship). As such, for Maori tourism, the value of *kotahitanga* was seen to reinforce strategic alliances and bring a sense of unity among Maori in tourism.

Kotahitanga (Unity, Solidarity)

Kotahitanga is the principle of Maori unity. "Despite diversity in affiliations and

Tuhono (Principle of Alignment)

Cross-sectoral alignment of Maori-centred businesses is the basis of the principle of *tuhono* (Durie, 2002, p. 7). Maori development, therefore, depends on the alignment of social, economic and cultural goals. An approach that integrates these goals is needed to align "Maori aspirations for advancement on all platforms, simultaneously" (Ibid).

In relation to Maori tourism as a values-based activity, respondents reported that the principle of *tuhono* describes how the business integrates different goals and/or values. This is consistent with Hinch *et al.* (1999), who have advocated that while economic independence is seen as a condition of cultural independence, this needs to be balanced with cultural and environmental performance. This approach can be reflected in a Maori tourism operator's company philosophy to, for example, "only undertake activities that are commercially viable, culturally acceptable and environmentally sustainable" (Kearsley *et al.*, 1999, p. 10).

As such, the principle of *tuhono* advocates Maori tourism, "that is culturally authentic and sustainable relative to local Maori culture, communities, environment, and their economic well-being" (J.H.M.R.C., 1998, p. 17). This includes fostering local employment, preservation of culture, maintenance of environment, education, family values, profit, service development, sense of community and Maori control or ownership. Furthermore, one respondent described how, "*Tuhuno* is also evident in how the support of *whanau* (extended family) or *hapu* (Maori sub-tribe) tourism initiatives by *iwi* (Maori tribe) is part of a comprehensive, integrated approach, that is, social, economic, environmental and cultural to development by *iwi*". The principle of *tuhuno* thus serves to ensure the alignment of the economic, social, cultural and environmental goals of a business to achieve sustainable development.

Purotu (Principle of Transparency)

Purotu is the principle of transparency or accountability. Maori businesses are seen to have responsibilities and levels of accountability, including a direct responsibility to shareholders or stakeholders and with the non-Maori legal accountabilities such as rules and regulations (Durie, 2002).

Analysis of the in-depth interviews revealed that when Maori values are involved, a majority of respondents felt that a Maori tourism business is accountable and responsible to the Maori community, that is, *whanau* (extended family) and *hapu* (Maori sub-tribe). Respondents described how, "For *iwi* (Maori tribe) based tourism initiatives, there are responsibilities and roles that come with working within a Maori customary framework"; "They have to comply with established guidelines unique to Maori". As such, it was felt that the need to address Maori accountabilities and responsibilities was an important feature of a Maori tourism business. In addition, it was reported by respondents that Maori tourism businesses also need to address non-Maori responsibilities. For example, one respondent from a Maori tourism operators association stated that "it is important for us to provide support for Maori operators in the non-Maori accountabilities such as developing strategic plans, budgeting, monitoring and understanding rules and regulations". In this way, Maori tourism was seen to involve a dual accountability in terms of maintaining Maori cultural practice in addition to adopting a western business structure.

Puawaitanga (Principle of Best Outcomes)

Puawaitanga, or the principle of best outcomes, is about "endorsing the use of multiple measures for the 'best possible return' in a Maori-centred business" (Durie, 2002, p. 8). According to a Maori-centred model therefore, a good outcome will be reflected in several aspects; namely, social, economic, cultural and environmental aspects of a business. Indicators of business performance need to be developed to measure social, cultural, and broader economic goals to give a "comprehensive" picture of outcome. Therefore, the principle of *puawaitanga* potentially reflects the approach advocated in models of sustainable ethnic tourism. That is, that attention must be given to incorporating ways to measure not only socio-cultural impacts and capacity to retain or reproduce authenticity, but also ways to measure the financial viability of a venture (see Sofield, 1993).

As such, a majority of respondents felt that measures, standards or indicators for Maori tourism are needed. However, the lack of standards and clear guidelines for the objectives of Maori in the tourism industry that have been decided by Maori for Maori has been noted in the published literature (see Stafford Group *et al.*, 2000). Respondents viewed suitable guidelines as involving "acceptability", "retention of culture and values", "environmental preservation", "local ownership, employment and control", "improved living standards and social well-being" and "education". Maori-centred tourism would thus involve evaluation of best outcomes for Maori in tourism, as decided by Maori.

Conclusion

The incorporation of Maori cultural values and practices into commercial development is advocated as essential for sustainable Maori self-determined development (see Durie, 2000, 2002; Henare, 1999). However, a values-based perspective of Maori tourism

from a Maori perspective has not been attempted. More commonly, Maori tourism has been associated with the quantification of Maori involvement in tourism, or the extent of Maori theme evident in the tourism product. The overall aim of this paper was therefore to seek conceptual clarification of "Maori tourism" by identifying and describing common values identified by Maori as defining Maori tourism in terms of their own criteria. To this end, the paper introduced the concept of "Maori-centred tourism" as an alternative to defining Maori tourism in terms of general Maori participation in tourism. Maori-centred tourism is a concept founded on a list of Maori values that seeks to recognise the desire among Maori to protect and develop Maori cultural and intellectual property and the need for self-determined tourism development.

Adopting a Kaupapa Maori research approach to ensure the research was culturally acceptable and founded on characteristics important to Maori, commonly expressed cultural values were identified and described from the empirical data collected. These included: *nga matatini Maori* (Maori diversity), *kotahitanga* (unity, solidarity), *tino rangatiratanga* (self-determination), *whanaungatanga* (relationship, kinship), *kaitiakitanga* (guardianship), *manaakitanga* (hospitality), *wairuatanga* (state of being spiritual), *tuhono* (principle of alignment), *puawaitanga* (principle of best outcomes) and *purotu* (principle of transparency). These values were expressed as both principles and outcomes. Furthermore, the dynamic relationships between values were expressed symbolically as a *koru* (spiral) of values. The list of values are not seen as exhaustive, nor are they set in concrete; rather they represent a starting point to document some commonalities of a collective values-based Maori tourism, termed here, "Maori-centred tourism". Whilst further research is needed to identify appropriate strategies for achieving a Maori-centred tourism business ethic, the epistemology offered here ensures a culturally relevant clarification of Maori tourism can be moved forward and further evaluated by Maori. It may, potentially, also be relevant as an approach to foster sustainable self-determined tourism development for indigenous populations elsewhere.

Acknowledgements

The authors would like to acknowledge that the knowledge gained in this research belongs to the Maori who participated. The research was funded by the New Zealand Foundation for Research Science & Technology; Tourism Strategic Portfolio Output.

References

Aotearoa Maori Tourism Federation (A.M.T.F.). (1996). *A Report on the Current Market Position of Maori Tourism Product.* A.M.T.F., Rotorua.

Asplet, M. & Cooper, M. (2000). Cultural Designs in New Zealand Clothing: The Question of Authenticity. *Tourism Management*, 21, 307–312.

Barnett, S. (1997). Maori Tourism. *Tourism Management*, 18(7), 471–473.

Barnett, S. (2001). Manaakitanga: Maori hospitality – A Case Study of Maori Accommodation Providers. *Tourism Management*, 22, 83–92.

Berno, T. (1996). Cross-Cultural Research Methods: Content or Context? A Cook Islands Example. In R. Butler & T. Hinch (eds), *Tourism and Indigenous Peoples* (pp. 376–395). International Thomson Business Press, London.

Butler, R. & Hinch, T. (eds) (1996). *Tourism and Indigenous Peoples.* International Thomson Business Press, London.

Chan, M., Webber, G., Bassett, B., Wilks, D., Schollmann, A., Ratana-Walser, S. & Moore, M. (2002). *Defining Maori Tourism for Compilation of Statistics.* Working Paper of the Maori Tourism Statistics Project, November 2002. Ministry of Tourism, Wellington, New Zealand.

Durie, M. H. (1995). Te Hoe Nuku Roa Framework – A Maori Identity Measure. *Journal of the Polynesian Society*, 104, 461–470.

Durie, M. H. (2000). *Contemporary Maori Development: Issues and Broad Directions. Working Paper/2000.* Department of Development Studies – Te Tari Whanaketanga, School of Maori and Pacific Development – Te Pua Wananga ki to Ao, University of Waikato – Te Whare Wananga o Waikato, New Zealand.

Durie, M. H. (2002). The Business Ethic and Maori Development. *MaungaTu MaungaOra: Economic Summit 2002*, 21 March 2002. School of Maori Studies, Massey University Auckland, New Zealand.

Hall, C. M. (1996). Tourism and the Maori of Aoteaora, New Zealand. In R. Butler & T. Hinch (eds), *Tourism and Indigenous Peoples* (pp. 155–175). International Thomson Business Press, London.

Hall, C. M., Mitchell, I. & Keelan, N. (1993). The Implications of Maori Perspectives for the Management of Promotion of Heritage Tourism in New Zealand. *Geo-Journal*, 29(3), 315–322.

Henare, M. (1999). Sustainable Social Policy. In J. Boston, P. Dalziel & S. St John (eds), *Redesigning the Welfare State in New Zealand: Problems, Policies and Prospects* (pp. 39–59). Oxford University Press, Auckland.

Hinch, T., McIntosh, A. & Ingram, T. (1999). *Maori Attractions in Aotearoa: Setting a Context for Sustainable Tourism.* Research Paper Number 6. Centre for Tourism, University of Otago, Dunedin, New Zealand.

Ingram, T. (1997). Tapoi Tangata Whenua: Tapoi Maori ki Aotearoa (Indigenous Tourism: Maori Tourism in Aotearoa). Proceedings of *Trails, Tourism and Regional Development Conference*, 2–5 December, Centre for Tourism, University of Otago, New Zealand.

James Henare Maori Research Centre (J.H.M.R.C.). (1997). *Sustainable Maori Tourism in Tai Tokerau. Collection of Reports for Case Study Three: West Ngati Kahu.* Foundation for Research Science and Technology, University of Auckland, Auckland.

James Henare Maori Research Centre (J.H.M.R.C.). (1998). *Sustainable Maori Tourism in Tai Tokerau, Collection of Reports for the South Hooking and Kamikaze Regions.* Foundation for Research Science and Technology, University of Auckland, Auckland.

James Henare Maori Research Centre (J.H.M.R.C.). (1999). *Sustainable Development in Tai Tokerau. Collection of Reports for the Ngati Whatua Region.*

Foundation for Research Science and Technology funded project, University of Auckland, Auckland.

Kearsley, G., Carr, A. & McIntosh, A. (1999). *Maori Myths, Beliefs and Values: Products and Constraints for New Zealand Tourism.* Proceedings of Tourism Industry and Education Symposium. September 23–26, Jyväskylä, Finland.

Keelan, N. (1996). Maori Heritage: Visitor Management and Interpretation. In C. M. Hall & S. McArthur (eds), *Heritage Management in New Zealand and Australia. The Human Dimension* (pp. 195–201). Oxford University Press, Oxford.

Loomis, T. (1999). Indigenous Populations and sustainable Development: Building on indigenous approaches to holistic, self-determined development. Working Paper 3/99. Department of Development Studies – Te Tari Whanaketanga, School of Maori and Pacific Development – Te Pua Wanangaki te Ao, University of Waikato – Te Whare Wanangao Waikato, New Zealand.

Maaka, R. & Fleras, A. (2000). Engaging with Indigeneity: Tino Rangatiratanga in Aotearoa. In P. Ivison, P. Patton & W. Sanders (eds), *Political Theory and the Rights of Indigenous Peoples* (pp. 89–108). Cambridge University Press, Cambridge.

Mahuta, R. T. (1987). *Tourism and Culture: The Maaori Case.* Unpublished Paper, Centre for Maori Studies and Research, University of Waikato, New Zealand.

McIntosh, A. J. (2004). Tourists' Appreciation of Maori Culture in New Zealand. *Tourism Management, 25,* 1–15

McIntosh, A. J., Hinch, T. & Ingram, T. (2002). Cultural Identity and Tourism. *International Journal of Arts Management,* 4(2), 39–49.

Page, A. J., Forer, P. & Lawton, G. R. (1999). Small Business Development and Tourism: Terra Incognita? *Tourism Management,* 20(4), 435–459.

Parliamentary Commissioner for the Environment, (1997). *Management of the Environmental Effects Associated with the Tourism Sector.* Office of the Parliamentary Commissioner for the Environment, Wellington.

Patton, M. Q. (1990). *Qualitative Evaluation and Research Methods. Second Edition.* Sage Publications, London.

Poharama, A., Henley, M., Smith, A., Fairweather, J. R. & Simmons, D. G. (1998). *Impact of Tourism on the Maori Community in Kaikoura.* Report No. 7. Tourism Recreation Research and Education Centre (T.R.R.E.C.), Lincoln University, New Zealand.

Roberts, M., Norman, W., Minhinnick, N., Wihongi, D. & Kirkwood, C. (1995). Kaitikitanga: Maori Perspectives on Conservation. *Pacific Conservation Biology,* 2(1), 7–20.

Ryan, C. (1997). Maori and Tourism: A Relationship of History, Constitutions and Rites. *Journal of Sustainable Tourism,* 5(4), 257–278.

Ryan, C. (1999). Some Dimensions of Maori Involvement in Tourism. In M. Robinson & P. Boniface (eds), *Tourism and Cultural Conflicts* (pp. 229–245). CABI Publishing, London.

Ryan, C. & Crotts, J. (1997). Carving and Tourism. A Maori Perspective. *Annals of Tourism Research,* 24(4), 898–918.

Smith, L. T. (1999). *Decolonising Methodologies: Research and Indigenous Peoples.* University of Otago Press, Dunedin.

Sofield, T. H. B. (1993). Indigenous Tourism Development. *Annals of Tourism Research,* 20, 729–750.

Stafford Group, te Hau, H. & McIntosh, A. (2000). *Closing the Gaps – He Matai Tapoi Maori, Barriers and Impediments Short Report.* A report prepared for the Office of Tourism and Sport and Te Puni Kokiri, November 2000, Wellington, New Zealand.

Stafford Group, te Hau, H. & McIntosh, A. (2001). *A Study of Barriers, Impediments and Opportunities for Maori in Tourism – He Matai Tapoi Maori.* A report prepared for the Office of Tourism and Sport and Te Puni Kokiri, June 2001, Wellington, New Zealand.

Tahana, N., Grant, K. T. O. K., Simmons, D. G. & Fairweather, J. R. (2000). *Tourism and Maori Development in Rotorua.* Report No. 15. Tourism Recreation Research and Education Centre (T.R.R.E.C.), Lincoln University, New Zealand.

Tahana, N. & Mariu, S. (undated). Proceedings of *Dreaming Visions.* International Indigenous Business and Economic Development Conference, 21–26 September, Cairns, Australia.

Tahana, N. & Oppermann, M. (1998). Maori Cultural Performances and Tourism. *Tourism Recreation Research,* 23(1), 23–30.

Taylor, J. P. (2001). Authenticity and Sincerity in Tourism. *Annals of Tourism Research,* 28(1), 7–26.

Te Puni Kokiri (T.P.K.). (2000). *Maori in the New Zealand Economy, Second Edition.* Te Puni Kokiri, Ministry of Maori Development, Wellington.

Zeppel, H. (1997). Maori Tourism in New Zealand. *Tourism Management*, 18(7), 475–478.

Zygadlo, F., Matunga, H., Simmons, D. & Fairweather, J. R. (2001). *Tourism and Maori Development in Westland*. Report No. 25. Tourism Recreation Research and Education Centre (T.R.R.E.C.), Lincoln University, New Zealand.

Managing Heritage Resources as Tourism Products

Pamela S. Y. Ho and Bob McKercher

Introduction

We already have a changed language in which we talk about the arts. We no longer discuss them as expressions of imagination or creativity, we talk about "product"; we are no longer moved by the experiences the arts have to offer, we "consume" them. Culture has become a commodity. (Hewison, 1988: 240)

In contemporary society, heritage is often treated as a commodity for economic uses, especially for tourism (Graham, Ashworth & Tunbridge, 2000). Although the value of heritage assets is far more complex than that of most goods and services, it is believed that exploiting heritage for tourism consumption, if not managed properly and cautiously, may commercialise, trivialize, and standardize the intangible cultural meanings born by the physical manifestations. The term "product" is often used to describe different types of culture and heritage consumed by tourists, such as ruins, museums, historic sites, arts, and cultural performances. This may seem ridiculous and unacceptable to some cultural heritage experts, as Hewison lamented. However, when considering the inherited nature of culture

and heritage as a resource of economic and cultural capital (Graham, Ashworth & Tunbridge, 2000), one may notice the legitimacy of treating cultural heritage assets as products when they are used for tourism. As echoed by Shackley (2001), although describing a journey to a sacred site as a service "product" being consumed by its "customers" convey a very commercial feel, this is however true.

The idea of managing cultural heritage assets as products for tourism consumption is relatively new, for cultural tourism professionals and scholars have been advocating this idea only since the late 1990s (Ashworth, 1994; Hughes, 1989; McKercher & du Cros, 2002; Richards, 1996; Shackley, 2001). This idea centres in the goal of providing an enriching experience to satisfy tourists' needs. Through understanding customers' needs and using marketing to elicit desirable exchanges, organizations are able to achieve the prescribed goals and objectives. These underlying concepts of product and marketing do not only provide incentives for tourism, but also help to achieve cultural heritage management goals. However, to what extent the cultural heritage sector and even tourism sector embrace the concept is a question. This is crucial as the ultimate goal of the tourism industry is to facilitate one's travel out of the usual environment and to create satisfactory holiday experiences.

The fundamental differences between the two disciplines, namely cultural heritage management and tourism, is a great hurdle, for the cultural heritage sector may find it hard to accept the notion of treating valuable inheritance as product, a resource of economic capital. In fact, treating cultural heritage assets as products does not simply mean pricing and selling in the market. It also does not imply that "cultural heritage assets" is a synonym to "cultural tourism products" in which the assets automatically become a product once they are promoted to and consumed by tourists. The term "product" is often misunderstood in reality, even by tourism players. As indicated by Gunn (1988: 10), "Misunderstanding of the tourism product is often a constraint in a smoothly functioning tourism system". Only if the true nature of a product is appreciated, will the management of it be successful and fruitful.

Without a clear understanding of what product means and how product functions, satisfactory experiences for cultural tourists may becomes elusive for both tourism and cultural heritage management sectors. While many of the site managers wish to promote their assets for tourism consumption, results are often not as expected such that either there are too many or too few tourists, or tourists consume the assets in a wrong way. In theory, treating cultural heritage assets as product is reasonable and logical. In practice, though, it is much harder to achieve. The challenges for successful cultural tourism development are the different mandates of the two disciplines, namely tourism and

cultural heritage management, as well as the valuable nature of heritage assets which cannot be replaced or reinvented.

Methodology

Given the importance of embracing the concepts of product and marketing, this study sought to explore challenges in developing cultural heritage assets as products by using Hong Kong as a case. As a descriptive and exploratory study, single-case (embedded) design, a qualitative research strategy has been adopted. Both primary and secondary data were collected for the study. Secondary data collection includes review on existing tourism marketing strategies for Hong Kong and the identification of cultural tourism products available for the market. Additionally, tourism statistics from Hong Kong Tourism Board were used to analyse the market demand for various cultural tourism products.

Twelve cultural heritage sites were identified from the cultural tourism visitor survey conducted by the School of Hotel and Tourism Management at the Hong Kong Polytechnic University in November 2000 as units for analysis. For primary data collection, a total of 28 interviews were conducted from two rounds of in-depth interviews with tour operators, the Hong Kong Tourism Board, museum curators and site managers. The site list encompasses a spectrum of different cultural heritage places appealing to different market segments in Hong Kong including museums, temples, and marketplaces. The purpose of these interviews and plan reviews is to determine the cultural and tourism goals established for the organization, identify the organization's perception of the cultural tourism markets and to develop an understanding of why and how the product is presented and marketed in the present manner.

Tourism versus Cultural Heritage Management

The critical challenge in cultural tourism development is therefore the need to manage heritage assets to become successful tourism products, mostly not originally intended for tourist consumption and managed by non-tourism public sector or non-profit organisations. For cultural heritage management, the intrinsic appeal and the significance, and sometimes rather than the physical manifestations, of the heritage to the host community are regarded as the core elements in their mandate (Lowenthal, 1996). For the tourism sector, cultural tourism products are those extrinsically appealing to tourists and can be consumed by them from which an enriched experience is gained after visitation. As such, sometimes a cultural asset is treated as a commodity for sale.

One of the differences between the cultural heritage and tourism sectors is noted by Ap and Mak (1999: 5): "tourism is a market-driven industry and is more consumer-friendly while the cultural industry appears to be more product and supply oriented". This poses a difficult task for cultural tourism development as cultural heritage management professionals and site managers are the ones who directly manage the assets. Unlike other products where one sector or organization is responsible for supply and marketing efforts, cultural tourism requires inputs from the two different sectors, with different mandates guiding their management practices. It is often the case that the cultural heritage management sector is responsible for providing and managing the assets, while the tourism sector is responsible for marketing. This arrangement, however, creates problems and conflicts.

A Product Approach

The idea of a product is defined under marketing as anything that is offered to consumers for attention, acquisition, use, or consumption that might satisfy a need or want (Kotler, 1997: 9). The key concept of product is its ability to provide a solution to a need and is not limited to physical objects. Anything that may satisfy one's need can be termed a product. Thus, the term "product", might be substituted by "satisfier", "resource", or "offer" (Kotler & Armstrong, 1991).

Knowing the true function of a product, it may then be inferred that the physical embodiment of the product is actually not what customers are purchasing. It is the benefits provided by consuming the products that customers are purchasing in order to satisfy their inner needs and wants. Just as the case of cultural tourism, tourists come to the heritage site not because of the physical asset, but seeking for various cultural experiences, be it personal emotional connection with the heritage, or out of an interest in witnessing national ideals and pride (Timothy, 1997). As such, the more the site manager knows what benefits tourists are seeking and shapes the products accordingly, the higher the chance of success a heritage site has.

A product exists because there is demand for the benefit offered. Having a good understanding of the market demand enables marketers and site managers to have a better match between potential customers and products, i.e. heritage sites. The essence of a product is thus not the product itself but the customers who need it. Cultural tourism products are developed because of the existence of cultural tourists regardless of varying needs they have and experiences they pursue.

To become successful in achieving financial and non-financial management goals, the tourism product must be manipulated and managed in such a way that can be easily consumed by the visitors (Reynolds, 1999). It is a mistake to compare tourists, who are pleasure-seekers, temporarily unemployed, and above all consumers, with anthropologists or any other researchers (de Kadt, 1979 cited in Reynolds 1999). A proper cultural tourism product therefore needs to be developed, from its original form not designed for tourist use into something that can offer a satisfactory cultural experience able to satisfy tourists' needs. To actualise the potential of a heritage asset, the asset should be transformed and developed into a product that can be explicitly consumed by tourists. Jansen-Verbeke and Lievois (1999) identified the following as the key factors influencing the success of the product development in cultural tourism.

1. Stakeholders' values and objectives
2. Morphological characteristics of cultural heritage assets
3. Accessibility and functionality
4. Integration with other tourism activities and supporting elements

du Cros (2001), however, argues that before any heritage asset is transformed, assessment of the asset with regard to its market appeal and robusticity is more important. The key and foremost effort for any cultural tourism development is therefore the examination of market size, tourist profile and how the heritage site may fit into various niche segments for tourists seeking different types of experiences with consideration of its level of robusticity. Careful investigation of the demand prevents the consequences of not enough or too many tourists while assessing the robusticity ensures the asset has the ability to withstand certain level of visitation without significant deterioration. This step is important, for any negative visitor impact will evoke a series of problems for the asset, such as becoming commercially non-viable, lacking financial support for conservation, or overwhelming tourists damaging the irreplaceable heritage, which detracts from the satisfactory tourist experience.

While visitors are the core element of cultural tourism, most heritage management, however, focuses only on developing the physical attributes of the resources without taking into consideration the visitor experience, which Hall and McArthur (1993: 13) argued, "should be placed at the centre of any heritage management process".

Marketing Management

Although the product needs to be developed and managed to satisfy the customer needs and wants, these should, however, be compatible with the nature of the product and, more importantly, the organization's visions and goals. Perhaps the most frequent accusations for adopting marketing in tourism development are, as Mill and Morrison (1985: 360) contend:

The uniqueness of tourism suggests that a philosophy that concentrates solely on the needs of the market is not the best orientation, even for the market itself. Tourism supply is oriented towards the resources of a community. To become totally marketing oriented, all aspects of the community would have to be oriented toward satisfying the needs and wants of the tourist. The risk for the community as well as for the tourist ultimately is that by orienting strictly and totally for the tourists' needs, the needs and integrity of the community may be abused...

Haywood (1990) provides a comprehensive defence for marketing. Paradoxically, the key element in the marketing concept should be the exchanges through which organisations attain the stated objectives and goals. The best way for the organisation to accomplish desirable exchanges is through gaining a knowledge of customers' needs and then create products to fulfil those needs.

Marketing is, in fact, not only a function of an organization, like human resources, finance, etc., but is a philosophy, which guides the management and operational directions, both short and long term, by the idea of exchange. In a generic sense, marketers seek to elicit behavioural responses from the consumers. At its simplest, marketing can be interpreted as a process of achieving voluntary exchanges between two individual parties (Middleton, 1994). For a heritage site, visitation by tourists is the behavioural response the site manager seeks, while patronage as revenue, appreciation and learning of the intrinsic cultural value, reverential behaviour and support for heritage conservation may be the real things they want consumers to offer in return.

However, a complete understanding of the underlying ideas and concepts of marketing is seldom found in reality. Many of the adverse impacts in cultural tourism are indeed the result of the failure to adopt a marketing management approach (McKercher & du Cros, 2002: 201–202). Very often, the term "marketing" is equated to increasing visitation, promotion and sales maximization, which in fact is about adopting a customer-focused management tool that can be used to achieve organizational goals, whether financial or non-financial, by matching demand with resources. In reality, many non-profit organisations have

started to value and adopt marketing as their management philosophy. Instead of tourists, the intrinsic values and interpretation of the heritage asset should underpin any management, marketing and financial decisions and strategies (Millar, 1989).

The meaning of product implies that heritage assets need to be managed for tourism consumption to fulfil some set of objectives and goals. To elicit desirable exchanges, therein lies a communication challenge between the heritage sites and tourists. Effective communication is necessary, for it can convey correct messages and images to attract the right types of tourists seeking travel experiences compatible with the interpretation of the site and provide an education experience, which may prevent inappropriate use of assets.

Hong Kong – The Cultural Tourism Market

This study uses Hong Kong as a case study because it represents a mature tourism destination with a series of well-established tourism attractions. While much of the emphasis on cultural tourism studies has been on emerging destinations, there is relatively little research on mature urban tourism destinations. While tourism has been developed for a long time in Hong Kong, it was only recently that the local government announced the development of cultural tourism in this international city famous for its diversity of cultures and traditions. Unlike other countries with world heritage sites and a rich array of cultural resources with potent development potential for international tourist arrivals, Hong Kong does not have significant large-scale heritage able to attract tourists internationally. Given these conditions, Hong Kong is therefore a representative case for most of the urban destinations around the world worth studying to fill a research void.

Since the Second World War, the Hong Kong economy has undergone a series of structural changes and has gradually been developed into one largely depending on service businesses. The tourism industry has always been a mainstream economic activity in Hong Kong with its ability to generate huge amount of foreign exchange earnings. For decades, Hong Kong was praised as the "Pearl of the Orient" appealing especially to visitors from the West. During the 1970s and 1980s, it enjoyed the reputation as a Shopping Paradise until economic turmoil occurred in 1997 with the Asian Financial Crisis. A dramatic decrease in the number of tourist aroused the attention of different sectors in the Hong Kong tourism industry that there was a need to reformulate a long-term strategy to regain the position of a leading tourist destination in the Asia Pacific region. To revitalize the tourism industry, the Hong Kong government identified cultural tourism as one of the key options to pursue. Indeed in the January 2003 industry briefing, culture/heritage and festivals were identified as one of the four pillars of Hong Kong tourism. According to Mike Rowse (International Conference: Heritage and Tourism, 13th–15th December 1999, Hong Kong) former Commissioner for Tourism of Hong Kong, the Government of the Hong Kong Special Administrative Region has adopted a three-pronged strategy as follows to enhance the local tourism business, of which heritage tourism has been identified as one of the key options to pursue.

- To provide easy access for visitors to come to Hong Kong;
- To enhance attractiveness by facilitating the development of tourism products;

- To promote Hong Kong as an attractive tourist destination.

As he commented, preservation and planning of cultural tourism attractions and products are key components of cultural tourism development, and marketing is deemed equally important. A five-Ps approach to successful cultural tourism development was delivered in the same speech:

- Preservation
- Planning
- Packaging
- Promotion
- Partnership

Looking at the cultural tourism market in Hong Kong, according to a visitors survey conducted by the Hong Kong Tourist Association in 1999, performing arts and arts/cultural exhibits, traditional Chinese festivals, gourmet and heritage are among the top five interests of Hong Kong inbound tourists. However, at present, over one third of the inbound tourists in Hong Kong came from Mainland China and the overall average length of stay was three nights. While shopping is the most popular activity for the Mainland tourists, most of their activities focus mainly in the tourist areas. In two studies by McKercher *et al.* (2002) and McKercher (2002), it was found that cultural tourism sites are only secondary attractions in Hong Kong as there were only 33% of tourists having participated in cultural tourism activities during their stay, with more than half of them being incidental or casual cultural tourists for whom cultural reasons played little role in their decision to visit the destination. While the cultural experiences these tourists pursued were different, most of them were looking for a shallow understanding of Hong Kong's cultural heritage. Their activities were also confined to icon attractions, convenience-based attractions located in inner city tourism areas, and purpose-built attractions such as theme parks. This reflects a high demand for commodified attractions from which cultural values can be consumed explicitly and possibly in an entertaining manner.

In examining the six source markets, namely Chinese Taipei, Mainland China, Singapore, the United Kingdom, the United States, and Australia, results from the study by McKercher and Chow (2001) showed that there were remarkable differences in the participation rates among different markets. While Western tourists demonstrated a higher propensity to participate in cultural tourism activities and regarded the opportunity to learn something about Hong Kong's culture as more important in their decision to visit, Asian tourists showed lesser interest in participating in cultural tourism activities and regarded cultural reasons as less important in their decision to visit Hong Kong. Although the motivation and psychographic factors showed significant differences between Western and Asian source markets, demographic and trip profile demonstrated no difference among tourists, which was opposite to what the literature suggested on the uniqueness of cultural tourists including higher spending power and longer stays (Canadian Tourism Commission, 1997; Leask & Yeoman, 1999; Silberberg, 1995).

While Asian markets contribute more than three quarters of all tourists to Hong Kong, Mainland China is now the number one source market and its share is expected to increase (Hong Kong Tourism Board, 2001). It is doubtful whether cultural tourism, as suggested by Mike Rowse, can be pursued as a key market for the Hong Kong tourism industry.

Unrealistic Expectation

In fact, most of the heritage sites promoted by the Hong Kong Tourism Board face the problem of under demand. A Heritage Tourism Task Force (HTTF) was established in 1998 responsible for developing and promoting Hong Kong heritage tourism. Although one of the components identified by HTTF in the development strategy is to take stock and identify distinctive heritage elements that may have tourism potential, it is interesting to find that the cultural heritage sites promoted by the Hong Kong Tourism Board in the promotion brochure titled *Museums and Heritage* includes a long list of 63 declared monuments and 20 museums found in Hong Kong. While some of the sites were popular among tourists, many of them were not even mentioned once by the respondents in the studies. The question becomes whether there is any demand for these unvisited sites and whether the sites have necessary potential to be developed as tourism products.

Physical Attributes

Some site managers felt that certain attractions promoted in the brochures, were not suitable as tourism products at all. One of the major reasons was that these attractions were not situated in accessible locations near downtown or tourist areas such that tourists might not gain access to them easily by public transport. The Hung Shing Temple is one of those remote attractions located on the island of Kau Sai Chau in Sai Kung. Having been recommended by the local community and then promoted by the Hong Kong Tourism Board and Mass Transit Railway, the temple was criticized in a local newspaper (Chan, 2001) as an attraction that tourists and local day-trippers found was almost impossible to reach by public transport. The promotional campaign, named "City of Life: Hong Kong is it!", highlighted 18 attractions where visitors could collect the chops and enter a lucky draw for prizes. However, some visitors felt frustrated and commented that the organisers should examine in advance the places before they came up with the recommendations.

Besides accessibility, size and scale were also important considerations as commented by some site managers. The example of Law Uk Hakka House and Folk Museum was given by the chief curator of the Museum of History. Owing to the small size and unattractive environment in which the building was surrounded by trucks, factories, and food stores, the museum was being considered for closure because attendance was dropping. Moreover, similar types of Hakka houses can be found elsewhere in Hong Kong. The curator thought that, although the museum was just five minutes walk from the subway station, the building suffered from lack of uniqueness and attractiveness to provide a compelling reason for tourists to visit within their short length of stay. Its limited size, scale, as well as space in the city centre, also imply significant limitations to expanding the existing facilities to enhance attractiveness.

Facilities and Services

Another comment from some site managers was that the attractions sometimes were oversold by outdated pictures and inaccurate information. The Ping Shan Heritage Trail was one of the attractions criticized in a local newspaper which found that construction sites and garbage were surrounding the trail and signage was not clear such that visitors might have easily got lost (Button, 2002).

When asking site managers whether tourism was an item on the agenda in their management plan, most of them indicated that tourists were welcome, but their operations would not specifically cater for tourists, as local audiences were their main market because of the public funding from the government. This probably accounts for the lack of facilities and services available for tourists on site. Although most of the museums provided pamphlets and leaflets in different languages, other facilities and services for tourists were inadequate, such as parking spaces, guided tours, and an information desk.

The lack of tourist facilities and services was even more common for religious sites. Although tourists would not be prevented from visiting the sites, all religious site managers claimed that their main objective was to serve the worshippers. Chi Lin Nunnery, which is a private premise, was one of the examples where tourism was not part of the management's considerations. Although it has been promoted by the Hong Kong Tourism Board as a tourist attraction because of its excellent Tang dynasty architecture, the Public Relations Officer of the Nunnery said that they had already mentioned to the tourism sector that Chi Lin is a religious place only and would not be considered for commercial use. However, the unexpected large number of tourists still places great pressure on the daily operations of the site. If the problem persists, tourists will not only cause disturbance to the Chi Lin, but also the overuse problem will affect the tourist experience.

Gaps Between the Stakeholders

Although cultural tourism necessitates input and partnership between tourism and cultural heritage management, gaps were found

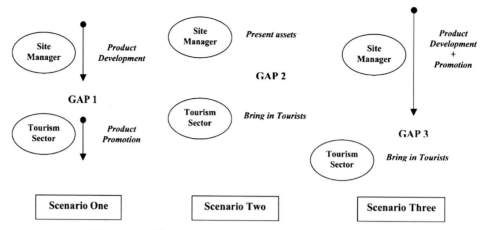

Figure 1   Three Scenarios in Cultural Tourism.

between the stakeholders, which is one of the key factors hindering the development of successful cultural tourism products. Three scenarios were identified as shown in Figure 1.

The most common scenario was that both sectors separately performed their own duties. While site managers regarded any operation of site development as their in-house issue, the tourism sector assumed the duty for all the promotion efforts. As such, the process of product development and product marketing were functionally separated by two sectors without knowing what the other was doing. The site managers were not aware of the market demand and the tourism industry was not aware of the intrinsic cultural value and interpretation of the assets. Without communication between parties, a wrong image is often shaped by the inappropriate messages conveyed by the tourism sector to the tourists.

The second scenario was that both parties did nothing for the tourists. The site managers simply presented and managed the assets while tourism operators brought in tourists and let them shape their own experiences. The lack of information, services and infrastructure made it hard for tourists to consume the product resulting in unsatisfactory or shallow experience.

In the last scenario, the site managers grew tourism alone without consulting the tourism sector about the market demand, or tourist profile and behaviour. Owing to the different nature of their discipline and their lack of training in tourism management, the lack of market information, the product was often not successfully developed. Without the input from the tourism industry, product development and marketing efforts were often inefficient and ineffective.

Conclusions

Buhalis (1999) indicated that destination marketing should consider the balance of the strategic objectives of all stakeholders involved in tourism development, as well as the valuable local resources. Besides, a successful marketing plan must lead to the optimisation of tourism impacts, especially on the host community. This paper explored the issues in relation to product development and marketing in cultural tourism.

In Hong Kong, most of the museums and all declared monuments are publicly funded and managed by two government departments, namely the Leisure and Cultural Services Department and the Antiquities and Monuments Office. Although subsidy level sometimes run up to 90% from which the heritage sites can operate without the need for a profit or return from the tourist market, site managers admitted that being a prominent tourist attraction could politically justify the values of the sites and secure future subsidies from the government. As such, site managers are willing and, sometimes eager, to have their sites promoted as tourism products.

However, in any of the identified three scenarios in Figure 1, the heritage sites being promoted as tourism attractions were virtually not meant to be tourism products. This paper demonstrates that misunderstanding the meaning of a tourism product and the goal of marketing is a major barrier to the success of cultural tourism as it can prevent both site managers and the tourism industry from achieving their desirable management objectives.

Based on the discussions, four factors leading to failure in cultural tourism development can be identified from this study. First is the lack of understanding of market demand. Not only does the final visitation involve tourists' participation, considerations of the tourists should start form the beginning for developing cultural tourism. The key step of cultural tourism development is the success of identifying the underlying needs of cultural tourists and introducing cultural tourism products into the mental map of tourists and eventually into their activity space (Jansen-Verbeke & Lievois, 1999). The challenge faced by tourism players and cultural heritage management is not only a matter of place marketing. Prior to any effort in cultural tourism promotion and communication is the understanding of the tourist attraction system and the way cultural heritage assets can become core elements of the destination tourist products. Understanding the market demand in terms of its nature and volume by analysing the tourist profile and preferences for activities they participate in and places they visit is therefore extremely important.

The second factor is the lack of asset evaluation. Knowing that there is huge demand for cultural experiences is not enough. How attractive the asset is and how much visitation the asset can withstand are also vital considerations. Before product development, there should be collective efforts in assessing heritage assets. This task cannot be done by site managers individually but should be directed by local governments to avoid duplication of products in which many sites are competing for the same groups of tourists.

The third factor is the lack of clearly defined management objectives and priorities. To recap, the essence of marketing lies on the idea of exchange. By knowing the tourists' needs and developing products to satisfy the tourists, site managers and the tourism industry aim to achieve their organisation goals. However, without clearly defined management objectives and priorities whether development or conservation should be emphasized, it is impossible for the development of cultural tourism to be successful.

The last factor is the isolation of product development. Ideally, marketing is a management philosophy guiding all aspects of an organisation. Product development, as well as product promotion should function together under the control of the same organisation. However, owing to the special nature of cultural tourism that two different disciplines are involved, isolation of product development often happens. Until these barriers are tackled, successful cultural tourism is less likely to occur.

References

Ap, J. & Mak, B. (1999). *Balancing Cultural Heritage, Conservation and Tourism Development in a Sustainable Manner.* Paper presented at the International Conference: Heritage and Tourism, 13th–15th December, Hong Kong.

Ashworth, G. J. (1994). From History to Heritage – From Heritage to Identity. In G. J. Ashworth & P. J. Larkham (eds), *Building a New Heritage: Tourism Culture and Identity in the New Europe* (pp. 13–30) Routledge, London.

Buhalis, D. (1999). Marketing the Competitive Destination of the Future. *Tourism Management*, 21(1), 97–116.

Button, V. (2002). Ramshackle Trail of the Unexpected. *South China Morning Post*, 3 March.

Canadian Tourism Commission (1997). *Fulfilling the Promise: A Report on Six Regional Round Tables on Cultural and Heritage Tourism.* Canadian Tourism Commission, Canada.

Chan, F. (2001). Tour Promotion Sites "an Obstacle Course". *South China Morning Post*, 15 October.

de Kadt, E. (1979). *Tourism: Passport to Development?* Oxford University Press, New York.

du Cros, H. (2001). A New Model to Assist in Planning for Sustainable Cultural Heritage Tourism. *International Journal of Tourism Research*, 3, 165–170.

Graham, B., Ashworth, G. J. & Tunbridge, J. E. (2000). *A Geography of Heritage: Power, Culture, and Economy.* Arnold, London.

Gunn, C. A. (1988). *Tourism Planning.* 2nd edn, Taylor and Francis, New York.

Hall, C. M. & McArthur, S. (1993). Heritage Management: An Introductory Framework. In C. M. Hall & S. McArthur (eds), *Heritage Management in New Zealand an Australia* (pp. 1–19). Oxford University Press, Oxford.

Haywood, K. M. (1990). Revising and Implementing the Marketing Concept as It Applies to Tourism. *Tourism Management*, 11(3), 195–205.

Hewison, R. (1988). Great Expectations-hyping Heritage. *Tourism Management*, 9(3), 239–240.

Hong Kong Tourism Board (2001). *Visitor Profile Report 2001.* Hong Kong Tourism Board.

Hughes, H. L. (1989). Tourism and the Arts: A Potentially Destructive Relationship? *Tourism Management*, 10(2), 97–99.

Jansen-Verbeke, M. & Lievois, E. (1999). Analyzing Heritage Resources for Urban Tourism in European Cities. In D. G. Pearce & R. W. Butler (eds), *Contemporary Issues in Tourism Development* (pp. 81–107) Routledge, London.

Kotler, P. (1997). *Marketing Management: Analysis, Planning, Implementation, and Control*, 9th edn. Prentice Hall, Englewood Cliffs, NJ.

Kotler, P. & Armstrong, G. (1991). *Principles of Marketing.* 5th edn. Prentice Hall, Englewood Cliffs, NJ.

Leask, A. & Yeoman, I. (1999). *Heritage Visitor Attraction: An Operations Management Perspective.* Cassell, New York.

Lowenthal, D. (1996). *The Heritage Crusade and the Spoils of History.* The Free Press, New York.

McKercher, B. (2002). Towards a Classification of Cultural Tourists. *International Journal of Tourism Research*, 4, 29–38.

McKercher, B. & Chow, B. (2001). Cultural Distance and Participation in Cultural Tourism. *Pacific Tourism Review*, 5, 23–32.

McKercher, B. & du Cros, H. (2002). *Cultural Tourism: The Partnership Between Tourism and Cultural Heritage Management.* The Haworth Press, New York.

McKercher, B., Ho, P., du Cros, H. & Chow, B. (2002). Activities-Based Segmentation of the Cultural Tourism Market. *Journal of Travel and Tourism Marketing*, 12(1), 23–46.

Middleton, V. T. C. (1994). *Marketing in Travel and Tourism.* 2nd edn. Butterworth Heinemann, Oxford.

Mill, R. C. & Morrison, A. M. (1985). *The Tourism System: An Introductory Text.* Prentice Hall, Englewood Cliffs, NJ.

Millar, S. (1989). Heritage Management of Heritage Tourism. *Tourism Management*, 10(1), 9–14.

Reynolds, P. (1999). Design of the Process and Product Interface. In A. Leask & I. Yeoman (eds), *Heritage Visitor Attractions* (pp. 110–126) Cassell, New York.

Richards, G. (1996). Production and Consumption of European Cultural Tourism. *Annals of Tourism Research*, 23(2), 261–283.

Shackley, M. (2001). *Managing Sacred Sites.* Continuum, London.

Silberberg, T. (1995). Cultural Tourism and Business Opportunities for Museums and Heritage Sites. *Tourism Management*, 16(5), 361–365.

Timothy, D. J. (1997). Tourism and the Personal Heritage Experience. *Annals of Tourism Research*, 24(3), 751–754.

Heritage Tourism and Community Participation: A Case Study of Sindhudurg Fort, India

Ilika Chakravarty

Introduction

Tourism is an increasingly complex and multi-dimensional social, political, economic, and ecological phenomenon. The realization of mutually beneficial interactions between the potentially conflicting expectations and aspirations of the tourists and those of the destination community presents myriad challenges and opportunities. Excessive or poorly managed development of tourism resources, including living cultures, can threaten the existence of the very base on which tourism survives (Mathieson and Wall, 1982). Ideally, tourism should benefit host communities and provide an important means and motivation for them to care for and maintain their heritage and cultural practices. In this context, the involvement and co-operation of local and/or indigenous community representatives, environmental conservationists, tourism operators, heritage enthusiasts, policy makers and other stakeholders becomes crucial for ensuring sustainable tourism development and the protection of heritage resources (Brooks, 2002; Timothy, 1998). Nowhere is this more

evident than in small islands and peripheral areas.

Small islands that are part of larger political units are often characterized by peripheral locations, fragile ecologies, small populations, traditional socio-economic structures, limited resource bases and under-developed infrastructure (Jordan, 2004; Liew, 1980; Weaver, 1998). In the absence of alternative forms of economic development, island economies often depend on tourism, more so if supported by significant cultural heritage resources. The ability of tourism to generate revenues and employment provides political and social legitimacy for the industry in such areas. However, increasing pressures on resources from tourists and the industry itself often deprive indigenous people in parks, historic sites and protected areas from using the resources as they become increasingly important tourist attractions.

Environmental capital, in terms of natural resources, and the more intangible and aesthetic constructs of landscapes, as well as built heritage, is clearly recognized as a platform for tourism development. Cultural capital is also being increasingly recognized as a foundation for growth. The economic benefits of tourism are the result of a fundamental process by which expressions and forms of environmental and cultural capital are traded. Conflicts over the exploitation, over-use, and contested use of environment and culture for tourism purposes have increased significantly in recent years. This has attracted considerable attention and led to wider public and political debates (Robinson, 1999). The tourist element in heritage has in many instances spawned contradictions. The growth of tourism and the commercialization of heritage have evoked controversial economic debates that often conflict with the conservation and educational goals of heritage places. Although tourists possess different motives for visiting historic sites, people who live in and around the sites have their own representations and attachments that often go unrecognised (Timothy, 1999). Heritage and heritage tourism are highly political phenomena (Hall, 1997; 2003; Timothy and Boyd, 2003). Often, powerful local and regional (even national or international) interest groups impose formal representations that disagree with the economic and ideological agendas of the resident communities themselves. This sometimes leads to conflicts between partners in the development process, possibly ending in alienation and at worst, violence (Porter, Sanday and Salazar, 2003).

In the context of cultural landscapes, tourism promotion, heritage preservation and site development involving planning and partnerships between governments, non-government organisations and local communities have gained considerable importance in recent times. Such associations have often helped in evolving issues of shared management, resolving challenges, and suggesting policy prescriptions for long-term development

(Wilkinson, 1989). Land ownership and economic opportunities constitute important goals for indigenous people in addition to cultural survival and right of self-determination (Johnston, 2003). Other issues, such as those related to sacred sites, are very much intertwined with indigenous attitudes toward, and involvement in, tourism (Brechin, West, Harmon and Kutay, 1991; Johnston, 2003).

The primary objective of cultural heritage sites is to identify, protect and preserve places and relics of historical importance. While tourism is economically beneficial to destinations at various scales, concerns over its environmental impacts and other effects on heritage sites are well founded. The rapid growth of culture-based tourism has resulted in culture primarily being promoted for economic, rather than cultural, ends (Richards, 1996). From a business perspective, cultural and heritage tourists are now considered a distinct market segment (Stebbins, 1996) that comprises a significant portion of demand ($>50\%$) for tourism products worldwide (McKercher and du Cros, 2002; Timothy and Boyd, 2003). The debate as to whether heritage and culture should be protected 'for tourism' or 'from tourism' has so far remained inconclusive.

Against this backdrop, this chapter examines issues related to a small indigenous community that lives within a heritage site in India (Sindhudurg Fort) and its prospects for benefiting from tourism, given its peripheral, dependant location, limited resource base and small population.

Sindhudurg Fort: A Profile

With an economy driven primarily by tourism, which has profoundly influenced the fragile ecology and ancient heritage, there is growing concern that the island fort of

Sindhudurg as a heritage site and tourist attraction is under severe threat from tourism and other forces of change. As such, it presents an ideal setting for examining the relationship between a tourism-based livelihood and heritage preservation through community involvement. The twin perspectives that emerge in this context are the cultural content of heritage preservation, which discourages the pure tourist appeal of the site and prescribes the promotion and development of alternative sites for tourism (Jayakar, 1997) and second, the synthesis of heritage conservation, tourism promotion and the economic interests of the community for sustainable development (Young, 1997). Although the two perspectives suggest alternative approaches to heritage tourism, the singular objective of conservation constitutes the crucial theme in both (Sengupta, 1998). Ownership and the role residents play in the management of their area in terms of designation and delimitation of protected areas, indigenous uses of existing resources, employment opportunities, and exclusion of visitors from specific sites, are other important concerns.

The coastal district of Sindhudurg is an economically depressed area in the state of Maharashtra. Its declaration as a 'tourism district' by the state and a Special Tourism Area (encompassing coastal Malvan) by the government of India in 1996 is the first instance of a district being selected for development focusing exclusively on a tourism-led strategy. The Malvan integrated tourism development plan has identified Sindhudurg District as having great potential (Tata Consultancy Services, 1998). Although the beaches in Tarkarli and Devbaugh appear to have been conceived as the main plank in tourism development in Malvan, Sindhudurg Fort has also been fingered as an important asset. Incidentally, the district derives its name from the historic sea

fort, *Sindhudurg*, built by the *Maratha* emperor Chatrapati Shivaji in 1664 AD on a rocky 48-acre island, 1.6 km from the Malvan coast. The fort bears immense significance to admirers of Shivaji, tourists, and other heritage enthusiasts. Seized by the British in 1765 and renamed Fort Augustus, construction of this maritime fort reflects the involvement of Shivaji on a site personally selected by him to counter the powerful *Siddhi* rulers of neighbouring Murud Janjira (MTDC, 1998). During the three-year building process no efforts were spared in ensuring that the sea would not encroach on the fort or allow the enemy to prevail (MTDC, 1995). Iron and lead were used for casting the foundation stones. The two-mile rampart walls are 30 feet high and 12 feet thick, and 52 semi-circular towers house a collection of cannons. The fort is presently in ruins except for a temple dedicated to its builder (built by his son Rajaram). Incidentally, this is the only shrine of Shivaji in the country, made more important by his hand and feet imprints on a limestone slab. In addition, there are temples in the fort dedicated to Hindu deities, such as *Maruti*, *Bhavani*, *Mahadeo*, *Jarimai*, and *Mahapurush*. There is also a small artificial beach – *Rani Tarabai* – on the island, that was built for the queen.

The island is forested, in contrast to the Malvan hinterland, and largely underdeveloped. It supports a small population of approximately 35 people in eight households. Different government departments administer different areas of the fort complex and are involved either directly or indirectly in its development. The heritage monument is under the jurisdiction of the Archaeological Survey of India (ASI), which oversees all construction and refurbishing and has been cited in recent years for the derelict condition of the fort. The Maharashtra Tourism Development Council

(MTDC) handles tourism promotion. The green spaces are administered by the Maharashtra Forest Department. The Port Authority manages the jetty from which boats sail to the fort from Malvan. Ferry operators run the boats, while the minor Ports Authority issues licenses for them. The District Collector and *tehsildar* (administrative officer) of Malvan in association with the *Sindhudurg Killa Rahivashi Sangh* – SKRS (village organization) – looks after the overall development of the fort and island. As an ecologically sensitive area, all developments are governed by Coastal Zone Regulations. Being a No Development Zone, permanent construction is not allowed within the fort premises.

Fort Residents

It is impossible to consider heritage conservation, tourism promotion or, for that matter, sustainable development on Sindhudurg without taking into consideration other areas of interest. To understand living conditions and resident attitudes to tourism, and in the complete absence of data from secondary sources, fieldwork was undertaken in February 2001 to establish baseline information about the small community and the heritage site it occupies. Interviews were conducted with all heads of households as well as with community leaders of the SKRS. In all cases, interviews were done with adult males because women were hesitant to come forward. Participants were asked about community views of tourism, socio-economic information, and other pertinent information about the community at large.

Group interviews were also conducted with SKRS members in public meetings. The SKRS members provided information about their present and proposed activities in heritage conservation, tourism promotion and environmental regeneration for improving the fort environs and local living conditions. They also provided information about difficulties on the island and suggestions for improving the situation. Based on the data collected, Table 1 provides a profile of the Sindhudurg village and its 35 residents.

The population has declined significantly in recent years. Birth and death rates and sex ratio figures for the island's population are not recorded by the Indian census. According to the SKRS, however, the population has declined from 104 (18 households) in 1981 to 35 (8 households) in 2000. Death and out-migration for work were seen as the principal reasons behind this declining trend. Six of the household heads reported male members of their families having migrated to Bombay/Mumbai and Goa for employment. In-migration appears to be non-existent.

There is a lack of adequate natural resources for local sustenance, and the absence of cultivable land on the island has restricted agricultural activities. As such, tourism was seen as the most viable source of income for most households. The spontaneous development of tourism and lack of government planning have collectively contributed to the predominance of petty tourism businesses. Fifteen men and six women (87.5 per cent of the total working population) derive their livelihoods from tourism-related occupations such as boatmen, tourist guides and vendors. The *pujari* (priest), carpenter, photographer and fishermen, are the other income categories. Otherwise, the island is largely devoid of skilled individuals in other occupations.

With a larger share in occupations and incomes, tourism-related work is expected to contribute substantially to the overall economic conditions of the community. A comparison between tourism and non

Table 1   Socio-Economic Profile of the Sindhudurg Fort Residents

Characteristic	Description of the characteristic	
Area	48 acres	
Population	Total	35
	Males	22
	Females	13
	Adults	25
	Children	9 (4 males, 5 females)
Population Density	0.72 persons/acre	
Households (No.)	18 (8 inhabited)	
Average Household Size	4	
Type of Family	Nuclear	5
	Joint	3
Age group of the Population	Less than 15	9
	15–30	8
	31–45	12
	46–60	4
	60 plus	2
Marital Status	Married	21
	Unmarried	12
Education Level	Literate	20
	Primary	9
	Middle/VIII	11
	Illiterate	15
Primary school	0	
Balwadi (children's school)	0	
Public Health Centre	0	
Water Supply	Wells	3
	Ponds	2
Power Supply	Electricity available	
Animal Assets	0	
Persons earning from tourism-based occupations (No.)	Total	21
	Males	15
	Females	6
Persons earning from non-tourist based primary occupation (No.)	3	
Income from tourist-based occupations (monthly)	Rs. 1,500 (approx.)	
Income from non tourist-based occupations (monthly)	Rs. 700 (approx.)	
Unemployed	2	

Source: Sindhudurg Fort resident survey.

tourism-based earnings indicates monthly incomes from the former being greater than the latter. Although tourism is the primary means of livelihood for most residents, about 12.5 per cent of the population is engaged in secondary activities. Hawking is most important among these, and all vendors selling to tourists are unlicensed. It is also unlikely to expect licensing in a primarily rural set up with a meagre population of 35 inhabitants. Fishing is the dominant non tourism-based occupation among the *Kolis* (fishers), the traditional residents of the region. However, economic necessity has also forced several non-*Kolis* to adopt fishing to make ends meet. This is despite the difficulties involved during the monsoons and the absence of good boats.

In terms of ethnic characteristics the residents form a fairly homogenous society. All of them speak *Marathi*, the regional language, in the local *Malvani* dialect. Most residents are Hindus except two Muslim families on the island. An interesting aspect is their participation in all matters of local interest. Regardless of caste or religion, all residents visit the temples within the fort premises and participate in community festivals (e.g. *Shivaji Jayanti, Eid* and *Holi).*

Living Conditions, Tourism Promotion and Heritage Conservation

Although the residents of Sindhudurg Fort are not poor in strict economic terms (as revealed from monthly expenditures), vulnerability exists on many fronts. Five of the eight mud houses with thatched roofs have only two rooms and there is a severe space shortage. Four houses are permanent concrete structures with tin roofs, a violation of ASI heritage guidelines. Seven household heads noted that they

had been living in the fort for generations and had no plans to relocate. Only one head of household informed that he owned land outside the fort, in Malvan. The residents are plagued by various civic problems, which have crippled tourism development on the island. There is a severe shortage of clean drinking water. The island's three sweet-water wells and two ponds as sources of potable water are unfit for drinking. Moreover, in winter, their water level reduces drastically, causing severe hardships for the local residents. Health care is often associated with water supply, and approximately 40 per cent of the residents were reported as having suffered from common water-borne diseases and stomach disorders, as apparently none of the families boil water before drinking it. Most of the houses lack toilets with running water. In the absence of adequate sanitation facilities, 85 per cent of the residents use open spaces for defecation. Domestic wastes, including non-biodegradable rubbish, are dumped inside the fort in places convenient to residents. Two households mentioned having dug pits in the back yard where litter was burnt at regular intervals. More than three quarters of the households use kerosene and firewood as fuel, which contributes to air pollution. There is no post office or telephone facility in the island. There are, however, good electricity connections.

Facilities for social development, which enhance human capital, are largely inadequate in Sindhudurg Fort. Nearly half of the residents are illiterate with only 11 having attended middle school in Malvan. The rest only made it to primary school. Presently the small primary school is closed with a previous enrollment of less than ten pupils, a high rate of absenteeism and a temporary teacher. With no secondary school to serve the small population, for those interested in pursuing higher education, Malvan remains the only option. Health facilities are also inadequate. There is no physician, public health centre or even a first aid centre on the island. Again, Malvan is the only option for regular treatment and emergency care. These issues are of utmost concern for island residents. According to them, a public health centre, a toilet, a school and a post office are the community's most imminent needs. This is in sharp contrast to most Indian rural settings where poverty and unemployment-related problems appear more urgent.

About three quarters of the population feel that tourist facilities are grossly inadequate and poorly managed on the island. The boats that transport tourists and residents to the fort are in bad condition. There are no accommodation facilities for tourists who might wish to stay overnight, and there are no pavilions or benches for tourists to rest on during their visit. Of the five residents working as tourist guides, three have received training from MTDC. Their fees vary between Rs. 40–50 during peak season and Rs. 25–35 at other times. The only person with a camera on the island takes photographs on request and charges a minimum of Rs. 50. Three temporary stalls sell food and drinks to visitors, which adds considerably to litter in the absence of garbage bins on the island. The pathway leading to the fort is also dirty and badly maintained.

A mere description of the social structure and living conditions fails to capture the interest of the community in tourism promotion and heritage preservation. During discussions with fort residents about their living conditions, inadequate civic facilities emerged as a crucial element. Residents noted that they wanted development of the fort and a change in their living standard not as an alternative to tourism but as a reasonable share in the existing tourism industry. Political manipulation by the state for economic gains has been evident through the Sindhudurg *Mahotsav*, the annual tourism festival, which was first organised by the MTDC in 1999. Although conceived to highlight the distinct cultural identity of the region, for some of the residents the festival is nothing more than a cosmetic facelift for the fort. The general feeling among residents was that the MTDC neither encouraged them to participate in the festival or share the monetary gains. Alienation of residents by the MTDC is viewed as a bureaucratic hold over the island, which has culturally distanced the small population from the positive elements of the festival. Moreover, the event has capitalized on the cultural rights of the residents. As an outsider, the MTDC often fails to understand indigenous institutions, although its effective management holds a crucial key in development. The local people cannot be divorced from the social structures of which they are a part. As such, new approaches to resolving disputes may be necessary if the community is to participate meaningfully and provide shared solutions to meet its needs and protect its traditional rights, which has been recognized in other parts of the developing world as a substantial concern (Johnston, 2003; Timothy, 1999). However, indigenous institutional arrangements may need reinforcing or rehabilitating so that they can meet the challenges of a changing world (Wall, 1999).

Members of the host society and tourists usually have very different relationships to the land and resources it supports. Thus, they have divergent attitudes concerning what can be shared or preserved, which activities are appropriate or inappropriate, whose heritage is being protected and the roles of indigenous and scientific knowledge in understanding and interpreting heritage. Such issues can easily lead to conflict between groups who value a site for different reasons and would like to use it in different ways and for different purposes. Power-related concepts of rights and ownerships often lead to cultural conflicts between the tourism industry and destination communities and are strongly influenced by the political-economic circumstances and the extent to which the communities are dependent on tourism. The political economy in Sindhudurg Fort is inextricably linked to unequal access to resources generated from tourism. For example, the *pujari* of the Shivaji temple suggested construction of a 340 m low-water rope bridge connecting Malvan town with the fort (160 metres from Malvan to Padamgad and 180 metres from Padamgad to Sindhudurg) to ensure easy access for tourists and residents during the monsoons. The toll tax collected from its use would generate revenues for the government. However, the proposal seemed against the interests of the boat operators, who viewed the bridge as a threat to their livelihoods. This clearly indicates an asymmetry of relations between the local elite and the masses who work for the tourism industry or between competing community groups and thereby accentuates differences and creates an apparent permanent backdrop for conflict (Craik, 1997).

Residents fear unrestricted tourist inflows (especially foreigners) would cause irreparable damage to the fort and their cultural identity and bring in social vices such as drug abuse, prostitution, and paedophilia. Some residents shared the view that it would be difficult to restrain foreign tourists from immodest sun bathing on the beach, which locals use for their daily activity space. Any act of trespassing by foreigners into their territory was feared to degrade moral values, particularly among the younger generation as already

evident in the beaches of nearby Goa (Brammer and Beech, 2004; Noronha, 1999). The likely impacts of tourism also evoked considerable resistance as regards changes in local resource-based lifestyles and livelihood patterns. With the government's thrust towards maximising economic benefits from tourism by attracting high-spending foreign clients, such apprehension seems justified. Yet, there were others who felt that foreign tourists should visit the fort and its surroundings to learn about its historical significance, bring in money for the local economy, and understand better the lifestyle of the inhabitants. The handful of residents who were not involved directly in tourism seemed to know little about what to expect from tourists as passive stakeholders.

Development of Sindhudurg Fort

The more a livelihood is dependent on tourism, the greater the need for strong coping mechanisms in the event of things going wrong. Communities that maintain a diversity of economic activities can more easily channel their time and assets into other activities. Their investments are also likely to be those that can be readily turned into cash as opposed to ones with long-term fixed assets. Working for others, migrating, and switching to alternative business activities to supplement incomes are the most common coping strategies among fort residents. Such a phenomenon becomes almost a reflex action, particularly during the monsoon months: a slack season for tourists and the tourist trade. Most respondents indicated diversification being particularly effective in the initial stages of decline as it helped in prolonging their survival while awaiting a possible upturn in tourist arrivals. Several factors influence the effectiveness of such coping strategies (e.g. skills diversity, management skills, access to land, credit, personal savings and markets through social networks), in enhancing opportunities for surviving annual declines (Kareithi, 2003).

State Involvement

Presently tourism at Sindhudurg Fort is not a financial burden for the MTDC. Conservation seems to have been accorded considerable priority as reflected in terms of financial allocation, with 91 per cent of the proposed investment. This far surpasses the amount allocated for the development of tourist facilities (Table 2).

However, for the ASI, a lack of adequate funds, administrative bottlenecks and sheer negligence have restricted renovation work on the fort's existing walls and towers. Although the foundations of the bastions still exist, most of the remaining structures are in ruins. The idol of *Jarimai* is missing, and the *Maruti* temple at the fort entrance lies in a derelict condition amidst a few cannons strewn about. The Padamgad Fort (200 metres away from Sindhudurg Fort), once used for constructing naval ships and protecting Sindhudurg, was in the past connected to Sindhudurg via an underground tunnel. This too lies in ruins. The forts of Ramgad, Yashwantgad Reddi, Sarjekot, Rajkot, Nivti Vengurla, Bhagwantgad and Bharatgad, also built for the protection of Sindhudurg Fort, are in dismal shape. The limestone slab with the hand and feet imprints of Shivaji is in an obscure corner of the fort and bears no plaque proclaiming its significance. As a result, it often goes unnoticed. Moreover, there is no signage highlighting the historical significance of Sindhudurg.

The most recent renovation work on the fort was undertaken in 1907 under royal patronage from the *Sahu* of Kolhapur. The offices of the ASI Superintending Archaeologist in Aurangabad (375 km away) and the Conservation Assistant in Panhala (180 km away) have achieved little as regards heritage preservation since that time. There is only one ASI guard in charge of the entire fort although residents petitioned for a full-time conservation assistant. Plans to improve the landing facilities have been abandoned by the Port Authority owing to cost considerations. Likewise, the State Forest Department has done little to improve vegetation cover on the island. The

Table 2   Investment Required For Developing The Sindhudurg Fort

Type of investment	Investment (in Rs.)	
Wooden Jetty at the Low Tide Level	2,00,000	(7.27%)
Monument Conservation	25,00,000	(90.90%)
Signage	50,000	(1.83%)
Total	27,50,000	

Note: Figures in parentheses indicate percentages of the total.
Source: Tata Consultancy Services, 1998.

MTDC with its limited financial and human resources has also failed to ensure adequate tourist facilities at the fort. Its seeming indifference to heritage preservation is also evident, with the fort being an ASI protected monument and technically outside its jurisdiction. Thus, an absence of bureaucratic coordination among different government departments and local policy makers, complexities of site management, and the potential of political conflicts are clearly visible. This has resulted in a piecemeal approach to development, with state interventions confined merely to verbal proclamations and delays in policy agreements and implementation.

Role of the Sindhudurg Killa Rahivashi Sangh

Established in 1999, the SKRS comprises 150 members including fort residents and others from outside. The organization has a head office in Prabhadevi (Mumbai) and a local office on the island. Donations are the main source of funding in addition to plays staged by its members in Malvan and other places. In 2001, the SKRS had a cash balance of Rs. 50,000. The SKRS was established with the objective of exerting community pressure on the state government in its development activities. Some 15 residents held the view that the government had been ineffective in solving the problems of the fort. According to one member, the concern of the community organization is not just the fort itself but, more importantly, its people-oriented and holistic approach to development. As such, the members wanted authority to look after their own place, improve their living conditions and gain a more equitable share from tourism.

With opportunities for resident participation in state-sponsored tourism appearing limited, the government should emphasize involving the local community in tourism development. Nineteen residents expressed their eagerness to participate in activities related to the beautification of the fort. They proposed cleaning the accumulated garbage and banning plastic from the premises. Development of a well-planned garden for ornamental plants was suggested, as was installing adequate signage to highlight the history of the fort. Others suggested a museum for the display and preservation of swords, cannons, and turbans associated with Shivaji. Besides being an added attraction for tourists, the museum could serve as an educational tool for students visiting on school field trips. Some members were eager to prepare models of ancient ships and boats that would highlight the naval history of Sindhudurg. Others suggested exploring the sea passage connecting the Sindhudurg and Padamgad forts. One member also proposed a *son-et-lumiere* (sound and light show) like the one at Shaniwarwada Fort in Pune (Maharashtra) funded by corporate sponsors. Some members also proposed the development of accommodation facilities for tourists wishing to stay overnight, although this would not be permitted by current heritage regulations stipulated for the fort. Some members were also eager to popularize sunrise and sunset trips to the fort for tourists by commencing special ferry services. Some boat operators proposed extending mooring times more than an hour to allow the tourists more leisure time to view the fort.

Local Participation in Community Development

Although most of the islanders seemed to be aware of the varied problems associated with

Sindhudurg, a social and moral responsibility for addressing the issues seemed largely absent. For instance, litter is a major problem for residents, further exacerbated by tourists' garbage, which invariably includes non-biodegradable plastics. Nonetheless, 40 per cent of the fort's residents did not think that tourist garbage posed a serious problem on the island. Residents' suggestions for improving the tourism product included reduction in ferry rates, improvement in water supply, better sanitation facilities, laying out attractive gardens, and constructing a bridge between Malvan jetty and Sindhudurg, thereby reflecting the livelihood-tourism equation in the perception of the community for the development of the fort.

Despite the lamentations of heritage degradation, the force of tourism seems to have its own logic. The majority of the islanders shared the view that they were surviving because of tourism. This has in turn built a strong awareness among them about the importance of tourism for the local economy. Nearly all of the residents expressed a willingness to participate as volunteers in community development programmes, such as re-forestation and garbage cleanup, and several noted their willingness to work as security guards. Others willing to work as tourist guides were keen to receive professional training from the MTDC. This reflected a willingness to improve their local area and living conditions. Some felt that it was important to educate the villagers and the tourists about the existing problems on the island and to seek participation in rescuing the fort.

Discussion and Conclusion

The uniqueness of Sindhudurg Fort rests on the fact that it represents a 'living' heritage monument where a population has been residing for generations. The equation between the heritage and tourism-oriented interests in the fort appears tricky and the challenges in reconciling the same may prove difficult. Protection of the heritage monument without any cultural invasion from the tourists and the generation of economic benefits from tourism for the resident community are the issues at hand. The primary responsibility for heritage conservation will have to be shouldered by the government (MTDC in particular), which needs to take advantage of the bonds shared with the site by local community groups like the SKRS. The multiplicity of government departments and their lack of co-ordination seem to be hindering development activities at the fort. There is nothing wrong *per se* in utilizing tourism as an instrument for development as it could be the least disturbing of development options. The host communities may freely choose tourism as an agent of modernization among other options (de Burlo, 1996). It is possible to protect heritage monuments through tourism promotion, which can generate revenues for conservation work when government funds are largely inadequate. However, tourism development should not be done to the extent that it destroys the heritage value of the fort. So far, tourism has not been a major cause of physical deterioration for Sindhudurg. Although the fort attracts a large number of tourists (excluding the monsoon months), to date they appear to have left the natural environment largely undisturbed. The thrust of tourism planners should be towards improvement of the tourism resource base of the fort so that tourism does not complicate and contradict the heritage element and pose additional problems in the future.

Heritage preservation if accompanied by tangible benefits for the residents would also have more socio-economic appeal than otherwise. The fort residents, although above the officially defined poverty line in India, presently seem to be living more of a subsistence existence. Their dependence on tourism as a primary occupation is severely affected by seasonality problems coupled with difficulties related to poor tourism infrastructure and civic amenities. The bureaucratic hold of the government on the fort also seems to have been distancing the community, as exemplified from the *Sindhudurg Mahotsav*. So far only lip service has been paid to tourism promotion and heritage preservation at the fort. As such, the threat to the local community's culture is almost non-existent. In the long term, assuming that the natural conservation policy is based on sound principles, it is reasonable to expect a diminution of environmental problems as litter accumulates. Involving the local community and the SKRS (both in their individual capacity and as a group to the mutual benefit of the wide range of disparate stakeholders) in the development process is more likely to succeed than fail in reaping long-lasting and sustainable outcomes.

Tourism involves introducing people with very different value systems into the areas inhabited by indigenous groups, which in turn raises questions concerning control over resources, the rights of indigenous people to determine appropriate uses of resources, their interests in becoming involved in or discouraging tourism development, and acceptable mechanisms for arriving at such decisions. In inter-cultural encounters, an already complex situation is exacerbated by lack of awareness, and/or misunderstandings of cultural behaviour, standards of language or of relational dimensions such as confidentiality or status. All these represent points of potential misunderstanding and conflict (Robinson, 1999). This too is overlain with a mesh of variables representing value systems, social classes, attitudes and patterns of tourist behaviour and those held by the host community. Thus, although tourism involves experiencing cultural differences, whether it is desired or not, the experience of difference has the potential to be rewarding, but at the same time, can induce fear often accompanied by desire and envy (Hall, 1987).

These encounters are characterized by relatively short and *ad hoc* periods of contact, a form of acting by both parties, in which they conform to their respective roles in leisure and work, and an implicit, if not explicit, moment of power on the part of the tourist (Robinson, 1999). In reality, relatively few prospective tourists seek total immersion in a different culture and few host societies seek to adapt wholly to the needs of the tourists. Instead, tourists seek safe glimpses of cultural differences, which may or may not be accompanied by a desire to understand the culture of one another. As such, the acculturation process, through the influence of foreign tourists, appears to be relatively limited. Thus, although direct tourist-host encounters may be limited, chances of indirect encounters are far greater and arguably more pervasive.

Community involvement in tourism is a positive element in regional development when it provides improved economic conditions and a gradual change in lifestyle for those who depend on it (Timothy, 1999). Furthermore, distributions of personal incomes from tourism may lead to improvements in living standards and thus limit the propensity to migrate to distant areas for employment (Brumbaugh, 1979). The most important aspect of any community-based tourism rests in ensuring ongoing community involvement. However, public participation demands considerable resources and time, which often prolong the planning process and paradoxically limit the degree of community participation in tourism. In many instances, local governments or corporations provide leadership to local communities in developing or expanding community-based tourism activities and in reaping mutual benefits from the same. However, the fear of loss of control by allowing more people with diverse interests to participate in the process often incites more conflicts, making the situation more difficult to control and less amenable for satisfactory resolutions.

References

Brammer, N. and Beech, J. (2004) Use and abuse of tourism: the Goan experience. *Tourism, Culture and Communications*, 5(1): 23–35.

Brechin. S.R., West, P.C., Harmon, D. and Kutay, K. (1991) Resident peoples and protected areas: a framework for inquiry. In P. West and S. Brechin (eds) *Resident People's and National Parks: Social Dilemmas and Strategies in International Conservation*, pp. 5–30, Tucson: University of Arizona Press.

Brooks, G. (2003) Heritage and Risk from Tourism, *Heritage and Risk 2001–2002*. Paris: ICOMOS International Committee on Cultural Tourism.

Brumbaugh, M. (1979) Paleohora, Crete: a case for grassroots tourism development. *Tourism Recreation Research*, pp. 23–26.

Craik, J. (1997) The culture of tourism. In C. Rojek and J. Urry (eds) *Touring Cultures: Transformations of Travel and Theory*, pp. 113–136, London: Routledge.

de Burlo, C. (1996) Cultural resistance and ethnic tourism on South Pentecost, Vanuatu. In R.W. Butler and T. Hinch (eds) *Tourism and Indigenous Peoples*, pp. 255–276, London: Routledge.

Hall, C.M. (1997) The politics of heritage tourism: place, power and the representation of values in the urban context. In P.E. Murphy (ed.) *Quality Management in Urban Tourism*, pp. 91–101. Chichester: Wiley.

Hall, C.M. (2003) Politics and place: an analysis of power in tourism communities. In S. Singh, D.J. Timothy and R.K. Dowling (eds) *Tourism in Destination Communities*, pp. 99–114. Wallingford: CABI.

Hall, S. (1987) *Minimal Selves in Identity: The Real Me*. London: Institute of Contemporary Arts.

Jayakar, P. (1997) Inaugural Address, Seminar on Elephanta Caves – Management of a World Heritage Site, (1st March), Indian National Trust for Art and Cultural Heritage, Mumbai, India.

Johnston, A.M. (2003) Self-determination: exercising indigenous rights in tourism. In S. Singh, D.J. Timothy and R.K. Dowling (eds) *Tourism in Destination Communities*, pp. 115–134. Wallingford: CABI.

Jordan, L.A. (2004) Institutional arrangements for tourism in small twin-island states of the Caribbean. In D.T. Duval (ed.) *Tourism in the Caribbean: Trends, Development, Prospects*, pp. 99–118. London: Routledge.

Kareithi, S. (2003) *Coping with Declining Tourism: Examples from Communities in Kenya*. Pro Poor Tourism Working Paper 13, Luton: University of Luton.

Keller, P. (1996) General trends in tourism today. In *Proceedings of the Round Table on Culture, Tourism, Development: Critical Issues for the 21st Century*. Paris: UNESCO/AIEST.

Liew, J. (1980) Tourism and development: a re-examination of tourism in the South Pacific. In D. Pearce (ed.) *Tourism in the South Pacific: The Contribution of Research to Development and Planning*, pp. 13–17, Christchurch: Department of Geography, University of Canterbury.

Mathieson, A. and Wall, G. (1982) *Tourism: Economic, Physical and Social Impacts*. London: Longman.

McKercher, B. and du Cros, H. (2002) *Cultural Tourism: The Partnership between Tourism and Cultural Heritage Management*. New York: Haworth.

MTDC (1995) *Tourism Policy for Maharashtra-1993*. Mumbai: Maharashtra Tourism Development Corporation.

MTDC (1998) *Integrated Tourism Development Plan for Sindhudurg District*, Final Report. Mumbai: Tata Consultancy Services.

Noronha, F. (1999) Ten years later, Goa still uneasy over the impact of tourism. *International Journal of Contemporary Hospitality Management*, 11(2/3): 100–106.

Porter, A., Sanday, P.R. and Salazar, N. (2003) Resolving conflicts in heritage tourism: a public interest approach. Paper presented at the Annual Meetings of the American Anthropological Association (22nd November), Chicago.

Richards, G. (1996) The scope and significance of cultural tourism. In G. Richards (ed.) *Cultural Tourism in Europe*, pp. 21–38, Wallingford: CABI.

Robinson, M. (1999) Cultural conflicts in tourism: inevitability and inequality. In M. Robinson and

P. Boniface (eds) *Tourism and Cultural Conflicts: Inevitability and Inequality*, pp. 1–32, Northumberland: Centre for Travel and Tourism, University of Northumbria.

Sengupta, C. (1998) *Elephanta Island-Heritage and Livelihood*, Report prepared for the Indian National Trust for Art and Cultural Heritage. Mumbai: Tata Institute of Social Sciences.

Stebbins, R. (1996) Cultural tourism as serious leisure. *Annals of Tourism Research*, 23: 948–950.

Tata Consultancy Services (1998) *Integrated Tourism Development Plan for Sindhudurg District*, I, Final Report. Mumbai.

Timothy, D.J. (1998) Cooperative tourism planning in a developing destination. *Journal of Sustainable Tourism*, 6(1): 52–68.

Timothy, D.J. (1999) Participatory planning: a view of tourism in Indonesia. *Annals of Tourism Research*, 26: 371–391.

Timothy, D.J. and Boyd, S.W. (2003) *Heritage Tourism*. Harlow: Prentice Hall.

Wall, G. (1999) Partnerships involving indigenous peoples in the management of heritage sites. In M. Robinson and P. Boniface (eds) *Cultural Conflicts in Tourism: Inevitability and Inequality*, pp. 269–286, Northumberland: Centre for Travel and Tourism, University of Northumbria.

Walters, G. (2005) Elephanta Island: world heritage, cultural conservation and options for nature conservation. In M. Hitchcock and D. Harrison (eds) *The Politics of World Heritage: Negotiating Tourism and Conservation*, pp. 176–180. Clevedon, UK: Channel View.

Weaver, D. (1998) Peripheries of the periphery: tourism in Tobago and Barbuda. *Annals of Tourism Research*, 25: 292–313.

Wilkinson, P. (1989) Strategies for tourism in the island microstates. *Annals of Tourism Research*, 16: 153–177.

Young, C. (1997) *On the Experience of Managing a World Heritage Site*. Paper presented in the Seminar on Elephanta Caves – Management of a World Heritage Site (1st March), Mumbai, Indian National Trust for Art and Cultural Heritage.

Part Three
Planning, Managing and Enterprise

Tourism Enterprises, the State, and the Construction of Multiple Dai Cultures in Contemporary Xishuang Banna, China

Jing Li

Ethnic Tourism, Modernity, and the Government-Guiding Principle

Achieving modernization has become a pivotal task for the Chinese state since the 1978 reforms. After highlighting the contribution of tourism to economic growth in government policies (CCP, 1993), tourism has been advocated as an appealing "short-cut" for the poverty-stricken, "backward" ethnic minorities. It is expected to assist minorities to catch up with China's market economy and modernization through the commercializing of ethnic cultures (Jiang, 1992a, b; Sofield & Li, 1998). The current West-Development policy of the state gives tourism in ethnic minority areas an even more important role by recognizing it as one of the major forces to promote economic prosperity in development blueprints for these regions (West Development Office of the State Council, 2002; He, 2002). The development of ethnic tourism, as part of the modernization agenda, is causing profound impacts on the

crafting of Chinese ethnic cultures and identities in this era (Guan, 1989; Swain, 1990; Oakes, 1998; Walsh, 2001; Li, 2003).

As an officially promoted industry in a socialist market economy, the development of China's ethnic tourism has shown the active involvement of different agents of control – the state, local governmental tourism bureaus, and tourism enterprises. The administrative decentralization trend in China's tourism after the late-1980s (Oakes, 1998; Wen & Tisdell, 2001; Zhang, 2003) enables local authorities and entrepreneurs to be more independent in the operation of the industry regarding the issues of investment, infrastructure construction, and the plural formats of tourism development in different regions (Xu, 1999). However, what occurs in most developing countries is that the state practices its macro-control power through direct or managerial or developmental involvement in the industry (Jenkins & Henry, 1982; Harrison, 2001; Timothy, 1999; Timothy & Tosun, 2003; Tosun, 2000). It is

the same case in China's tourism development in recent years. The state's policies or
programs regarding tourism development
effectively direct the practices of local governmental tourism bureaus as guiding rules,
and, further, shape the specific operations of
tourism enterprises with authorized, official
regulations (Zhang, 2003, p. 26).

In ethnic tourism, the power relationship
between these agents of control and their
specific administrative and commercial involvement in the industry strongly determine the
ways of staging, packaging, and further
re-producing ethnic cultures and identities in
tourist zones. This paper, using the Dai
Yuan – an officially supported tourism enterprise in Xishuang Banna (hereafter, Banna)
in southwest China – as a case study, explores
this proposition in the context of social and
economic reform in China. It seeks to clarify
how tourism enterprises manage and construct
ethnic tourist sites in a government-supervised
market at local level; how profit-driven enterprises play with the market and official
tourism bureaus in order to achieve both politics and economic capital; and, more importantly, how the possible collaboration
between the state and tourism enterprises
exert influence on the representations of
ethnic cultures and the local cultural reality
of ethnic groups.

The Dai Yuan

The Xishuang Banna Dai Garden Ltd Co. (*the
Xishuang Banna Dai Zu Yuan Youxian
Gongsi*, hereafter, the Dai Yuan) is located
in Menghan town (also called Ganlanba),
thirty kilometers from the prefecture capital
of Banna. The tourist site managed by the
Dai Yuan, the Dai Garden, is called
"premium or top quality works (*jingpin*)" of

exhibiting Dai minority culture in Banna's
tourism market. The particularity of the Dai
Garden lies in the fact that it consists of five
natural Dai villages: Manchunman, Manjiang,
Manting, Manzha, and Manga. The villagers'
way of life is displayed in the typical features
of Dai culture, including Dai-style bamboo
houses on stilt foundations, Dai cuisine, Theravada Buddhism and related religious activities, women's *xing* (Dai skirt) wearing and
hairdressing. The Dai Yuan built a splendid
gate at the entrance to the five villages to indicate the integrated nature of this destination.

As a local enterprise, the Dai Yuan has a
strong tie to the state-run Ganlanba Farm,
which is the largest state-run enterprise in
Menghan town and a branch of the Yunnan
Farm Bureau of the State. The Ganlanba
Farm played an important role in the foundation of the Dai Yuan. A private Guangdongese company initially invested the Dai Garden
in 1998. The Ganlanba Farm, with the
approval of the Yunnan Farm Bureau and
the coordination of the Menghan Town
government, became a co-investor when the
Guangdongese company was short of investment capital in 1999. With 60% of the stock
in the Dai Garden, the Ganlanba Farm also
appointed the executive manager. At the end
of 2000, the Ganlanba Farm purchased all
the stock and became the sole owner and operator of the Dai Garden.

On 28 January 2002, the Dai Yuan experienced one of the most significant moments in
its development since it started its tourism
business in 1999. The Dai Garden under its
management received the title of "the
AAAA-level tourist destination" in the nationwide government rating program presided
over by China's National Tourism Administration (CNTA). This is the highest rank in
the Chinese rating system of tourist sites.
After only a two-year development period,

the Dai Garden became the only AAAA-level ethnic tourist destination in Banna. Currently, it receives 350,000 tourists per year.

Tourist Sites Rating and the Government's Involvement in Banna's Tourism Market

CNTA launched the national rating program in late 1999 for the purpose of promoting high-quality tourist destinations in China (He, 2002:3), building the image of China's tourism, and accelerating the modernization and internationalization of China's tourism industry. As a policy-maker, CNTA promulgated *The Regulation for Rating and Evaluating Tourist Sites* (*Luyouqu [dian] Zhiliang Dengji de Huafen yu Pingding*, hereafter, *The Regulation*) in that year as a guideline for governmental tourism bureaus at different administrative levels to carry out the rating program nationwide. Specifically, all tourist sites in China that have formally registered and received tourists for over one year are eligible for participating in the governmental rating. Under the inspections of the national, provincial or local governmental tourism bureaus, tourist sites will be rated A, AA, AAA, and AAAA, according to the quality of the sites' tourist products (resources, landscapes, and events), services, environment and the degree of tourist satisfaction. *The Regulation* lists detailed criteria for each category and each criterion is given a grade. The sum of the assessed grades determines its rating level for that category. For example, *The Regulation* stipulates that an AAAA rating for a site's service and environment requires 800 grade points (the highest possible is 1000). While A and AA titles can be issued by regional tourism bureaus, the tourist sites who apply for AAA and AAAA titles will be inspected jointly by the national, provincial, and local tourism bureaus (Article 3, *Specific Methods For Carrying Out the Regulation for Rating and Evaluating Tourist Sites*). By 2002, 43 tourist sites nationwide had met the requirements for AAAA titles and 107 sites were rated AAA (He, 2002, p. 3).

The significance of being highly ranked in this program lies in the fact that governmental recognition is associated with augmented commercial value of the sites in the tourism market. In a government-guiding tourism industry, the governmental rating will bring prestige and authority for a highly ranked tourist site and promote its popularity in the market. CNTA will publicize top quality tourist sites both domestically and internationally through official promotion campaigns. CNTA also issues title plaques for the rated sites, which are required to be placed in an eye-catching position at the entrance of the sites and to be indicated clearly in tourist brochures of the sites. Therefore, receiving the AAAA or AAA plaque implies added political and economic capital for a tourist site to achieve or to strengthen its leading status in the market. The efforts of tourist sites to gain governmental recognition simultaneously reflect the macro control power of governmental tourism bureaus in terms of guiding the construction and management of tourist sites from top to bottom.

Being a branch of CNTA at the prefecture level, the Banna Prefecture Tourism Bureau (BPTB) has been actively carrying out the principles and policies of the central bureau to regulate Banna's tourism development since its foundation in 1991. The rating program has been emphasized as one of the major tasks on BPTB's work agenda since Banna formally started this program in September 2001. All the tourist sites in Banna were required to participate in the governmental rating. By early 2002, Banna had three AAAA tourist sites including the Dai Garden, two AAA sites, three AA sites, and two A sites. In his talk at the 2002 Banna's governmental tourism conferences, Shifu Li, the director of BPTB, further highlighted the importance of continuing the rating program and regarded it is a step leading to the professionalization and standardization of Banna's tourism industry (Li, 2002, p. 22).

Yet, the conducting of the rating program in Banna is not limited to promoting high-quality tourist sites. Pushing the governmental rating one step forward, BPTB also attempts to reinforce its administrative effectiveness in regulating Banna's tourism market, such as fighting against the commission-oriented operations and protecting the highly ranked sites to survive market competition.

After the opening of Banna to outsiders in the late 1980s, this mysterious borderland in the Chinese imagination became a well-known tourist destination because of its unique subtropical setting, rich fauna, colorful ethnic minority cultures, and border-crossing tours to Burma and Laos. In the early 1990s when Banna's domestic tourism market entered its rapid growth period, the commission-oriented behaviors and operations, also called "*huiyong*" (commission), which mainly involved tour guides, travel agencies, tourism enterprises managing tourist sites, and souvenir businesses started to emerge and formed a trend. To compete for more tourists, enterprises or businesses at tourist sites contended for establishing reciprocal relationships with travel agencies, tour guides, and bus drivers through sharing the profits from tourist expenditures. The Dai Yuan charged 35 RMB per person to enter the site with 25 RMB (70%) returned to travel agencies as *huiyong* in early 2001 when it had not received its AAAA rating. Tour guides received their *huiyong*

mainly in the souvenir shopping center of the Dai Garden by way of free meals, fruits, and a certain percentage of tourist expenditures.

Why do travel agencies and tour guides hold an advantageous position in the *huiyong* trend? It is closely related to their considerably powerful role in controlling the flow of tourists in Banna's tourism industry. Because tourist sites in Banna are scattered and cannot be reached by public transportation, most tourists have to depend heavily on tour groups organized by local travel agencies during a three- or four-day stay in Banna. Travel agencies usually provide a complete set of tourist services, including assigning guides for tour groups, designing itineraries, arranging transport and accommodation, and visa applications for border-crossing tours. The assigned tour guide is required to accompany each group throughout trips from arrival to departure. During tours, the guide is in charge of specific activities of a tour group, including making changes to itineraries, deciding where to shop for souvenirs, where to eat, how long to stay and what to see at a site. Unfamiliar with the destinations, tourists tend to follow and trust tour guides' opinions or suggestions on values of sites, making purchases, or even choosing the best spots for taking photos. Thus, travel agencies and tour guides have tightly controlled the flow of tourists and influenced tourists' expenditure since the inception Banna's tourism industry due to the geographical distribution of Banna's tourist sites. Tourist sites, whose successes are largely determined by the number of tourists received, have employed the *huiyong* system to allure the favors of travel agencies and tour guides to increase the number of tour groups. The fact that tour guides with most travel agencies in Banna are unpaid, contracted employees also solidifies the *huiyong* system because it is essential income for those involved in profit sharing. Without acceptable commissions, travel agencies or tour guides could alter their itineraries to bypass certain attractions and thus threaten the survival of tourist sites in the market.

The *huiyong* behaviors and operations in the past decade have led to a diminishing consideration of tourists' interests and to a deterioration of product quality in Banna's tourism industry. In the author's fieldwork in residence from 2001 to 2002, there was a popular saying among tourists "If you never visit Banna, you will always regret it (*budao Banna zhongsheng yihan*), but if you do visit Banna, you will always regret it (*daole Banna yihan zhongsheng*)". Complaints from tourists about the quality of the sites and some commission-oriented behaviors were exposed on national television and other mass media. This endangers Banna's image as a domestic destination, as well as its economic development, given that tourism is one of Banna's leading industries. Furthermore, the *huiyong* system directly works against the ultimate goal of the governmental rating program, which is to promote high quality tourist products and experience. The AAA or AAAA ratings with their associated prestige and governmental support, to a great extent, improve the commercial value of the sites in the market. However, the rated sites still face the dominant game rule of *huiyong* in Banna's tourism industry that is oriented by the percentage of profit sharing instead of the qualities of the sites. Thus, after the rating program started in late 1999, the tourist sites, including those rated AAA or AAAA, insisted on keeping the *huiyong* practices. The *huiyong* system endows travel agencies and tour guides with more control of the tourism market than governmental tourism bureaus in terms of what will be displayed for tourists. Banna's tourism images and

tourist products are consistently devalued and dissociated with their notoriety of being associated with the *huiyong* trend.

The negative impacts of *huiyong* practices have caused BPTB considerable anxiety and pushed it to seek effective regulations of tourism through administrative intervention. After Guangwei He, the director of CNTA, emphasized putting tourism in order as a major task of China's tourism development in his keynote talk at the 2002 annual national governmental tourism conference, BPTB endeavored to practice this principle in its work agenda by drafting and promulgating restrictive polices to macro control the tourism market. One of the most influential regulations is *The Management for Rated and Designated Tourist Sites* (*Dengji Dingdian Guanli*), which refers to preferential regulations for the rated and designated tourist sites. Policy implementation through regulation has been effectively applied to tourism since April 2002. Mainly, BPTB designates the AAAA and AAA rating sites as "must-visit" destinations on tour itineraries. The regulation forbids travel agencies taking tour groups to non-rated sites. To fully exhibit Banna's top quality tourist sites, tour groups visiting the AAAA sites must be guided by the sites' tour guides rather than travel agency guides to guarantee tour quality and length of time at the site.

By designating and protecting AAAA sites with administrative authority, the regulation places these sites advantageously in Banna's tourism market through increasing their control of tour groups. The AAAA sites can be secure in receiving desired numbers of tourists without playing the game rule of *huiyong*, which equals "a green aisle" for their further economic growth and for improving the construction of tourism products (discussed in detail later). With the regulations, the Dai

Yuan stopped giving commissions to travel agencies in April 2002 and significantly lightened its burden of investment capital in the early stage of development. Wenwu Fan, the president of the Dai Yuan, praised the regulations as a way of standardizing the market and sustaining the development of the best-qualified tourist sites (conversation with Fan on 28 March, 2002). The AAAA rating and its associated prestige and governmental support result in tangible and significant economic and political capital for the preferentially positioned sites.

BPTB's efforts to combine the governmental rating and market regulating in *The Management for Rated and Designated Tourist Sites* reinforces its bureaucratic power to interfere with market operations. Its designation and protection of "must-visit" sites influence the relationships between travel agencies and enterprises managing tourist sites and among tourist sites themselves in Banna. A or AA tourist sites, which are primarily theme parks or entertainment parks, argue against their unequal status since BPTB only protects AAA or AAAA sites from *huiyong* practices. It will intensify *huiyong* practices when the lower level sites struggle to receive more tourist groups controlled by travel agencies and make their survival more difficult in the market. Moreover, when the market economy makes its way in China, the degree to which governmental tourism bureaus should exercise their administrative power through regulations of the tourism industry also causes debate among some tourism entrepreneurs and officials in Banna. It is argued that the market forces are more effective regulators of quality than government control functions or formal regulations. BPTB as a governmental bureau holds a contrary opinion though some of its officials disagree on its stance. However, it is such a sensitive topic in BPTB that the disagreement never emerges on the surface to the best of the researcher's knowledge. BPTB acts as an active follower of the state's guiding principles attempting to achieve the goal of regulating the market and building up Banna's tourism brand image as a quality destination.

The Title Makes a Difference: Tourism Enterprises and the Inventing of Multiple Dai Cultures

Among the three AAAA tourist sites in Banna, the Dai Yuan is the only one dedicated to displaying Dai ethnic culture with which Banna's popularity is always associated as a famed destination in China (Blum, 2001; Wen & Tisdell, 2001). *The Management for Rated and Designated Tourist Sites* turns the Dai Yuan into the only officially authorized site to present "authentic" Dai culture to tourists. What does this golden AAAA title, which denotes the high quality of the site's tourist resources, mean to the Dai Yuan when it packages the Dai villages as a tourist fairyland?

The Dai Garden is based on five natural Dai villages that are famous for the Dai-style bamboo houses, the subtropical yard scene, and the Dai's village life. Yet, the Dai Yuan did not actively promote these resources before its participation in the governmental rating program in late 2001. Instead, consistent with the dominant representations of Dai culture in Chinese society, the Dai Yuan tended to produce a fragmented showcase through staged performances and events to present a feminized, exotic, and timeless Dai culture.

Prior to the application for the AAAA rating, tourist activities in the Dai Garden were basically confined to a square called "the Center for Dai Folk Performances" built between Manchunman and Manga. The Center contained a large-scale theatre for staged dance performances, a fountain square for tourists to participate in the water-splashing event, and several Dai-style houses for a staged Dai-wedding ceremony. In tourist zones, the colorful *xing*-wearing Dai women occupied the central stage, greeting and entertaining tourists with their singing and dancing. Several groups of young girls took turns splashing in the water with tourists on the fountain square of the Center. The water, laughter, and Dai young girls' liveliness and vigor were intertwined for the tourists' enjoyment. In the staged performance of the Dai wedding ceremony, male tourists were encouraged to experience the custom by "marrying" a *saoduoli* (beautiful young girl) in the show. The show would ask the "bridegrooms" to purchase a piece of pre-prepared jewelry, such as ring, silver belt, or jade bracelet, for their "brides". After the ceremony, the "bridegrooms" received their "wedding photos" with that year's calendar printed on the lower half of the paper as a souvenir. The beauty, affection, and sexual attraction of Dai women were packaged and labeled as a desirable commodity for tourist consumption. As the designer and director of these events, the Dai Yuan, by employing the centered and idealized image of Dai women as an ethnic symbol, presented a feminized exotic Dai culture in the showcase.

Another ethnic symbol highlighted to increase the distinctiveness of Dai culture in the Dai Garden was Theravada Buddhism before the rating. The Manchunman Theravada Buddhist Temple enjoyed great favor in Banna's tourism with its unique wooden structure and noteworthy position in the history of Banna's Theravada Buddhism. The temple had been open to tourists since the inception of Banna's tourism industry in the late 1980s, but the village elders who were in charge of religious affairs and the temple priests insisted on keeping the management of the Dai Yuan outside of the temple walls. The Dai Yuan was only allowed to rent the open space in front of the temple entrance to serve tourists. Groups visited the temple with their tour guides and developed their understanding of the temple and Theravada Buddhism from their guides' commentaries, given that the temple did not give much information on its uniqueness except a brief introduction to its history on a bulletin board. Based on the author's participation in a tour group in September 2001 and observations after starting residency in the village, the temple tour typically included a 15-minute (or shorter) visit to the main hall looking at the indoor wooden structure and the Buddha figure or burning incense sticks in front of the Buddha for blessings. Tour guides, who accompanied their groups in the tour of the hall, commonly emphasized things that were foreign to most Han Chinese and their understanding of Buddhism, such as meat in the diet and the custom of living as a monk for a period of time in a man's life. Many guides even quoted a popularly circulated, but inaccurate, saying "A Dai monk can have a girlfriend" in Banna to intensify the exoticness of Theravada Buddhism. The cultural significance of the custom of sending young boys to the temple and the important role of Theravada Buddhism in the Dai people's lives were erased from the presented picture of the temple and the robe-wearing young monks. What impressed tourists was the exoticness of the land where they saw the young faces in the dim temple and listened to the chants flowing in the shade of tropical tress. The Dai Yuan, who staged tourist activities in front of the temple, did not make efforts to promoting a better understanding of Dai Theravada

Buddhism. It provided two stalls serving to take photos of the temple for tourists to perpetuate their experiences, although the whole tour in the Dai Garden lasted about 45 minutes or less than one hour.

In this tour, few tourists had the opportunity to walk into the villages or even to talk to the villagers who built the elegant bamboo houses and practiced Theravada Buddhism in the temple. Tourists were guided to experience Dai culture through the young girls' dancing, the water splashing, and the monks' chanting – all of which presented a fragmented picture signifying a joyful, feminized, and exotic fairyland where "the culture of the Dai for over 1,000 years deposits" (Dai Yuan, 2002, p. 96).

Most surprising, however, was that Dai Yuan's managers were well aware of their showcased representations of Dai culture when the author discussed with them her own experience of visiting the Dai Garden as a member of a tour group. The managers claimed that their construction of the site was not directed by the goal of presenting top quality tourist events but the need to survive Banna's *huiyong*-oriented tourism economy. As mentioned above, travel agencies and tour guides tightly controlled the flow of tourists due to the scattered distribution of Banna's tourist sites and thus determined where tourists would visit. To compete for the business of travel agencies and tour guides, the Dai Yuan, as well as other tourist sites, not only returned a certain percentage of the ticket profits to travel agencies but also tended to promote the *huiyong*-generating tourist events at the site to attract tour guides such as the staged Dai wedding ceremony. In the performance, tourist-bride-grooms were asked to purchase a piece of jewelry for their "brides" as a wedding gift, and tour guides who brought the tourists to

attend the show would share a certain ratio of this expenditure. The same *huiyong*-oriented activities also occurred in the souvenir shopping center of the Dai Garden. Still, the Dai Yuan's managers complained that some tour buses did not even enter their site because of fewer *huiyong*-involved events compared to other sites. Thus, despite fully understanding the value of the village life-centered tourist events, President Fan and Chief Manager Deng pointed out that they had to consider market demand above the integrity and quality of presented tourist events. Unless taking control of tour groups, the Dai Yuan had to rely on the force of commission to receive more tour groups and prolong lengths of stay.

The operation "choice" of the Dai Yuan in representing Dai culture pushes us to dwell on the academic critique of the showcased representations of a culture in the tourism industry, which has been extensively discussed since Greenwood's perspective of "Culture by the Pound" (Greenwood, 1997; Van de Berge & Keyes, 1984; Picard, 1993). Scholars condemn that ethnic cultures tend to be romanticized and standardized as unchanging, exotic, and pleasant (Adams, 1984; Silver, 1993; Linnekin, 1997). Tourism entrepreneurs are regarded as an essential actor in producing stereotyped images and causes the fetishization of a culture (Mowforth & Munt, 1998). However, this perspective does not fully reveal what drives tourism entrepreneurs to represent a culture in a particular way in tourist zones. In addition to satisfying tourists' thirst for authenticity in ethnic tourism, tourism enterprises, being a knot in the market network, constantly adjust their operations to accommodate change in their positions in the industry and relationships with other sectors. In the case of the Dai Yuan, its unfavorable position in controlling tour groups in the *huiyong*-oriented tourism market, to some extent, limits its efforts to promote top quality tourist products. By the same token, BPTB's administrative regulation of Banna's tourism market, such as the governmental rating and *The Management for Rated and Designated Tourist Sites*, unavoidably changes the Dai Yuan's construction of its site by influencing *huiyong* practices.

With the filtering of the national rating program of tourist sites to the provincial and local levels, improving the quality of tourist events and landscapes becomes a core issue for tourism entrepreneurs required to participate in the rating program in Banna. In late 2001, the Dai Yuan applied for an official evaluation of its candidacy for an AAA-level tourist site. To serve this goal, it developed new tourist activities and redesigned its tour route to bring the Dai's village life and folk arts to the foreground.

The new route goes through two villages that are most accessible from the main entrance of the Dai Garden. After a group of tourists steps out of buses, a tour guide of the Dai Yuan dressed in Dai costumes will bring the group to the heart of where the villagers live. On the winding road that connects one bamboo house to another, the guide will introduce the names of different kinds of subtropical trees, fruits, and flowers blossoming in the villagers' luxuriant yards. In some yards, one or two Dai villagers are working on silver jewelry crafting while some old secularized monks are carving Theravada Buddhist scripts on dried palm leaves with an iron made pen. Tourists will learn the history of Dai Theravada Buddhism and the production and preservation process of Buddhist scripts from the guide. Along the road, tourists can also observe the Dai's traditional production skills of sugar pressing, thread spinning, and cloth dyeing performed by the villagers.

Tourists are encouraged to try the tools with the help of the villagers. From time to time, tourists can hear beautiful melodies of Dai gourd flutes and folksongs echoing in the villages. The last stop is the Manchunman Theravada Buddhist temple where tourists will learn the legends of the Buddha, mural stories, and some important religious rituals and festivals of the Dai people from the guide. Dance performances, once held in the theatre before the route was re-designed, are relocated to the open space in front of the temple. Tourists can appreciate the dances up close. Some of them even stood among the performing dancers to take photos to memorize their experiences. Various aspects of Dai culture are presented and integrated into the natural scene of the villages. The direct interactions between guests and hosts strengthen the connection between tourists and the landscape when tourists walk through the picturesque villages. Particularly, the Dai Yuan employs some native villagers as tour guides. The guides can tell tourists in which bamboo houses they live, which school they attended, which of their brothers serve as monks in the temple, at what age they start to learn gourd flute playing, and that the old man who is carving Buddhist script is his/her grandfather. Their presence and narratives greatly increase the sense of authenticity as an integral part of the village life.

The presented scenes, of course, do not escape from the tendency to narrow the totality of Dai culture down to a collection of artistic expressions, not to mention the failure to represent the diversity that asserts competing economic and political interests of ethnic groups (Wood, 1984; Picard, 1997). Yet, compared to the feminized and exotic showcases in the previous representations, the newly designed route endeavors to present a relatively complete, rich and contexualized Dai culture that cannot be duplicated or fabricated in any theatre, theme park, or staged performance. The Dai Yuan intends to perform the Dai culture on an invisible stage that is structured on the ideal of the villagers' ordinary life.

As the producer of different tour routes, the Dai Yuan demonstrates its power to determine how to stage and represent Dai culture in tourist zones. But its representations are conditioned and shifted by its position in Banna's tourism market, which is further effectively controlled by governmental bureaus. At the AAAA plaque-awarding ceremony of the Dai Yuan in January 2002, the officials from Banna's tourism bureaus, the prefecture and township governments, and the Ganlanba Farm toured the new route to show their approval and support to the Dai Yuan's marketing of Dai culture. This gesture reveals the powerful role of governmental tourism bureaus in macro controlling the tourism market and thus influencing the ways in which tourism entrepreneurs stage and represent a minority culture. In Banna, the governmental rating of tourist sites and BPTB's preferential regulations for the highly-rated tourist sites like the Dai Yuan directly result in the construction of multiple versions of Dai culture in tourist zones.

Role of Cultural Protector: Modernity and Traditionality

As a tourism enterprise that manages five villages, the Dai Yuan not only has the authority to represent the villagers' culture in tourist zones, but it also actively constructs the cultural reality of the villages through its ideology-laden operations.

The slogan "to protect [Dai culture] is to develop [Dai culture] (*Baohu Jiushi*

Fazhang)" is defined as the fundamental principle in the Dai Yuan's management approach.

To preserve (*baochi*) the rich folk customs; to preserve the typical architectural feature of the Dai minority – the Dai-style bamboo houses; to retain the traditional lifestyle of the Dai and their guest-receiving etiquette; to protect historical relics and the Dai religious culture; to design and to package the excellent (*youxiu*) Dai ethnic culture as a whole and to create a unified [cultural] image; make efforts to turn [the Dai Garden] into a historic and cultural heritage in China and even in the world; to make it serve tourism in a better way (Dai Yuan, 2001, p. 150).

For the purpose of presenting cultural heritage and serving tourism, the issue of developing Dai culture means the preservation of Dai culture – especially its traditional and ethnic characteristics. The specific operation of preserving Dai culture is carried out in two ways. One is to promote the revival of Dai culture through organizing festivals or cultural events for the villagers. The other is to regulate cultural "alienation" to guarantee the "purity" of Dai culture.

As the powerful sponsor and organizer, the Dai Yuan has arranged and invented various events to produce more tourist programs and to revive Dai traditions. On 15 April 2001, the Chinese Central Television (CCTV) successfully broadcasted a one-hour live documentary on the grand Dai New Year celebration in the Dai Garden. The Dai Yuan was one of the main agencies involved in designing celebration activities and directing the villagers as performers in the process of broadcasting. It rearranged the times and locations of some activities and required all the young villagers to attend specific events, such as the water-splashing event, to enhance the joyful atmosphere of the festival. Though the show kept silent about how the festival was organized to maintain the "authentic" or "natural" picture it depicted, it could not erase the fact that the Dai Yuan has been an active force shaping the cultural production of the Dai's most important festival in the local area.

The villagers seem to accept readily the Dai Yuan as part of their cultural practices. The VCD version of CCTV's one-hour live show of the Dai New Year celebration is popularly circulated among the villagers. They watch it repeatedly with excitement, especially when they see their relatives, friends, or themselves on the show. In other cultural events organized by the Dai Yuan, the villagers also show their strong interest in participation. One of the most influential events is the folk performance competition held among the five Dai villages in the Dai Garden in early 2002. Each village participated in the competition as a unit, and all the participants were required to perform ethnic programs with "ethnic characteristics (*minzu tese*)". The villagers were motivated to be part of this event mainly because the Dai Yuan set up monetary prizes for winners, but in the process of designing programs, training performers, and rehearsing for the competition, the villagers showed their enjoyment in the demanding practices. The performers, mostly women, would not miss the practices every evening unless their household duties were not finished. The Dai people are famed for their singing and dancing talents, but most cannot perform Dai songs or dances without professional training. The practices for the competition became an opportunity for the villagers to learn their own culture and entertain themselves. The learned dances or songs are continuously performed in various occasions for village affairs held by the villagers themselves after the competition. The Dai Yuan's role in

producing the local cultural reality is greatly enhanced with the villagers' willingness to be involved.

Yet, the process of cultural revival or production in the Dai Garden is selectively and ideologically directed compared to what occurs in many other Chinese minority areas (Schein, 2000; Mueggler, 2002). After the promulgation of the 1984 minority law, the state has shown a lenient attitude to ethnic affairs. Ethnic minorities are encouraged to revive their culture and to display *minzu tese* as the family members of a multi-national China. However, not all the aspects of ethnic culture are supported or accepted in the process. What should be promoted is evaluated against certain official or dominant (Han) ideologies (White, 1998). Among these, the discourses of nation building, upholding the Party's government, and achieving modernity run through the Dai Yuan's practices of cultural revival as a salient theme.

With the need to cooperate with the government to gain political capital, the Dai Yuan is well aware of advocating the official discourses of the state in organizing cultural events. In the folk performance competition mentioned above, all five villages chose to perform Dai songs which praise socialism, the improvement of Dai living conditions under the Party's leadership, and the management of the Dai Yuan. The songs were composed and written by a Manchunman villager, a master of Dai folksong in the local area. This villager was also employed by the Dai Yuan to work for the performance department including composing songs or instructing gourd flute playing. Through adopting some melodies of Dai folksong, this master filled in the "right and good" content to teach the villager performers. Here, the "right and good" content referred to the messages that accorded with the official discourses of the state. In the songs, the Party was described as a leader and protector who brought happiness for the Dai ethnic group. "The benefits of socialism and tourism benefited every household like wind blowing through the villages and stars shining from the sky. We [the villagers] would love the Dai Yuan and keep it clean and beautiful in the way we took care of our eyes".

According to the composer's viewpoint that was identified by other villagers, the songs with a "right and good" content would most possibly receive higher scores in the competition because the Dai Yuan's managers served as judges of the villagers' performances. The perceived need to gain favor with Dai Yuan illustrates the authoritative image of the Dai Yuan – not the Dai villagers – who can determine what kinds of songs would be encouraged and produced in the process of cultural revival.

The value-laden messages of the songs are further and repeatedly distributed when the villagers perform the learned songs in similar cultural practices, such as the events organized for celebrating national holidays. On 1 October 2001, the Chinese National Day, the Dai Yuan held a Karaoke competition and a dance party with the participation of the villagers, the frontier soldiers of the People's Liberation Army posted in Menghan, and its employees. In his opening speech, Wenwu Fan, the president of the Dai Yuan, emphasized the status of the Dai as a minority on the borderland and the importance of making progress together with other ethnic groups in China. The villagers did not participate in the competition, but they were invited to perform the nationalism-tuned Dai songs for the audience. The main stage was dominated by Mandarin songs and fashionable singers wearing jeans and tight tops. In celebration of the Chinese National Day, the Dai as a whole are presented in contrast to

being Han Chinese and being modern. The scene where the *xing*-wearing Dai girls danced with the soldiers in military uniform vividly illustrates the imbalanced relationship between the two sides. To the villagers who only performed the learned songs and then applauded for others' performances as viewers, this event becomes an occasion for them to experience the distance between the center and the margin, the modern and the traditional through entertainment. The Dai Yuan, the organizer and judge of the performances, functions as an effective "speaker" of the government conveying and disseminating the message of nation building and the marginalized status of the Dai minority.

With the discourse of depicting the Dai ethnic group as the opposite site of modernity, to preserve "authentic" Dai culture is to rule out cultural assimilation or "alienation" to guarantee its "pure" ethnic and traditional features. As Fan (2001, p. 152) points out, "... facing the onslaught of modern culture, ethnic culture that is engendered in a specific living environment will be assimilated in a unavoidable way. In order to prevent the negative influences on the development of the Dai Garden from cultural assimilation, it is necessary to maintain the purity of the Dai ethnic culture".

The modernization trend had entered the villagers' lives in Menghan region long before the existence of the Dai Yuan through education, mass media, public health, and a series of economic and political movements and reforms. However, it is the arrival of tourism that accelerated the process of modernization in the villages. Tourists come with their cameras, money, and higher education and present a different world. Tourism also creates opportunities for the villagers to change their farming-based traditional lifestyle. Before large-scale tourism enterprises like the Dai Yuan entered the villages, some Han business people and a few villagers had started tourism businesses including the Dai house visiting, petty trade, or food stalls. With the inception of the Dai Yuan and the further development of tourism in the past several years, some villagers – especially in Manchunman – have stopped farming and become fully engaged in tourism-related businesses. Meanwhile, the Dai Yuan also employs some villagers and helps some households in the villages construct modern bathrooms and solar bathing equipment to serve visiting tourists. The profits from tourism, as well as the income from farming and rubber tapping, allow many Dai villagers to modernize their lives in a down-to-earth way, such as purchasing the wall-to-wall combination cabinets that are popular in Banna's urban areas, VCD players and motorcycles. Even for less-affluent families without economic strength, the trend-following habit is so powerful in the villages that almost all families have similar house decorations and modern furniture. The pursuit of modernity is quite visible in the villagers' daily life.

While tourism effectively promotes the discourse of modernity in the villages, it also produces a dilemma for its own development – especially in the case of the Dai Yuan whose tourist resources contain the totality of the Dai villagers' daily life. A corresponding tension between the pursuit of modernity and the preserving of tradition is intensified in the destination community. The intension started to cause anxiety in Dai Yuan management when a Manting villager built the first "alienated (*yihua*)" house among the five villages in 2001. The building, with its domed roof, brightly colored walls, and grand manner, formed a striking contrast with the surrounding Dai bamboo houses. More importantly, this house was regarded as a symbol of being affluent and modern among the villagers. The Dai Yuan was very concerned that other villagers would follow this example and build more "alienated" buildings in the Dai Garden if they could afford it. Thus, besides negotiating with the house owner, the Dai Yuan even turned to the Menghan Bureau of City Planning to prevent the construction of the house. However, the owner insisted on his right to build his own house on his own land. The failure to guarantee the "purity" of Dai culture in this incident forced the Dai Yuan to consider the possible negative impacts on its business in the future. According to the author's questionnaire on the issue of "alienated" buildings in the Dai Garden conducted between 7 March and 14 March, 2002, of 165 households in the five villages, 89% of the villagers would choose the modern (or urbanized) indoor decorations if they could afford to do so. Twenty percent of the villagers expressed that the government should not interfere with their right to construct houses, including the choice of house styles. In meetings with the governmental officials, the managers of the Dai Yuan often cited the incident of the Manting "alienated" house as an example of demanding the forceful macro-regulation and legislation to run the ethnic tourism business smoothly.

Though the Dai Yuan's efforts to rule out "alienated" houses failed in this incident, it shows the influential role of the Dai Yuan in constructing the local cultural reality regarding who has the authority to define what are essential elements of an "authentic" Dai culture. Consciously acting as a cultural protector, the Dai Yuan determines what should be revived, developed, and preserved with its economic and political power in the villages. Its cultural events and management become an effective way to shape cultural production of the Dai villages in the context of nation building and modernity. While the villagers' active involvement makes this process more complete, their resistance appears to be relatively weak and silent given their inferior economic and political status.

Conclusion

Administrative decentralization has been one of the essential issues in the development of China's tourism since the mid-1980s. By devolving administrative power from top to bottom, it facilitates the participation of provincial and local governments in the tourism industry in terms of having the determinate authority on investments, the construction of infrastructure, and the plural development of tourism in different regions (Xu, 1999). Yet, the state's principles, policies, and directions relating to tourism development still shape the practices of local government tourism bureaus as guiding rules. The effective implementation of the national rating program of tourist sites in Banna gives an example of how the state practices its macro-control of the tourism industry through its regional bureaus.

As an official channel for regulating Banna's tourism market, the rating program and BPTB's preferential regulations directly influence the operations of tourism enterprises in terms of representing and marketing ethnic cultures in tourist zones. To receive the AAAA title and to gain the government's protection, the Dai Yuan modified its feminized and exotic representation of Dai culture to improve the quality of tourist resources and events at the site. The newly designed tour route leads tourists through the Dai village life to experience a contexualized Dai culture. The Dai Yuan, with its golden AAAA title, also consciously advocates the official discourses of nationalism and modernity among the Dai villagers through cultural events and management. The cooperation of the Dai Yuan with the government displays its active and effective role in shaping cultural production of a contemporary Dai community in the context of pursuing modernity.

Acknowledgements

This article is based on fieldwork research conducted between September 2001 and April 2002 in Xishuang Banna, Yunnan, P.R. China. The Dai Yuan grants me permission to use the real name of the corporation. I would like to express my greatest thanks to the villagers, the Dai Yuan, and BPTB for their generous support, warm help, and provoking insights on Banna's tourism development in my fieldwork research. I am indebted to the Penfield Fellowship of the University of Pennsylvania that makes my fieldwork possible and to Dr. Maggie Kruesi, Dr. Jay Dautcher, and the reviewers of this article for their comments and support during my writing and revising of this article. Part of this article was first presented at the International Conference on Tourism Development and Management in Developing Countries, Guilin, P.R. China, November 2001.

References

Adams, K. (1984). Come to Tana Toraja, "Land of the Heavenly Kings": Travel Agents as Brokers in Ethnicity. *Annals of Tourism Research*, 11, 469–485.
Blum, S. (2001). *Portraits of "Primitives"*. Rowman and Littlefield, New York.
CCP (Chinese Communist Party) (1993). *Decision of the Central Committee of the CCP and the State Council on Speeding Up the Development of Tertiary Industries.* June 16 (in Chinese), Beijing.

Dai Yuan (the Xishuang Banna Dai Garden Tourism Ltd. Co.) (2001). The Guiding Principles of Constructing the Dai Garden (*Dai Zu Yuan Jianshe de Zhidao Sixiang*). In J. Yan (ed), *Miraculous Menbalanaxi* (*Shenqi de Menbalanaxi*) (p. 150). Sichuan Renmin Press, Chengdu.

Dai Yuan (the Xishuang Banna Dai Garden Tourism Ltd. Co.) (2002). *The Dai Garden in Xishuang Banna (Xishuang Banna Dai Zu Yuan)*. Xishuang Banna Dai Garden Tourism Ltd, Menghan.

Fan, W. (2001). Preservation and Development (*baohu yu fazhang*). In J. Yan (ed), *Miraculous Menbalanaxi* (*Shenqi de Menbalanaxi*) (pp. 151–154). Sichuan Renmin Press, Chengdu.

Greenwood, D. (1977). Culture by the Pound. In V. Smith (ed), *Hosts and Guests* (pp. 171–185). University of Pennsylvania Press, Philadelphia.

Guan, J. (1989). Tourism, cultural survival and host ethnic participation. *New Asia Academic Bulletin*, 8, 75–78.

Harrison, D. (2001). Tourism and less developed countries: Key issues. In D. Harrison (ed), *Tourism and the Less Developed World: Issues and Case Studies* (pp. 23–46). CAB International, Wallingford, UK.

He, G. (2002). *Keep up with the World, Greet Challenges, and Struggle for the Better and Faster Development of China's Tourism (yushi jujin, yingjie tiaozhan, lizheng woguo luluye gengkuai gengda de fazhan)*. Speech presented at the 2002 national governmental tourism conference on 8 January, Beijing.

Jenkins, C. L. & Henry, B. M. (1982). Government involvement in tourism in developing countries. *Annual of Tourism Research*, 9(4), 499–521.

Jiang, Z. (1992a). *Speed up Revolutionary Change to Increase the Pace of Modernization to Achieve a Greater Victory for Socialism with Chinese Characteristics*. Report to the Fourteenth National People's Congress of the Communist Party of China. People's Press, Beijing.

Jiang, Z. (1992b). To strengthen ethnic minority cooperation: Let's hold hands together and carch forward in order to develop socialism with Chinese characteristics. In Chinese Communist Party Central Documents Study Center (ed), *Important Documents Collections since the Thirteenth National People's Congress 1987* (Vol. 3, pp. 1832–1850). People's Press, Beijing.

Li, J. (2003). Playing upon fantasy: Women, ethnic tourism and the politics of identity construction in contemporary Xishuang Banna, China. *Tourism Recreation Research*, 28(2), 51–65.

Li, S. (2002). *Analysis of the Situation of Tourism Development, Keep up with the World, Promote the Faster Development of Banna Tourism in a New Era (renqing xingshi, yushijujin, tuijin wozhou luyouye zai xinshiqi de geng kuai fazhan)*. Speech presented at the 2002 Banna's Governmental Tourism Conference, 5 February.

Linnekin, J. (1997). Consuming cultures: Tourism and the commoditization of cultural identity in the Island Pacific. In M. Picard & R. Wood (eds), *Tourism, Ethnicity, and the State in Asian and Pacific Societies* (pp. 215–250). University of Hawaii Press, Honolulu.

Mowforth, M. & Munt, L. (1998). *Tourism and Sustainability: New Tourism in the Third World*. Routledge, London.

Mueggler, E. (2002). Dancing fools: Politics of culture and place in a "Traditional Nationality Festival." *Modern China*, 28(3), 3–39.

Oakes, T. (1998). *Tourism and Modernity in China*. Routledge, London.

Picard, M. (1993). Cultural tourism in Bali. In M. Hitchcock, V. King & M. Parnwell (eds), *Tourism in South-East Asia* (pp. 71–98). Routledge, London.

Picard, M. (1997). Cultural tourism, nation-building, and regional culture: The making of a Balinese identity. In M. Picard & R. Wood (eds), *Tourism, Ethnicity, and the State in Asian and Pacific Societies* (pp. 181–214). University of Hawaii Press, Honolulu.

Schein, L. (2000). *Minority Rules: The Miao and the Feminine in China's Cultural Politics*. Duke University Press, Durham.

Silver, I. (1993). Marketing authenticity in third world cultures. *Annals of Tourism Research*, 20, 301–318.

Sofield, T. & Li. F. M. (1998). Tourism development and cultural policies in China. *Annals of Tourism Research*, 25, 362–392.

Swain, M. (1990). Commoditizing ethnicity in Southwest China. *Cultural Survival Quarterly*, 14(1), 26–30.

Timothy, D. J. (1999). Participatory planning: A view of tourism in Indonesia. *Annals of Tourism Research*, 26(2), 371–391.

Timothy, D. J. & Tosun, C. (2003) Appropriate planning for tourism in destination communities: Participation, incremental growth and collaboration. In S. Singh, D. J. Timothy & R. K. Dowling (eds), *Tourism in Destination Communities* (pp. 181–204). CAB International, Wallingford, UK.

Tosun, C. (2000) Limits to community participation in the tourism development process in developing countries. *Tourism Management*, 21, 613–633.

Van den Berghe, P. & Keyes, C. (eds). (1984). Tourism and ethnicity. Special issue of *Annals of Tourism Research*, 11(3).

Walsh, E. (2001). *The Mosuo-Beyond the Myths of Matriarchy: Gender Transformation and Economic Development*. Unpublished doctoral dissertation, Temple University, Philadelphia.

Wen, J. & Tisdell C. (2001). *Tourism and China's Development: Policies, Regional Economic Growth and Ecotourism*. World Scientific Publishing, Singapore.

West Development Office of the State Council (*Xibu Kaifa Bangongshi*). (2002). *Six Tasks in the Future West Development* [Online]. Available: http://news.sina. com.cn/c/2002-11-12/1959805848.html, News Center for the 16th Party Congress. Accessed on 12 November, 2002.

Wood, R. (1984). Ethnic tourism, the state and cultural change in Southeast Asia. *Annals of Tourism Research*, 11(3), 353–374.

White, S. (1998). State discourse, minority policies, and the politics of identity in the Lijiang Naxi People's Autonomy County. *Nationalism and Ethnic Politics*, 4(1/2), 1–27.

Xu, G. (1999). *Tourism and Local Economic Development in China*. Curzon press, Surrey.

Zhang, G. (2003). China's tourism since 1978: Policies, experiences, and lessons learned. In A. Lew, L. Yu, J. Ap & G. Zhang (eds), *Tourism in China* (pp. 13–34). Haworth Hospitality Press, New York.

Intangible Heritage and Sustainable Tourism Planning: A Critique of a Tourism Resort Development Proposal for Lugu Lake, China

Sandra Leong and Hilary du Cros

Introduction

Yunnan is a southwestern province in China rich in tourism resources and noted not only for its highland plateau landscapes, snowy mountains and canyons, but also for its variety of ethnic cultures and striking scenery. Collectively, these features have helped establish Yunnan as an extremely mysterious and attractive destination for tourists. A large percentage of these tourists are domestic Chinese, although growing numbers of international visitors have been attracted to the province since it became more accessible more than 15 years ago.

Recognizing Yunnan's immense potential for further tourism development and the province's need for proper structural planning to realise this potential better, the World Tourism Organization (UNWTO) launched the Yunnan Provincial Tourism Master Plan in the year 2000 (WTO, 2002). As part of this master plan, the UNWTO's consultants conducted a series of pre-feasibility studies to examine proposed tourism development projects for the province. Commissioned by the China National Tourism Administration (CNTA) and the Yunnan Provincial Tourism Administration (YPTA), one of the pre-feasibility studies focused on tourism development in Yunnan's Lugu Lake area and the proposal of a new resort development along its shores.

Lugu Lake is located in Ninglang County in the northernmost part of the province that borders Sichuan and Tibet. The lake itself has high aesthetic value and is designated a scenic spot of high provincial significance. The population comprises a number of different ethnic nationalities, particularly Yi and Mosuo. The Mosuo number around 40,000 and are believed to have migrated from Tibet. It is their custom of 'walking marriage', classified as a type of matrilineal tradition, by anthropologists that has generated so much interest in the area and which YPTA and local tourism officials seek to develop further for tourism (Walsh, 2001).

Originally, tourism development at Lugu Lake was restricted to one section of its southern shore since it first opened to tourists, but local officials, some of whom are Mosuo people, have managed to expand the area where commercial enterprises, such as guesthouses, can be established (Forney, 2002). Concerns were raised amongst Chinese anthropologists and others regarding the impact of increased exposure to tourism on this ethnic group (Walsh, 2001; Lugu Lake Institute, 2005). The authors also share these concerns about impacts and undertook a review of the pre-feasibility study vision and development strategies in light of current sustainable tourism and heritage literature to evaluate the following:

1. The applicability of the vision of developing a resort in the area.
2. The stakeholder consultation process recommended.
3. The success of the development strategy recommended in terms of market appeal.
4. Whether there are any features of the strategy that could be changed to minimise the impact on Mosuo intangible heritage and living culture without losing the economic benefits of tourism for the region.

Finally, some brief conclusions were reached regarding whether the development strategy in the study has merit for replication in other situations in China, for instance where tourists may want to travel long distances to visit unique attractions, such as World Heritage sites also rich in living culture.

The Pre-Feasibility Study (PFS)

The main master plan notes that all work, including the pre-feasibility studies, was carried out using an internationally derived sustainable tourism development framework to manage the socio-cultural impacts of tourism development (WTO *et al.*, 2001:

34–37). As part of the study, a situation analysis was conducted, giving a detailed appraisal of the strengths, weaknesses, opportunities and threats with regards to tourism development in the Lugu Lake area. One of the opportunities was for a new tourism development to be planned and located outside of the water catchment for Lugu Lake (WTO *et al.*, 2001: 11) instead of allowing tourism to continue in an unplanned fashion.

A resort was planned to follow this suggestion with plans to have it located on a secondary lake approximately one kilometer from Lugu Lake. It would be a resort town built to international standards with environmental controls, amenities, and visual experiences. The resort would also provide a significant space for the Mosuo and other ethnic people for performance, handicrafts and demonstrations of their cultural life. It is envisioned as a self-contained, fully-sufficient resort development that will include five hotels ranging from two to four stars, commercial and residential areas, restaurants, cafes and foreshore promenade, amusement areas and a hospital (WTO *et al.*, 2001: 14). Aware of the need for tourism to develop sustainably, the PFS also recommends a list of environmental management measures and cultural heritage strategies to prevent negative socio-cultural impacts and reinforce positive ones. The study also strongly advises that a thorough stakeholder consultation process be implemented that addresses the views of the local community (WTO *et al.*, 2001: 42–50).

The Mosuo People and Their Culture

Lugu Lake is the cultural cradle of the Yongning Mosuo people, more often referred to as just the Mosuo (Pun, 2002). Known to most Chinese as "the Kingdom of the Daughters" and described as "a world without fathers or husbands" (Chen, 2002), the Mosuo-dominated villages are home to a unique ethnic cultural group which has managed to maintained a matrilineal lifestyle for centuries. Courtships among the young are more easygoing than in some other parts of China and the majority of Mosuo still practice a "separated couple marriage system" in which the man lives in his home and the woman lives in hers. Should a couple produce a child, he or she takes after the mother's family name and experiences very minimal contact (if not none) with his or her father (RTHK, 1999). This system is also known as the "walking marriage" (Walsh, 2001). Together, both their matrilineal family system and unusual marriage system makes them highly distinctive and therefore, one of Yunnan's most interesting ethnic minority groups to study and/or visit.

While Mosuo women are the linchpins of their society and "decision-makers, the business managers, just as they are the inheritors of property and controllers of the family purse" (Wintle, 2001: 20), they currently do the majority of hard work at home and in the fields. Added to this workload, some women are expected to escort tours, maintain small hotels or become involved in prostitution with little say in the tourism decision-making process. While most of this activity is limited to one area at present, it should also be seen as evidence of how the existing level of tourism is already causing socio-cultural impacts (Walsh, 2001).

The Tourism Product

What is to be Sold to the Tourist?

According to the PFS, it is expected that the rich and interesting culture of the Mosuo people complements a "stand-alone ecotour experience featuring the Lijiang Ancient Town, the rich Naxi culture, natural attractions of the Tiger Leaping Gorge, [and the] White Water Terrace" (WTO *et al.*, 2001: 13). Hence, it would be consumed as a niche ecotourism and/or cultural experience. The proposed resort project would allow the tourist a more controlled experience than what is currently available, in which the tourism product will be modified and standardised.

The PFS (WTO *et al.*, 2001: 14) states that provision for a small theatre in the resort will be made for the Mosuo people to put on a play for the tourists. It recommends that "no presentation areas should be established in any of the towns as this small theater and its presentations will be the main and only introductory experience for understanding Mosuo culture". Moreover, there will be also be restricted access (if any at all) for tourists to the Mosuo cultural villages not already open to tourism. They are not a tourism product in the same sense as the proposed resort and its recreational facilities (boat, canoe, kayak, lakeshore and amusement facilities). The short (and controlled) experience that the tourists will have with Mosuo culture, by way of the play, could almost be considered ancillary to this main tourism product.

Market Appeal

Over 70 percent of the overseas tour operators, interviewed by the WTO consultants for market research, ranked Lugu Lake as their most preferred attraction out of seven key sites (WTO *et al.*, 2001: 12). This highlights that, as it stands, Lugu Lake is already well known outside the local area and holds strong market appeal. The marketing the resort as a tourism attraction within the area could rely on three key factors:

1. Destination Associated with Culture. Given the locational context of the proposed resort development project, it should be able to thrive off the market appeal that the area already possesses. This is because the area is strongly associated with culture. It is viewed within China as a tourist haven not only because of its natural scenic beauty, but also because of the matrilineal culture of the Mosuo (*China Daily*, Feb 13 2002). However, if the tourists (especially those who are keen to learn more about Mosuo culture) are aware that the most they would get is a theatrical presentation of the Mosuo's lifestyle, and not a real-life authentic experience, this market appeal would definitely fall.

2. Tourism Activity in the Region. On the national scale, China is already presently experiencing spectacular tourism growth rates. With such a vast territory, huge population, long-standing history, brilliant ancient civilization and multiethnic culture (Zhang, 1995), as well as with increasingly relaxed travel entry formalities now, it is set to become the leading country for scheduled domestic and international travel by 2010 (Page, 1999: 63). Many parts of China will see greater tourist numbers and the uniquely combined natural and cultural resource base of Yunnan Province makes it one that will correspondingly generate much more tourism activity as well. There are 390 listed sites and attractions in Yunnan, of which Dayan, Lijiang's ancient town, has also been listed by UNESCO as a World Heritage Site (UNESCO, 2002). Against this backdrop, the proposed resort development in Lugu Lake holds high market appeal.

3. Appeals to Special Needs or Uses. The proposed resort development also exudes market appeal in the arena of specialist

tourism products as it has the capacity to accommodate a host of recreational activities made possible through proposed facilities such as the boat, canoe, kayak, lakeshore and amusement facilities. More than a self-contained resort development, the myriad of additional sports and recreational facilities would allow for the place to be marketed as a new destination for water sports enthusiasts and for other mass tourists who may be looking for fun and excitement.

Consequences of Unplanned Tourism Development

"Tourism is like fire. It can cook your food, or burn your house down" (Robbin Fox in UNESCO, 2003). This statement is found to be all too true in many cases. If planned tourism strategies for sustainable tourism are not implemented at Lugu Lake, it is highly likely that spontaneous and unplanned tourism development will occur and result in uncontrollable socio-cultural repercussions on the Mosuo people. Wong How Man, founder of the China Exploration Society, had this to say about tourism development in Lugu Lake,

"Tourism has had quite an impact on the area and if the dozen of so villages change themselves to accommodate tourism, their traditional culture will very soon disappear. While life is being improved, old culture is sure to be challenged." (RTHK video-recording, 1999)

As can be seen, the rich cultural resource base which draws tourists to the Lugu Lake faces eminent challenges to its very sustainability and therefore the consequences of unplanned tourism development have to be understood and controlled by way of planning if sustainable development is to emerge.

The Local–Tourist Divide

Firstly, with unplanned tourism development taking place in and around Lakeside village, with more locals (and outsiders) exploiting it by providing accommodation, performances and other activities for the tourists, there is an increase in "contact zones" between hosts and guests (Pratt, 1992). Although cultural interaction is what most of the tourists yearn for, if tourism increases and spreads to all the Mosuo villages it could lead to "contested landscapes" (Relph, 1976), wherein locals feel increasingly marginalised and displaced by the influx of tourists. There will be a further-pronounced local–tourist divide as "zoofica-tion" (Mowforth and Munt, 1998) takes place, with the Lugu Lake area being deni-grated to a mere "theme park" and the Mosuo people mere objects for the "tourist gaze" (Urry, 1990). Butler and Hinch (1996: 3) note even more seriously that the exposure which many tourists now have to indigenous cultures and peoples is limited to a master/servant relationship, or to a fleeting, often staged and inauthentic, representation of traditional lifestyles. This is particularly true of the sometimes unequal relationship between Han Chinese tourists and ethnic hosts maintained through domestic tourism in the more economically backward parts of China in the west and south. If unplanned tourism development is allowed to continue many villagers may find themselves having to play a servant role to the "tourist-king".

The insensitivity that some tourists may display could further exacerbate the resident–tourist divide. Craik (2000: 115) regards tourism as an egocentric pursuit, involving a fascination with self-indulgence and self-delusion. Some tourists may be aware of their monetary right and therefore behave in a con-descending and demanding style, interrupting the lives of destination residents. The Mosuo people might strongly resent such intrusions but continue to serve them because the tourist dollar does, after all, bring them economic benefits. Social discontent on the locals' part would result, and the problem of social incom-patibility with tourism will arise, with locals feeling a general sense of unhappiness towards having to "put up with" the tourists (Mathieson and Wall, 1982).

Tourism Dependency

Encloe (1989) notes that resident populations sometimes go to extraordinary lengths to meet the needs of tourists. With tourists flock-ing to Lugu Lake, and unplanned tourism development taking place to cater to those increasing numbers, larger sections of the com-munity (aware of how lucrative the tourist dollar is) will become increasingly dependent on tourism. In some cases, local households give up other kinds of economic activities, such as agriculture or local services, in an effort to take advantage of employment oppor-tunities in tourism. There are also situations where people abandon their values and shed their dignity (e.g. undertaking sex work) in their quest for the cash that tourists provide. Thus as a resulting consequence, they lose their self-reliance and are placed in a state of socio-cultural and economic vulnerability.

Challenges to Mosuo Culture and Identity

With more grounds for interaction between the residents and tourists, challenges are

made to their own identity as it is now sub-
jected to "on-going negotiation between state
policies, popular representations of the
Mosuo, tourists' desires and Mosuo notions
of their own identity" (Walsh, 2001: 94).
They have to present to outsiders different
'masks' or 'faces' that incorporate key concerns with gender, sexuality, family and cultural continuity and possibly have to tailor
their culture to give tourists what they want.

Moreover, with reference to discourses on
ethnic tourism in China's villages, it has been
suggested that in their own quest for modernity, local ethnic minorities have to paradoxically "perform a delicate balancing act in
appearing un-modern for the purposes of
modernization" (Oakes, 1995: 217). To have
sufficient funds to develop economically and
achieve higher standards of living, there is an
unstated requirement for them to appear
"stuck in time" for the perusal of tourists.
To a certain extent, it is true that ethnic
tourism has brought about a rejuvenation of
traditional cultures, which could have been
lost if they were not retained for the tourists.

In the case of the Mosuo, showcasing such
intangible heritage also exposes details of
their private affairs and sexuality. Their
"Walking Marriage" customs comprise a
different kind of heritage asset to those such
as stories, dances or songs that are normally
commodified for tourist consumption. Tourists wishing to "experience" it can lead to a
certain kind of social interaction that goes
beyond costume animation or cultural performance. Hence it was stated as important
in the PFS that Mosuo themselves decide
what should and should not be interpreted
for a wider audience and set limits that they
can monitor. Setting limits of acceptable
change (LAC) is a concept that is contained
in the ICOMOS Cultural Tourism Charter
(1999) that was used by the PFS authors,

although it was not stated clearly how the
Mosuo should undertake such a task.

Discontent within the Community

Another negative consequence of unplanned
tourism activity is that discontent could arise
within the community regarding equity issues.
Hitchcock (1997: 99) writes that inflows of
cash into communities can sometimes cause
disagreements, especially when the distributions of the benefits are inequitable. While
tourism may indeed expand incomes and
create additional employment opportunities,
it may also cause social stratification and
exacerbate problems of factionalism in local
communities. This is especially so if some of
the Mosuo people are excluded from the economic benefits of tourism and are not able to
earn as much out of it than others. However,
despite the problems described, there could
also be some avenue for optimism as counter-
vailing trends could allow the Mosuo a rising
pride in their cultural traditions and some
respect within China, particularly, for their
ethnic identity (Forney, 2002).

The Proposed Resort Development Project

The Vision

As social and environmental risks often associated with tourism development have become
more apparent worldwide, increased attention
has been paid to strategies for encouraging a
more sustainable approach to tourism, one
that will permit planning that facilitates development without jeopardizing the resources
upon which the industry depends. The
Pre-Feasibility Study for proposed resort

development on Lake Lugu assesses the project as a demand-based, environmentally sustainable and culturally sensitive development. More than a vision to create a resort town that will be built to international standards, the proposed project aimed to minimise existing negative tourism impacts and pre-empt future ones.

Ultimately, the PFS vision was to bring about sustainable tourism development at Lugu Lake by concentrating development away from sensitive areas. The idea was similar to that tried at Yulara Resort, which was constructed outside, but adjacent to, the Uluru-Kata Tjuta National Park in Australia.

The PFS stated that tourism will expand at Lugu Lake, with or without the implementation of the resort development proposal. It stated that, "unplanned development will surely lead to severe environmental and cultural problems (and therefore) to preserve both the unique environment and cultural aspects of the region, there will have to be some kind of planned development along the lines of this proposal" (WTO *et al.*, 2001: 49–50).

The Advised Stakeholder Consultation Process

Butler and Hinch (1996: 6) put forward that "very careful planning and management are required by host destinations, if they are to capture their fair share of the benefits of tourism and ensure that they do not have to suffer more than their fair share of the negative consequences". As an underlying strategy to prevent negative impacts and reinforce positive ones on the Mosuo group, the PFS continually emphasizes the need for stakeholder consultation to be regarded as an integral part of the development and implementation process for the proposed resort. This is

because acceptance by, and the cooperation of, the host community is essential to the success of any resort as a sustainable tourism development project, and therefore, resident opinions and local impacts must be carefully addressed in the development and management of resorts (Stynes and Susan, 1996: 240).

The UNWTO PFS states that "a stakeholder consultation process should be adopted before developing the area further and the role of the non-Mosuo individuals should be better defined" (WTO *et al.*, 2001: 46). Current international practice (e.g. Pearson and Sullivan, 1995; ICOMOS, 1999) recommends that consultation be started early in the planning process. The study follows this practice with a valuable recommendation that consultation must indeed commence from the outset and be a regular part of the on-going management of the asset. However, it notes there may have to be some compromises if Mosuo stakeholders are asked to expose their culture by commodifying it, so as to achieve its tourism potential (in this case, a theatrical presentation of the group's matrilineal culture).

The PFS (pp. 46–49) also notes that stakeholder consultation has to be carried out in a broad range of areas with regards to proposed tourism developments. Some of these include:

1. The addition of extra lake activities for tourists.
2. The development of trails around the lake.
3. The presentation of cultural life at new resort-town.
4. The development of local handicrafts for tourists to buy and in fixing prices for the handicraft sales and demonstration area of the resort.
5. Monitoring the impacts of tourism through the regular discussion of the results of impact surveys and studies for amendment to existing strategies when necessary.

Review of the Stakeholder Consultation Process

McKercher and du Cros (2002: 180) observe that the consultative process should not be a mere one-off process and highlights that "for an asset to be truly sustainable, ongoing feedback from stakeholders must be encouraged so that emerging issues can be resolved". The PFS takes this into consideration and allows for amendments to be made to existing strategies when the need arises (as described in point number five above). Continual and regular communication has to be facilitated for, in all stages of tourism development, and a stakeholder consultation framework that contains this aspect is worthy of praise.

However, this aside, the study at its best only gives a very simplified and general framework for the stakeholder consultation process, and fails to address the complexity of the stakeholder consultation process. It highlights that the stakeholders "should be better defined" (WTO *et al.*, 2001: 46), but makes no attempt to define who the possible stakeholders are in this resort development project as a guide.

The stakeholders referred to in PFS seem to be only the indigenous people who theoretically are able to negotiate their involvement in tourism from a position of strength because they form the cultural base, which attracts the tourists to the area. However, as Jenkins (1996) and Timothy (1999) point out, in developing countries the idea of community involvement in tourism is very different from that of the developed countries, because decision-making by many of these communities may be based on the traditional elite rather than on a whole community.

Will a majority of the Mosuo people be excluded from the consultation process then? If the majority of them are indeed included

in the process, what would be the actual breadth and depth of their participation? Moreover, in reality, there are definitely more stakeholder groups than expressed in the study. These groups include the hosts, the guests, and the tourism facilitators (the industry) who serve as "prime movers in effecting innovation and change" (Smith, 2001: 199). This is because increasingly the tourists are responding to suggestions of environmental and social conscience, and the tourism industry, with its many facilitators, now takes greater pride in the promotion and certification of sound ecological practices. In addition, there will also be the government officials and professionals, who while they are generally not involved as investors in tourist enterprises, or as direct employees of the industry, nevertheless still play important roles in determining both the direction and ideology of tourism's future for the area. To complicate matters, each stakeholder group could also display varying perspectives and degrees of power over the development project (McKercher and du Cros, 2002). Implementation in practice is often a long way from planning for it in theory. Therefore, given the complexity of the stakeholder process, difficulties to its implementation should have been more clearly anticipated and recommendations made accordingly.

The pre-feasibility study provided an extensive list of strategies that would be undertaken to reinforce the former, while preventing the latter. To minimize the impact on Mosuo living culture without losing economic benefits of tourism for the region, two additional features should be made to existing plans. These comprise a greater dedication to eco-tourism and a better understanding of the needs of the community by tourism developers and the government.

A Greater Dedication to Eco-tourism

With its pristine natural beauty and awe-inspiring mountains, Lugu Lake is an excellent place for eco-tourism. An earlier part of the PFS notes this and highlights that the Lugu Lake could be marketed as a stand alone eco-tour experience. However, in the proposed strategies, no mention was given to the development of eco-tourism initiatives. In the authors' opinion, more effort should be made to market the resort development to eco-tourists. Although true eco-tourists currently form a small market segment, their numbers are set to grow in the times to come as China becomes more urbanised. It has been noted that eco-tourists travel with an ethic of responsibility toward local ecosystems and cultures, thereby lessening the social and environmental costs often associated with tourism development (Ryel and Grasse 1991).

Better Understanding the Needs of the Local Community

An established resort development that can be used as a comparison is the Laguna Phuket. The resort has mitigated its environmental impact by transforming a ruined former tin mining area into a verdant landscape. Besides implementing a variety of environmentally sensitive practices and energy conservation measures in its daily operations, the resort development also makes very substantial contributions to the 'human environment'. To ensure that the development benefits the local community, a large proportion of the workforce comprises locals. A variety of social projects have been implemented, including a provision of childcare, medical services, educational scholarships, language classes and other community-related activities (*Laguna Resorts and Hotels*, 2000; Piprell, 1997).

Conclusion

A PFS seems the best option to many tourism authorities for integrating international advice into a local environment. In practice this does not always turn out to be the case. No matter how praiseworthy the vision of the PFS for minimizing tourism impacts at the local level, it had nothing to cause government authorities and developers to implement it to satisfy their desire for short-term gain; hence, it was ignored. The tourist numbers, particularly from Mainland domestic tourism, still continue to increase along with the associated negative social impacts, particularly prostitution. In 2001, the Ninglang County government constructed a new hotel near the Lake (Forney, 2002). The PFS has been a failure at the local level. It was not truly supported at the provincial level either, as the change of governor in 2001 removed its champion.

By 2005, little had been done that was sustainable or likely to mitigate social impacts on the Mosuo. A local nongovernmental organization, Lugu Lake Institute of Matriarchal Culture of Mosuo People, had been trying to increase international and national support for mitigating impacts through its web site (LLIMCP, 2005). Although the PFS recognizes stakeholder consultation as an important element of the planning and management process, the study would have been improved by providing more detail on the nature of that process and the nature of the stakeholders likely to be involved, and provided an idea of incentives for undertaking such a process in the first place.

Finally, there is a need for international projects of this kind to continue to pay attention to such important dilemmas of maintaining equilibrium in the sustainable tourism development of intangible heritage. Even though this one has had problems, it is important not to give up completely. This is a very new area of conservation and planning practice, and a mechanism needs to be put in place to provide more peer reviews of such studies. Even when these studies appear to be in line with current 'best practice' codes and charters, there is still much to be done in terms of 'selling' the idea on the ground.

Acknowledgements

The authors would like to thank Dr Chang Tou Chuang (Department of Geography, University of Singapore) and Bob McKercher (School of Hotel and Tourism Management, Hong Kong Polytechnic University) for their comments on the manuscript.

References

Butler, R. and Hinch, T. (1996) *Tourism and Indigenous Peoples*. London: International Thomson Business Press.

Chen, K. (2002) A World without Fathers or Husbands. *Library Journal* 127(8): 146.

China Daily (Feb 13, 2001) Ripples of Change on Lake Lugu [North American Edition] p. 9.

Craik, J. (2000) The culture of tourism. In C. Rojek and J. Urry (eds) *Touring Cultures: Transformations of travel and theory*, pp. 113–136. London: Routledge.

Encloe, C. (1989) *Bananas, Beaches and Bases: Making Feminist Sense of International Relations*. Berkeley: University of California Press.

Forney, M. (2002) Minority Report. *Time Magazine*, November.

Hitchcock, R.K. (1997) Cultural, economic and environmental impacts of tourism among Kalahari Bushmen. In E. Chambers (ed.) *Tourism and Culture: An Applied Perspective*, pp. 93–128. Albany: State University of New York Press.

ICOMOS (1999) *Cultural Tourism Charter*. Paris: ICOMOS.

Jenkins, C.L. (1996) Incorporating cultural assets in tourism development planning. In W. Nuryanti (ed.) *Tourism and Culture: Global Civilization in Change?*, pp. 248–269. Yogyakarta: Gadjah Mada University Press.

Laguna Resorts and Hotels (2000) Corporate Citizenship and Environmental Policy < /// > Accessed 16 December 2000.

MacClancy, J. (2002) Paradise postponed: the predicaments of tourism. In J. MacClancy (ed.) *Exotic No More: Anthropology on the Front Lines*, pp. 418–429. Chicago: The University of Chicago Press.

Mathieson, A. and Wall, G. (1982) *Tourism: Economic, Physical and Social Impacts*. London: Longman.

McKercher, B. and du Cros, H. (2002) *Cultural Tourism: The Partnership between Tourism and Cultural Heritage Management*. New York: Haworth.

Mowforth, M. and Munt, I. (1998) *Tourism and Sustainability: New Tourism in the Third World*, London: Routledge.

Oakes, T. (1995) Tourism in Guizhou: the legacy of internal colonialism. In A.A. Lew and L. Yu (eds) *Tourism in China: Geographic, Political, and Economic Perspectives*, pp. 203–222. Boulder, CO: Westview Press.

Page, S. (1999) Transport and infrastructure issues in Southeast and South Asian tourism. In C.M. Hall and S. Page (eds) *Tourism in South and Southeast Asia: Issues and Cases*, pp. 58–73. Oxford: Butterworth–Heinemann.

Pearson, M. and Sullivan, S. (1995) *Looking After Heritage Places: The Basics of Heritage Planning for Managers Landowners and Administrators*. Melbourne: Melbourne University Press.

Piprell, C. (1997) Laguna in the sun. *Sawasdee*, January: 42–47.

Pratt, M.L. (1992) *Imperial Eyes: Travel Writing and Transculturation*. London: Routledge.

Pun, P. (2002) Lijiang gears up for tourist boom, *Hong Kong iMail*, 20 May.

Relph, E. (1976) *Place and Placelessness*. London: Pion.

RTHK video-recording (Produced in 1999 by Sharon Chiu) Where Women Rule, Parts 1 & 2.

Ryel, R. and Grasse, T. (1991) Marketing ecotourism: attracting the elusive ecotourist. In T. Whelan (ed.) *Nature Tourism*, pp. 164–186. Washington, DC: Island Press.

Smith, V.L. (2001) Sustainability. In V. Smith and M. Brent (eds) *Hosts and Guests Revisited: Tourism Issues of the 21st Century*, pp. 187–200. New York: Cognizant.

Stynes, D. and Stewart, S. (1996) Impacts of the Grand Traverse Resort, Michigan, USA: are perceptions consistent with "reality"? In L. Harrison and W. Husbands (eds) *Practicing Responsible Tourism: International Case Studies in Tourism Planning*, pp. 239–260. New York: Wiley.

Timothy, D.J. (1999) Participatory planning: a view of tourism in Indonesia. *Annals of Tourism Research*, 26(2): 371–391.

Urry, J. (1990) *The Tourist Gaze: Leisure and Travel in Contemporary Societies*. London: Sage.

Walsh, E. (2001) Living with the myth of matriarchy: the Mosuo and tourism. In C. Tan, S. Cheung, and H. Yang (eds) *Tourism, Anthropology and China*, pp. 93–124. Bangkok: White Lotus Press.

Wintle, J. (2001) My date with the free-loving mountain nymphs: Justin Wintle experiences an 'extraordinary flotation' as he examines the myths surrounding the 'Kingdom of the Daughters'. [London edition] *Financial Times*, 11 August: 20.

World Tourism Organization (2005) *Congestion Management at Natural and Cultural Sites*. Madrid: World Tourism Organization.

World Tourism Organization, China National Tourism Administration, and Yunnan Provincial Tourism Administration (2001) *Yunnan Province Tourism Development Master Plan and Pre-Feasibility Studies*. Madrid: World Tourism Organization, China National Tourism Administration, and Yunnan Provincial Tourism Administration.

Zhang, Y. (1995) An assessment of China's tourism resources. In A.A. Lew and L. Yu (eds) *Tourism and China: Geographic, Political and Economic Perspectives*, pp. 42–59. Boulder, CO: Westview Press.

Development, Economy and Culture: Cultural Heritage Tourism Planning, Liangzhu, China

Dianne Dredge

Introduction

There is a small but growing body of literature that deals with tourism in China. Understandably so, given that, in 2000, China received 83.44 million international arrivals, making it the fifth largest destination in the world. By 2020 the World Tourism Organisation (WTO) projects that China will become the most important destination in the world (World Tourism Organization, 1997). To date, academic attention has focused mainly on the national context, especially the progressive dismantling of barriers to inbound tourism (e.g. Tisdell & Wen, 1991; Lew & Yu, 1995; Zhang, 1997; Sofield & Li, 1998; Guangrui, 2003), regional economic analyses (e.g. Wen & Tisdell, 2001; Zhang, 2001), resource and product development issues (e.g. Zhang, 1995; Sofield & Li, 1998), and the unfolding of latent domestic markets (e.g. Qiao, 1995; Zhang, 1997). There has also been some case study investigation into the challenges associated with the planning and development of tourism products at the local level (e.g. Li, 2002; Sofield & Li, 2003) and on the effects of tourism on the commodification of Chinese culture and ethnic minorities (e.g. Swain, 1990; Li, 2002).

A common thread that may be drawn through this research, explicit or otherwise, is an enquiry into the way in which global-local relations impact upon tourism planning and decision-making. In China, tourism development occurs within quite distinct political, economic and cultural frameworks that filter global-local relations and make this dialectic play out in different ways to the way that they might play out in liberal economies. Accordingly, different interests, values and ideas are empowered over others in the planning process. It is essential that planners undertaking work in countries other than their own understand these subtle complexities, otherwise the lack of fit between their efforts and the political, institutional, socio-cultural and economic frameworks in the recipient country will ensure little comes of their efforts (e.g. Verhelst & Tyndale, 2002; Sofield & Li, 2003). In this context, this paper interrogates the global-local dialectic as it is played out in the planning for a potential world cultural heritage site in Zhejiang Province, China.

Underpinning this paper is the notion that greater appreciation of the interplay between tourism development, economy and culture across space is required. This dynamic relationship between tourism development, economy, culture and space is frequently embedded in discussions of the global-local nexus. However, these relationships are rarely teased out, resulting in a situation where the global-local nexus, or dialectic, has come to be accepted as academic dogma explaining complex influences on policy-making.

In essence, the notion of a global-local nexus has developed out of critical discussions of globalisation by those observing that geopolitical faultlines are resilient and are challenging the cultural homogenisation of globalised production and distribution systems (e.g. Massey, 1984; Featherstone, 1995; Robertson, 1995; Urry, 1995). These observers note that localities have been able to mobilise local political, economic and social resources in unique ways to counter the dominance of global capital, to assert local interests and actively shape their own transformation. In tourism, the dialectical tensions associated with the global-local nexus are receiving increased attention (e.g. Urry, 1990, 1995; Chang, Milne, Fallon & Pohlmann, 1996; Milne & Ateljevic, 2001; Teo & Li, 2003), especially in relation to cultural heritage tourism (Nuryanti, 1996; Sofield & Li, 1998). Cultural heritage tourism is one vehicle through which localities can harness local culture and traditions to engage in and shape their developmental direction within broader global processes. Teo and Li (2003) observe that globalisation is constituted by different agents, interpreted at different scales, combines internal and external

responses and occurs dialectically over time such that the global-local nexus cannot be understood without knowledge of the particular characteristics of place. This paper is conceptualised in response to this complexity, and will argue that notions of, and connections between, development, economy and culture, embedded in the global-local dialectic, need to be unpacked before tourism planning and policy-making can adequately respond.

The growing interest in cultural heritage tourism in China is a case in point. Since 1978, the top-down drive to engage in more diverse forms of economic production has been matched with a diversification of economic pursuits in both urban and rural areas (e.g. Lin, 2002). Industrialisation of the countryside has been a grass-roots response derived from two main factors. Firstly, the concept of development, especially during the late reform period, has been dominated by an economic discourse, which has focused on industrialisation and economic wealth creation (e.g. Ogden, 1992). Industrial development, which represents a shift from China's historical focus on rural production, has been a consequence. Secondly, the cultural importance of the rural class in China has historically been enshrined in government policy resulting in a large rural population. However, the mechanisation of agriculture, decreasing arable land, improper use of farmland, environmental deterioration and the absorption of peasants from China's communes in the 1980s has led to an employment oversupply in rural areas (Li, 1999). While there has been some shift toward the cities, the new political economy in China, combined with the cultural importance of the rural population, has created conditions conducive to rural industrialisation (Lin, 2002).

More recently, the central government's recognition of the potential role of tourism in economic development, combined with institutional reforms aimed at encouraging lower levels of administration to become actively involved in economic development, have boosted local tourism policy responses (Ma, 1997). Strong social and cultural meanings attached to localities have developed over the course of Chinese civilisation, and which are central to Chinese nationalism, provide a rich ground for the development of cultural heritage tourism products. Teasing out these dialectical relationships and understanding the interconnections between development, economy and culture across spatial scales are important in developing strong and responsive policy.

Support for this position comes from the literature. Richter (1983, 1989) argues that it is important to understand not only the broad context, but also the issue-drivers and socio-political influences at the local level where the drive for development and tourism intersect. Any macro-level research that fails to take into account local dynamics risks misrepresenting the real influences on development (e.g. Marton, 2000; Milne & Ateljevic, 2001). Furthermore, Clancy (2001) argues that the best level to understand the intersection between tourism and development is at the level in which tourism product planning and development are routinely undertaken.

This paper is the product of a recent consulting experience in Hangzhou, China. The project involved initial tourism and town planning advice with respect to the listing of a potential Cultural World Heritage Area to the north of Hangzhou City. The site is associated with an ancient Neolithic community known as the Liangzhu culture and has been included on the List of Cultural World Heritage in Danger. The site is one of the oldest and most significant archaeological finds in China, dating back some 5700 years. Little is known about the Liangzhu culture and archaeological investigations are proceeding slowly. Nevertheless, the Liangzhu cultural site is material proof that the Chinese civilisation is one of the oldest in the world, a notion that existed only in legend until Liangzhu relics were discovered in 1936.

Within the project a number of international specialists were brought in to conduct studies complementing and building upon existing archaeological studies. These included a landscape assessment, a tourism assessment and a land use assessment. All these studies were intended, in the first instance, to contribute to the development of the City's strategic land use planning framework. In the second instance, the studies were intended to provide preliminary direction with respect to the preparation of management plans required for application to the World Heritage Committee for World Cultural Heritage (see ICOMOS, 1999). Extensive research was undertaken prior to undertaking site inspections with respect to national and regional tourism issues, economic development and institutional arrangements for tourism. However, limited information concerning the cultural influences on tourism planning and development at the local level was available (Sofield & Li, 2003). This paper responds to this gap and reflects on the different values and approaches between international and domestic participants in the study.

In this project, Chinese planners and local administrators played an interactive and participatory role in the planning process. As the project proceeded, the author became acutely aware that the interpretation of the planning problem, the way in which issues were prioritised and agendas were derived from a complex range of internal and externally derived responses to both global-local and internal-external factors. Moreover, the author was an active agent in this dialectic. Verhelst and Tyndale (2002) observe that there is a degree of intrusiveness in all research and planning, but especially when consultants undertake projects in cultures distinct from their own. There is a risk of generating top-down planning solutions that reduces, or at worst, ignores, local cultural values, ideas, wisdoms, ideas and knowledge (Timothy, 1999; Verhelst & Tyndale, 2002; Sofield & Li, 2003) Moreover, there is a risk that local planners and administrators come to devalue their own knowledge of planning problems and possible solutions in the overwhelming face of 'international experts'. Accordingly, it was important to develop deep understandings of the abovementioned dialectical challenges and issue drivers that were underpinning the planning process.

In this context, this paper is an exploratory case study investigation. The paper draws from extensive research, site investigations and analysis, and interviews with Chinese town planners and tourism planning officials in developing understandings of the way in which endogenous and exogenous factors combine to influence local tourism planning and decision-making. Extensive note-taking was made during all meetings and site investigations, although the necessity of a translator meant that verbatim translation could not be guaranteed. To address these challenges, efforts were made to progressively elaborate upon and corroborate evidence at every opportunity throughout the investigative process. The resulting paper makes a contribution in three main areas. Firstly, the paper adds to a relatively scant body of case study

research that critically discusses local tourism planning and development in China. Secondly, it adds to the development studies and heritage tourism literature, by explicitly unpacking the concepts of, and relationships between, development, economy and culture that influence local tourism development. Thirdly, the paper provides useful background information for those who might be involved in China's burgeoning tourism consulting activity in the future. Heritage and cultural tourism are important components of China's tourism development strategy and there is a need to understand the pull and push forces that influence the planning of cultural heritage tourism.

Tourism in China

While travel in China dates back thousands of years, the 'Open Door' reform policies introduced in 1978 provide a useful starting point for many discussions on the development of contemporary Chinese tourism policy. In 1978, China initiated policy reforms aimed at opening up the country's economy and locating its place on the international stage. Prior to this, inbound tourism was restricted, outbound tourism was limited to diplomats and government officials, and domestic tourism hardly existed (e.g. Li, 2002). However, in 1978, tourism was officially recognised as a tool for foreign relations and economic development (e.g. Zhang, H. Q., 1995; Zhang, Chong & Ap, 1999; Wen & Tisdell, 2001). Principle emphasis was placed on the power of tourism to enhance foreign relations, and as such, international tourism was focused principally on compatriots (from Hong Kong, Macao and Taiwan) and overseas Chinese. Commencing in 1986, a second phase of reforms identified international tourism as an important source of foreign income and economic development. As a consequence, the emphasis of policy shifted from political to economic. Restrictions and impediments to both international and domestic tourism were eased in an effort to stimulate tourism on a massive scale (e.g. Zhang, 1995; Wen & Tisdell, 2001).

Since 1986, the importance of tourism to China's economic and social development has been reconfirmed on many occasions by the central government, and policies have been progressively rolled out to assist in attracting investment and in the planning, development and promotion of tourism (e.g. ICOMOS, 1999; China National Tourism Administration, 2002). Alongside these economic reforms, there has also been a decentralisation of policy-making, where provincial and city level administrations have become increasingly active in developing localised tourism policy planning and policy. This increasing activism among local administrations has been met by the emergence of a new breed of local developers and investors eager to take advantage of land release programs and other economic development opportunities and international investment.

A brief digression into the statistical profile of tourism illustrates the magnitude of growth. In 2000, China received 83.44 million international visitors, making it the fifth largest country in the world in term of visitor arrivals (World Tourism Organization, 2001). Moreover, as noted previously, the World Tourism Organisation has predicted that China will become the most important destination in terms of international arrivals by 2020 (World Tourism Organization, 1997). While much of this international tourism is derived from day-trips in the southern provinces, international visitors generated 31.23 million visitor nights in 2000.

The domestic tourism market has also grown strongly over this period. Rising disposable incomes, domestic and international investment in tourism product development, and the removal of barriers to travel have all stimulated domestic tourism. Vacation periods have been extended and staggered to reduce peak demands at May Day and National Day, and ten new paid holidays for workers have been introduced. In 2000, domestic tourists generated 740 million visitor trips. Average domestic expenditure is still relatively low at 426.6 Yuan per day, however, domestic and international tourism expenditure together was estimated to be 499 billion Yuan (60 billion US dollars) or five percent of GDP in 2000 (People's Daily, 2000).

The effects of this tourism growth, including trends in the expansion of tourism activity and patterns of tourism investment, have received keen interest by academics (e.g. Lew & Yu, 1995; Sofield & Li, 1998; Zhang et al., 1999; Lew, Yu, Ap & Guangrui, 2002). Much of this research focuses on the macro scale, reflecting on the impact of central policy, and the influence of world tourism trends. However, an emphasis on global and macro forces alone in explaining the development of tourism is China is dangerous. Sofield and Li (1998, p. 363) argue for a focus on the 'dynamics of centripetal and centrifugal internal forces exerted between socialist ideology and traditional culture rather than modernity and exogenous global forces'. Their arguments rightly recognise the powerful role that local Chinese culture plays in shaping tourism development and that the dynamics of internal forces (social, historical, political and cultural) cannot be denied in any discussion of the impetus for tourism development (Sofield & Li, 1998, p. 363). This position is supported in development studies literature in general (e.g. Marton, 2000), and in the case of tourism in particular (e.g. Clancy, 2001).

In the case study that follows, local influences on tourism planning and product development are explored. Central policy directives and international trends are also discussed but these appear to have an indirect, and much less significant, influence on local decision-making. Accordingly, it is dangerous to rely solely on examining the implications of macro trends to explain local tourism development initiatives, just as it is inaccurate to assume small-scale endogenous factors are subordinate to large-scale exogenous factors (Sofield & Li, 1998; Teo & Li, 2003). A balanced understanding of the dynamics between macro, meso and micro scales is necessary. To do this requires an understanding of how local officials perceive and interpret the range of internal and external influences on tourism planning, and the cultural frameworks within which tourism planning and decision-making takes place. A brief overview of the structure of government administrations and their roles and responsibilities with respect to tourism development sets the scene for developing this understanding.

The central government, through the China National Tourism Association (CNTA), provides direction for tourism development through its Five Year Plans, and through the development of decrees and regulations relating to particular tourism issues (CNTA 2002). Of interest to this project is that the CNTA has identified a number of 'top tourist cities', which are to be emphasised in the developing and marketing of tourism. Emphasis has also been placed on developing management guidelines and regulations for nationally designated scenic areas. Located within the city limits of Hangzhou, West Lake is a nationally designated scenic area.

Its cultural and heritage attractions have been instrumental in the identification of Hangzhou as one of China's top tourism cities.

Under the central government, there are five levels of administration in China. Subdivisions within these five levels are confusing and lead to considerable overlap in responsibilities and functions (e.g. see Lin, 2002). Firstly, the provinces have authority and jurisdiction sanctioned by the central government. This level of administration has a role in refining the CNTA policy directives and implementing particular projects and initiatives. In this case study, the Province of Zhejiang has indicated considerable commitment to the development of tourism in its Tourism Development Plan and a strong interest in recognising and protecting sites that are of potential World Cultural Heritage significance. Below the Provinces are prefectural or city level administrations which receive official designation and fiscal commitment from the provincial government to carry out a wide range of activities including infrastructure provision, economic development, and provision of social services. These prefectures are usually the seats of provincial government (i.e. the provincial capital), and their budgetary allocation is increasingly dependent upon their own revenue raising and generating capacity. These prefectures often include large tracts of countryside. In the case of Hangzhou, the City administration has an active tourism bureau that has developed a citywide master plan for the development and marketing of tourism. Below the prefectures there are county level administrations, which are administered directly by the prefectural level, are divided into two categories; "regular" level counties (predominantly rural) and county level cities (smaller than prefectures). Again using the case study as an example, Yuang County is a city level county within the limits of Hangzhou City but which also contains a significant rural area. Responsibility for economic development and management has been devolved to the county administration, which has developed comprehensive economic development and tourism strategies. Below the county level, townships include rural market towns, small towns and small cities. Township administrations report to their respective county administrations. Fifthly, village administrations, which, under the supervision of township level governments, have locally elected grass roots committees responsible for extensive aspects of village administration. These last three levels, counties, townships and villages, have not traditionally been involved in tourism development but are becoming increasingly active in this arena as will be discussed in the context of the case study. In sum, not only are there many overlapping levels of administration, but boundaries in some cases are not clearly defined. Overlapping roles and responsibilities, and spatial and bureaucratic complexities continue to beset policy development, especially at the local levels. In this paper, factors affecting the drive for local economic development in cities, counties and towns are discussed.

Impetus for Local Tourism Development

The 'Open Door' reform policies have had a transformative change in the geography of economic and social development in China (e.g. Marton, 2000; Lin, 2002). While this transformation is discussed elsewhere in detail (e.g. see Marton, 2000; Lin, 2002), a brief overview of the changes is worthy of discussion as they directly impact upon the values and interests embedded in local tourism planning and decision-making. Traditionally, Chinese culture has emphasised the

importance of rural areas and the rural population in servicing cities. In policy, there has been a deliberate de-emphasis on urban areas and what Marton (2000) describes as an ideological suspicion of large cities. The Chinese Communist Party (CCP), representing the union of peasants, has fully integrated this philosophy into its political strategies and policy-making by supporting and maintaining a large rural population to service a much smaller urban, industrialised workforce (Lin, 2002). Moreover, central policy has actively tried to maintain a large rural population, thereby inhibiting, to some extent, rural-urban migration and the rapid urbanisation witnessed in many other developing countries.

As a result of state restructuring, the social and economic characteristics of the rural population have changed dramatically, giving impetus to local interest in rural tourism development. In an ideological shift from earlier years, in 1978 the CCP began to relax state-control in many areas of policy. Decentralisation of decision-making powers has had a significant impact on local administrations where localities now have considerable powers in revenue collection, government expenditure, credit allocation, investment project approval, price and wage control, foreign trade management and industrial policy formation (Ma, 1997). Local tiers of administration now have greater responsibility and control over creating the right conditions for economic development, in securing investment, and in the provision of community infrastructure and servicing (e.g. Ogden, 1992; Li, 1999). Furthermore, there are strong incentives for involvement in economic entrepreneurship since complex revenue sharing arrangements permit the retention of a larger proportion of locally derived income (see Ma, 1997). This incentive is further strengthened by the fact that officials at the community or village level of administration are now popularly elected, and are eager to identify sources of alternative income.

In addition, the deregulation and marketisation of the economy since 1978 has opened up opportunities for local entrepreneurship at an individual level where opportunities have not previously existed (e.g. Guangrui, 2003; Lin, 2002). Where farmers have been given the freedom to decide upon their economic pursuits, there has been a shift observed from staple food production to more profitable occupations (Lin, 2002). While some have turned to market gardening, or have value added to their produce in other ways, others have also developed sideline businesses in, for example, trade, construction, manufacturing and tourism. The Dragon Well tea producers in the Xihu District of Hangzhou City are illustrative of this trend, where tea growing has been supplemented with teahouses, bed and breakfast establishments and secondary attractions such as recreation and ecotourism activities. As a result of this growth in rural entrepreneurialism, a trend toward the division of labour has been observed in rural households, where, for example, the elderly take care of agricultural production and younger family members are engaged in these types of entrepreneurial activities (Marton, 2000).

As a result of these conditions, new forms of rural-urban development are emerging in China. Chinese scholars refer to this as rural-urban integration, and Western scholars, as rural industrialisation (Lin, 2002). In essence, it refers to a trend toward the development of industrial plant and other types of urban development associated with these entrepreneurial activities in rural locations. The effect has been the development of clusters of rural settlements inter-dispersed with non-agricultural activities in what were formally relatively homogeneous rural landscapes (Marton,

2000). This is a phenomenon that distinguishes China from other developing countries, and has significant implications for local tourism development as small-scale tourism developers and operators emerge in rural areas in a relatively ad hoc manner, inter-dispersed with industrial development.

As a result of the implementation of these economic reforms, there has been the progressive reduction of the central government's involvement in local affairs and communities have received increased administrative autonomy. The mandate of community levels of government has broadened to include responsibility for employment creation and infrastructure development. In rural areas, this increased autonomy has been directed towards the expansion of economic development and employment opportunities, with county, town and village administrations becoming increasingly interested in providing and facilitating community-based production opportunities. Moreover, since the service sector has traditionally been relatively small in China, cultural interpretations of economic development have been closely associated with industrialisation, and specifically, factory development. One of the most pressing challenges, according to local officials associated with the following case study, is to open up people's perceptions of economic development beyond industrial factory development.

On the basis of the above discussion, the ideological shift occurring in the Chinese socialist system has brought with it new cultural and economic interpretations of development. Development are conceptualised in economic terms, and industrial-centred modernisation is its cultural companion. Together, the drive for local economic development and focus on creating a modern, diverse, efficient and competitive economy that can attract international investment and generate jobs have proven powerful stimuli for tourism entrepreneurialism in a fledgling political economy, and has created diverse challenges for local administrations. These challenges will be investigated in the following case of the Liangzhu project.

Liangzhu Case Study

Background

The site known as the Liangzhu Cultural Protection Area is located 16 kilometres northwest from the City of Hangzhou in Zhejiang Province. Hangzhou has a distinguished place in Chinese history. While settlement in the area associated with the Liangzhu culture dates back 5,000 years, the City's formal origins were as an administrative district during the Qin Dynasty (221–206BC). The construction of the Grand Canal in the Sui Dynasty (581–618AD) stimulated major cultural, economic and political development and it later became capital of the Southern Song Dynasty between 1127 and 1279AD. Due to the various roles that the City has played in the social, economic and political development of China, Hangzhou contains many cultural attractions and scenic spots. Many of these attractions are located around West Lake, which is said to have inspired many famous Chinese poets, artists and politicians. This rich history has contributed to the designation of Hangzhou as one of China's seven ancient cities (Chen, 2001).

The area inhabited by the Liangzhu culture is thought to have covered the lower Yangzi Valley and extended over 3650 square kilometres. As a Neolithic culture, the archaeological significance of the Liangzhu area is extremely high. Neolithic communities appeared as the agricultural revolution took

place between 7000 and 5000 years ago, when newly developed cultivation techniques permitted small clans and family groupings to produce surplus agricultural produce (Mumford, 1960). The storage of this surplus meant that larger communities could be supported. As communities grew, a division of labour occurred that stimulated further domestic and agricultural related invention. The result was cyclic with invention supporting further community growth. The humble container and its airtight lid, used for storage of grains, was a significant invention that allowed communities to overcome seasonal variations in food availability. An airtight container of rice, reported to be the first species of cultivated grain, has reportedly been found at the project site.

It is difficult to explain with certainty why the area was important to the Liangzhu culture and why a relatively concentrated settlement emerged at this location. However, it is thought that good quality agricultural land, the abundance of fresh water, the shallow sea that covered the present low lying areas and provided fertile fishing grounds, and the hilly topography made it attractive for settlement. It is also thought that the surrounding mountains protected the site from attack, since attackers would be clearly visible as they descended over the mountains. The site, which is the subject of this study, occupies 270 square kilometres, and is understood to be the centre of the Liangzhu civilisation. The size of the site distinguishes it from many other cultural heritage sites that are relatively well contained, and presents important challenges for visitor management and presentation of the site. Within this larger area there is a 33.8 square kilometre core protection area in which it is estimated some 119 heritage sites are located. High quality jade carvings, textiles, sculpture and black pottery artefacts have been uncovered at many of these sites. Many of these artefacts are displayed in a small local museum. The relics uncovered to date are generally small implements and agricultural tools. Many are ornately carved and are very fragile. A tomb and sacrifice alter are thought to have been identified, as have a military bund wall and man-made dykes for the purpose of water management and land reclamation.

There are a number of significant challenges to the planning, management and interpretation of the site. A population of 30,000 people currently live within the core protection area, predominantly within two townships, Liangzhu and Ping Yao. There is also extensive industrial development, in the form of small locally owned factories, situated within and around these settlements. A range of agricultural uses also characterises the non-urban land, including fruit orchards, fisheries and piggeries. There has also been extensive quarrying in nearby hillsides to obtain construction materials used in the expansion of nearby urban areas. All of these land use activities impact upon the visual quality and amenity of the subject site. Local officials estimate 100 industrial developments are currently located within the core protection area. Excavations associated with industrial and residential development in and around these townships frequently reveal new archaeological artefacts and sites. Humid soils and fragility of the artefacts make prolonged exposure of the tombs to air impossible. This makes interpretation of the site difficult.

Despite the impacts of current land uses and development pressures on the site, there is strong support at all levels of governments that this area should be planned and managed properly due to its extreme cultural significance. As an interim measure, a protection order has been placed over the core protection area so that no new development can take place. A special committee has also been established to examine the possibility of having the site listed as a World Cultural Heritage site under the World Heritage Convention (UNESCO, 1972). The consulting project in which this author was engaged required the development of a plan for the protection, management and presentation of the area within a land use planning framework. This plan was to be integrated with the Hangzhou City government's master plan that was being prepared by the City's planning academy. This was to be the first stage in moving the project toward World Heritage listing, as it is necessary as part of the listing process to illustrate that the proper planning framework for the protection of the site is in place before the listing process can proceed (ICOMOS, 1999).

Institutional Context

Hangzhou is the seat of the Zhejiang Provincial government. The City is divided into 15 districts. The subject site falls within Yuang District and two county administrations share control of the project site. As a result, a Liangzhu management committee, comprising members from both county administrations, was set up to oversee the preparation of the Liangzhu Management Plan. The interests of this committee and its individual officials were to balance the economic development potential of the site with the protection of its cultural value. They were keenly aware of the need to promote alternative forms of economic development. Since budgets depended on the estimated revenue generated by the locality, local administrators were eager to maximise and enhance the economic contribution of the site to local economies.

The Hangzhou City Planning and Design Academy was preparing the City's Master Plan and managed the consultancy. The Academy was most concerned with issues such as land use, transport and infrastructure provision, and how the planning for this area would fit within the overall urban planning framework. So, while the local socio-economic concerns of the Liangzhu Management Committee were important, the context in which the planning work was undertaken emphasised land use planning. Strategies for the protection, management and presentation of the site had to be embedded in a land use planning framework. This framework could later be "unpacked" to provide direction for visitor management strategies, local economic development initiatives, tourism marketing and the development of product synergies as the listing process unfolded and political and community support strengthened. In this case study, the use of a land use planning framework meant that all new development and land use change could be managed with a long term view to protecting relic sites and enhancing visual quality. Locations appropriate for tourist infrastructure and servicing could also be protected from intrusive or inconsistent development. This was extremely important given the rapid rate of rural-urbanisation that has been occurring.

In sum, the project involved the preparation of a land use planning strategy that not only recognised the planning requirements associated with World Heritage sites, but also addressed the challenge of managing the rapidly urbanising Yuang County. In the following section, the major directions and recommendations contained in the tourism component of the Liangzhu Plan are discussed and influences upon tourism planning and decision-making are identified.

The Liangzhu Plan

Information required for the planning process is not always pre-existing and freely available. In the case of the Liangzhu plan, further and more detailed archaeological information with respect to the relative significance, fragility/durability of the site would have been an advantage. Archaeological investigations were proceeding slowly and were subject to political and administrative processes outside the control of the consultants and the Hangzhou City Planning and Design Academy that commissioned the plan. Due to the large number of archaeological investigations being conducted in China, issues about illegal digs, black-marketing of relics and the overall management of the archaeological investigations, the relics and burial sites had received preliminary investigation and then had been sealed with concrete. Such a gap in information is a common challenge faced by planners attempting to plan for heritage sites that have not yet received detailed investigation, and is not necessarily unique to this project. However, gaps in information should not stop the planning process as the consequences of non-planning can be significant. In this case study, the rapid expansion of the urban and industrial complex on the outskirts of Hangzhou was a major threat to the protection of archaeological integrity and the development of a Liangzhu tourism product.

Derived from previous discussions, initial site investigations, interviews with Chinese planners, historians and archaeologists a range of issues and challenges were identified:

- The county administrations' economic and social concerns (e.g. local economic development, employment generation and conservation) were to be given priority.

- The potential impact of continued rural urbanisation in and around archaeological sites, both known and unknown, meant that extreme care had to be taken when considering changes in land use and development.
- Relocation of some housing and industry was inevitable. Possible locations needed to be carefully considered to minimise any potential social dislocation problems.
- The potential impact of rural urbanisation on the way in which the site could be interpreted and presented was an important management challenge. While significant landscape change had clearly taken place over the last 5,000 years, presentation of the site needed to emphasise the close association of the rural landscape to the Liangzhu culture. For this reason the continued urbanisation of the county was seen as a threat to the presentation of the site.
- The protection, management and presentation of the site's cultural values should meet World Cultural Heritage requirements.
- The size of the total site, the lack of detailed archaeological information and the fragility of the archaeological sites represented a significant challenge to on-site presentation. Moreover, the Neolithic people of the Liangzhu culture were emerging from the agricultural revolution. They were not advanced city builders. Nor were they builders of monumental structures. As a result, the heritage sites associated with the Liangzhu culture lack the visual impact of sites associated with more recent city-building civilisations (e.g. Greeks, Romans and Mayans).

While a lengthy discussion of the plan contents is not the object of this paper, it is nevertheless important to provide a brief overview of the general direction so that the dialectical influences upon local heritage tourism planning

can be discussed. The general approach taken in developing the plan was that a potential World Cultural Heritage site should be integrated with, and complementary to, the Hangzhou tourism product and associated tourism development strategy. As a designated top tourist city with a vast range of cultural heritage attractions located principally around West Lake, the development and presentation of the Liangzhu site was consistent with the overall direction for tourism development in the City. Due to the fragile nature of the sites, and the difficulty associated with on-site presentation, a museum was considered to be of central importance in visitor management and presentation. Underpinned by the Chinese drive for modernisation, local planners argued for the replacement of the existing museum with a larger building housing state-of-the-art interpretative displays of the Liangzhu culture. The museum would be the gateway to the site and would provide opportunities for all segments of the visitor market to learn about and appreciate the contribution of the Liangzhu culture to Chinese civilisation. The museum would house fragile relics and would provide for education and research needs.

The consultants were also asked to identify a location for a possible cultural heritage theme park. This was intended to be an artificially derived Liangzhu culture experience that mixes entertainment and education, authenticity and fabrication. A similar theme park exists to the south of Hangzhou where visitors can obtain a contrived 'authentic' experience of life during the Song Dynasty. The development of such parks has been a common response to the increased emphasis on tourism and serve important internal Chinese objectives: to strengthen cultural identity and to promote economic development (Sofield & Li, 1998; Ap, 2003). Discussions with local Chinese planners tended to support this view. They were keen to contribute to what they saw as China's modernisation process and to reinforce and validate the importance of the Liangzhu culture to modern China. These internally driven objectives were extremely important to local planners and administrators. Issues about the theme park's consistency with World Heritage market demands, long-term investment requirements associated with theme park development, profitability and authenticity were issues raised by the consultants (e.g. see Ap, 2003 for a discussion of these concerns). However, the Liangzhu Project Committee and local planners involved in the project quickly side-lined these issues, placing more emphasis instead upon the 'statement' that a theme park would make about the significance of the Liangzhu culture.

The Liangzhu culture had a close relationship with the landscape and it was clear that the site could not be interpreted through the museum and artificial attractions only. On-site interpretation opportunities were also included in the plan to cater for the demands of markets seeking authentic experiences and scholars. Despite the large number of archaeological sites that had been flagged, six main sites emerged from detailed analysis as being of core significance. Sites suitable for heavy, medium and light visitation were identified and a strategy developed for the presentation of these sites. Recommendations were made to manage the landscape and to present it in such a way that relationships between the land and the archaeological sites could tell the story of the Liangzhu culture. Successful interpretation relies on both the imagination of the viewer and the skill with which the interpretation strategy is implemented. In this case, international planners argued that it was important to reduce the 'clutter' of rural-urbanisation so that visitors could imagine the relationships between cultural and landscape elements. Recommendations for the removal of some buildings and powerlines, to introduce buffer zones around interpretive sites, to introduce screen planting and to rehabilitate degraded sites to reduce the impact of more distant incompatible elements were made.

Discussion

The aim of this paper has been to interrogate the global-local dialectic as it is played out in the planning for a potential world cultural heritage site in Zhejiang Province, China. It is based on the notion that we need to unpack this global-local nexus and investigate fundamental relationships between tourism development, economy and culture as they are played out in space in order to understand the issues, ideas and values that drive local tourism planning in China.

This case study suggests that connections between culture, economy and development have been mediated through changing ideas about socialism, just as in western democracies prevailing definitions and understandings of development are filtered through our own particular neo-liberal systems of politics and government. Throughout the course of this project, it became apparent that the meaning of development is shaped by an economic discourse, which is tied to cultural values and changing socialist ideologies. The emphasis has been on industrialisation, modernisation and wealth creation. This discourse has played out in economic and institutional reforms and has given rise to a set of relations between the central government and local administrations that shape the issue drivers and agendas of local stakeholders.

Accordingly, local tourism development occurring at the prefecture, city, county and town level are set within this economic development discourse. The way that this economic discourse intersects with culture, and specifically values about the environment, heritage and nationalism have important implications for tourism planning and product development.

Establishing Significance—Global or Local Agenda?

The 'Open Door' reforms introduced in 1978 have provided fertile grounds for the playing out of a curious set of global-local relations in which the central government and localities have been active agents. In essence, the central government has responded to the emerging global economy since 1978 by creating a powerful central and top-down drive for economic development. Economic development has been conceptualised within a framework that emphasises the diversification of economic activity, improved income generation, the stimulation of private sector employment, widespread deregulation across many sectors of the economy and the devolution of responsibilities to lower levels of administration. As a result, local administrations have a greater influence over local community well-being and prosperity. These economic reforms have filtered down into the lowest tiers of administration with budgetary incentives prompting all levels of government to eagerly pursue boosterist local economic development policy. This empowerment of 'the local' has fed parochialism, which remained somewhat suppressed under the strong central control of previous years, as localities try to establish their national significance (Marton, 2000).

Sofield and Li (1998) observe that cultural heritage tourism is a major element of China's tourism product. This paper argues that the emphasis on local economic development, which intersects with a drive for localities to assert their significance in a national context, will continue to stimulate the development of cultural heritage tourism products. In this case study, globally-induced economic influences such as attraction of mobile capital investment and the development of foreign income streams were much less important to local planners and decision-makers. The cultural imperative of proving national significance and asserting the locality's place in a rapidly changing China is a more powerful incentive to become involved in cultural heritage tourism planning and development.

The global local-nexus and the commodification of culture for the purposes of tourism have been discussed elsewhere (e.g. Urry, 1995; Milne & Ateljevic, 2001). In this literature, advances in technology and communication have empowered globalised production and distribution systems. The resulting time-space compression and the homogenisation of culture has promoted a view of the world as a single and finite place (Giddens, 1990). In contradiction, these globalising forces have led to greater awareness of diversity, and a reassertion of local interests (e.g. Featherstone, 1995; Appadurai, 1996). The term 'glocalisation' encapsulates this increasing emphasis on the local under the influence of global forces (Robertson, 1995). The development of cultural tourism products that emphasise uniqueness and sense of place has been one response by local governments to the unrelenting global imperative of economic development. Put simply, distinctiveness sells, and destinations, in an increasingly competitive global tourism marketplace, are increasingly pressured to construct local identities in order to competitively position themselves in the global context.

In this sense, the concept of World Heritage is a vehicle of the global-local dialectic. World heritage listing endows a site with international iconic value. In the majority of cases, inclusion on the Register of World Heritage has had the effect of elevating awareness, importance and image of a site within international tourist markets (e.g. Drost, 1996; Jenkins & McArthur, 1996; Shackley, 1998; ICOMOS, 1999; Dredge & Humphreys, 2003). In the case of the Liangzhu project, national pride and a drive to assert local significance at a national level has a substantial impact on the drive to prove international significance and to obtain World Cultural Heritage listing. China is in a stage of rapid and sustained change. Economic reforms, institutional change and the breakdown of the social and cultural isolation of the pre-1978 period have created a situation where the significance of place is constantly being negotiated and renegotiated at a domestic level. In essence, obtaining World Heritage listing would validate the importance of the Liangzhu culture and would reinforce the importance of the county and the city in a domestic context. The centralised institutional structures of the past reinforced solidarity, however the local county is now able to break from this generic Chineseness to promote its unique and highly significant place in China's history. As a result, the place promotion that is occurring does not represent a response to global forces, but rather a response to the centrifugal-centripetal forces associated with domestic restructuring and local empowerment. World Heritage is the vehicle to establish this cultural significance. It is a means to an end, and not the ultimate goal.

Environment, Modernisation and Authenticity

The push to facilitate local economic development, assert local difference and promote the domestic significance of locality has brought with it many environmental impacts. While air and water pollution, soil erosion, and deforestation are evident, the march of rural urbanisation and the modification of the landscape through quarrying and large-scale infrastructure development can have important visual and psychological impacts on tourism markets. In this context, the push for local economic development, which is closely associated with rural industrialisation and other forms of environmental change, has important implications for tourism product planning and development.

In this case study, the Liangzhu tourism project was underpinned by an uneasy tension between the desire to promote the mass production and consumption of the cultural heritage experience through an enlarged museum and cultural heritage park (a decontextualised experience in a modified environment) and the desire to protect landscape integrity scenic quality and provide on-site interpretation of selected archaeological sites (to contextualise and authenticate the tourism experience in a more natural environment). The former is to cater predominantly for the growing domestic market and the latter, an international market. The protection of the associative landscape becomes a central element for the planning of the tourism product, since the close association of the Liangzhu culture with its natural setting provides a rich understanding of daily life in the Neolithic era. However, it is also a point of difference that highlights Western planners' biocentric and Chinese planners' anthropocentric (Chinese) values towards the environment (Sofield & Li, 2003). These values have an important influence upon product planning and development.

China's long and rich cultural history provides many economic, social, political and artistic interpretations of place. As Petersen (1995) observes, much domestic tourism in China is driven by a desire to validate this poetic knowledge of place and to see and validate understandings of history that have been embedded over centuries in Chinese culture. To western consultants driven by biocentric interpretation of nature, this suggests that a high degree of authenticity is important for the domestic market and the preservation of landscape quality should be an important aspect of product planning. However, the Chinese have a different cultural relationship to the environment (see Sofield & Li, 2003). Instead of the biocentric approach inherent in Western ideology, which emphasises the maintenance and enhancement of natural systems and the reduction of evidence of human intrusion, the Chinese take an anthropocentric position. The anthropocentric position embraces the notion that improvements to the environment can enhance human use and enjoyment. To this end, the interest expressed by Chinese planners to incorporate built attractions into the Liangzhu cultural heritage product is consistent with their notions of authenticity.

Conclusion

This paper has sought to investigate and critically discuss relationships between economy, culture and tourism development in the case of the Liangzhu cultural heritage tourism project in Zhijiang Province, China. These relationships between economy, culture and development underpin the issues that shape

agendas, drive interests and, ultimately, influence decision-making processes. China's socialist system has undergone significant ideological shifts that have played out in its economic and institutional structures since the Open Door reform policies were introduced in 1978. Responding to global economic processes, there has been a reworking of conceptions of development resulting in an emerging focus on economic profitability and wealth creation. The decentralisation of decision-making has empowered localities to differentiate themselves and pursue local tourism development.

Nationalism and cultural conceptions of modernisation are also powerful influences upon local planners' and administrators' ideas and values about tourism development. The drive to assert national significance is a powerful internal force that shapes local responses. International vehicles, such as World Heritage listing, assist in procuring this internal goal. Moreover, World Heritage is also a mechanism to globalise the tourism product and achieve another internal goal: modernisation. In sum, local tourism planning in China is underpinned by the interplay of globalism, localism, nationalism and modernisation. The way that these are played out and impact upon local tourism planning and product development is dependent upon cultural and economic conceptions of development. Understandings of these parameters are essential for the development of appropriate and responsive policy.

References

Ap, J. (2003). An Assessment of Theme Park Development in China. In Z. Guangrui (ed), *Tourism in China* (pp. 195–214). New York: Haworth Hospitality Press.

Appadurai, A. (1996). *Modernity at Large: Cultural Dimensions of Globalisation.* Minneapolis: University of Minnesota Press.

Chang, T. C., Milne, S., Fallon, D. & Pohlmann, C. (1996). Urban Heritage Tourism: The Global-Local Nexus. *Annals of Tourism Research*, 23(2), 284–305.

Chen, G. (2001). *Greater Hangzhou: A New Travel Guide.* Hangzhou: n.p.

Clancy, M. (2001). *Exporting Paradise.* London: Pergamon Press.

Dredge, D. & Humphreys, J. (2003). Ecotourism Planning and Policy in the Wet Tropics. In R. Dowling (ed), *Ecotourism Policy and Planning.* (pp. 121–140) London: CABI.

Drost, A. (1996). Developing Sustainable Tourism for World Heritage Sites. *Annals of Tourism Research*, 23(2), 479–492.

Featherstone, M. (1995). *Undoing Culture: Globalization, postmodernism and identity.* London: Sage.

Giddens, A. (1990). *The Consequences of Modernity.* Cambridge, UK: Polity Press.

Guangrui, Z. (2003). China's Tourism Since 1978: Policies, experiences and lessons learned. In A. Lew, L. Yu, J. Ap & Z. Guangrui (eds), *Tourism in China* (pp. 67–82). New York: Haworth Hospitality Press.

ICOMOS. (1999). *Tourism at World Heritage Sites: Site Manager's Handbook (2nd Edition).* Madrid: World Tourism Organisation.

Jenkins, O. & McArthur, S. (1996). Marketing protected areas. *Australian Parks and Recreation Journal*, 10–15.

Lew, A. & Yu, L. (1995). *Tourism in China: Geographic, Political and Economic Perspectives.* Oxford: Westview.

Lew, A., Yu, L., Ap, J. & Guangrui, Z. (eds) (2003). *Tourism in China.* New York: Haworth Hospitality Press.

Li, C. (1999). 200 Million Mouths Too Many: China's Surplus Rural Production. In D. Shambaugh (ed), *The China Reader* (pp. 362–375). New York: Vintage Books.

Li, Y. (2002). The Impact of Tourism in China on Local Communities. *Asian Studies Review*, 26(4), 471–486.

Lin, G. (2002). The Growth and Structural Change of Chinese Cities: A contextual and geographic analysis. *Cities*, 19(5), 299–316.

Ma, J. (1997). *Intergovernmental Relations and Economic Management in China.* Houndmills: Macmillan Press.

Marton, A. (2000). *China's Spatial Economic Development: Restless Landscapes in the Lower Yangzi Delta.* London: Routledge.

Massey, D. (1984). *Spatial Divisions of Labour: Social Structures and the Geography of Production.* London: Macmillan.

Milne, S. & Ateljevic, I. (2001). Tourism, economic development and the global-local nexus: theory embracing complexity. *Tourism Geographies*, 3(4), 369–393.

Mumford, L. (1960). *The City in History: Its origins, its transformations and its prospects.* Harmondsworth: Penguin.

Nuryanti, W. (1996). Heritage and Postmodern Tourism. *Annals of Tourism Research*, 23(2), 249–260.

Ogden, S. (1992). *China's Unresolved Issues: Politics, Development and Culture.* Englewood Cliffs, NJ: Prentice Hall.

People's Daily. (2000). National Tourism Income to Hit \$15.5b. *People's Daily*, pp. 9 January, 2000.

Qiao, Y. (1995). Domestic Tourism in China. In A. Lew & L. Yu (eds), *Tourism in China: Geographical, Political and Economic Perspectives.* (pp. 121–130) Oxford: Westview Press.

Richter, L. (1983). Political Implications of Chinese Tourism Policy. *Annals of Tourism Research*, 10(3), 395–413.

Richter, L. (1989). *The Politics of Tourism in Asia.* Honolulu: University of Hawaii Press.

Robertson, R. (1995). Glocalisation: Time-space and homogeneity-heterogeneity. In R. Robertson (ed), *Global Modernities* (pp. 25–44). London: Sage.

Shackley, M. (1998). Introduction – World Cultural Heritage Sites, *Visitor Management: Case Studies from World Heritage Sites* (pp. 1–9). Oxford: Butterworth Heinemann.

Sofield, T. & Li, F. (1998). Tourism Development and Cultural Policies in China. Annals of Tourism Research, 25(2), 362–393.

Sofield, T. & Li, F. M. S. (2003). Processes in Formulating an Ecotourism Policy for Nature Reserves in Yunnan Province China. In R. K. Dowling (ed), *Ecotourism Policy and Planning* (pp. 141–167). Wallingford: CABI International.

Swain, M. (1990). Commoditizing ethnic tourism in Southwest China. *Cultural Survival Quarterly*, 14, 26–29.

Teo, P. & Li, L. H. (2003). Global and Local Interactions in Tourism. *Annals of Tourism Research*, 30(2), 287–306.

Timothy, D. J. (1999) Participatory planning: A view of tourism in Indonesia. *Annals of Tourism Research*, 26(2): 371–391.

Tisdell, C. & Wen, J. (1991). Investment in China's Tourism Industry: Its Scale, Nature and Policy Issues. *China Economic Review*, 2(2), 175–193.

UNESCO (1972). *Convention Concerning the Protection of the World Cultural and Natural Heritage.* Paris: UNESCO.

Urry, J. (1990). *The Tourist Gaze: Leisure and Travel in Contemporary Societies.* London: Sage Publications.

Urry, J. (1995). *Consuming Places.* London: Routledge.

Verhelst, T. & Tyndale, W. (2002). Culture, spirituality and development. In D. Eade (ed), Development and Culture: Selected Essays from Development in Practice (pp. 1–24). London: Oxfam.

Wen, J. & Tisdell, C. (2001). *Tourism and China's Development: Policies, Regional Economic Growth and Ecotourism.* Singapore: World Scientific.

World Tourism Organization (1997). *Tourism: 2020 Vision.* Madrid: WTO.

World Tourism Organization (2001). *Tourism Highlights 2001.* Madrid: WTO.

Zhang, H. Q. (1995). China's Tourism since 1978: Policies, experiences and lessons learned. In L. Yu (ed), *Tourism in China: Geographic, political and economic perspectives* (pp. 3–17). Boulder: Westview Press.

Zhang, H. Q., Chong, K. & Ap, J. (1999). An Analysis of Tourism Policy Development in Modern China. *Tourism Management*, 20, 471–485.

Zhang, W. (1997). China's Domestic Tourism: Impetus, Development and Trends. *Tourism Management*, 18(8), 565–571.

Zhang, Y. (1995). An Assessment of China's Tourism Resources. In A. Lew & L. Yu (eds), *Tourism in China: Geographic, Political and Economic Perspectives.* Oxford: Westview Press.

Zhang, Y. (2001). *Tourism and Regional Imbalance in Yunnan (China).* Paper presented at the CAUTHE Conference 2001: Capitalising on Research, Proceedings of the Eleventh Australian Tourism and Hospitality Research Conference, 7–10 February 2001. Canberra: University of Canberra.

Creating Opportunities and Ensuring Access to Desirable Heritage and Cultural Tourist Services and Leisure Experiences

Shane Pegg and Norma J. Stumbo

Introduction

"In the best of all possible worlds, individuals with disabilities would be able to board a plane or a cruise ship, or make reservations at a hotel or a resort without the slightest worry – knowing that all accommodations would be fully accessible. At some point in the future, perhaps that may become a reality"

(*Epstein, 1998, p. 61*)

There is no greater challenge to the global community than to acknowledge and optimise opportunity for all persons. Integral to creating such opportunity is the necessity of ensuring access and inclusion of all persons to appropriate heritage and cultural tourism services. However, as noted by James (1996), in economically, ethnically, and racially stratified societies, individuals' inability to gain access to and receive services that address their particular needs and expectations is not merely a result of their failure to take advantage of available services. Rather, it may be reflective of the barriers often inherent in the very societies in which they live. McAvoy (2000) and O'Neill and Knight (2000) charged that many tourism-driven agencies today may often unknowingly create these organisational and institutional barriers by way of their policies, practices, facilities and programs, as well as rules and regulations, that tend to exclude, restrict, or discriminate against persons with disabilities.

People with Disabilities: The Scope

Recognising that people are living longer and healthier, and are better educated than their predecessors, it is now commonly recognised that people with disabilities, be they old or young, are fast becoming influential players in all sectors of the world economy, not least of which is the leisure and tourism sectors (Burnett and Bender Baker, 2001; Grant, 2002). In the United States, a narrow definition of disability resulted in 48.9 million (19.4 percent of the population) being counted as individuals with disabilities in

1992 (Rimmer, Braddock, and Pitetti, 1996). A broader definition of disability, including such conditions as arthritis and mental disability, expands the percentage to nearly 30 percent of the 270 million individuals living in the US (Rimmer, Braddock, and Pitetti, 1996). Burnett and Bender Baker (2001) and Lach (1999) noted that by 2030, the number of people living with disabilities in the United States is expected to double with the aging of the baby boomers.

On the world stage the trends are not dissimilar, with the percentage of persons with disabilities in Japan growing from 4.9 percent in 1950 to 19.2 percent in 2000 (Ward, 2001). In Australia, the trends are similar, with some 3.6 million people (19% of the population) now recognised as having a disability (Australian Bureau of Statistics, 1998).

A market segment as large as 20 to 30 percent (or more) of all travellers is an enormous consideration for tourism operators in the Asia Pacific region. The World Tourism Organization (UNWTO) has projected that by the year 2020 international arrivals will reach over 1.56 billion, of which 1.18 billion will be intra-regional and 377 million will be long-haul travellers. Furthermore, the UNWTO acknowledged that in 2002, East Asia and the Pacific achieved international tourist arrivals of 115.2 million individuals, up from 109.2 million the prior year. Although it is forecasted that Europe will, for the short term at least, hold the largest share of world arrivals, it is forecasted that in coming years the Americas will decline from 19 to 18 percent and East Asia and the Pacific region will increase to 25 percent, from its 2001 level of 16.6 percent, of the market share. At the same time, East Asia and the Pacific, South Asia, the Middle East, and Africa are forecasted to record growth rates of over 5 percent per year, compared

with a worldwide average of 4.1 percent (UNWTO, 2003). If 20 to 30 percent of this travelling population is considered to have disabilities, the financial, social, and service implications are great.

Worth noting is the fact that individuals with disabilities are more financially independent than those of a similar demographic in the past and are much more discerning in their consumer choices. In the United States alone, individuals with disabilities account for some 50 to 80 million individuals with a discretionary income of some $200 billion per annum (Burnett and Bender Baker, 2001; O'Neill and Knight, 2000).

In a recent study of the trends and market scope of United States resident travellers with disabilities, Lipp and Keefe (2003) noted that people with disabilities could spend at least US$27 billion per year if certain travel needs were met. This was an increase of nearly 100% on the current industry estimate whereby people with disabilities spent US$13.6 billion on 31.7 million trips in the previous year. The study also found that currently travellers with disabilities generated a total of 194,000 travel-related jobs, $4.22 billion in payroll and $2.52 billion in tax revenues in the United States alone (Lipp and Keefe, 2003).

Despite the large numbers of individuals involved, their growing financial wealth, and their desire to travel to cultural and heritage locations, this group of consumers has largely been ignored by the leisure and tourism industry worldwide, especially in the Asia Pacific market. Failing to respond positively to the needs and desires of persons with disabilities may distance the tourism industry from a vibrant, active, and relatively affluent consumer group, costing the regional industry millions, potentially billions, of dollars per year.

People with Disabilities: A Case of Unmet Needs

A great irony exists when discussing the travel needs of people with disabilities. On one hand, they have been identified as *the* largest and fastest growing market segment for the travel and tourism industry, especially within the cultural and heritage sector (Burnett and Bender Baker, 2001). Although no accurate information is available on the travel volume of people with disabilities in the South Pacific region, this segment of the travel market is considered substantial in numbers (Cavinato and Cuckovich, 1992) and can, depending upon the region, represent over 20 to 30 percent of the travel market (Rimmer, Braddock, and Pitetti, 1996; Turco, Stumbo and Garncarz, 1998). It is apparent from a review of global travel figures that people with disability collectively represent a statistically significant number of travellers (Burnett and Bender Baker, 2001; Darcy and Daruwalla, 1999).

On the other hand, researchers across the world have repeatedly reported that persons with disabilities have not been adequately served by the travel and tourism industry (Burnett and Bender Baker, 2001; Darcy and Daruwalla, 1999; Turco, Stumbo and Garncarz, 1998). A variety of barriers exist to stymie full, active, and inclusive participation on the part of persons with disability. Travel researchers have noted such constraints as

- inaccessible transportation (Taylor, 2000; Turco, Stumbo and Garncarz, 1998; Vollmer, 1999);
- inaccessible accommodation (Burnett and Bender Baker, 2001; Turco, Stumbo and Garncarz, 1998; Vladimir, 1998);
- inaccessible attractions (Turco, Stumbo and Garncarz, 1998);

- misleading informational resources (McGuire, Dottavio and O'Leary, 1986; Turco, Stumbo and Garncarz, 1998); and
- negative staff attitudes and interactions (Burnett and Bender Baker, 2001; Turco, Stumbo and Garncarz, 1998; Vladimir, 1998).

It is clear that people with a disability can no longer be ignored by tourism operators in the Asia Pacific region given this group's economic clout and, of course, their recognised interest and growing passion for cultural and heritage experiences. In fact, research by Burnett and Bender Baker (2001) of the travel needs of people with disabilities supports the notion that this subgroup may be a most profitable segment for the travel and tourism industry to target, if properly positioned.

The researchers noted that, while not wealthy, these consumers have adequate resources to travel several times per year, especially for the purposes of vacations and family visits. Burnett and Bender Baker (2001) also noted that, as a group of consumers, people with disabilities were very loyal to destination institutions that were sensitive to their needs while not being patronising. Furthermore, they found that people with disabilities would travel a great deal more if they could find disability-friendly destinations. This researchers have found to be particularly true for respondents where opportunities were provided for individuals to receive personal and consistent satisfaction through their involvement and immersion in appropriate and relevant tourism services and settings (Burnett and Bender Baker, 2001; Fallon and Kriwoken, 2002).

Inclusive Leisure and Tourism Services in the Asia Pacific

Importantly, inclusive leisure and tourism services are those in which everyone, regardless of the presence of disability, has choices, social connections, and supports. In this context, inclusion has been defined as a process that enables an individual to be part of his or her physical and social environment by making choices, being supported in their endeavours, having friends and being valued (Bullock and Mahon, 2001; Datillo, 1994). Sayeed (1999, p. 14) argued "the word inclusion itself conjures up a picture of belonging, of being part of woven threads of colourful fabric which are the communities we live in."

Clearly, the key tenet of inclusion being expressed by the authors is that this process seeks to ensure everyone, regardless of level of ability or disability, the right to experience an enjoyable and satisfying life. Importantly, and as acknowledged by the National Recreation and Park Association (NRPA) (1999), inclusive leisure experiences encourage and enhance opportunities for people of varying abilities to participate and interact in life's activities together with dignity and respect. Dattilo has suggested that there are certain characteristics of inclusion that can be embraced by tourism and leisure service providers to their competitive advantage. These included:

- recognise we are one yet we are different;
- create chances for others to experience freedom to participate;
- value each person and value diversity; and
- support participation (2002, p. 26).

Yet it is clear that many travel and tourism operators, whilst accepting compliance with legislated national requirements such as the Americans with Disability Act (ADA) in the United States or the Australian Standards (1428) guidelines which relate to minimum standards of accessibility to facilities and venues in Australia, often do little to enhance the tourist experience of people with a disability (Devine and McGovern, 2001; Tan, 2002).

This issue was identified by Burnett and Bender Baker (2001) who in a study of the travel related behaviours of mobility-disabled consumers found that unfortunately the general response of the vast majority of businesses operating in the tourism and travel sector was mostly compliance with legislated minimum standards of service delivery. This is despite the fact that heritage and cultural visitor attractions also have a public obligation to ensure that their facilities are fully accessible, and that this should be accurately communicated to the tourist with a disability (Patterson, 1996).

However, people (or travellers) with disabilities, especially those with high support needs, tend to approach the information provided about tourist accommodations and visitor attractions with a great deal of apprehension, if not outright suspicion. Perhaps this can be explained in part by recent research by Darcy (1998), who concluded that about 45% of those with a disability surveyed found that most information about access that was provided by tourism operators was either inaccurate or outright misleading.

Darcy and Daruwalla (1999) documented a consistent lack of accurate information about accessible tourism features. For example, the authors noted the particular comments of one respondent who arrived into the City of Canberra at 8pm to find "that the 4-star motel with a disabled unit had two steps to gain entry to said room, plus hob and sliding screen on shower, great info, great holiday. I guess there are no politicians in wheelchairs" (Darcy and Daruwalla, 1999, p. 44).

Some travel and tourist accommodations have paid attention to these unnecessary barriers. One example is Microtel Inn and Suites in the United States, which has specifically targeted in recent years the needs of travellers with disabilities by implementing nationwide an "opening doors" training program designed to allow staff to better serve travellers with disabilities (Weiner, 1999). Significantly, the customer service program implemented placed a high importance on disability etiquette in addition to the physical accessibility of the facilities for guests. Accessibility in all its forms, from information resources to staff training to the physical environment, are all noted as important to individuals with disabilities (Schleien, 1993).

As difficult as it is for the many travellers with disabilities in countries where base standards have been legislated there are all too many examples in the Asia Pacific region where little has been done to support the needs of people with disabilities. For example, few accessibility laws exist in Japan that affect private buildings. In November 2000, the "Barrier-Free Transportation Law" took effect requiring public transit systems to be more accessible, and by 2010 the government hopes to make all transportation hubs with more than 5,000 daily users accessible. But Michiko Kikuchi, appointed to form disability policy for Toyko's metropolitan government, believes a barrier-free Japan is a long way off. "It is impossible to close all the vertical gaps in town," she lamented to the *Japan Times* last year. What the handicapped need, she said, "is a helping hand" (Ward, 2001, p. 46).

Dealing Effectively with a Diverse Range of Clients

As acknowledged by Allison (2000), clearly one of the greatest challenges today for service-based agencies providing cultural and heritage visitor experiences is to meet the needs of their diverse clients and participants. While an important consideration in the inclusionary process is the creation of opportunities for all people, it does not mean however that people must participate in groups characterised by their diversity (Dattilo, 2002; Schleien, Germ and McAvoy, 1996). Rather, what inclusion should mean to heritage and cultural tourism operators is that all people, regardless of ability or disability, should feel welcome and supported to participate in programs or activities of their choosing.

Dattilo (2002) urged service providers to understand that "choice" means freedom to choose among many available and equivalent options, not between lesser, poor quality, or no options at all. Darcy and Daruwalla (1999) emphasised that the improvement of access for people with disabilities, and the removal of constraints and barriers, is not just an issue of providing a legal solution to physical access issues. Indeed, access for tourists with disabilities is affected by a wide variety of intrinsic, environmental, and interactive factors affecting their comfort and enjoyment level (O'Neill and Knight, 2000; Smith, 1987).

Therefore it is paramount that tourism operators have a clear and thorough understanding of issues pertaining to inclusion, diversity, disability, attitudes and common barriers to leisure participation from the outset. To this end, tourist operators must be mindful of the need to facilitate participation in the full variety of cultural and heritage tourism activities by positively encouraging and advocating for inclusion, making adaptations to programs and infrastructure as and where necessary, training staff in welcoming diverse groups, and considering individual characteristics of participants when developing and implementing leisure services.

The Commonwealth Research Centre (CRC) for Sustainable Tourism (2002), in a study of the inbound practices affecting tourism product quality, reported that poor service quality and lack of understanding and appreciation of international service standards and visitor expectations were primary reasons for tourist dissatisfaction with their "holiday experience." Dattilo (2002, p. 18) noted that most people with disabilities are just regular people trying to lead meaningful lives, not to inspire, not to be pitied. That is to say that they simply seek to engage in typical community activities and enjoy life in the same manner as so many of us take for granted each and every day. Darcy and Daruwalla (1999, p. 46) contended that tourism operators must encompass the broadest notion of access if the ultimate goal of eliminating social injustice for people with disabilities is to become a reality.

The competitive advantage of any tourism operator lies in the uniqueness of its superior service, and the degree to which the organisation renders itself difficult to be duplicated by its competitors (Kandampully and Duddy, 2001). In recognising people with disabilities as a growing group of discerning and paying consumers seeking out opportunities to participate in various heritage and cultural tourism activities in the Asia Pacific, tourism operators have before them an ideal opportunity to seize that competitive advantage.

Researchers such as Weaver (2002) have identified the South Pacific tourism industry as being characterised by low visitor numbers and low tourist/resident ratios but with ample opportunity for future growth and sustainable development. While the industry would appear therefore to be in an excellent position to facilitate and enhance the leisure experiences of a broad cross section of tourists it has, with respect to people with

disabilities at least, failed to effectively do so (Devine and McGovern, 2001; Lipp and Keefe, 2003).

Conclusion

This paper has advanced the proposition that heritage and cultural tourism operators in the Asia Pacific must change their service philosophies and offerings to better facilitate the development of inclusive consumer-driven services. More particularly, it has also identified the need for operators in Asia Pacific countries that presently do not have accessibility mandates or legislation to take direct responsibility for such standards so as to be better positioned to serve the growing disabled tourist market within heritage and cultural locales.

Dattilo (2002) asserted that we need to provide tourism and leisure services that reach all members of the community, that treat everyone fairly, and that help to eliminate any form of discrimination. Moreover, the cultural and heritage tourism industry has matured to such a point whereby its leading operators must now recognise the need to augment quality (value of service), and hence the service offering, on a continuous basis (Kandampully and Duddy, 2001). The challenge therefore for tourism service providers in the Asia Pacific, and one argued by Schleien (1993) more generally, is that the time has come to adopt a new way of thinking, one founded on the premise that the community belongs to everyone, and everyone regardless of level and type of ability belongs to the community.

"Clearly the disabled would travel a great deal more often if they could find more disability-friendly destinations" (Burnett and Baker, 2001, p. 10). Inclusive cultural and heritage tourism services in the Asia Pacific region therefore can be a powerful and, might we add for the operators involved, a financially worthwhile vehicle for promoting such an ideal.

References

Australian Bureau of Statistics (ABS) (1998), *Catalogue No. 4430.0 – Disability, Ageing and Carers: Summary of findings*. Canberra: ABS.

Burnett, J., and Bender Baker, H. (2001), 'Assessing the travel-related behaviours of the mobility-disabled consumer', *Journal of Travel Research*, 40, 4–11.

Cavinato, J. L. and Cuckovich, M. L. (1992), 'Transportation and tourism for the disabled: An assessment, *Transportation Journal*, 31, (3), 46–53.

Commonwealth Research Centre for Sustainable Research (CRC) (2002), *Study into the Inbound Practices Affecting Tourism Product Quality in Australia's Tourism Industry*. Gold Coast: CRC for Sustainable Tourism.

Darcy, S., and Darawala, P. (1999), 'The trouble with travel: Tourism and people with disabilities', *Social Alternatives*, 18, (1), 41–48.

Dattilo, J. (2002), *Inclusive Leisure Services: Responding to the Rights of People With Disabilities* (2nd edn). State College, PA: Venture Publishing.

Devine, M., and McGovern, J. (2001), 'Inclusion of individuals with disabilities in public park and recreation programs: Are agencies ready?', *Journal of Park and Recreation Administration*, 19, 4, 60–82.

Epstein, R. (1998), 'Trouble-free vacations', *Exceptional Parent*, 28, (3), 61.

Fallon, L., and Kriwoken, L. (2002), *Key Elements Contributing to Effective and Sustainable Visitor Centres*. Gold Coast: CRC for Sustainable Tourism.

Grant B. (2002), 'Over 65 and ready to play'. *Australian Leisure Management*, 35, 36–38.

Henderson, J. (2003), 'Visitor attraction development in East Asia', in A. Fyall, B. Garrod, and A. Leask (eds), *Managing Visitor Attractions*. London: Butterworth Heinemann, pp. 73–85.

Kandampully, J., and Duddy, R. (2001), 'Service system: A strategic approach to gain a competitive advantage in the hospitality and tourism industry', *International Journal of Hospitality & Tourism Administration*, 2, (1), 27–47.

Lach, J. (1999), 'Disability – Liability', *American Demographics*, 2, 21–22.

Lip, E., and Keefe, C. (2003), *Study suggests travellers with disabilities would double their spending if airlines and hotels improved certain needs*, http://www.hotel-online.com/News/PR2003_1st_Jan03_Disabletravelers.html. Site visited 18th January 2003.

O'Neill, M., and Knight, J. (2000), 'Accessing the disability tourism dollar – Implications for hotel enterprises in Western Australia', Research Paper, *CAUTHE 2000 National Research Conference*, Canberra: CAUTHE, pp. 165–173.

Patterson, I. (1996), 'Tourism, travel and people with disabilities: Untapped market segment', Research Paper, *Leisure in the 21st Century: Challenges and Opportunities*. 2nd Gatton International Workshop, October 3–4, The University of Queensland, Gatton.

Rimmer, J.H., Braddock, D., and Pitteti, K.H. (1996). 'Research on physical activity and disability: An emerging national priority', *Medicine and Science in Sports and Exercise*, 28, (8), 1366–1372.

Sayeed, Z. (1999), 'A 1998 Tash Conference Keynote Address: Zuhy Sayeed', *TASH Newsletter*, 25, (1/2), 12–14.

Schleien, S. (1993), 'Access and inclusion in community services', *Parks and Recreation*, 28, (4), 66–72.

Schleien, S., Germ, P., and McAvoy, L. (1996), 'Inclusive community leisure services: Recommended professional practices and barriers encountered', *Therapeutic Recreation Journal*, 30, (4), 260–273.

Smith, R. (1987), 'Leisure of disabled tourists: Barriers to participation', *Annals of Tourism Research*, 14, 376, 389.

Tan, S. (2002), *Hotel Management Attitudes Toward People With Disabilities in Brisbane*. Unpublished Honours Thesis. Brisbane: The University of Queensland.

Turco, D.M., Stumbo, N.J. and Garncarz, J. (1998), 'Tourism constraints for people with disabilities', *Parks & Recreation*, 33, (9), 78–84.

Ward, J. (2001), 'Too little, too late', *Architecture*, 90, (7), 46.

Weaver, D. (2002), 'Perspectives on sustainable tourism in the South Pacific', in R. Harris, T. Griffin and P. Williams, *Sustainable Tourism: A Global Perspective*. London: Butterworth-Heinmann, pp. 121–139.

Weiner, B. (1999), Microtel Inn & Suites "open doors" to travellers with disabilities. http:///www.hotel-online.com/News/PressReleases1999_2ndMay99_Microtel-Doors.html Site visited 22nd January 2003.

World Tourism Organization. (2003). *Tourism highlights – 2002*. http://www.world-tourism.org/index.htm. Site visited 18th January, 2003.

Distribution Channels for Heritage and Cultural Tourism in New Zealand

Douglas G. Pearce and Raewyn Tan

Introduction

This paper examines the structure, functioning and challenges of managing distribution channels for heritage and cultural tourism. Distribution channels in tourism create the link between the suppliers and consumers of tourism services, providing information and a mechanism enabling consumers to make and pay for reservations (Buhalis, 2000; Gartner & Bachri, 1994; Wahab *et al.*, 1976). Developing an effective distribution system is critical to the successful development and marketing of any form of tourism, especially in times of increased competition (Knowles & Grabowski, 1999). Despite this importance, scarcely any attention has been given to this subject in the heritage and cultural tourism literature and the newly emerging literature on distribution channels has essentially ignored issues relating to this form of tourism. The paper seeks to fill this gap through a systematic exploration of distribution channels for heritage and cultural tourism in two New Zealand settings: Wellington, the capital, and Rotorua, a major resort destination renowned for its Maori culture and geothermal attractions.

The research on which the paper is based forms part of a larger project entitled "Innovation in New Zealand tourism through improved distribution channels" funded by the Foundation for Research Science and Technology (Pearce & Tan, 2002). Begun in July 2002, the central aim of the broader project is to develop a more systematic understanding of the diverse distribution channels for New Zealand tourism and to examine ways of increasing their effectiveness with regard to particular markets, regions and forms of tourism.

The significance of distribution channels was highlighted in the recent New Zealand Tourism Strategy 2010. The strategy identified a need to "develop a tourism distribution channel strategy so New Zealand tourism operators have an increased level of influence in the distribution channel" as one means of achieving the goal of marketing and managing a world-class visitor experience (Tourism Strategy Group, 2001: 41). This requires an increased understanding of the strengths, weaknesses and working of existing channels.

Distribution, as Wahab *et al.* (1976: 96) note, "is what makes the product available". The links between producers and consumers may be made directly or indirectly via one or more intermediaries (e.g. wholesalers, inbound and outbound operators, retail travel agencies, regional or local tourism organisations...) and a range of different channel structures may occur in any market or destination. The choice of direct or indirect sales and the selection of appropriate distribution channels essentially involve a trade-off between market coverage and cost.

Despite the strategic importance of distribution channels and their potential to serve as a unifying conceptual and analytical framework that spans markets and destinations (Pearce, 2002a), the literature in this field is relatively recent and remains rather fragmented (Buhalis and Laws, 2001; O'Connor, 1999; Pearce, 2002b). Most of the more detailed research has involved a two-stage or business-to-business approach dealing with such themes as buyer-seller relationships (March, 2000; Lumsdon & Swift, 1999), the role of supplier/intermediary characteristics (García-Falcón & Medina-Muñoz, 1999; Radburn & Goodall, 1990), concentration and conflict (Buhalis, 2000), and the potential for disintermediation through advances in information technology (Ali-Knight & Wild, 1999; Morrell, 1998). Research on distribution channels has been undertaken in a variety of contexts and with respect to various forms of tourism. Studies dealing with mass package tourism, particularly in coastal settings, have been the most common (Buhalis, 2000; March, 1996; Yamamoto & Gill, 2002). None appears to have focused yet on heritage and cultural tourism.

Similarly, the expanding literature on heritage and cultural tourism which has developed over the last fifteen years has essentially ignored questions of distribution associated with these forms of tourism. Much of the work in this field centres around issues of production and consumption, of development and demand (Richards, 1996; Wall & Nuryanti, 1996, Russo & van der Borg, 2002). In terms of production, a particular concern has been with the inherent tension between questions of heritage and cultural conservation and the development of sites for tourism purposes (Herbert, 1995; Nuryanti, 1997). One characteristic of this situation is the so-called "curatorial approach" to the heritage sector where the primary mission is "caring for the property and maintaining it in as pristine a state as possible", with questions of financial solvency and public access being secondary considerations (Garrod & Fyall, 2000: 684).

Middleton (1997: 217–218) argues many small heritage sites suffer from a "management deficit", especially in terms of marketing management: "The people responsible may be trained and knowledgeable about their particular resource but, for perfectly understandable reasons, they typically lack expertise in the management skills required to deal effectively with modern international tourism...". Indeed, marketing issues are largely ignored in the heritage and cultural tourism literature. Research on the demand side has generally been limited to establishing profile characteristics of visitors (Chandler & Costello, 2002; Prentice, 1993) or perhaps examining their motivations (Jansen-Verbeke & van Rekom, 1996), but the marketing implications of these findings are rarely developed in depth. Where the marketing of heritage and cultural tourism has been addressed it is often in terms of what is being promoted and how authentic the message is rather than how the marketing is being undertaken, by whom and with what results (Renucci, 1997; Waitt, 2000).

Research in New Zealand, the context for the present study, reflects these trends in the broader literature. Research on tourism distribution channels is very recent and so far limited in extent (Crotts *et al.*, 1998; Pearce, 2002b; Pearce & Tan, 2002; Tan, 2002). Studies on heritage and cultural tourism are more developed but far from voluminous and tend to focus on the broader issues of development and demand noted earlier (Balcar and Pearce, 1996; Blackler, 1998; Hall & McArthur, 1996; Ryan, 2002; Warren & Taylor, 2001). Warren & Taylor's (2001) report provides a recent, wide-ranging overview of heritage tourism in New Zealand, a sector they note that is still comparatively new. The report highlights the diversity of tourism products, with historic or heritage buildings, historic sites, heritage tours and museum or heritage collections being the most numerous while Maori tourism is relatively under-represented. Warren and Taylor also found that most heritage tourism enterprises rely on word of mouth and brochures in promoting their products.

The present paper then attempts to bridge these two literatures and reduce the gaps identified by examining distribution channels for heritage and cultural tourism. While the focus is on selected operations in New Zealand, the approach adopted and the lessons learnt have a more general application. The approach used will now be outlined before the findings are presented and discussed. Conclusions are then drawn.

Methodology

Given the paucity of existing information about distribution channels for heritage and cultural tourism and the exploratory nature of this study, intensive qualitative research focusing on a small number of heritage and cultural tourism operations was undertaken. The operations were located in Wellington (eight) and Rotorua (six), two of the case destinations for the larger distribution channels project (Pearce & Tan, 2002). In each destination a list of relevant sites or operations was established from information obtained from the regional tourism organizations. Reflecting the broader characteristics of the two destinations, the emphasis in Wellington was on museums and heritage sites while Rotorua also offered a variety of Maori cultural tourism experiences (Table 1). In Wellington these ranged in scale from the Museum of New Zealand Te Papa Tongarewa, with over one million visits annually, to much more modest sites and operations receiving under ten thousand visitors a year. The operations analysed in Rotorua were generally much larger, drawing 100,000 visitors or more a year. The large Maori cultural attractions tend to attract a greater proportion of international visitors (up to 80%), while the local and domestic market is generally more important for the museums. While some were primarily commercial tourism ventures, others were owned and managed by trusts or incorporated societies, often having conservation and/or education as their prime mission. These factors illustrate some of the diversity to be found in the heritage and cultural tourism sectors. To put these operations in context, background information was also sought from the National Historic Places Trust and the Wellington Museums Trust.

As in other distribution channel research, in-depth structured interviews constituted the main means of data collection, enabling a rich vein of information to be captured (Buhalis, 2000; March, 1996; Yamamoto & Gill, 2002). Interviews were sought with the managers or marketing managers. The

Table 1   Heritage and Cultural Tourism Attractions Analysed

Wellington
  Cable Car Museum
  Colonial Cottage Museum
  Katherine Mansfield Birthplace
  Maori Treasures
  Museum of Wellington City and Sea
  National Cricket Museum
  National Museum of New Zealand Te Papa Tongarewa
  Old St Paul's
Rotorua
  Buried Village of Te Wairoa Tarawera
  New Zealand Maori Arts and Crafts Institute
  Rotoiti Tours
  Rotorua Museum
  Tamaki Village Tours
  Whakarewarewa Thermal Village

interviews were structured around a checklist of questions which focused on the nature of each operation, the markets targeted, the distribution channels used and strategies followed, factors influencing these, relationships established and partnerships developed. Interviews lasted about an hour on average, taking a little longer for some of the bigger operations and less time for some of the smaller, less complex ones. Notes were taken at each interview and in the majority of cases the interviews were also taped (a few respondents declined to be recorded) and later transcribed in order to capture the full richness of the material. The notes and transcripts were then analysed in terms of recurring themes, especially any that might distinguish distribution issues in heritage and cultural tourism from those in other tourism sectors. Particular attention has been given to explanatory factors, for as Bitner & Booms (1982: 40) noted in a related context: "While structural factors give clues to how the system operates,

motivational and behavioural factors provide more complex explanations for why intermediaries do what they do, what influences their decisions, and how they interact with customers and suppliers". While most respondents were prepared to discuss their operations freely, in some cases they did not allow attribution of quotes or details to their business or property and this material has been treated more generally. As a result, not all points made can be illustrated in the text with reference to specific examples.

Distribution Channels for Heritage and Cultural Tourism

Reflecting the diversity noted above, the heritage and cultural tourism operations examined in Wellington and Rotorua vary considerably in the extent to which they have developed distribution channels. The larger, more commercially-oriented operations tend to have well-developed marketing plans, with active and explicit distribution strategies and practices. In contrast, the smaller museums and heritage properties often have very limited or ad hoc distribution strategies. Some managers spoke of having marketing plans but no means of implementing them. The small scale of the operations and the accompanying lack of resources in terms of staff time and budget are key factors in explaining the degree of activity undertaken. In some instances these factors are compounded by traditional curatorial attitudes to the properties concerned, with some managers commenting on the reluctance of some trust boards to engage actively in marketing. In several cases managers stressed that efforts were primarily still going into conservation and that further work to maintain the property or develop facilities for visitors was needed before a more concerted distribution strategy could be pursued.

Structure

The structure of the distribution channels reflects the different market segments drawn to or targetted by each operation and the relative importance of these. Different distribution channels are used for international and domestic visitors, and by the group and independent segments within these markets (Figure 1).

For some of the operations, especially some of the larger ones in Rotorua, tour group visitors can account for forty to sixty percent of the total visitors, mainly those from overseas. In other cases, international tour groups are much less significant (less than 20%) and in some instances virtually non-existent. The scale of the operation will influence the nature of the tour. The larger operations will deal primarily with series tours while the smaller ones will depend more on special interest tours or,

in the case of some of the museums and heritage properties in Wellington, groups of cruise ship visitors. Old St Paul's in Wellington is also included on the city tour itinerary of one of the local sightseeing tour operators.

For the international group tours the distribution channel structure is a classic and conventional one. The heritage or cultural attraction will deal directly with a New Zealand based inbound tour operator, offering them special rates. The inbound tour operator in turn puts together the land arrangements for package tours being offered by a wholesaler in one of the offshore markets. These tour packages are then sold to customers, sometimes through the wholesalers' own outlets, but more commonly through a retail travel agency. In some instances marketing staff from the larger heritage and cultural tourism operations will also make calls on offshore wholesalers to develop relationships with them so that the wholesalers will subsequently request or encourage their inbound operators to include the attraction on their New Zealand itineraries. Many, however, do not have the resources to do this and some also think it unnecessary.

It should be noted too that the major cultural tourism experience for many of the series tour visitors in Rotorua, especially the Asian ones, will consist of a *hangi* (a meal cooked in the traditional Maori fashion) and Maori cultural performance within the large hotel at which they are staying rather than a visit to one of the separate attractions examined here. These arrangements, along with accommodation and other meals, will be negotiated between the hotels and the inbound tour operators.

For many of the heritage and cultural tourism operations examined, the majority of their international visitors are independent travellers (FITs). In some cases, attempts are made to reach visitors in the overseas

Major Market Segments

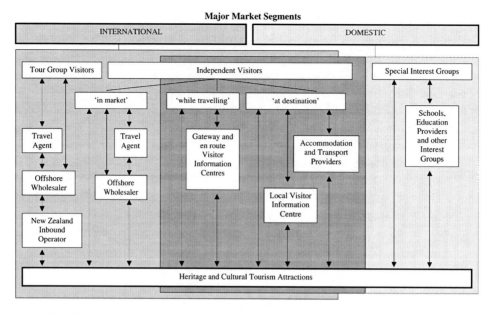

Figure 1 Distribution Channels for Heritage and Cultural Attractions in Rotorua and Wellington.

markets. Two of the Maori cultural attractions had developed or were endeavouring to develop pre-purchased products for sale to more upmarket independent travellers through offshore wholesalers and travel agents. In general, however, the pricing of the heritage and cultural tourism operations examined does not lend itself to this type of approach. In most other cases some information may be made available through websites and by other means to independent visitors while still at home but only one reported a significant amount (10–15%) of booking over the Internet. More commonly, FITs are targeted once they have reached New Zealand, either while travelling throughout the country or once they have arrived at the destination itself, in this case in either Rotorua or Wellington. Many bookings or sales may ultimately be made directly with the cultural or heritage attraction, with the

information distributed contributing to the purchase decision.

Several of the Rotorua operations are particularly active in distributing information about their product to travelling visitors through the placement of brochures in racks at the airport or visitor information centres in Auckland, the country's largest gateway, and at intervening points:

"... as soon as they get off the plane, we have things in place where they can see the Buried Village brand all the way through until they get to Rotorua"

"... as soon as they step off the plane they walk into one of the brochure stands. And we're in every single brochure stand and important accommodation up in Auckland there. So wherever they go, we try to make sure that they can't escape our product".

Brochure production and distribution in other locations is not without cost, however, and is not undertaken by some of the smaller operations even though they might recognize the benefits of doing so. Advertising in guidebooks and tourist newspapers is also undertaken. A number of respondents complained of the proliferation of brochures, guides and tourist newspapers and question the value and need to be represented in all of them.

Reaching international visitors once they have arrived at the destination is the most common distribution strategy and may be undertaken in conjunction with the foregoing or as the sole means of reaching these visitors. This is done with varying levels of intensity and in different ways. Reaching visitors at the destination is especially important to many of the smaller museums as the Wellington Museums Trust representative explained:

"Because of the nature of our facilities, because they are all low charge, the maximum is only five dollars normally a visit, they are quite different from where there's a hotel product or whatever it might be . . . We are not reliant on . . . that part of the chain to provide business for us as much as we are reliant on getting our information out there in the market once the visitors have arrived. We are reliant on others getting them here, and then we are reliant on the . . . information centre . . . or whatever else it is we are able to get out our information to the visitors."

The Cable Car Museum, one of the trust's properties, at present depends entirely on its location immediately adjacent to the summit terminal of the cable-car at one of the most visited look-out points in the city. With free admission it receives some 150,000 visitors a year, most on very short and largely serendipitous visits.

Use of the local visitor information centre for distribution of product information and, particularly in the case of Rotorua, a source of bookings, is widespread. In Rotorua, accommodation providers are another key source of referrals and bookings and the heritage and cultural tourism operations (as well as other attractions) actively recruit them to act as intermediaries, generally paying them a ten per cent commission on all bookings made. As the Rotorua Museum respondent observed:

"We just don't have the big bucks to be able to go offshore and do stuff out there. We know for the kind of markets we are looking for, specifically that FIT market, our money is much better spent knocking on accommodation providers' doors, than overseas'.

Effort is also directed at increasing awareness amongst local residents of what the museum has to offer with the goal of encouraging them to bring the international friends and relations they host to visit. Backpacker bus companies are another important distribution channel for several operations in Rotorua.

Use of accommodation providers as a distribution channel is not common in Wellington, possibly due to the smaller scale of the heritage and cultural tourism operations there and the importance of the business and other non-leisure segments in much of the capital's accommodation (Pearce & Tan, 2002). The Wellington Museums Trust, however, has tried to increase the awareness of its museums amongst local taxi-drivers.

The "while-travelling" or "at-destination" distribution channels are also used to reach domestic visitors. This activity may also be supplemented by advertising in some of the major population centres and by working with the regional tourism organization to promote the destination as a whole. Some of the museums and heritage sites will also cater for schools, international language students and special interest groups, both locally and from further afield, often working directly with the institutions or organizations concerned.

Factors Influencing Channel Structure

The varying emphasis on group or independent travellers and the channels used to reach these is a function of several inter-related factors associated with the nature of the heritage and cultural products and their related markets.

Breadth of product appeal. To be included in the itinerary of a series tour with a reasonably large volume of visitors, an attraction must have a reasonably broad appeal and be of interest to all or most members of the tour parties. Independent travellers have much greater flexibility to pick and choose what they will visit or what activities they will undertake. The different Maori cultural attractions in Rotorua clearly have a broad appeal by offering a distinctive cultural experience as part of a visit to New Zealand by international visitors, both group and independent. In contrast, many of the smaller museums and heritage properties in Wellington (and elsewhere) lack this breadth of appeal – interest in Katherine Mansfield's Birthplace, the colonial gothic architecture of Old St Paul's or the National Cricket Museum tends to be much more specific- and are thus less suitable to be packaged as part of a series tour. This was recognized by the representative of the Wellington Museums Trust who observed: "We are putting quite a bit

of effort into [assessing whether our product is what package groups want] and it may be at the end of the day that it's just the independent traveller who is the one that will be of any importance coming through Wellington anyway".

From a national perspective, the New Zealand Historic Places Trust respondent noted that inbound tour operators are:

"producing standard products, very standard products. They are producing product related to market expectations to some extent. ... What we are offering is different to their traditional product offer. ... We have to show them that there is a market for this product as well [and data are lacking] ... And that's even just placing one product within the ITOs' product mix. The actual notion of having ITOs develop product that is specifically heritage-based I think is another step on."

Until this occurs, targeting independent travellers or particular niches or special interest groups may be a more effective distribution strategy. This point was well made by the Maori Treasures representative who commented with respect to one of the American wholesalers: "... his client base is mid upper market, the people who are interested in culture and art and that's what we offer ...". Similarly, the manager of one of the heritage properties in Wellington claimed elderly American cruise ship visitors were appreciative of that type of product. However, a willingness to open the property at 8 am when cruise ships were in port also appeared to be an equally decisive factor in being able to attract these groups.

Capacity issues. Capacity constraints limit the ability of a number of the heritage and cultural tourism operations to develop a group tour market. This is particularly the case with some of the heritage properties and museums that cannot handle large coachloads of visitors, either in terms of the physical degradation of the property or the diminished enjoyment of visitors. The Rotorua Museum respondent explained the choice of distribution channels in these terms: "Our push is for the FIT market because we can't physically cope with too many groups through here. As soon as you get a couple of schools here, to try and push through another big group just puts constraints on our resources and means that their experience is not as good as it should be". Similarly, at Old St Paul's competing demands are sometimes experienced between the property's wedding operations and tour group visitors, a problem that might be alleviated were a visitor centre developed there to manage the flow of visitors better. Some of the Maori cultural tourism operations, especially the purpose-built ones such as the Tamaki Maori Village or the in-hotel performances, are able to handle large numbers of visitors, including groups. Others recognize capacity constraints on their product and do not market to group tours in part because of the nature of the cultural experience they offer. The respondent from the thermal village at Whakarewarewa observed that because of the time needed "... the FIT market is more suited to the package we deliver because it involves a lot of history, education, cultural interaction ... Large tour companies tend to like have 25 minutes; they want to come and see the geyser, a mud pool and taste a corn on the cob cooked in geothermal waters but they rarely have time for our history".

Commissionable products. The economic interests of the various parties – the heritage and cultural tourism operations and the different intermediaries – also play a key role in determining the nature and extent of the different distribution channels used. Many heritage and some cultural tourism products are characterized by their low entrance fees – entrance to some museums and heritage sites is free or by donation, many are less than NZ$10, few are more than NZ$20. Where distribution structures are founded on a system of booking commissions (usually in the range of 10–20%) or special rates to inbound tour operators and wholesalers enabling them to include a mark-up on their packaged products, free admission or low entry fees to heritage and cultural attractions are less likely to stimulate interest from these intermediaries than other operations where rates are much greater and commissions or mark-ups are accordingly higher. This is especially the case in Rotorua where there are many competing commercial tourism attractions. One reason why accommodation providers there appear keen on booking guests on a Tamaki Maori Village tour is that the price is much more substantial ($70). This issue was expressed by the marketing managers spoken to in various ways:

"... why does a tour company want to take tours out of their visitors" time to go somewhere that's free when they can fit maybe two attractions in that they could get a $10 commission on, or a $5 dollar commission on".

"... you have to have more of a product than just a visit to the museum for five bucks a head. You need to package something together ... so you get a more marketable thing. So you have got to package thirty bucks or whatever it is so that it's commissionable – An operator in tourism will be more interested in picking up something like that."

"I don't think the [heritage] sector can even talk about commissionable products. ... It's often the case, as with Old St Paul's, that it's free entry. ... So the only way they can place themselves is by the strength as a product itself, and that it will add value to and therefore be more attractive to clients of the ITOs on the basis of their existing offer. For example, if the Wellington package was enhanced and would attract more custom simply by the fact that Old St Paul's was in the programme then that's really the only valid argument we can give them actually."

However, where the attraction is a major one, the issue of free admission may be addressed differently:

"Free admission ... They [the inbound operators and wholesalers] like that. But at the same time they will also want some money and the advantage in Wellington is that our hotel rates are quite high. So even if they don't get commissions from here [a museum] they'll get if from the hotels if they stay and the downside of that is that the rest of the costs are quite considerable. So we have to provide them with compelling reasons why they should spend more time to come and see Wellington."

One response to this, especially for the FIT wholesale market, is to package together several related products to generate a higher overall cost and provide a more commissionable pre-purchase product. Thus in Rotorua three operations – the museum, Buried Village and Whakarewarewa village tours – have combined to offer a Tarawera Legacy package which is linked by a common heritage theme and offers a more commissionable product ($38.50 self-drive, $49 with shuttle). Similarly in Wellington, discussions are being held to examine the possibility of creating a cluster of heritage products to meet these marketing needs better.

At the same time, some of the heritage and cultural tourism operations are pursuing the independent travellers through the ways outlined earlier as direct marketing to them, or through the lower commissions of the accommodation providers and information centres, is seen to offer a higher yield compared with offering special rates to inbound operators or wholesalers.

Other factors. Other factors also come into play in terms of determining the balance between using direct channels or intermediaries. While appreciating the "enormous amount of extra reach" which inbound operators offer, one museum marketing manager observed:

"I can go out and train up a few Visitor Information Centre [staff] and I know immediately they will be talking to somebody who is in here next day. So it's a very quick response time. It's a lot cheaper than travelling offshore. And we have a lot more control. You can provide a lot more in-depth information because they are local. They tend to have a better understanding and they are also focused on the detail".

Another marketing manager also saw the benefit of direct marketing in heritage tourism in these terms:

"... you are actually getting your own message across. You are not relying on somebody else. Particularly with heritage that could be a bit of a difficulty because not a lot of people will understand and appreciate it. They act like they do but they don't".

Conclusions

One of the more established heritage managers interviewed commented with regard to distribution channels: "Probably the biggest minus is trying to work it all out ... I just feel it should not have to be that complicated". It is hoped that this systematic analysis of distribution channels for heritage and cultural tourism in Wellington and Rotorua will assist others to "work it all out" through having identified and outlined the key distribution structures currently operating and explaining why they have come about.

Distribution channels for heritage and cultural tourism are complicated. Much of this complexity arises from the diverse nature of heritage and cultural tourism and the use of different channels to reach different market segments (Figure 1). Notable differences occur between group and independent travellers. Factors accounting for these differences include: the breadth of product appeal, capacity issues and the level of commissionable product.

To a certain extent these factors appear to be to be a particular function of the nature of heritage and cultural tourism but further work is now required to examine the generality of the structures and factors presented here. In terms of the current literature, the distribution channels for group tours to heritage and cultural attractions in Wellington and Rotorua are not dissimilar to those for mass package travel to coastal and ski resorts (Buhalis, 2000; March, 1996; Yamamoto & Gill, 2002). It is the diversity of channels for independent travellers that is novel, although further research may reveal other forms of tourism, such as nature-based tourism, may also share some of these characteristics.

The "management deficit" highlighted by Middleton (1997) did not appear to be a particular issue with regard to the development and management of distribution channels in the cases examined here. Certainly, the larger operations tended to have more developed and more explicit distribution strategies but even amongst the smaller ones there was generally a reasonable appreciation of the key issues and how to tackle these. More limiting than individual managerial ability were constraints relating to issues of conservation versus visitor management, availability of resources and the nature of the product and market demand. What is clear is that if further growth in visitor numbers is desired, more effort will need to be directed at addressing these issues and implementing more active distribution strategies. If more tour groups are to be targeted then issues of demand, capacity and pricing need to be tackled. Initiatives currently being explored and put in place to develop larger packages and more commissionable products appear to offer one way forward. In other instances where capacity and other constraints associated with heritage and cultural tourism remain, concentration on improving distribution channels to independent travellers will be appropriate. In most cases, achieving an appropriate mix of segments and reaching these through a variety of channels will be the goal.

References

Ali-Knight, J. & Wild, S. (1999). British Airways' Inbound Leisure Market to Manchester, England: Is Direct Marketing the Answer? *Journal of Vacation Marketing*, 6(1), 9–20.

Balcar, M. J. O. & Pearce, D. G. (1996). Heritage Tourism on the West Coast of New Zealand. *Tourism Management*, 17(1), 203–212.

Bitner, M. J. & Booms, B. H. (1982). Trends in Travel and Tourism Marketing: The Changing Structure of Distribution Channels. *Journal of Travel Research*, 20(4), 39–44.

Blackler, G. (1998). Heritage Tourism In Christchurch. Unpublished MSc Thesis, University of Canterbury, Christchurch.

Buhalis, D. (2000). Relationships in the Distribution Channel of Tourism: Conflicts Between Hoteliers and Tour Operators in the Mediterranean Region.

International Journal of Hospitality & Tourism Administration, 1(1), 113–139.

Buhalis, D. & Laws, E. (eds) (2001). *Tourism Distribution Channels; Practices, Issues and Transformations*. Continuum, London.

Chandler, J. A. & Costello, C. A. (2002). A Profile of Visitors at Heritage Tourism Destinations in East Tennessee According to Plog's Lifestyle and Activity level Preferences Model. *Journal of Travel Research*, 41(2), 161–166.

Crotts, J. C., Aziz, A. & Raschid, A. (1998). Antecedents of Supplier's Commitment to Wholesale Buyers in the International Travel Trade. *Tourism Management*, 19(2), 127–134.

García-Falcón, J. M. & Medina-Muñoz, D. (1999). The Relationship Between Hotel Companies and Travel Agencies: an Empirical Assessment of the United States Market. *The Service Industries Journal*, 19(4), 102–122.

Garrod, B. & Fyall, A. (2000). Managing Heritage Tourism. *Annals of Tourism Research*, 27(3), 682–708.

Gartner, W. C. & Bachri, T. (1994). Tour Operators' Role in the Tourism Distribution System: an Indonesian Case Study. *Journal of International Consumer Marketing*, 6(3/4), 161–179.

Hall, C. M. & McArthur, S. (eds) (1996). *Heritage Management in Australia and New Zealand – the Human Dimension*. Oxford University Press, Melbourne.

Herbert, D. T. (ed) (1995). *Heritage, Tourism and Society*. Mansell Publishing, London.

Jansen-Verbeke, M. & van Rekom, J. (1996). Scanning Museum Visitors: Urban Tourism Marketing. *Annals of Tourism Research*, 23(2), 361–375.

Knowles, T. & Grabowski, P. (1999). Strategic Marketing in the Tour Operator Sector. In F. Vellas & L. Bécherel (eds), *The International Marketing of Travel and Tourism: a Strategic Approach* (pp. 249–262). St Martins Press, New York.

Lumsdon, L. M. & Swift, J. W. (1999). The Role of the Tour Operator in South America: Argentina, Chile, Paraguay and Uruguay. *International Journal of Tourism Research*, 4(1), 429–439.

March, R. (1996). Organisational Linkages in Australia's Japanese Inbound Travel Market. In G. Prosser (ed), *Tourism and Hospitality Research: Australian and International Perspectives* (pp. 337–349). Bureau of Travel Research, Canberra.

March, R. (2000). Buyer Decision-Making Behavior in International Tourism Channels. *International Journal of Hospitality & Tourism Administration*, 1(1), 11–25.

Middleton, V. (1997). Marketing Issues in Heritage Tourism: An International Perspective. In W. Nuryanti (ed), *Tourism and Heritage Management* (pp. 213–220). Gadjah Mada University Press, Yogyakarta.

Morrell, P. S. (1998). Airline Sales and Distribution Channels: the impact of new technology. *Tourism Economics*, 4(1), 5–19.

O'Connor, P. (1999). *Electronic Information Distribution in Tourism and Hospitality*. CABI Publishing, Wallingford.

Nuryanti, W. (ed) (1997). *Tourism and Heritage Management*. Gadjah Mada University Press, Yogyakarta.

Pearce, D. G. (2002a). Current and future directions in tourism research. *Japanese Journal of Tourism Research*, 1(1), 9–19.

Pearce, D. G. (2002b). New Zealand holiday travel to Samoa: a distribution channels approach. *Journal of Travel Research*, 41(2), 197–205.

Pearce, D. G. & Tan, R. (2002). Tourism distribution channels: a destination perspective. In W. G. Croy (ed), *New Zealand Tourism and Hospitality Conference Proceedings* (pp. 242–250). Waiariki Institute of Technology, Rotorua.

Prentice, R. (1993). *Tourism and Heritage Attractions*. Routledge, London.

Radburn, M. & Goodall, B. (1990). Marketing Through Travel Agencies. In G. Ashworth & B. Goodall (eds), *Marketing Tourism Places* (pp. 237–255). Routledge, London.

Renucci, J. (1997). Aperçus sur le Tourisme Culturel Urbain en Region Rhône-Alpes: L'Exemple de Lyon et de Vienne. *Revue de Géographie de Lyon (Observations on urban cultural tourism in the Rhone-Alps: the examples of Lyon and Vienne)*, 67(1), 5–18.

Richards, G. (ed) (1996). *Cultural Tourism in Europe*. CAB International, Wallingford.

Russo, A. P. & van der Borg, J. (2002). Planning Considerations for Cultural Tourism: A case Study of Four European Cities. *Tourism Management*, 23(6), 631–638.

Ryan, C. (2002). Tourism and Cultural Proximity: Examples from New Zealand. *Annals of Tourism Research*, 29(4), 952–971.

Tan, R. (2002). Channels of Distribution Characterising Singapore Holiday to New Zealand: structure and implications. Unpublished MTM Thesis, Victoria University of Wellington, Wellington.

Tourism Strategy Group (2001). *New Zealand Tourism Strategy 2010*. Tourism Strategy Group, Wellington.

Wall, G. & Nuryanti, W. (eds) (1996). Heritage and Tourism (Special Issue). *Annals of Tourism Research*, 23(2), 249–478.

Warren, J. A. N. & Taylor, C. N. (2001). *Developing Heritage Tourism in New Zealand*. Centre for Research, Evaluation and Social Assessment, Wellington.

Wahab, S., Crampon, L. J. & Rothfield, L. M. (1976). *Tourism Marketing*. Tourism International Press, London.

Waitt, G. (2000). Consuming heritage: perceived historical authenticity. *Annals of Tourism Research*, 27(4), 835–862.

Yamamoto, D. & Gill, A. (2002). Issues of globalisation and reflexivity in the Japanese tourism production system: the case of Whistler, British Columbia. *The Professional Geographer*, 54(1), 83–93.

Part Four

Marketing

The Poignancy of Times Past: Heritage Travel Motivation Among Seniors

Glenn F. Ross

'People like you and I, though mortal of course like everyone else, do not grow old no matter how long we live.... (We) never cease to stand like curious children before the great mystery into which we were born.'

Einstein, from a letter to Otto Juliusberger.

Introduction

It was the philosopher Heraclitus who, in approximately 600 BC, described the human psyche as a quite prodigious phenomenon, the boundaries of which may never be entirely mapped nor understood. Now, many centuries later, we still have relatively little knowledge and understanding as to what it is that constitutes essential human attributes and states such as personal well-being, or even why individuals act in the ways that they do. In recent times, however, a number of commentators such as Argyle (1991, 1999), Deci and Ryan (2000), Kahneman (1999), Seligman (2002) and Seligman *et al.* (2005) have been variously engaged in describing, examining and evaluating many of the more important 'why' and 'how' questions associated with human

motivation, with the making of meaning in each individual's life, and with the overall experience of well-being. Essentially the need to find or to construct meaning within one's life would seem to be an indispensable activity associated with human well-being. This making of meaning is therefore central within the process, and is commonly understood as the creation of an understanding or narrative, the outcome of which is to provide organization, structure and significance in the life of the individual. The construction of meaning is now widely regarded as a powerful life motive in the attainment of personal well-being (Deci and Ryan, 2000; Diener, 2000; Kahneman, 1999; Seligman, 2002). It is also suggested that this meaning-making can take many forms, can be encountered in a wide variety of contexts, and is pursued by people of all ages and life-stages. It is, moreover, as Lyubomirsky *et al.* (2005) point out, sought not only to attain affective states such as joy, contentment and serenity, all emotional attributes frequently associated with human well-being, but also to eschew actively those relatively common yet unwelcome emotional states concerned with pessimism, failure and an enduring unhappiness.

This chapter examines issues associated with motivation as meaning-making as it may adumbrate the perceptions, expectations and behaviours of senior travelers to heritage sites. The chapter commences with coverage of heritage travel, particularly the issues concerned with motivations to visit historic sites. The chapter then focuses upon senior citizens, examining how seniors maximize their life outcomes; this section will present an understanding of role theory that may be frequently applied to senior motivation. The following section also examines senior tourism, particularly research findings from studies that have xamined senior travel motivation; this section will highlight motivations that have a strong resonance with meaning-making. Finally, the chapter presents a model, in graphical form, which explicates the various influences upon senior heritage travelers in respect of meaning-making motivation. This chapter will, in particular, seek to demonstrate that senior travelers are typically not passive, nor are they mostly diffident people who are said to shun participation, preferring to shelter from the vicissitudes of life; this false image does however linger, in no small measure due to the persistent and pernicious stereotypes appearing in advertising and other media. Rather, as Einstein so acutely perceived about himself and his friend, many senior citizens are perennially curious about the world in which they live, and have lost no desire to find out more about it and its mysteries and meanings. Moreover, seniors are frequently active decision-makers who much prefer to play no small part in meaning-making that vitally reflects upon the direction of their lives and upon the well-being that they derive from their experiences. Central among

these experiences are those to do with heritage and its visitation.

Heritage Travel Motivation

Heritage is, according to a variety of commentators such as Alzua *et al.* (1998), Palmer (1999, 2003, 2005) and Timothy and Boyd (2003), a prominent and increasingly important part of tourism. Not only is it receiving scrutiny within a range of interdisciplinary contexts, but it is also now regarded as a vital phenomenon in understanding individual social behaviour for many travelers (Nuryanti, 1996). Heritage tourism, moreover, has a number of identifiable components, such as the built environment (Laws, 1998), the cultural environment (Richards, 1996, 2002) and the natural environment (Hall, 2000). Each of these various elements, suggests Hewison (1987), has major relevance not only to tourism but to the wider society in which it is embedded. The desire to experience historical and cultural places is now a prominent motivation among tourists of all ages and from a diversity of backgrounds. And whilst many continue to debate what it is that constitutes heritage tourism (see, for example, Garrod and Fyall, 2000, 2001 and Poria *et al.* 2000), there is, as Poria *et al.* (2003) conclude, now little doubt as to its power as a social phenomenon. A part of this potency, Johnson (1999) would assert, comes from core aspects of the heritage site, such as scenic beauty and historic interest that, together, can imbue the visitor with a sense of enrichment and even completion.

Nuryanti (1996) approaches this understanding of heritage tourism from a different perspective, and suggests that it is possible to gain a greater understanding of the power of heritage by examining the derivation of the word; the provenance of the word, Nuryanti suggests, is to be found in the idea of inheritance. Thus heritage may be understood as something of great value that is passed down through the generations of people with whom the site or the phenomenon has been associated. Developing on this theme, Nuryanti points out that heritage allows people, including tourists, to experience the past, represented in the present and simultaneously illuminating the future. Heritage is, moreover, intimately connected with the wider society, and is not simply an isolated place or event in one geographical location. This wider significance, posits Nuryanti, makes a diversity of heritage relevant and intensely meaningful to visitors who have no immediate connection to the spot where at the site or event happens to be located. For many visitors, cultural tourism is closely identified with that form of heritage generally described as built, assembled or arranged by people, particularly in a previous era (Seale, 1996); for the most part this form of heritage pertains to buildings and other similar edifices. Nuryanti would hold that most prominent heritage sites of this kind have often been deliberately constructed by humans, have a permanency about them, and have acquired historical and venerable attributes that have, over time, permeated the societies thereabouts, and have even assumed ascribed meaning at national and international levels.

Other approaches to the understanding of the power of heritage tourism suggest that local cultural traditions also need to be taken into account, as too do arts, crafts, festivals and historical reenactments (Hollinshead, 1988). Such an approach would broaden the definition and therefore expand the range of motivational factors associated with travelers' needs to experience not only the past and its physical manifestations, but also to experience and even participate in cultural phenomena

and their settings. It is also asserted by Smith (1991) that heritage tourism not only encapsulates a desire to visit the past in the present, but also a desire to participate in indigenous culture through a variety of manifestations such as authentic objects. Such views are reflective of McCannell (1976) who asserted that tourists generally have an intention to experience an authentic interaction with another society or culture. Commentators such as Cohen (1988) and Pearce and Moscardo (1986) argue that this strong desire for authenticity, as described by scholars such as McCannell, is a potent motivational force in respect of the visitation to historical and cultural sites, those entities that are typically deemed as being encompassed by the notion of heritage.

Heritage as Meaning and Identity

Understanding what motivates heritage tourists may also be achieved by examining reactions to the site itself. Tourists at heritage places, according to McIntosh and Prentice (1999), demonstrated insightfulness as to the past; these visitors, moreover, were found to experience an enhancement of their own particular identity, and also a deepening of their appreciation of their unique role in regard to place and time. McIntosh and Prentice further report that cultural and heritage tourism may generally be characterized by individual role interpretations that go to forge and construct an individual's meaningful life environment; meanings, therefore, particularly those meanings to do with the interpretation of the individual traveler's life narrative, are seen as being enriched, even ontologically driven by heritage experiences. There would thus seem a clear experiential aspect to heritage tourism that places it, potentially, with other life-affirming dimensions. These reactions, according to Prentice *et al.* (1998), are most salient for the visitor who perceives some affinity with the venue; benefits such as learning and identity-development are said to follow from contact. Tourists, suggest McIntosh and Prentice (1999), have experiences that involve a number of cognitive, reflective and emotional reactions; insightfulness, McIntosh *et al.* hold, is a major benefit from such processes experienced by visitors to a heritage site deemed of particular importance by that visitor.

Commentators such as Poria *et al.* (2000, 2001, 2006) and Timothy and Boyd (2003) have variously pointed out that two principal approaches to the explication of heritage tourism may be identified. The first is that pertaining to the supply side of heritage; this line of inquiry focuses upon the individual *vis a vis* artifacts of historical and cultural interest, as well as sites deemed to be of heritage interest and value. This approach often involves issues concerning management of places, of objects and of cultural events. There is, however, as Poria *et al.* (2006) and Timothy and Boyd (2003) conclude, another perspective in the understanding of heritage travel: the demand aspects. This typically involves issues concerning individual desires for travel. Motivational formulations are asserted to be of central importance in this perspective (Swarbrooke, 1994; Richards, 2002; Prentice *et al.* 1998). Notwithstanding the relatively small number of studies that have sought to adumbrate motivational forces associated with heritage travel, researchers such as Prentice *et al.* (1998) and Richards (2002) make the point that this is an area of research likely to reveal a rich diversity of factors occasioning visitation to a heritage site or event. In regard to legacy tourism or personal heritage tourism, McCain and Ray (2003) and Timothy (1997) point out that many individuals are impelled by a deep desire for

connection with ancestors and with the contexts wherein they lived; such a quest, they argue, goes much deeper than simply a quest for information or enjoyment. In regard to sacred sites and events, Shackley (2001) concludes that many people travel not only to participate in worship events, but also because of the aesthetic emotional power of architecture, and of art in its many forms.

Motivation is seldom if ever singular, uniform or unchanging in respect of particular heritage sites. Uzzell (1996), commenting on visitation to battlefield sites, suggests that some people may visit in order to remember their experiences at that battlefield long ago. Others may travel so as to pay respect to a parent or relative who fought or even died at that place; yet others, with little specific connection to the site, may come out of curiosity, as part of a tour group simply to see what the field looks like, or even be there because the tour included a stop at that place. It is also the case that the battlefield site will, over time, draw visitors with different motivations to those who fought there, or indeed have immediate relatives with this association; there will come a time when those particular people are no longer able to visit.

Heritage as Connection

This great variety of motivational causes raise the complex issue of connection; a site may be deemed as heritage by local people, by national authorities, and also by those charged with the preservation of the site, but if it evokes little heritage significance in the people visiting, it will evoke no deep attractiveness nor life-affirming reaction; neither will it have any lasting impact upon the individual's life narrative. If, however, the site has profound significance to the individual traveler, the motivation to travel there to is of a much more ontological kind, and the experiences at the site are considerably more likely to have a lasting meaning for the traveler. It might therefore be suggested that travel to heritage sites needs to be seen not only as recreational and leisure experiences occasioned by hedonic motivation; there is also another form of heritage motivation, occasioned by the purposes of ontology and producing what the psychiatrist Frankl (1963) described as life-meaning.

The experiences of visitors to heritage sites may be influenced by a number of factors, two of which are the quality and the sensitivity of the interpretation provided, and the personal and the professional skills of the tour and site guides (Moscardo, 1996; Timothy and Boyd, 2003). In regard to interpretation, studies have focused upon content and expectation; and Timothy and Boyd aver that content can sometimes be portrayed to visitors in such a manner that the visitors are left with a lingering sense of inauthenticity. The role of tour guides is thus of considerable importance in contexts such as heritage. Ap and Wong (2001) and Cohen *et al.* (2002) conclude that tour guides have a determining influence upon the overall experience of the visitor, particularly in regard to informativeness and sincerity. Dahles (2002) goes further and advocates that guides at such sites ought to adopt the role of mediator between the visitors and the local social and physical environment. Guides are thus exhorted to be facilitators, not only in the supply of information, but also in respect of the understanding and the experiencing of the site or context visited. Whilst this set of goals is indeed ambitious, it is nonetheless likely to add markedly to the enrichment of the visitors.

Heritage Motivation: Visitor Needs, Site Specific Characteristics and Enduring Memory

It has been suggested that tourists desire to attend heritage sites for a variety of reasons, and do so with a wide range of perceptions and expectations. This complexity may partially be explained by reference to cultural background (Ashworth, 1998). There are however yet other factors that assist in accounting for the diversity; Poria *et al.* (2003) argue that certain sites have the power to produce heightened emotional reactions in some individuals. In similar vein Timothy (1997) and McCain and Ray (2003) hold that people may travel to heritage sites and contexts for reasons to do with finding their roots, with coming to know and to understand their ancestors. This would suggest that many people are impelled to travel, particularly to heritage sites and contexts, so as to set in train a process of deepening in regard to self-understanding. Uzzell (1988) makes the point that this process is facilitated by the symbolic meaning imbued in place and the objects and phenomena found there. Poria, Butler and Airey (2003, 2004) develop these notions further and argue that individual perception must also be included in any understanding of heritage tourism in regard to both motivation to visit and also the behaviour at the heritage site. They persuasively argue that perceptions of a heritage site, particularly in relation to an individual's own heritage understandings, is indispensable in the comprehension of why they choose to travel to the place, and also what they do whilst at the site.

Within the heritage travel arena memory may also be regarded as a form of motivation. Basu (2001, 2004a, 2004b, 2005), examining heritage tourism in the Scottish Highlands, has argued that there are many sites of memory such as the battlefield of Culloden or the ruined villages of the Highlands that were emptied at the clearances. Phenomena such as these, Basu posits, have an aura for many people; they are said to hold and widely epitomize memories of a past that draws people to them. These places have *animus loci* that arise out of the interaction between the visitor and the place. Basu further describes the mechanism of this encounter as memory of place and event becoming internalized by way of encounter, of engagement and of identification. This process, particularly when repeated at sites of memory, becomes the vehicle of ontological meaning and so is embedded as salient threads in an individual's life narrative.

Senior Citizens

Bandura (1995) has ably made the point that perceptions of personal agency and competence have a powerful impact upon well-being; this is so for all people, both young and old. Individuals who have the belief that they are able to have some reasonable effect upon the circumstances and events of their daily lives are much more likely to report being happier, better able to deal with the vicissitudes of daily life, and to enjoy a higher level of health (Mendes de Leon 2005). For senior citizens, as Bowling and Dieppe (2005) conclude, successfully negotiating the ageing process involves attaining a number of important milestones, a most important one being a concern with the ongoing perception of well-being. Schulz and Heckhausen (1996) have offered a life-span model wherein the processes of successful ageing can be explicated. Their model seeks basically to understand and explain how

perceptions of personal agency change as a person ages, yet also serve to provide the individual with feelings of well-being. Schulz and Heckhausen clearly differentiate primary and secondary agency at the personal level: primary perceptions of control refer to actions taken to alter one's surrounding environment, whilst secondary perceptions pertain to changes made to the manner by which the individual conceives of and typically thinks about a situation, problem, threat or dilemma.

They make the point that, as people age, so personal resources often diminish; the balance between acquisitions and losses may frequently not be in the older person's favour, and may invoke a diminution in both physical and mental skills formerly prized by that individual. Whilst these changing circumstances do not happen according to some invariant schedule, and may affect some seniors more than others, they are nonetheless not uncommon and are major challenges that lie in the way of well-being. All, however, is not bleakness in this developmental process; many seniors actively seek to maximize the assets they retain. They do so, according to Schulz and Heckhausen, by a process of incremental relinquishment of primary control of areas that are of lesser importance to them, diverting personal assets and skills toward a fewer number of domains over which they most highly value primary control. A valuable framework in which this process may be understood is role theory.

Role Theory and Individual Identity

To ascertain the causal agents that are likely to be the engines of such choice, it is worthwhile to examine role theory and identity as suggested by Burke (1991) and Thoits (1995). In this formulation an individual's identity, particularly as it may be expressed within social roles, assumes a central position in the understanding of human motivation. Each person has certain identifiable roles *vis-à-vis* others, particularly others within the person's particular group or community. A person may be a mother, uncle, friend, public official, or tour guide; each person, moreover, has his or her identity constructed from the sum of these various roles and role recognitions. Furthermore, each role is typically accompanied by a range of identifiable behaviours and expectations of behaviour; these behaviours and expectations of their appearance are the building blocks of an individual's identity. They provide widely recognized criteria by which a person is frequently evaluated in regard to the competent discharge of his or her role. In particular, it is concluded that the identifiable and widely-recognizable aspects of role allows individuals to gain feedback as to their competency and success, and provides them with an awareness of meaning, purpose and even life direction.

Role theory has a direct and illuminating effect upon Schulz and Heckhausen's formulation of successful ageing among older citizens. As people age and more carefully marshal their personal resources, they focus upon the roles that are identified as more vital to their particular well-being, and are prepared to devote less time and energy to the roles that they now regard as being of lesser relevance. It may also be reasonably inferred that, as senior citizens seek to retain primary control over fewer and more central roles in regard to their happiness, they also invest a much higher level of commitment to these remaining forms of self expression. The demonstration of competency in respect of these roles becomes incrementally more important to them as they age; it is from these fewer roles that life meanings are derived. Roles that lead to meaning,

to fulfillment and to the provision of an ongoing significance in a person's life are the ones likely to be favoured.

Senior citizens, through the deliberate focus on limited resources, are afforded a mechanism by which they show that they can demonstrate personal competency in critically important areas of life, and thereby enhance their sense of well-being. In this manner seniors can eschew dependency upon those around them and maintain perceptions of competency and independence in regard to their life course. Indeed, as many seniors know or sense to some degree, accelerated dependency upon family, friends and those around them vitiates a sense of personal competency (Baltes and Wahl, 1992). It is also the case that understanding the environment surrounding them as having qualities of malleability and reactivity to effort reinforces goal-setting and perseverance. The more that seniors entertain the perception that they do have, by way of their favoured role(s), some control or agency over their lives, the more they will attain this perception of meaning and direction (Ryff and Singer, 1998). Evidence for such a powerful effect emanates from a variety of sources, such as Seligman (2002) and Frankl (1963). The psychiatrist Frankl survived the horrors of WWII concentration camps, and concluded that people more likely to survive hardship and suffering were those who sought and found meaning and purpose to go on in the face of overwhelming desperation.

Not only does the successful performance of role requirements most often lead to the discovery of meaning and to personal resilience, it does, suggest Nunn (1996), Seligman (2002) and Peterson *et al.* (2005), result in an enhanced degree of hope and optimism for the future. They would argue that a strong conviction of meaning and purpose in a person's life, produced as the result of role proficiency, will most likely foster perceptions that events and outcomes will be positive and beneficent as they age. Future role attainments will more likely be expected as will happiness and well-being. It is, however the case that many society-level factors increase the probability of a diminution of personal, professional and community responsibility among older citizens. Role attrition, as Cummings and Henry (1961) and Rosow (1976) have pointed out, is frequently experienced by many older people, robbing them of meaning, of perceived competency and ultimately of optimism. Retirement, the loss of a partner, of family, of friends, even of familiar community structures, aggravates the loss of roles; many seniors cannot find new and meaningful roles. They do, moreover, often receive relatively little help to do so by much of the wider society (Rowe and Kahn, 1998). Such a situation is compounded by media and advertising stereotypes of older people as useless, as odd and even as objects of ridicule. Yet, there is also now a growing awareness that a person's senior years can be interesting, exciting, happy and fulfilling; these years can offer roles leading to the experience of such states (Bowling and Dieppe, 2005). Moreover, as Schulz and Heckhausen propose, those roles that are available, particularly those of a significant nature, tend to be invested with an even greater degree of commitment, for it is these deliberately selected roles that carry the capacity to provide both purpose and well-being among senior citizens. This is no less true of senior citizens in the tourism arena.

Seniors Tourism

A number of researchers such as Reece (2004) and Sellick (2004) have concluded that senior tourists represent a major and growing market presenting abundant opportunities for the travel and tourism industry. Seniors, as Sellick (2004) suggests, desire to learn more about themselves and the physical and cultural environments of many parts of their own country and indeed other parts of the world; older travelers have also been found to believe passionately that travel can enable them to reach higher levels of life satisfaction and fulfillment through their encounters with other people and other environments. Moschis *et al.* (1997) and Shoemaker (1989) have argued that seniors should not be seen as one large homogenous group; every life stage, including those experienced by older people, is characterized by change and adaptation in both the physiological and psychological arenas. Life-affirming roles, and the flowering of varied interpersonal relationships within such roles, are important characteristics among seniors (Birren and Schaie, 2004). Thus, an understanding of the range of travel motivators that characterize seniors is of use in providing a better understanding of what heritage travel represents to members of this group.

There are now a variety of studies reported in respect of the travel motives of seniors (Backman *et al.* 1999; Cleaver *et al.* 1999; Prideaux *et al.* 2004; Stone and Nichol, 1999). Motivation in tourism has been addressed in various ways. Push and pull factors, as a motivational schema, has been examined in a number of studies: Dann (1981), Goodall (1991), and Turnbull and Uysal (1995). Within this schema the distinction is made between a push factor (i.e. a personal travel motive such as the sociability need), and a pull factor (i.e. a salient destination attribute). Both push and pull factors typically motivate personal travel. Commentators such as Iso-Ahola (1989) argue for the importance of other motivating factors such as escape and seeking, with some potential travelers wishing to escape the circumstances of their everyday life, whilst others yearn for meaningful and illuminating experiences; older tourists, it can be noted, are said more likely to be seekers rather than escapers.

Various researchers have attempted to identify particular motivational sets; it can be concluded that social, relational and personal meaning factors feature prominently. Shoemaker (1989) highlights three components: family travelers, active resters and an older group, whilst Kim *et al.* (1996) identify knowledge, escape and kinship. Stone and Nichol (1999) articulate four senior travel motives: recreation, self-esteem, escape, and social interaction. Within an Australian context, Cleaver *et al.* (1999) suggest the following motivational typology: nostalgics, friendlies, learners, escapists, thinkers, status-seekers and physicals. Pearce (1999) concludes that senior self-drive tourists may exhibit implicit motives associated with self-discovery, achievement and also possibly sociability. Within nature tourism, Moisey and Bichis (1999) suggest that senior nature trail visitors were more likely to reveal the wish to meet new people, and to have insightful and evocative experiences as motivations to visit than were non-senior visitors to a national park. It might be thus concluded that personal meaning and self discovery are compelling motivators within a variety of studies.

Seniors Travel: Constraints and Possibilities

Beliefs concerning personal agency are able to influence both behavior and well-being (Gollwitzer and Moskowitz, 1996; Schmuck and Sheldon, 2001). Impediments to personal agency, at any stage of the life-span, can be occasioned by a variety of factors including resource limitations, conflicting personal demands and societal strictures. Moreover, barriers to the attainment of personal goals may result in dysfunctional behavior and a diminution in feelings of contentment and happiness (Hobfoll, 1998; Kahneman and Tversky, 1984; Riediger and Freund, 2004). The literature would suggest that senior travel patterns show evidence of a variety of factors that inhibit members of this group from traveling. And, just as a range of studies suggest that seniors are not homogenous as a group and reveal sundry motives for travel, it has also been reported that senior travelers encounter many barriers to travel, including ill-health, limited financial resources and home-based commitments that afford them insufficient time. Five major constraints to senior travel have been highlighted by McGuire (1984): insufficient resources, time demands at home, lack of approval from significant others, lack of social support whilst traveling, and limitations regarding physical capacity. Several authors (e.g. Blazey, 1987; Fleischer and Pizam, 2002; Huang and Tsai, 2003; Jang and Wu, 2006; McGuire *et al.*, 1986; and Mayo and Jarvis, 1985) have also elaborated major barriers to senior travel, including a lack of resources, time constraints, competing physical and emotional demands, paucity of travel information and health impediments. These findings have also been reflected in the works of Rose and Graesser (1981), McGuire (1984), Romsa and Blenman (1989) and Shoemaker (1989).

There is considerable disagreement about who constitutes a senior traveler; researchers such as Cleaver *et al.* (1999), Javalji *et al.* (1992), Moisey and Bichis (1999) and Shoemaker (1989) reflect clear differences in regard to who comprises this group of tourists. Some would opt for a starting point of 50 years of age, whilst others choose 55 years or even 60. Whilst cogent reasons often accompany each choice of age level, the clear lack of an agreed age boundary would seem to make comparisons among studies problematic. It is also the case that senior travelers cannot be identified by a single or predominant motivator or reason for travel. Indeed, it has been found that travel motivators represent an effective dimension for segmenting this group into various sub-groups and special interest segments. Neither can any simple differentiation be made between those travelers less than 50 years of age and those who are older (Horneman *et al.* 2002; Javalji *et al.* 1992; Moisey and Bichis, 1999). Javalji *et al.* (1992) have reported that over 50 travelers were more motivated by physical fitness oriented activities, by understandings of nature, and by opportunities for personal enrichment than were those travelers under 50 years of age. Moisey and Bichis (1999) have found that older travelers could be differentiated from younger travelers according to a range of factors, including cruising, touring, personal meaning, as well as visiting friends and relatives; visiting theme parks, they report, was an activity more likely to be favoured by the under 50s. It might thus be concluded that the pursuit of life enrichment and of ontologically significant experiences clearly characterize senior travel motivations.

Seniors and the Notion of Time: Problem-Solving and Personal Agency Issues

The problem-solving process adopted by most adults may be characterized by both subjective and objective modes of thinking. Subjective thought basically arises from the personal experiences and perceptions of each individual, and is typically set within an interpersonal and social network context. In contrast, the form of thought termed objective proceeds by way of abstract and impersonal logic. It has been argued that many traditional models of higher cognitive functioning place relatively little value on emotional experience and exchange, and are said to overly or exclusively esteem logical thinking (Argyle, 1991, 1999; Goleman, 1999). Many commentators would not want to dismiss the value of objective understandings gained by way of reasoning; indeed Sinnot (1998) would suggest that objective thinking can be a corrective mechanism for processes such as prejudice and emotional bias. Yet as Labouvie-Vief (1985, 1992) has argued, purely objective and logical modes of problem-solving can become maladaptive when individuals attempt to comprehend the complexities involved in those events and communications that are to do with deeply meaningful life experiences. Subjective feelings and interpersonal experiences are important yet often undervalued components in the understanding of human behaviour. Explanatory models that do not adequately take into account such factors, Sinnott (1998) suggests, will result in an understanding of behaviour that is limited, rigid and impoverished; comprehension of the complexities of everyday human decision-making will be inhibited without taking into account both types of problem-solving.

Pearce, Morrison and Rutledge (1998) make the point that many tourism studies focus upon images, information processing and decision-making choices of travelers who are assumed to decide important vacation issues solely by way of fact and logic, and *in vacuo*. They would suggest that a more compelling understanding of these mechanisms may be gained by taking into account meaningful social processes and events that surround and influence people when they come to making travel decisions. Partners, children, family members, co-workers and friends also form an influential context wherein these decisions are made. The decision-making process for many travelers most often begins with the quest for information. Solutions need to be found for dilemmas involving the selection of a destination, for transportation to and within destinations, and for issues such as accommodation, touring and sundry activities at or *en route* to the destination (Chen and Gursoy, 2000; Fodness and Murray, 1998; Gursoy and Chen, 2000). The initial step in this problem-solving process would seem to involve a recall of previous experiences and information regarding possible travel options (Vogt and Fesenmaier, 1998). Commentators such as Fodness and Murray (1997) have made the point that, for many travel decisions, particularly those involving new destinations and contexts, a turning to external sources is typical for many would-be travelers; family members and friends are an important source of and influence upon decision-making. Other factors found to be influential include travel party composition, purpose of trip, and culture of origin (Snepenger and Snepenger, 1993; Schmidt and Spreng, 1996; Vogt and Fesenmaier, 1998; Gursoy and Chen, 2000; and Uysal *et al.* 1990). Variables such as age, gender, life stage and desired network relationship type and intensity are also factors associated with travel decision-making. Moreover, so too are those motivational factors associated with events and experiences that give purpose and direction to an individual's life.

There is now a growing corpus of behavioural research focusing upon decision-making; many scholars would regard the notion of time and perceptions of both its elasticity and its immutability, as being of major explanatory consequence (Carlson and Pearo, 2004; Kesting, 2004; Reid and Reid, 2004). Time, when conceptualized as a finite entity, has long been regarded as playing a vital role in human problem-solving (Berger, 2001; Kail and Cavanaugh, 2004). Through all stages of the lifespan and in many contexts such as work, leisure and interpersonal relationships, time is seen as a crucial factor to be taken into account in the understanding of decision-making. Time is, moreover, a major explanatory notion in understanding human stress (Cooper and Robertson, 2001; Schaufeli and Buunk, 2003; Spurgeon and Cooper, 2001), with many individuals, perceiving themselves to be time-poor or time-pressured, believe that they must make decisions under pressure and with insufficient attention to considerations deemed important in determining outcomes. For others, however, time may not be such a pressing issue; this may be so for many people in leisure or travel contexts. Some travelers may prefer to make decisions on the spur of the moment, to be reactive to the changing circumstances of the vacation, and to be constantly mindful of the opportunities for forging new networks that may serendipitously present themselves during a journey. Travel for these individuals can be conceived as entering into new, spontaneous and more exciting or rewarding social realities (Krippendorf, 1987).

In regard to particular travel planning timeframes, Murphy (1996) found that, whilst backpacker tourists typically select the country they will visit some months beforehand, destinations within the chosen country were found to be selected only a few days prior to the visit. The image of younger travelers, as portrayed by commentators such as

Cohen (1973), Mukarji (1978) and Riley (1988), as well as authors such as Jack Kerouac and Alex Garland, is often of a group, the members of which typically approach decision-making and problem-solving with a timeframe that is immediate and spontaneous; decisions are made and problems addressed only when they arise. They would seem to require little or no time to prepare or plan strategies. Moreover, personal relationships established and social networks joined are often critical influences in evaluating travel experiences (Noy, 2004; Ross, 1996, 1997; Ryan *et al.*, 2003).

By way of contrast, travel-planning time frames may be quite different for other groups such as older travelers, sometimes termed snowbirds or grey nomads (Javalgi *et al.*, 1992; Mings, 1997; Zimmer *et al.*, 1995). Here it has been suggested that pre-travel planning is regarded as much more necessary, with decision-making delayed to later stages only for unforeseeable issues and problems. Indeed Muller (1996) would suggest a major reason for this desire for pre-planning involves stronger perceptions of personal agency and predictability; middle and older adulthood for many brings with it, he suggests, a greater sense of control of one's life, the possibility and the utility of preparation, and thus a willingness to plan ahead. It is also the case that groups such as older travelers take into account social networks and sociability when making travel decisions, often returning to destinations at which friends and acquaintances may again be found (Mings, 1997). Thus many senior travelers prefer preparation and preplanning. This for seniors is a signifier of personal agency, a method whereby they may channel personal resources into maximizing the likelihood that their most important travel goals are attained. Senior travelers therefore are held more likely

to perceive their role as ideally involving maximal preparation and it is by way of this perceived role requirement that meaning-making is most likely to be realized.

A Summary Model of Salient Motivational Factors Relevant to Senior Travelers

Many commentators suggest that we now know more about human functioning than was known in the time of Heraclitus in 600 BC, though the degree to which we know more, and can confidently assert so, will continue to be a matter of some debate. It is, however, undeniable that a great deal of research has in recent decades taken place in crucial areas such as heritage tourism motivation, the personal efficacy of senior citizens, and motivational forces that represent the engines of personal well-being. This chapter has sought to examine elements of heritage tourism motivation among seniors in light of what are now represented as central domains, the operation of which critically determines human well-being. The model in Figure 1 represents motivations associated with senior heritage tourists to be of two types: that which may be described as positive and acts as an impulsion toward a heritage site or context, and the type of motivation that might be described as negative, as having an element of avoidance energizing it. This latter motivational force suggests that individuals may act to avoid aversive consequences such as the deprivation associated with missing those experiences that will be of the meaning-making type.

The model also encompasses three types of meaning-making processes: those associated with enduring dispositional elements pertaining to the individual, those processes

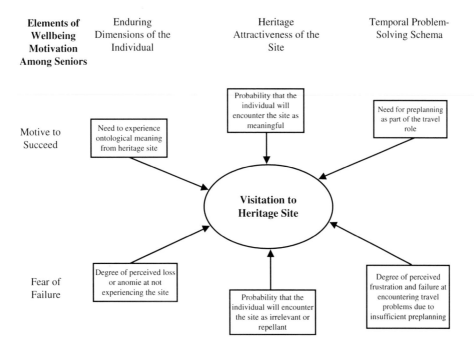

Figure 1   Structural Model Involving Motivational Factors Associated with Ontological Travel Undertaken by Seniors.

concerned with the perceived meaning-making potency of the heritage site or context, and those processes involved with individual temporal problem-solving schemas. The first of these processes, enduring dispositions, suggests that senior heritage tourists will likely exhibit various levels of needs to visit heritage places, both because they have a clear intent and need to do so, and also because they realize that the power of meaning-making is of sufficient importance to their functioning, that not to do so will likely occasion personal loss and anomie at their life-stage. The second process, that pertaining to the power of the place, *animus loci* as Basu would describe it, has been investigated by a range of tourism researchers, many of whom would argue that there are salient aspects of the site that attract particular

visitors. Should those prized elements not be present as expected, the model would suggest that many of these senior visitors will likely encounter the site as disappointing or even perhaps egregiously inauthentic.

There is now a considerable awareness in regard to the importance of heritage travel among many communities and nations within the Asia Pacific region. Li (2003) notes that in Hong Kong heritage tourism is presently recognized as a valuable strategy for promoting Hong Kong to the world at large. Indeed Li and Lo (2004) point out that approximately 27% of visitors to Hong Kong report an interest in heritage and traditional Chinese festivals, and moreover would rank this interest as second or third in their hierarchy of travel aspirations with respect to Hong Kong as a vacation destination. McKercher, Ho and du Cros (2005) similarly recognize the importance of heritage tourism to this region of the world, and would argue for a more constructive engagement between tourism and cultural heritage management. Heritage tourism, they aver, not only reacquaints travelers with their historical and cultural origins, but also has the effect of revivifying a widespread interest in history and culture, to the benefit of many peoples and destinations such as Hong Kong. A variety of commentators have similarly examined heritage issues in other Asia Pacific contexts, such as Japan (Cunningham, 2006), Taiwan (Huang and Tsai, 2003), Indonesia (Dahles, 2002), Australia (Onyx and Leonard, 2005; Ross, 2005), China (Lam and Hsu, 2004), Singapore (Teo and Leong, 2006) and Laos (Aas, Ladkin and Fletcher, 2005). These various studies and commentaries would conclude that the desire for heritage tourism experiences is a salient component of the overall visitor motivation profile.

Sellick (2004) and Goulding (1999) have both concluded that nostalgia is a potent motivator among older travelers throughout the world: the wish to discover the past and thereby an aspect of themselves long dormant or not yet fully appreciated. This heritage may be perceived as taking the form of buildings, artifacts, cultural displays and reenactments. It might also be understood by the senior traveler as being essentially within the communities and peoples that he or she wishes to visit and to understand better. This process, the present model would suggest, is optimally perceived by many older travelers in the Asia Pacific region as leading to their self understanding, a sense of completeness, and thus their overall sense of well-being.

Finally well-being motivational processes among senior heritage travelers, this model posits, will also involve temporal problem-solving schemas. Senior heritage tourists, it is suggested, are more likely to display a need for preplanning as an essential component of their role as a traveler. Being prevented from doing so, and encountering travel problems occasioned by too little pre-travel preparation, will as this model suggests, lead to disappointment and a perceived diminution of personal agency that frustrates meaning-making and therefore well-being. Senior travelers are now, perhaps more than ever before, seeking to exert a degree of personal agency or competence in their lives in areas such as travel experiences. They do, moreover, regard heritage and associated travel as a prime source of meaning-making around which this personal agency is able to be expressed. The derivation of meaning and thence personal well-being is, for senior travelers, of fundamental importance. Many seniors are therefore ever curious about the great mysteries of their lives and of the world about them; they, like Einstein and his friend, frequently experience no attenuation of the drive to engage with the mysteries of the world. Heritage travel, it is concluded, is thus likely to see an even greater number of senior tourists in contexts such as the Asia Pacific region actively engaged in this quest for meaning-making.

References

Aas, C, Ladkin, A. and Fletcher, J. (2005) Stakeholder collaboration and heritage management. *Annals of Tourism Research* 32: 567–593.

Alzua, A, O'Leary, J. and Morrison, A. (1998) Cultural heritage and tourism: Identifying niches for international travelers. *Journal of Tourism Studies* 9: 2–13.

Ap, J. and Wong, K. (2001) Case study on tour guiding: Professionalism, issues and problems. *Tourism Management* 22: 551–563.

Argyle, M. (1991) *Cooperation – The Basis of Sociability*. London: Routledge.

Argyle, M. (1999) Causes and correlates of happiness. In D. Kaneman, E. Diener and N. Schwarz (eds) *Well-Being: The Foundations of Hedonic Psychology*. New York: Sage.

Ashworth, G.J. (1998) The conserved European city as cultural symbol: the meaning of the text. In B. Graham (ed.) *Modern Europe: Place, Culture, Identity*, pp. 261–286. London: Arnold.

Backman, K.F., Backman, S.J., and Silverberg, K.E. (1999) Investigations into the psychographics of senior nature-based travelers. *Tourism Recreation Research* 24: 13–22.

Baltes, M.M. and Wahl, H.W. (1992) The dependency-support script in institutions: Generalization to community settings. *Psychology and Aging* 7: 409–418.

Bandura, A. (1995) *Self-efficacy in Changing Societies*. New York: Cambridge University Press.

Basu, P. (2001) Hunting down home: Reflections on homeland and the search for identity in the Scottish Diaspora. In B. Bender and M. Winer (eds) *Contested Landscapes*, pp. 333–344. Oxford: Berg.

Basu, P. (2004a) Route metaphors of roots-tourism in the Scottish Diaspora. In S. Coleman and J. Eade (eds) *Reframing Pilgrimage: Cultures in Motion*, pp.150–174. London: Routledge.

Basu, P. (2004b) My own island home: The Orkney homecoming. *Journal of Material Culture* 9: 27–42.

Basu, P. (2005) Pilgrims to the Far Country: North American roots-tourists in the Scottish Highlands and Islands. In C. Ray (ed.) *Transatlantic Scots*, pp. 286–317. Tuscaloosa: Alabama University Press.

Berger, K. S. (2001) *The Developing Person through the Life Span*. New York: Worth.

Birren, J.E. and Schaie, K.W. (2004) *Guidelines for Psychological Practice with Older People*. Washington, DC: American Psychological Association.

Blazey, M. (1987) The difference between participants and non-participants in a senior travel program. *Journal of Travel Research* 26(1): 7–12.

Bowling, A. and Dieppe, P. (2005) What is successful ageing and who should define it? *British Medical Journal* 331: 1548–1551.

Burke, P.J. (1991) Identity process and social stress. *American Sociological Review* 56: 836–849.

Carlson, K.A. and Pearo, L.K. (2004) Limiting predecisional distortion by prior valuation of attribute components. *Organizational Behavior and Human Decision Processes* 94: 48–59.

Chen, J.S. and Gursoy, D. (2000) Cross-cultural comparison of the information sources used by first-time and repeat travelers and its marketing implications. *International Journal of Hospitality Management* 19: 191–203.

Cleaver, M., Muller, T.E., Ruys, H.F.M. and Wei, S. (1999) Tourism product development for the senior market based on travel motive research. *Tourism Recreation Research* 24: 5–11.

Cohen, E. (1973) Nomads from affluence: Notes on the phenomenon of drifter-tourism. *International Journal of Comparative Sociology*, 14: 89–103.

Cohen, E. (1988) Authenticity and commoditization in tourism. *Annals of tourism research*, 15: 371–386.

Cohen, E., Ifergan, M. and Cohen, E. (2002) A new paradigm in guiding: The Madrich as a role model. *Annals of Tourism Research*, 29: 919–932.

Cooper, C.L. and Robertson, I.T. (2001). *Well-Being in Organizations*. Chichester: Wiley.

Cummings, E. and Henry, W.E. (1961) *Growing Old: The Process of Disengagement*. New York: Basic Books.

Cunningham, P. (2006) Social valuing for Ogasawara as a place and space among ethnic host. *Tourism Management*, 27: 505–516.

Dahles, H. (2002) The politics of tour guiding: Image management in Indonesia. *Annals of Tourism Research* 29: 783–800.

Dann, G.M.S. (1981) Tourism motivation: An appraisal. *Annals of Tourism Research*, 8: 187–219.

Deci, E. and Ryan, R.M. (2000) The 'what' and 'why' of human goal pursuits: Human needs and the self-determination of behavior. *Psychological Inquiry*, 11: 227–268.

Diener, E. (2000) Subjective well-being: The science of happiness and a proposal for a national index. *American Psychologist*, 55: 34–43.

Fleischer, A. and Pizam, A. (2002) Tourism constraints among Israeli seniors. *Annals of Tourism Research*, 29: 106–123.

Fodness, D and Murray, B. (1997) Tourist information search. *Annals of Tourism Research*, 24: 503–523.

Fodness, D. and Murray, B. (1998) A typology of tourism information search strategies. *Journal of Travel Research*, 37: 108–119.

Frankl, V. (1963) *Man's Search for Meaning*. New York: Simon & Schuster.

Garrod, B. and Fyall, A. (2000) Managing heritage tourism. *Annals of tourism research*, 27: 682–708.

Garrod, B. and Fyall, A. (2001) Heritage tourism: A question of definition. *Annals of tourism*, 28: 1949–1052.

Goleman, D. (1999) *Working with Emotional Intelligence*. London: Bloomsbury.

Gollwitzer, P.M. and Moskowitz, G.B. (1996) Goal effects on actions and cognition. In E.T. Higgins and A.W. Kruglanski (eds) *Social Psychology: Handbook of Basic Principles*, pp. 361–399. New York: Guilford.

Goodall, B. (1991) Understanding holiday choice. In C.P. Cooper (ed.) *Progress in Tourism, Recreation and Hospitality Management*, Vol 3, pp. 58–77. London: Belhaven.

Goulding, C. (1999) Heritage, nostalgia, and the "grey" consumer. *Journal of Marketing Practice: Applied Marketing Science*, 5: 177–199.

Gursoy, D. and Chen, J.S. (2000) Competitive analysis of cross cultural information search behavior, *Tourism Management*, 21: 583–590.

Hall, C.M. (2000) Tourism and the establishment of national parks in Australia. In R. Butler and S. Boyd (eds), *Tourism and National Parks: Issues and Implications*, pp. 29–38. Chichester: Wiley.

Hewison, R. (1987) *The Heritage Industry: Britain in a Climate of Decline*. London: Methuen.

Horneman, L., Carter, R.W., Wei, S. and Ruys, H. (2002) Profiling the senior traveler: An Australian perspective. *Journal of Travel Research*, 41(1): 23–27.

Hobfoll, S.E. (1998) *Stress, Culture and Community*. New York: Plenum.

Hollinshead, K. (1988) First-blush of the longtime: The market development of Australia's living Aboriginal heritage. Tourism research: Expanding Boundaries. In Proceedings of the 19th annual conference of the Tourism Research Association, pp. 83–198. Salt Lake City: University of Utah.

Huang, L. and Tsai, H-T. (2003) The study of senior traveler behavior in Taiwan. *Tourism Management*, 24: 561–574.

Iso-Ahola, S.E. (1989) Motivation for leisure. In E.L. Jackson and T.L. Burton (eds) *Understanding Leisure and Recreation: Mapping the Past, Charting the Future*, pp.247–271. State College, PA: Venture.

Jang, S. and Wu, C-M.E. (2006) Seniors' travel motivation and the influential factors: An examination of Taiwanese seniors. *Tourism Management*, 27: 306–316.

Javalgi, R.G., Thomas, E.G. and Rao, S.R. (1992) Consumer behavior in the U.S. pleasure travel marketplace: An analysis of senior and nonsenior travelers. *Journal of Travel Research*, 31(2): 14–19.

Johnson, N. (1999) Framing the past: time, space and the politics of heritage tourism in Ireland. *Political Geography*, 18: 187–207.

Kahneman, D. (1999) Objective happiness. In D. Kahneman, E. Diener and N. Schwarz (eds) *Well-being: The Foundations of Hedonic Psychology*, pp. 3–25. New York: Sage.

Kahneman, D. and Tversky, A. (1984) Choices, values, frames of reference. *American Psychologist*, 39: 341–350.

Kail, R. V. and Cavanaugh, J.C. (2004) *Human Development*. Belmont, CA: Wadsworth/Thomson.

Kesting, P. (2004) The relation between routine and decision: An action-based approach. Paper Presented at the Cambridge Realist Workshop, May, 2004.

Kim, Y., Weaver, P. and McCleary, K. (1996) A structural equation model: The relationship between travel motivation and information sources in the senior travel market. *Journal of Vacation Marketing*, 3: 55–66.

Krippendorf, J. (1987) *The Holiday Makers*. London: Heinemann.

Labouvie-Vief, G. (1985) Intelligence and cognition. In J.E. Birren and K.W. Schaie (eds) *Handbook of the Psychology of Aging*, pp. 500–530. New York: Van Nostrand Reinhold.

Lam, T. and Hsu, C.H.C. (2004). Theory of planned behavior: Potential travelers from China. *Journal of Hospitality and Tourism Research*, 28: 463–482.

Laws, E. (1998) Conceptualizing visitor satisfaction management in heritage settings: An exploratory blueprinting analysis of Leeds Castle, Kent. *Tourism Management*, 19: 545–554.

Li, Y. (2003) Heritage tourism: the contradictions between conservation and change. *Tourism and Hospitality Research*, 4: 241–261.

Li, Y. and Lo, R.L.B. (2004) Applicability of the market appeal–robusticity matrix: A case study of heritage tourism. *Tourism Management*, 25: 789–800.

Lyubomirsky, S., Sheldon, K.M. and Schkade, D. (2005) Pursuing happiness: the architecture of sustainable change. *Review of General Psychology*, 9: 111–131.

McCain, G. and Ray, N.M. (2003) Legacy tourism: The search for personal meaning in heritage travel. *Tourism Management*, 24: 713–717.

McCannell, D. (1976) *The visitor: A new theory of the leisure class*. New York: Schocken Books.

McKercher, B., Ho, P.S.Y. and du Cros, H. (2005) Relationship between tourism and cultural heritage management: Evidence from Hong Kong. *Tourism Management*, 26: 539–548.

McGuire, F.A. (1984) A factor analysis study of leisure constraints in advanced adulthood. *Leisure Science*, 6: 313–326.

McGuire, F.A., Dottavio, D. and O'Leary, J.T. (1986) Constraints to participation in outdoor recreation across the life span: A nationwide study of limits and prohibitors. *The Gerontologist*, 26: 538–544.

McIntosh, A. and Prentice, R. (1999) Affirming authenticity: Consuming cultural heritage. *Annals of tourism research*, 26: 589–612.

Mayo, E.J. and Jarvis, P. (1985) *The Psychology of Leisure*. Boston, MA: CABI Publishing.

Mendes de Leon, C.F. (2005) Why do friendships matter for survival? *Journal of Epidemiology and Community Health*, 59: 538–539.

Mings, R.C. (1997) Tracking snowbirds in Australia: Winter sun seekers in Far North Queensland. *Australian Geographical Studies*, 35: 168–182.

Moisey, R.N. and Bichis, M. (1999) Psychographics of senior nature tourists: The Katy nature trail. *Tourism Recreation Research*, 24: 69–76.

Moscardo, G. (1996) Mindful visitors: Heritage tourism. *Annals of Tourism Research*, 23: 376–397.

Moschis, G.P., Lee, E. and Mathur, A. (1997) Targeting the mature market: Opportunities and challenges. *Journal of Consumer Marketing*, 14: 282–293.

Muller, T. (1996) Baby boomer lifestyle segments and the imminence of eight trends. *New Zealand Journal of Business*, 18: 1–25.

Murkarji, C. (1978) Bullshitting: Road lore among hitch-hikers. *Social Problems*, 25: 241–252.

Murphy, L. (1996) *Backpackers and the Decisions They Make*. Townsville: Department of Tourism, James Cook University.

Nunn, K.P. (1996) Personal hopefulness: A conceptual review of the relevance of the perceived future to psychiatry. *British Journal of Medical Psychology*, 69: 227–245.

Nuryanti, W. (1996) Heritage and post-modern tourism. *Annals of Tourism Research*, 23: 249–260.

Noy, C. (2004) This trip really changed me: Backpacker's narratives of self-change. *Annals of Tourism Research*, 31: 78–102.

Onyx, J. and Leonard, R. (2005) Australian grey nomads and American Snowbirds: Similarities and differences. *Journal of Tourism Studies*, 16: 61–68.

Palmer, C. (1999) Tourism and the symbols of identity. *Tourism Management*, 20: 313–321.

Palmer, C. (2003) Touring Churchill's England. *Annals of Tourism Research*, 30: 426–445.

Palmer, C. (2005) An ethnography of Englishness. *Annals of Tourism Research*, 32: 7–27.

Pearce, P.L. (1999) Touring for pleasure: Studies of the senior self-drive travel market. *Tourism Recreation Research*, 24: 35–42.

Pearce, P.L. and Moscardo, G.M. (1986) The concept of authenticity in tourists' experiences. *Australian and New Zealand Journal of Sociology*, 22: 121–132.

Pearce, P.L., Morrison, A.M. and Rutledge, J.L. (1998) *Tourism: Bridges Across Continents*. New York: McGraw-Hill.

Peterson, C., Park, N. and Seligman, M.E. (2005) Orientations to happiness and life satisfaction: The full life versus the empty life. *Journal of Happiness Studies*, 6: 25–41.

Poria, Y., Butler, R. and Airey, D. (2000) Clarifying heritage tourism: A distinction between heritage tourism and tourism in historic places. *Annals of Tourism Research*, 28: 1047–1049.

Poria, Y., Butler, R. and Airey, D. (2001). Tourism sub-groups: Do they exist? *Tourism Today*, 1: 14–22.

Poria, Y., Butler, R. and Airey, D. (2003) The core of heritage tourism: Distinguishing heritage tourists from tourists in heritage places. *Annals of Tourism Research*, 30: 238–254.

Poria, Y., Butler, R. and Airey, D. (2004) Links between tourism, heritage, and reasons for visiting heritage sites. *Journal of Travel Research*, 43: 19–28.

Poria, Y., Reichel, A. and Biran, A. (2006) Heritage site management motivations and expectations. *Annals of Tourism Research*, 33: 162–178.

Prentice, R.C., Witt, S.C. and Hamer, C. (1998) Tourism as experience: The case of heritage parks. *Annals of tourism research*, 25: 1–24.

Prideaux, B., Wei, S. and Ruys, H. (2004) Tour coach operations in the Australian seniors market. *Asean Journal of Hospitality and Tourism*, 3: 135–148.

Reece, W.S. (2004) Are senior leisure travelers different? *Journal of Travel Research*, 43: 11–18.

Reid, D. and Reid, N.L. (2004) Time discounting over the lifespan. *Organizational Behavior and Human Decision Processes*, 94: 22–32.

Richards, G. (1996) Production and consumption of European cultural tourism. *Annals of tourism research*, 23: 261–283.

Richards, G. (2002) Tourism attraction systems: Exploring cultural behaviour. *Annals of Tourism Research*, 29: 1048–1064.

Riedeger, M. and Freund, A.M. (2004) Interference and facilitation among personal goals: Differential associations with subjective well-being and persistent goal pursuit. *Personality and Social Psychology Bulletin*, 30: 1511–1523.

Riley, P.J. (1988) Road culture of international long-term budget travelers. *Annals of Tourism Research*, 13: 313–328.

Romsa, G. and Blenman, M. (1989) Vacation patterns in the elderly Germans. *Annals of Tourism Research*, 16: 178–188.

Rose, C. and Graesser, C.C. (1981) *Adult Participation in Life-Long Learning Activities in California*. Los Angeles: Evaluation and Training Institute.

Rosow, I. (1976) Status and role change throughout the life span. In R.H. Binstock and E. Shanas (eds) *Handbook of Aging and the Social Sciences*, pp. 457–483. New York: Van Nostrand Rienhold.

Ross, G.F. (1996) Personality needs as predictors of service quality judgements among backpacker visitors to the Wet Tropics region of Far North Queensland. *Australian Leisure*, March: 35–41.

Ross, G.F. (1997) Backpacker achievement and environmental controllability as visitor motivation. *Journal of Travel and Tourism Marketing*, 6: 69–82.

Ross, G.F. (2005) Senior tourists sociability and travel preparation. *Tourism Review*, 60: 6–15.

Rowe, J.W. and Kahn, R.L. (1998) *Successful Aging*. New York: Pantheon Books.

Ryan, C., Trauer, B., Kave, J., Sharma, A. and Sharma, S. (2003) Backpackers: What is the peak experience. *Tourism Recreation Research*, 28: 93–98.

Ryff, C.D. and Singer, B. (1998) The contours of positive human health. *Psychological Inquiry*, 9: 1–28.

Schaufeli, W. B. and Buunk, B.P. (2003) Burnout: An overview of 25 years of research and theorizing. In M.J. Schabracq, J.A.M. Winnubst and C.L. Cooper (eds) *The Handbook of Work and Health Psychology*, pp. 383–425. London: Wiley.

Schmidt, J.B. and Spreng, R.A. (1996) A proposed model of external consumer information search. *Journal of the Academy of Marketing Science*, 24: 246–256.

Schmuck, P. and Sheldon, K.M. (2001) *Life Goals and Well-being*. New York: Hogrefe and Huber.

Schultz, R. and Heckhausen, J. (1996) A life span model of successful aging. *American Psychologist*, 51: 702–714.

Seale, R. (1996) A perspective from Canada on heritage tourism. *Annals of Tourism Research*, 23: 484–488.

Seligman, M.E.P. (2002) *Authentic Happiness*. New York: Free Press.

Seligman, M.E.P., Steen, T.A., Park, N. and Peterson, C. (2005) Positive psychology progress. *American Psychologist*, 60: 410–421.

Sellick, M. C. (2004) Discovery, connection, nostalgia: Key travel motives within the senior market. *Journal of Travel and Tourism Marketing*, 17: 55–71.

Shackley, M. (2001) *Managing Sacred Sites: Service Provision and Visitor Experience*. London: Continuum.

Shoemaker, S.A. (1989) Segmentation of the senior pleasure travel market. *Journal of Travel Research*, 27(3): 14–21.

Sinnott, J.D. (1998) *The Development of Logic in Adulthood*. New York: Plenum.

Smith, A. (1991) *National identity*. London: Penguin.

Snepenger, D. and Snepenger, M. (1993) Information search by pleasure travelers. In M.A. Kahn, M.D. Olsen, and T. Var (eds) *Encyclopedia of Hospitality and Tourism*, pp. 830–835. New York: Van Nostrand Reinhold.

Spurgeon, A. and Cooper, C.A. (2001) Working time, health and performance. In C.L. Cooper and I.T. Robertson (eds) *Well-Being in Organizations*, pp. 189–222. Chichester: Wiley.

Stone, G.J. and Nichol, S. (1999) Older, Single female holiday makers in the United Kingdom: Who Needs Them? *Journal of Vacation Marketing* 5: 7–17.

Swarbrooke, J. (1994) The future of the past: Heritage tourism into the 21st century. In A.V. Seaton (ed.) *Tourism: The State of the Art*. pp. 222–229. Chichester: Wiley.

Teo, P. and Leong, S. (2006) A postcolonial analysis of backpacking. *Annals of Tourism Research*, 33: 109–131.

Thoits, P.A. (1995) Stress, coping and social support processes: Where are we? What next? *Journal of Health and Social Behavior*, 35: 53–79.

Timothy, D.J. (1997) Tourism and the personal heritage experience. *Annals of Tourism Research*, 34: 751–754.

Timothy, D.J. and Boyd, S. (2003) *Heritage Tourism*. Harlow: Prentice Hall.

Turnbull, R.D. and Uysal, M. (1995) An explanatory study of German visitors to the Caribbean: Push and pull motivations. *Journal of Travel and Tourism Marketing*, 4: 85–92.

Uysal, M., McDonald, C.D. and Reid, L.J. (1990) Sources of information used by international visitors to US parks and natural areas. *Journal of Park and Recreation Administration*, 8: 51–59.

Uzzell, D. (1989) *Heritage Interpretation: The Natural and Built Environments*. London: Belhaven.

Uzzell, D. (1996) Creating place identity through heritage interpretation. *The International Journal of Heritage Studies*, 1: 219–228.

Vogt, C.A. and Fesenmaier, D.R. (1998) Expanding the functional information search model. *Annals of Tourism Research*, 25: 551–578.

Zimmer, Z., Brayley, R.E. and Searle, M.S. (1995) Whether to go and where to go: Identification of important influences on senior's decisions to travel. *Journal of Travel Research*, 33(3): 3–10.

Sustainable Tourism Competitiveness Clusters: Application to World Heritage Sites Network Development in Indonesia

Donald E. Hawkins

Introduction

In September 2002, the United Nations Environmental Programme (UNEP) and United Nations Educational, Scientific and Cultural Organisation (UNESCO) World Heritage Centre held a three-day workshop at Ujung Kulon World Heritage site in Indonesia in order to explore the actions needed to design and implement networks of World Heritage sites in Indonesia and throughout Asia. The rationale for the workshop was that the establishment of linkages between World Heritage sites can increase local economic development, enable distribution of visitors from well-known sites to those with fewer visitations, raise awareness of the World Heritage program, and enrich the visitor experience. Some preliminary suggestions for linkages included shared interpretation, promotional materials, management practices, and branding based upon the World Heritage label. The idea of creating these networks of sites is largely based upon the concept of competitive clusters.

In recent years, this approach has become increasingly more common in the tourism industry, with numerous success stories to support its continued application.

The purpose of this article is to describe how Indonesia can utilize World Heritage networks to enhance its competitiveness, based upon findings of the workshop at Ujung Kulon, as well as a review of other cases around the world. First, however, the World Heritage program will be explained, highlighting specific sites in Indonesia. Also, the competitive cluster approach will be described in detail.

World Heritage Network Development

UNESCO's World Heritage Program

UNESCO created the World Heritage program as part of its mission to identify, protect, and preserve "cultural and natural heritage around the world considered to be of outstanding value to humanity" (UNESCO World Heritage Website, 2003). Since the program's inception in 1972, the UNESCO's World Heritage Committee has convened annually to determine which sites will be added to the World Heritage List.

Nominations, which can only be submitted by countries, are evaluated by two advisory bodies, the International Council on Monuments and Sites (ICOMOS) and the World Conservation Union (IUCN). Cultural heritage sites are evaluated on their "historical, aesthetic, archaeological, scientific, ethnological, or anthropological value" (ibid). Natural heritage sites must be "outstanding physical, biological, and geographic formation, habitats of threatened species of animals and plants and areas with scientific, conservation, or aesthetic value" (ibid).

To date, the World Heritage Committee has accepted the applications of 730 sites worldwide. There are numerous benefits associated with being on the World Heritage list. First, accepted sites attain a heightened public awareness and a certain prestige that comes with the World Heritage name. Second, they receive expert advice and technical assistance from UNESCO. Some of the advice comes in the form of an extensive site manager's handbook. It provides recommendations on a wide range of managerial issues such as staffing, budgeting, interpretation, marketing, and visitor recording. Also, in some cases, UNESCO provides financial assistance to sites on the World Heritage list (ibid).

Indonesia's World Heritage Sites

Like most other East Asian countries, Indonesia experienced tremendous tourism growth throughout the 80's and most of the 90's. Increasing tourism receipts resulted in further investment, especially in mass tourism infrastructure. But in 1997, growth throughout the

region was severely stunted as a result of the Asian economic crisis. In Indonesia, tourism receipts declined 15.6% in 1997, from US$6.3 billion to US$5.3 billion. Receipts fell another 18.6% in 1998. During the previous five years, Indonesia had experienced average tourism revenue growth rates of 20.3% and over the previous ten years, 27.5% (Department of Culture and Tourism of the Republic of Indonesia, 2001).

While most tourism revenues in most other East Asian countries returned to pre-crisis levels within a few years, Indonesia has had a much more difficult time recovering. This has been due to negative media attention stemming from massacres in East Timor, two other major separatist movements in Irian Jaya and Aceh (Infoplease Website, 2003), widespread environmental damage by the logging and mining industries, and most recently, the acknowledged harboring of al-Qaeda members. To rescue the ailing industry, Indonesia is looking to follow the lead of other successful East Asian countries such as Cambodia and Thailand, which have built lucrative and sustainable tourism industries based on their wealth of natural and cultural assets. Certainly, the World Heritage Sites network will be instrumental to their efforts.

Currently, Indonesia has six World Heritage sites, three cultural and three natural. Descriptions are provided below. Readers should note that visitation statistics are available only for Komodo National Park and Ujung Kulon National Park.

Borobudur Temple Compounds

This famous 8th century Buddhist temple, restored with the help of UNESCO, was inscribed as a cultural heritage site in 1991. It was built under the supervision of the Sailendra Dynasty, which controlled Java in the 8th and 9th centuries. The temple's incredible workmanship can be seen in the 432 Buddha statues, 100 gargoyles, 1,212 decorative panels, and 1,460 narrative panels. The walls and balustrades, adorned with bas-reliefs, cover an area of 2,500 square meters (UNESCO World Heritage Website, 1998).

Prambanan Temple Compounds

This site, located in Java, contains three temples dedicated to the major Hindu divine figures (Shiva, Vishnu, and Brahma) and three temples dedicated to the animals that serve them. The former are decorated with elaborate relieves illustrating the entire epic of *Ramayana*. All temples in the compound are believed to have been built in the 10th century. Prambanan was inscribed as a cultural heritage site in 1991 (UNESCO World Heritage Website, 2001).

Sangiran Early Man Site

Also located in Java, this site is where the first hominid fossil was discovered. During a period of excavations between 1936 and 1941, 50 *Meganthropus paleo* and *Pithecanthropus erectus/Homo erectus* were found. This represents over half of the world's known hominid fossils. They are dated at around a million and a half years old. Sangiran was inscribed as a cultural heritage site in 1996 (ibid).

Komodo National Park

This 173,500 hectare national park is best known for its population of 5,700 giant lizards known as Komodo dragons. Endemic to the four islands of the park, they are of great interest to evolutionary scientists. One

problem they face is the depletion of their stocks through predation by feral dogs and poaching from the park's roughly 1,500 human inhabitants. Another threat to the park's natural equilibrium is the dynamite fishing of the coral reefs by fishermen from surrounding islands (ibid). Komodo National Park was inscribed as a natural heritage site in 1991. Consistent with overall tourism trends in Indonesia, visitation to Komodo has declined steadily in recent years. In the 1997–1998 seasons, the park received roughly 28,000 international visitors and 3,000 domestic visitors. By the 2001–2002 season, these figures dropped to roughly 11,000 and 1,500, respectively (Rare, 2002).

Lorentz National Park

Covering an area of 2.5 million hectares, this is the largest protected area in Southeast Asia. It is also the only protected area in the world with a continuous transect from snowcap to tropical marine environment. As such, it has tremendous biodiversity, including many endemic species. In its five altitudinal vegetation zones reside 324 species of reptiles, 650 species of birds, and 164 species of mammals. The park, however, faces several problems that have significantly reduced tourism arrivals. One is the negative environmental impact of open cast gold mines. Another is the civil unrest on the Irian Jaya. Lorentz National Park was inscribed as a natural heritage site in 1999 (UNESCO World Heritage Website, 2001).

Ujung Kulon National Park

This 120,550 hectare park in southwest Java is known for its natural beauty and the presence of several endangered plants and animals. The park represents the last natural refuge for the Javan rhinoceros, of which only 60 remain. The park's other notable mammals include the leopard, fishing cat, Javan mongoose and three endemic primates species (Javan gibbon, Javan leaf monkey, and silvered leaf monkey). Also, the coastal coral reef environment ranks among the richest in Indonesia. The park's most serious threats come from illegal logging and rhinoceros poaching. Ujung Kulon was inscribed as a natural heritage site in 1991 (ibid). As in many other Indonesian sites, visitation has declined in recent years. In 1997, it received roughly 4,000 domestic visitors and 2,000 international visitors. By 2001, these numbers decreased to approximately 3,000 and 1,000, respectively (Rare, 2002).

Competitive Cluster Approach

Destination Competitiveness

The strategic issues of cost leadership, differentiation, and focus emerged from the initial discussions on areas of common concern and the prospects for collaborative action. Porter's Diamond Model (1996) affirms that the competitive advantage of a firm or a group of firms at the destination level is determined by four fundamental elements, which when combined form the four points of the "Competitive Diamond" shown in Figure 1. These elements and their interaction with one another explain how an industry remains innovative and competitive within a localized area. The four points are (1) factor conditions; (2) demand conditions; (3) related support sectors; (4) strategy, structure and rivalry among firms. In addition to the four principal elements, government and chance or

unplanned factors also play a large role as described in the following figure:

Factor Conditions. Classic economic theory suggests that a destination's basic resources, which include land, human resources and capital, determine competitive advantage. However, this does not explain why any one area would lead the world in a particular industry. Instead, it is specialized factors, which are not inherited but created by each destination, such as educational systems, technological "know-how", specialized infrastructure, and other capabilities, which respond to the specific needs of an industry.

Demand Conditions. It would appear as globalization advances that local demand would become insignificant. However, research has shown exactly the opposite. High expectations by local consumers seem to drive firms to a more competitive and innovative position.

Related Support Sectors. The existence of specialized and efficient support industries helps foster competition in destinations by allowing the "cluster" to have lower costs, superior quality and rapid product turn-over rates. In order for a "cluster" to be competitive, it is vital that there be an innovative, dynamic support system.

Firm Strategy, Structure and Rivalry. Competition is dependent upon an environment that promotes innovation and efficiency. An effective cluster forces firms to reduce costs, improve quality, and develop new markets.

Additional Factors. More important than each individual sector or element of the diamond is the interaction of each linked together. This creates a complex system where imitation is virtually impossible. Government and chance also play

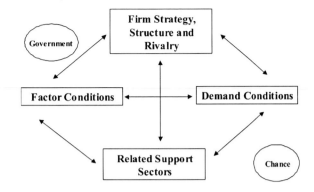

Figure 1   Determinants of Competitive Advantage.
Source: Michael E. Porter. The Competitive Advantage of Nations, 1996.

significant roles in cluster development. Chance is nothing more than unplanned events that influence product development. These could include technological advances, market changes, political decisions, terrorist attacks, natural or mad-made disasters, among others. Of course, government regulation and attitude will influence competitive advantage regardless of the industry. At the same time, government may, in turn, be influenced by the factors in the diamond, as well.

Building upon Porter's Diamond, Crouch and Ritchie (1999) created a systemic model for destination competitiveness within the tourism industry. The model has four main components: Core Resources & Attractions, Supporting Factors & Resources, Destination Management, and Qualifying Determinants. Each is further broken down into subcategories.

Core Resources & Attractors such as culture and history are the fundamental reasons visitors choose one destination over another. The Supporting Factors & Resources such as infrastructure provide a firm foundation upon which a destination's tourism industry can be established. Whereas the preceding two components are largely

beyond the control of tourism professionals, Destination Management refers to the specific decisions and actions tourism managers can take in order to enhance the destination's core and supporting resources. The last component, Qualifying Determinants, refers to situational conditions such as location and safety, which determine the scale, limit, or potential of the destination. These are also largely out of the control of destination managers.

Crouch and Richie (2000) added a fifth component focused on Destination Policy, Planning and Development. One of its key subcategories is Competitive and Collaborative Analysis. This reflects the growing "importance that members of the tourism industry now place on carefully chosen strategic alliances", both at the local and regional level. This concept is also one of the principal components of the competitive cluster approach.

Competitive Clusters

The competitive cluster approach is now being employed in developing and transitional

296   *D. E. Hawkins*

countries. "A cluster is a geographically proximate group of companies and associated institutions in a particular field, linked by commonalities and complementarities" (Porter, 1996).

Industries tend to cluster. It may seem a paradox but global competition can be fostered with local elements of competitive advantage. A cluster allows SME's to compete globally thanks to a better access to information and specialized resources, flexibility and rapid adoption of innovations. The key for competitive success is strategy. "Competitive strategy is about being different. It means deliberately choosing a different set of activities to deliver a unique mix of value" (ibid).

The "competitive cluster" concept is a strategic set of activities and services organized as an effective sustainable tourism supply chain. In the case of World Heritage Sites, the core of the "cluster" is the comparative advantage represented by their cultural or natural

attractions. The competitive cluster is used to examine and support a set of strategic relationships between the private sector, NGOs and government in a specific program of support to sustainable tourism development linked to improved management of World Heritage Sites. This concept may have merit as a key element of national tourism development as well as an essential element of formulating a World Heritage sustainable tourism strategy, as a means of linking heritage preservation and biodiversity conservation to local enterprise development. Figure 2 describes these relationships.

In the cluster development process, it is essential to define niche sustainable tourism market segments through market research and then to provide services resulting in high levels of customer satisfaction. The identification and pursuit of those sustainable tourism niches where the destination can be most successful is essential.

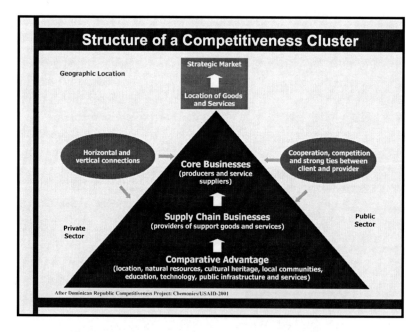

Figure 2   Structure of a Competitiveness Cluster.

The focus of market research and analysis should be on all phases of the travel experience that are relevant to forming the cluster, as described in Figure 3.

Examples of Heritage Clusters and Networks

Linking historical and cultural destinations is a concept that has received increased attention in recent years. A common thread among nearly all of these projects is the cooperation of the governmental and private sectors. A good example of such an initiative at the local level is the Chesapeake Bay Gateways Network. In the Chesapeake Bay Initiative Act of 1998, the US Congress called for the establishment of this network to link important sites in the region. The Congress's motivation was to maintain interest in and therefore aid conservation efforts of the

country's largest and most biologically diverse estuary. The Act provides grant money for all individual sites and organizations that participate in the network.

The network consists of four key components: gateway hubs, the primary locations for introduction to and transport through the region; regional information centers, to orient people to the particular region of the network; gateway sites, the cultural, historical, natural, and recreational places where tourists experience and learn about the Chesapeake; and connecting routes, a network of driving, walking, biking, or water trails to link the other three components. The initiative also calls for the creation of a broadly distributed map/guide of the region, a network web site, signage along connecting routes, and consistent promotional materials for all members. Additionally, certain network members will be linked by themes such as "The Living, Natural Bay" and

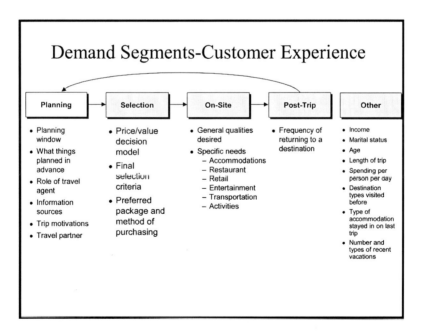

Figure 3 Demand Segments-Customer Experience.

"Peoples of the Bay" (Chesapeake Bay Gateways Network Working Group, 2000).

At the regional level, an example of a partnership between government and private tourism industry stakeholders is the Canadian Tourism Commission's (CTC) Product Club Program. The CTC launched the initiative in 1996 to encourage cooperative ventures among small and medium-size tourism enterprises. They believe that the resulting "critical-mass" will help improve the competitiveness of the geographic area or sector. To date, the CTC has accepted 35 product club proposals. Most involve the packaging of niche tours that link multiple destinations within a specific region. For example, *The Heritage Product Club* offers packages showcasing French culture in Western and Northern Canada. The club is composed of many stakeholders including tour operators, travel agencies, transportation companies and accommodation providers (Canadian Tourism Commission Website, 2003).

At a transnational level, an example of linking heritage sites comes from the Silk Road initiative, organized by the World Tourism Organization (WTO) and aided by UNESCO and the United Nations Development Programme (UNDP). In 1993, representatives from nineteen countries signed the Samarkand Declaration of Silk Road Tourism, which called for their governments to "create and implement joint strategies and programs to promote both international and domestic tourism" along the Silk Road. The old trading route's potential as a tourist destination lies in its tremendous historical importance. For nearly two thousand years, it facilitated not only economic, but also cultural and religious exchanges between China and nations throughout Central, South, and West Asia. To promote tourism along the route, the nineteen countries agreed upon efforts

such as joint marketing and publicity efforts to the travel trade and consumers, press familiarization trips, relaxed border restrictions for travelers, and the involvement of air carriers to create convenient air schedules (World Tourism Organization, 1997).

In Uzbekistan, a smaller-scale competitive cluster has formed among the country's two Silk Road World Heritage Sites, Bukhara and Khiva, along with another important town on the route, Samarkand. Uzbekhistan's tourism ministry, recognizing the potential of the cluster, began to promote the country as "the center of the ancient Silk Road". This promotion, combined with improved air access and ground transport, has created a significant increase in heritage tourism to the three cities, with estimates for significant growth over the next decade (Shackley, 1998).

Yet another transnational example of linking sites is the IDB – OMM Circuit (Inter-American Development Bank and Munda Maya Organization). Ten years ago, National Geographic created the Maya Route concept to link the Maya archaeological sites it was working on. The five counties involved (Belize, Guatemala, Honduras, El Salvador and Mexico) then created the Munda Maya Organization (OMM) to implement the circuit.

One of OMM's major initiatives is for all destinations to develop unified marketing efforts that include a web site, logo, site management programs, and entrepreneurial programs like archaeological site concessions. Additionally, the OMM has identified eight priority areas in the region, each with a circuit where secondary archaeological monuments (or lesser known sites) will be linked to either World Heritage Sites or well-known sites.

For example, in Tikal National Park (UNESCO World Heritage Site, 2003) the OMM is linking the ruins of Tikal to another Maya site and community, Uaxactun. In the past, Uaxactun has not received many tourists due to a variety of infrastructure problems. But the OMM proposal improves Uaxactun's situation dramatically through improvements on the road to Tikal, placement of water systems, archaeological restoration and conservation efforts, training programs, and micro-enterprise development. Ultimately, linking Uaxactun to Tikal will benefit both sites because tourists will stay longer in the area (instead of visiting for the day) and therefore spend more money.

UNEP-UNESCO Tour Operator's Initiative Workshop

This three-day workshop, held at the Ujung Kulon World Heritage site in September, 2002, was initiated by UNEP and UNESCO to explore opportunities for linking World Heritage sites in Indonesia and beyond. Participants included World Heritage site managers, government officials from Asia, hoteliers, ground transport operators, and members of the Tour Operators Initiative (TOI), a network of tour operators dedicated to improving the sustainability of the tourism industry.

Several perceived benefits have stimulated interest in developing networks of World Heritage sites. First, it is thought that much needed financing for conservation activities could be generated at less visited sites by linking them to more popular sites. Second, linked sites could share management strategies and reduce costs by jointly producing brochures, interpretation, and web sites. Third, the visitor experience would be enhanced, as connecting sites allows important themes or stories to emerge, some of which helping to communicate important conservation issues.

The workshop began on September 11, during which presentations were given to introduce World Heritage and tourism needs, the current situation of the Indonesian tourism market, and the current relationship between tour operators and World Heritage site managers. The second day consisted primarily of group discussions, each group being responsible for developing one component of the overall World Heritage site network strategy. The five groups discussed creation of a tour of Indonesian World Heritage sites, interpretation materials, promotional/marketing materials, Internet and web site development, and shared management activities. Each group had to generate and then present an action plan that included specific recommendations, responsibilities, time requirements, and estimated costs. Some of the more innovative recommendations included introducing training and exchange programs for World Heritage guides, twinning strategies for linking popular and less visited sites, a passport program to encourage visits to multiple sites, and the creation of integrated visitor centers.

On the third day, workshop participants took a tour of Ujung Kulon National Park. The idea was for participants to develop a sample tour and also incorporate the park into an action plan for designing and implementing a pilot network of World Heritage sites in Indonesia. The two major outputs of the workshop were an action plan to pilot test a network of World Heritage sites in Indonesia and a report outlining the recommendations for network design and implementation.

Lessons Learned

As a result of the Indonesia workshop and related case study analyses conducted at

George Washington University, it is evident that several "lessons learned" can be derived. These lessons learned could be paired with different sustainable tourism "collaborative tools" linked to World Heritage Sites, as described in the following section:

Collaborative Tool #1: Develop an inclusive stakeholder group.   Failure to include all key stakeholders within a destination is the most common cause of discord and ultimately, failure of a tourism destination. Stakeholders must participate in the planning process so that their needs can be developed in a manner that protects the natural and social environment in an economically sustainable way.

There are several methods of fostering stakeholder participation. Recently, Conservation International and the George Washington University with support from USAID developed the Tourism Rapid Assessment (TRA) Tool. This tool is designed to perform a rapid assessment and analysis of a tourism destination linked to sensitive cultural, natural or related biodiversity resources through a participatory planning process. The assessment can be used for policy debates, for developing a conservation strategy, for determining focus areas for development assistance, and for planning and implementing tourism development. The TRA is currently being tested in both Ghana and Niger (RAISE Website, 2003). In general, it is most applicable in the developing world and certainly Indonesia is no exception.

Collaborative Tool #2: Foster education and awareness within gateway communities near World Heritage Sites.   In Indonesia, visits to World Heritage sites tend to be quite short, which is indicative of their not being enough opportunities to expand visits in gateway communities. This is particularly the case in the

Borobudur and Prambanan World Heritage sites. Awareness of the World Heritage sites and the tourism opportunities associated with the sites must be promoted within gateway communities. This could lead to more meaningful relationships with the World Heritage sites and the development of tourism products within the gateway communities, which in turn will result in increased lengths of stay in the area.

Also, indications are that community awareness promotes sustainable practices. Educating the local community, and in some cases, the tourist, is increasingly crucial. By understanding why it is important to protect an area, residents are given the opportunity to make educated decisions about their quality of life and to comprehend the reasons why tourists visit their destination.

One of the most common ways of fostering education and community awareness is through benchmarks or best practices. There are many sources of best practices. The World Travel and Tourism Council has developed an on-going series entitled Steps to Success. Steps to Success offers practical information through a variety of "real-life" case studies in key areas of management and training. Many examples have a direct relationship to World Heritage Site applications (WTTC Website, 2003).

An additional tool for best practice identification has been developed by Business Enterprises for Sustainable Travel (BEST). Through a monthly publication, BEST highlights successful business practices utilized by travel and tourism companies that advance their business objectives while enhancing the social and economic well being of destination communities (BEST Website, 2003).

Collaborative Tool #3: Create strategic partnerships to promote a World Heritage

global brand through competitive clusters, tour packaging, standards, marketing and reservation systems. As the world moves towards a global economy and boundaries continue to blur, it is no longer effective to operate with the "each man is an island" mentality. Creating strategic partnerships and competitive clusters strengthens a destination and enables it to compete on a greater plain while reducing individual economic liability.

For example, the Organization of American States (OAS) Inter-Sectoral Unit for Tourism and USAID in 2001 began a partnership involving the packaging of a "Caribbean experiences" brand with sites, attractions, events, festivals and related activities of interest to the marketplace. An adaptation of the OAS STEP (Small Tourism Enterprises Project) approach to Indonesia and other countries with World Heritage Sites might encompass the following elements:

- Best practices identification and dissemination;
- A coaching system and walk-in centers to support product development;
- Occupational standards for small hotels and receptive tour operators;
- A comprehensive environmental management program;
- An investment fund;
- Volunteer programs and partnerships;
- Needs assessment related to World Heritage Sites; and
- An international marketing system, built upon the brand "World Heritage" as the overall brand for the small hotels sector.

Collaborative Tool #4: Establish a product enhancement strategy linking World Heritage Sites to other less visited protected areas. A tool to assist destinations, as well as small and medium size businesses foster product development and differentiation is the *Product Development Workbook* developed for ARD, Inc. for use in the gateway communities of the Rila and Balkan National Parks. This workbook was designed to provide a step-by-step process from which local participants could strategically develop their own tourism product. It utilized a product development approach designed to add value to the core product which focused on the natural attractions represented by the Rila and Central Balkans National Parks.

This augmentation approach might include packaging of nature-based or cultural heritage experiences offered by other less popular sites with World Heritage Sites. This was in fact the major focus of the workshop in Ujung Kulon, as Indonesia has a wealth of lesser known protected areas that could be linked with more popular World Heritage sites such as Ujung Kulon and Komodo National Parks.

A replicable model has been developed by the United States National Park Service (NPS) National Office of Tourism. In early 1999, it initiated the "Hidden Treasures" program to highlight lesser-known areas within the NPS system as a means to alleviate overcrowding at the larger well-known parks. Tourists have been encouraged to visit lesser-known parks in the Grand Canyon area, such as Canyon de Chelly or Capitol Reef National Parks in Utah instead of Brice Canyon or Zion, and so on. This has been done through the publication of a quarterly tourism magazine, "Destinations" which gives a pictorial and brief history of certain areas. This magazine is sent to a mailing list of approximately 80 thousand subscribers, and distributed widely at both national and international travel and trade shows.

Collaborative Tool #5: Implement an environmental management and certification program at the destination level. Environmental certification programs exist for an array of consumer products. Tourism is no different. Environmental certification programs or environmental management systems (EMS) have increased dramatically in the last 10 years. In a recent study, the WTO identified 59 eco-label initiatives, some global and others locally-based (WTO, 2002).

There are two main reasons why a destination or an operating tourism enterprise would wish to involve themselves with a certification or environmental management program. First, consumers may demand a certification of some sort, although at present consumer pressure has been minimal in the tourism industry. Secondly, the implementation of an Environmental Management System (EMS) can save significant resources, including contributing to the "bottom line." Most the changes made during the implementation of an EMS will pay for themselves in energy, waste removal and sanitary savings.

There are many certification programs available to the individual property owner. One example is the Costa Rican Certification in Sustainable Tourism. The Certification in Sustainable Tourism Program (CST) is a product of the Costa Rican Tourism Institute (ICT). CST was designed to differentiate tourism sector businesses based on the degree to which they comply with a sustainable model of natural, cultural and social resource management. CST is regulated by the Costa Rican National Accreditation Commission and consists of a scale of 5 "levels" of sustainable tourism achievement (CST Website, 2003).

Collaborative Tool # 6: Expand financing for World Heritage Sites. For a World Heritage Site sustainable tourism cluster approach to work, it is essential to establish resource rents, taxation regimes and other financing mechanisms to support improved World Heritage Site management systems.

The Caribbean Group for Cooperation in Economic Development and the Environment Department of the World Bank in collaboration with The European Union (2000) called attention to the relationship between improved environmental management and the ability to continue to generate revenues for Caribbean countries. Their report concluded that there is an argument to be made for the existence of resource rents arising from tourism assets, and for taxation schemes to capture these rents. These resource taxes should be considered as fees or user charges for the enjoyment and preservation of the environment.

In establishing a model for taxing tourism, their report recommends measures such as elimination of tax holidays for tourism investments, a moderate-rate corporate income tax, arrival taxes for cruise ship passengers, room taxes, departure taxes, and user fees at World Heritage Sites.

Collaborative Tool #7: Use the Internet for linking and branding the network. It is no longer possible to deny the tremendous importance of the Internet to the tourism industry. Any effective tourism organization must harness its power in order to compete in the global market. In the case of Indonesian World Heritage Sites, creation of a unified Internet site can be an especially effective tool for organizationally linking sites. It also serves as a cost-effective means of mass marketing, taking advantage of the World Heritage brand.

The basis of the Indonesian World Heritage Sites' Internet presence should be a single portal that encompasses the individual heritage sites' web pages, designed in a single motif and format. They should contain an overview of the destinations (ideally in several major languages), frequently-updated accommodations and transport information, package tour offers (if applicable), high-quality photos or videos, a chat-room or other forums for sharing experiences, searchable archives, links to related web sites, and press information. To enhance the branding effort, it is important that the domain name, logos, images, and even fonts are consistent with a clearly defined marketing position. Another recommended practice is the collection of visitors' e-mail addresses. The resulting database can then be used to send newsletters or promotional messages. A website that has put into practice many of the suggestions above is www.belizenet.com (2003).

Collaborative Tool #8: Develop indicator or monitoring systems. Although the development of a monitoring system might be the least exciting element to tourism development, it is extremely important in the long run. Monitoring a destination allows its stakeholders to adequately access the impact (both positive and negative) tourism is having on the natural, social and economic environments of a destination.

A useful guideline for monitoring development has been developed as part of the Urban Environmental Management Project of the Canadian Universities Consortium at the Asian Institute of Technology under the supervision of Dr. Walter Jamieson. *Indicators in Monitoring Tourism in Small Communities* (2000) is a manual intended for use by those involved in monitoring tourism development in a village or small community. This manual may be used by a community member who has been designated as the person responsible for monitoring tourism change in the community, a local government official given the same task, someone from outside of the community who has been brought in to conduct the monitoring, or anyone else charged with this task. The manual addresses common impacts affecting small communities as tourism grows and begins to have an effect on community life.

Discussion

The dialogue generated at the intervention workshop clearly confirmed the importance of linking World Heritage Sites in Indonesia and the rest of the world. In order to be successful, the links must occur at several levels. First, there must be transport links between sites for the purpose of facilitating tour circuits. Second, there must be marketing links that allow for effective, low-cost ways of reaching potential visitors. These marketing links should be present through traditional initiatives such as brochures, as well as through an integrated Internet portal that contains web pages of all sites, including available reservation systems.

Regardless of the medium, the development and use of a "World Heritage" global brand will be central to the marketing effort. The World Heritage global brand should define what will be presented to the marketplace through international, regional and national marketing efforts. The "rooted ness" of the global brand can be the basis of its power – strength of identity, cultural or natural provenance, and the image which already exists in the consumer's mind (Morgan, 2002). The World Heritage branding should use lessons learned (successes and failures) from other global branding initiatives. Examples may include the use of the "Olympics" brand by destinations that formerly hosted summer or winter Olympic events or the European Union's "Cultural Capital of Europe" brand by cities that currently hold or formerly held that distinction.

In the case of the World Heritage sites, it is recommended that they collaborate with the UNEP/UNESCO/WTO Tour Operators Initiative to market tour packages under the overall World Heritage supra-brand. Sub-brands could be associated with regional transnational corridors, nations, types of sites (historic forts, coral reefs, religious sites, etc), and events. These packages can use direct marketing to match their brands with specialty markets. The Tour Operators Initiative would be especially useful in delivering product development and training programs for all involved tourism enterprises, as well as in the construction of a World Heritage web portal for purposes of marketing the supra-brand and sub brands.

Despite the progress made in the Indonesia intervention workshop, it is clear that additional workshops and pilot projects are needed in order for industry stakeholders in all regions of the world to exchange information from ongoing research and practices relating to World Heritage Site networks. Issues such as branding, benchmarking, and the role of the Tour Operators Initiative will need to be focal points in these future discussions.

References

ARD, Inc. (2001, October) *Tourism Competitive Cluster*, Biodiversity Conservation and Economic Growth Project [Online]. Available: http://www.ardinc.com/htm/projects/p_bceg.htm

Belizenet (2003, June). [Online]. Available: www.belizenet.com.

Business Enterprises for Sustainable Travel (2003, June). *Best Practices* [Online]. Available: www.sustainable-travel.org.

Canadian Tourism Commission Website (2003, June). *Product Clubs* [Online]. Available: www.canada-tourism.com.

Caribbean Group for Cooperation in Economic Development and the Environment Department of the World Bank in collaboration with The European Union (2000, June), *Tourism and the Environment in the Caribbean: An Economic Framework Discussion Draft.*

Certification in Sustainable Tourism (2003, June), *Costa Rican Certification System* [Online]. Available: http://www.turismo-sostenible.co.cr/EN/home.shtml

Chesapeake Bay Gateways Network Working Group (2000). *Chesapeake Bay Gateways Network Framework.* Annapolis, Maryland.

Crouch, G. I. & Ritchie, J. R. B. (1999). Tourism, Competitiveness, and Social Prosperity. *Journal of Business Research*, 44, 137–142.

Crouch, G. I. & Ritchie, J. R. B. (2000). The Competitive Destination: A Sustainability Perspective. *Tourism Management*, 21, 1–7.

Department of Culture and Tourism of the Republic of Indonesia (2001). *Indonesia Tourism Market Database 2001.* Jakarta, Indonesia.

Infoplease Website (2003, June). *Indonesia* [Online]. Available: http://www.infoplease.com/ipa/A0107634.html.

Jamieson, W. (2000). *Indicators in Monitoring Tourism in Small Communities.* Urban Environmental Management Project of the Canadian Universities Consortium, at the Asian Institute of Technology.

Lindberg, K. & Hawkins, D. (1999). *Sustainable Tourism and Cultural Heritage: A Review of Development Assistance and its Potential to Promote Sustainability.* World Heritage Office, Oslo.

Morgan, N. (2002). *Destination Branding*, Butterworth Heinemann, Oxford.

Porter, M. (1996). Competitive Advantage of Nations; On Competition, What is strategy? *Harvard Business Review*, Nov–Dec, 61–78.

Rare (2002, December). *Linking Biodiversity Conservation and Sustainable Tourism in World Heritage Sites.* Internal report, Washington, D.C.

Shackley, M. (1998). *Visitor Management: Case studies from World Heritage Sites.* Butterworth Heinemann, Oxford.

Simpson, K. (2001). Strategic Planning and Community Involvement as Contributors to Sustainable Tourism Development. *Current Issues in Tourism*, 4(1).

UNESCO World Heritage Website (2003, June) [Online]. Available: http://whc.unesco.org/.

USAID Website (2003, June). *Tourism Rapid Assessment.* [Online]. Available: www.raise.org/tourism.

World Tourism Organization (1997). *WTO Silk Road Forum: Xi'an China 17–20 June 1996.* Madrid, Spain.

World Tourism Organization (2002). *Voluntary Initiatives for Sustainable Tourism.* Madrid, Spain.

World Travel and Tourism Council (2003, June). *Steps to Success.* [Online]. Available: http://www.wttc.org/resourceCentre/publications.asp.

Heritage Tourism on Australia's Asian Shore: A Case Study of Pearl Luggers, Broome

Warwick Frost

Introduction

Broome is a town which has had two boom periods. In the late nineteenth and early twentieth centuries, Broome was the pearling capital of the world. Hundreds of divers, at first mainly Aboriginal and later primarily Asian indentured labourers, collected wild oysters for the shell (*mother of pearl*), which was popular for buttons and other ornaments. Occasionally they would find pearls, which due to their rarity, were extremely valuable. Due to the value of the industry, Broome's extreme isolation (it is 2,500 kilometres from the state capital of Perth) and the risks of diving, pearling was exempted from the restrictions on Asian immigration contained in the White Australia Policy. After World War One, pearling and Broome declined, primarily due to the development of plastic substitutes for pearlshell.

In the late twentieth century, Broome boomed again, this time as a tourist destination. Its development was a result of a combination of local and general factors. Much credit has been given to Alistair McAlpine for

his establishment of the Cable Beach Resort and generation of publicity for Broome. More generally the boom in Australian tourism and strong interest in heritage, Aboriginal culture and multiculturalism focussed attention on this old pearling town with a perfect tropical beach at the entrance to the wild Kimberley region (McAlpine, 1997: 136–144; Davidson & Spearritt, 2000: 305–7).

Broome differs from other Australian coastal destinations in the high degree which its culture and heritage contributes to its tourist appeal. In Australian terms, Broome sits on a distant periphery, essentially the most remote destination in the country. However, it is the closest part of Australia to Asia, being only 500 kilometres from Indonesia and East Timor. Broome's culture and physical fabric are strongly influenced by a multicultural history based on its closeness to Asia and isolation from the rest of Australia. At the 2001 Census, 23 percent of its resident population were indigenous, compared with two percent for Australia. A further six percent of Broome's population were of

Asian ancestry (Australian Bureau of Statistics, 2002). Chinatown is its main tourism and shopping precinct.

Pearls are still a major industry, though now farmed, and provide an iconic symbol of the town. In 2000 Pearl Luggers opened as a tourist attraction focussing on the history of pearling. It is owned and operated by the Arrow Pearling Company, which has pearling interests in Broome and the Kimberley. Its aim was to preserve the last two remaining pearling luggers and allow visitors to understand Broome's rich history and culture.

The purpose of this article is to utilise Pearl Luggers as a case study to examine how Australian heritage attractions deal with Australia's non-European history. This article is divided into four sections. The first considers the current literature on heritage tourism in Australia, particularly as it relates to issues of Eurocentricity. The second describes the main features and characteristics of Pearl Luggers. The third considers how Pearl Luggers interprets the stories of the many different cultures involved in pearling. The fourth examines ownership issues and how they may influence interpretation.

Heritage and Tourism in Australia

A common criticism of tourism development is its tendency to be destructive of local heritage, culture and environment (see for examples, Craik, 1991; Croall, 1995; Mowforth & Munt, 1998; Wheeller, 1994). This criticism is often applied to beach resorts, where a universal resort culture based on sun, sand and fun blots out all local cultural features and development may modify the environment (for this tendency in Australia see, Craik, 1991; King, 1997; Mercer, 1999). Broome is no exception to such concerns. As

tourism has developed there have been widely held fears that mass beach resort tourism will overwhelm all of Broome's special cultural and heritage attractions. Whilst there has been little academic analysis of Broome, this notion that tourism is overpowering Broome's distinct culture can be seen in general works such as *Broomtime* (Coombs & Varga, 2001). The importance of preserving its culture and heritage was recognised by Alistair McAlpine, Broome's chief developer:

The snag ... in a small town is that unless great care is taken, the need for constructing accommodation for both new residents and visitors destroys the very reason for tourists coming there in the first place. It is the atmosphere in Broome that is so valuable, an intangible but fragile asset, which could be destroyed by accident or simply by turning the town into just another hell of high-rise hotels and apartments edging the most beautiful beach in the world (McAlpine, 1997: 140).

Heritage tourism in Australia is often seen as Eurocentric. A well-known example of such a focus and the resultant problems was the 1988 Bicentenary of European Settlement. Its organisers were so concerned that they avoid controversy over the effect of European settlement on the Aborigines, that much of the historical context was removed from their celebrations. Even then the celebration remained highly divisive (Bennett *et al.*, 1992; Davison, 2000: 71–72; Hall, 1992: 93–94; Lowenthal, 1998: 90; see also Frost, 2001: 154–156 for similar problems with California's recent Sesquicentenary). Other heritage attractions have been criticised for presenting interpretations of Australian history and culture that are primarily European and conservative, even though there were opportunities for giving more diverse

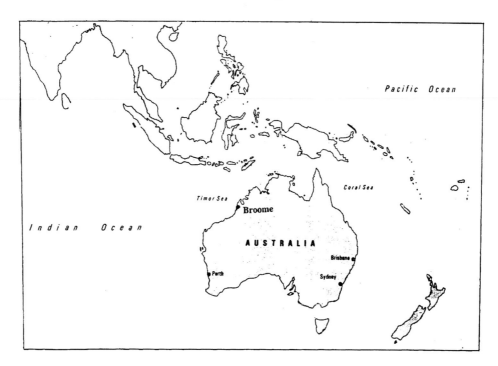

Figure 1   Broome in relation to Asia and Australia.

emphases. Examples include the Stockman's Hall of Fame (Trotter, 1992); the Rocks historic port area in Sydney (Waitt, 2000) and the Bradman Museum (Hutchins, 2002). Such issues are not confined to just Australia. Worldwide the trend is for dominant cultural and ethnic groups in society to claim, interpret and present heritage in such a way that reinforces their position (Lowenthal, 1998; Richter, 1999; Timothy & Boyd, 2003).

However, the culture and heritage of smaller or marginal groups are also of interest to tourists. For Australia, tourism and Aboriginal culture have been examined in a large and growing literature (including Altman, 1989; Boyd & Ward, 1996; Griffiths, 1996; Hall, 2000; Mercer, 1998; Ryle, 1996; Staiff *et al.*, 2002; Venbrux, 2000; Wells, 1996). Unfortunately, there is a tendency to present Aboriginal heritage as removed from Australian history and mainstream culture. This is

manifested through presenting Aboriginal culture as occurring in an ahistorical "Dreamtime" rather than the modern world (Ryle, 1996) and the common failure to provide "alternative narratives" by Aborigines which contrast with or even contradict those of European settlers (Staiff *et al.*, 2002). Furthermore, despite the growth in this literature, there are still significant gaps. There has been almost no consideration of Aboriginal heritage in an urban context, such as Broome. Nor has there been much analysis of "cultural displacement", particularly where indigenous people do not benefit from tourism interest in their culture (see Ashworth, 1998, for a case from New Mexico in the USA).

In contrast, there has been very little consideration of Australian tourist attractions featuring the experiences of Asian migrants. One exception is that of Sovereign Hill, an outdoor museum which recreates the Victorian Gold

Rushes of the 1850s and has the largest number of visitors of any history based attraction in Australia. A study by Evans (1991) explains how Sovereign Hill's recreation includes a Chinese village and staff acting out the characters of Chinese miners. However, Evans' article is now over a decade old and since it was written Sovereign Hill have developed attractions specifically for Chinese tour groups. While Sovereign Hill is a leader in presenting Chinese heritage, it has been criticised for failing to develop interpretation featuring the experiences of Aborigines in the Gold Rushes (Frost, 2001: 151).

Some care must be taken in considering the literature on heritage and cultural tourism in Australia, for there are only a limited number of case studies. Researchers have tended to choose case studies in which attractions focus on a Eurocentric view, but this does not necessarily mean that most attractions present such an interpretation. The clumsy handling of Aboriginal issues during the Bicentenary has rightly attracted a great deal of academic interest (see above). In contrast, the highly successful and sympathetic integration of Aboriginal themes into the Opening Ceremony of the 2000 Sydney Olympics has attracted little academic analysis. Other attractions with strong Asian themes, such as Melbourne's Chinese Museum, the Golden Dragon Museum in the historic gold town of Bendigo, the newly established Castlemaine Diggings National Heritage Park and the Chinatown precincts in Sydney and Melbourne (and indeed Broome's), have also hardly been considered. Furthermore, it is notable that Australian researchers have not explored heritage attractions dealing with death and forced labour, which elsewhere in the world have been categorised as dark tourism or thanatourism (Lennon and Foley, 2000)

In the context of these limitations in the literature, Pearl Luggers provides a valuable case study for two reasons. First, it is located in a rapidly growing coastal resort where there are strong fears that tourism development will diminish a strong and unique local culture and history. Second, it is an excellent example where its location and subject matter have led its operators to consider the interaction of Aboriginals, Asians and Europeans in the history of the pearling industry. As such, it provides an instructive counter to a literature which focuses on case studies where heritage is accused of being sanitised.

The Luggers and the Tour

Pearl Luggers is located in Chinatown, the busy commercial and tourist centre of Broome. The attraction centres on two old pearl luggers, the *Sam Male* and the *D. McD.*, both named after old pearlers. Luggers were the sailing boats from which the pearlshell divers operated. In the early twentieth century there were hundreds operating out of Broome, but the decline in the industry and World War Two greatly reduced their numbers to only a handful. At Pearl Luggers, these two are permanently fixed on dry land, but only metres from the tidal flats where the lugger fleets used to moor.

One of the luggers is owned by the local council, the other by the Arrow Pearling Company. As part of the arrangement between the council and the Arrow Pearling Company, visitors are welcome to enter the property and inspect the luggers without charge. The luggers are surrounded by a decking allowing viewing at different levels, but due to the fragility of the luggers, visitors are not allowed on them. Initially the Arrow's intention was just to preserve the luggers, but in developing the project it was realised that the best option for providing high quality interpretation and protection of the luggers was through regular guided tours.

Tours are run throughout the day during the tourist season. The charge in 2001 was $15 per adult. Tours last for about 75 minutes. They are conducted by a number of former pearl divers. The main guide is Richard "Salty Dog" Baillieu, who was a pearl diver throughout the 1980s (Blundell, 2002; Trevor, 2000). Presenting an appropriate seafaring character, Baillieu has become the "public face" of Pearl Luggers, appearing frequently in the media and providing the inspiration for a new BBC-Channel 10 co-produced children's drama set in Broome and called *Ocean Star* (Blundell, 2002). The guides are a popular feature of the attraction and Pearl Luggers provides a good example of tourists being motivated not so much by "the ease and convenience of travelling with a guide, but by the opportunity to learn something" from a knowledgeable source (Weiler & Ham, 2001: 259).

The tour commences in the tender's store. Tender is short for attender, each diver had an attender who stayed on the surface. This recreated store is a corrugated iron shed or small warehouse, not intended to be exactly authentic, but suggestive of the corrugated iron building style associated with Broome. In its centre are rows of benches for the visitors and around the walls there is an extensive range of historical photos, paintings and artefacts.

The tour consists of three sections. The first is an explanation of the historical development of pearling and the luggers. Originally pearlshell was found right along the shoreline. For centuries Aborigines made extensive decorative use of it. In the late nineteenth century Europeans began to collect it. As they quickly stripped the beaches they were forced to go just offshore, using Aborigines to free dive. As pearlshell became scarce close to shore, extensive beds were discovered in deeper water. Exploiting these required helmeted divers. Japanese, Timorese, Malays and Indonesians were recruited as divers. Diving was highly dangerous, the *bends* were a common complaint and there was an extremely high mortality rate. To illustrate the discomfort of diving, a volunteer from the audience is invited to don a diver's woollen underclothes and then a helmet.

For the second section the tour moves outside to view the luggers. The guide explains the chief features of the boats and also details life on board. With multicultural crews interesting traditions quickly developed, some examples include that bananas were forbidden and that rice had to be served at every meal.

In the final part of the tour, the party returns to the tender's store. The guide relates some of the recent history of the luggers and the stories of some of the main artefacts and pictures in the collection. In the case of Baillieu he tells some stories of his experiences as a diver in the 1980s. A short documentary film from the 1970s is shown. Finally pearls are discussed, which in the old pearl shelling days were really a rare byproduct. Today they are grown on pearl farms and an example of a pearl is passed around for tour members to hold and inspect. In addition to the tours, a number of special functions are held, usually at night. These include pearl meat tastings and screenings of old pearling films on the canvas sails of the luggers.

Like many tourist attractions, Pearl Luggers has a number of practical difficulties. Being in the sub-tropics, tourism is confined to the dry season. Its management has found it difficult to develop a name which accurately describes what it offers. Occasionally visitors arrive expecting they will be on a cruise. Indeed the photo captions in the travel article by Blundell (2002) state that it is a "floating museum". Their capacity is limited, each tour has a maximum of 20 people, though Pearl Luggers is considering the logistics of operating two tours at once.

A Multicultural Story

The story of pearling in Broome is a multicultural one. It is also a dark story of forced labour, high mortality rates, lingering illnesses and Australia's infamous White Australia Policy. Such themes are interlaced throughout the interpretation provided at Broome Pearling Luggers. The content includes:

- At first Europeans harvested pearl shell close to shore using local Aborigines as forced labour with a consequent high death rate. Richard Baillieu does not mince words, calling this slavery.
- As pearling moved into deeper water, helmeted divers operating off luggers were used. While the work was lucrative it was highly dangerous. The "bends" killed and horribly maimed many divers. The mortality rate may have been as high as 50%.
- The high risks and isolation of Broome made it very difficult to recruit Australian divers. Instead they came from Asia, particularly from Japan and Kupang in West Timor, only 500 kilometres north. In addition there was an influx of Chinese traders.
- Broome became an exception to the Asian immigration restrictions of the White Australia Policy. However, while the Asian divers were effectively in command of the pearling luggers, they were required to carry European captains who were nominally in charge.
- In an attempt to reassert the White Australia policy, in 1912 the Australian Government recruited 12 divers from the British Navy ("the white divers of Broome", see Bailey, 2001). However, nearly all of these divers died and the experiment was not repeated.

These racial divisions continued into modern times. Towards the end of the tour Richard Baillieu tells a number of stories *against himself*. Keen to collect as much shell as possible he learnt a number of tricks in order to distract other divers. For example, when diving with a Thursday Islander (from the Torres Strait Islands between Australia and Papua-New Guinea), Baillieu would indicate by gesture that there was a sea snake nearby. As these were taboo to the Thursday Islander he would be frightened away. Now Baillieu regrets such behaviour, but as a young man it just seemed part of the culture.

In its emphasis on death, disease and racial tension, the interpretation at Pearl Luggers may be seen as an example of dark tourism (Lennon & Foley, 2000). The experience of Pearl Luggers suggests that tourists do not want a sanitised heritage, rather they do value authenticity, even if it is violent and confronting. It also suggests that they will not be satisfied with historical interpretation written purely from the perspective of history's winners (Lowenthal, 1998: 102). That Broome is a coastal resort with a strong emphasis on its beach and tropical climate does not seem to diminish the interest of tourists in these matters. Certainly it is beginning to feature heavily in popular travel writing. In a recent book on Broome and the Kimberley by the well known travel writer, Tim Bowden, a great deal of attention is given to massacres, killings and mistreatment of Aborigines (Bowden, 2001). In an article on Richard Baillieu the emphasis is on tales of death and disaster during diving (Blundell, 2002).

In its discussion of European treatment of Aborigines, Pearl Luggers contrasts starkly with Sovereign Hill. Recreating the Gold Rushes between 1851 and 1861, its management has given a great deal of emphasis to authentic recreation, which is its major selling point (Davison, 2000; Evans, 1991; Frost, 2003b; Moscardo & Pearce, 1986). However, its great dilemma is in how to depict Aborigines. Under extreme pressure from European settlement, traditional Aboriginal society had collapsed just prior to the Gold Rushes, with consequent increases in disease, drunkenness and mortality. Afraid of upsetting visitors with such issues, Sovereign Hill has chosen not to depict Aborigines at all, though it does emphasise death and disease amongst European miners.

The author discussed the Sovereign Hill case with Stephen Arrow, the manager of the Arrow Pearling Company. He was surprised with their decision. He felt that the pain and suffering of the various non-European groups were integral to the story of pearling and the pearl luggers and indeed of Broome. In developing the attraction it had not occurred to him to leave any parts out because it might upset the visitors.

In 2001 the historian David Goodman, a noted critic of historic attractions such as Sovereign Hill, took the opportunity of the 150th Anniversary of the Australian Gold Rushes to call for changes in which these episodes in Australian history were viewed. Complaining of the tendency to see the Gold Rushes as a comfortable and prosperous period of European settlement and expansion, Goodman argued for an "edgier" approach focussing on uncertainty and those groups, such as Aborigines and Chinese, who had tended to be consigned to the periphery (Goodman, 2001). Goodman's comments echo a developing trend in

Australian historiography. Recent research is changing the way that groups such as the Chinese are viewed. Instead of being seen as passive victims of European exploitation, there is an increasing focus on their technical, management and entrepreneurial skills and their ability to adapt to Australian conditions in mining and agriculture (Curthoys, 2001; Frost, 2002). Pearl Luggers demonstrates this trend. Asians and Aborigines are integral to the stories told. Their skills and flexibility are emphasised. The Japanese, in particular, are portrayed as skilled divers who often effectively skippered the luggers and even secretly owned them. These stories are of a type rarely told at heritage attractions in the past. Adapting Goodman's terminology, it can be said that Pearl Luggers presents an "edgier" history of pearling.

Ownership

Pearl Luggers is a privately-owned tourist attraction. In Australia, historic tourism attractions are generally publicly-owned, either by community groups or government agencies. For example, Sovereign Hill is owned and operated by a community association, Swan Hill Pioneer Settlement and the Historic Port of Echuca by local councils. Unfortunately, the fairly sparse literature on the business of heritage tourist attractions has little consideration of the advantages and disadvantages of public or private ownership, or how ownership may affect interpretation (Frost, 2003a). An interesting exception is a case study of privately-owned Old Sydney Town, a historic recreation of the convict era. Despite never being likely to return a profit Old Sydney Town kept in operation due to the passionate commitment of its owner

(Davidson & Spearritt, 2000: 266–267), although Old Sydney Town closed in 2003.

Why do private businesses operate historic tourism attractions? Are they intended as profitable enterprises? Or are there other reasons (as at Old Sydney Town) for the establishment of the attraction? It is important to understand what the objectives are, for they should determine how the attraction is run and the interpretation is presented. Furthermore, the objectives set the criteria for success or failure.

Identifying why the Arrow family set up Pearl Luggers and what they were seeking from its operation was a lengthy and complex process. It quickly became apparent that there were a number of different though inter-related factors at work. Different family members gave different opinions and some had different perspectives at different times.

In early discussions, they consistently emphasised that Pearl Luggers was a business, was run on commercial lines and was intended to eventually make money. Of course such a position is understandable, the Arrow family has a wide range of business interests and would not wish to be associated with a project which lost them money and showed them in a poor light. However, they also emphasised that Pearl Luggers was more than just a purely commercial venture. If they were just interested in another good investment, there were other alternatives. For example, one of their competitors, Kailis Pearls, has recently built a large modern shopping centre in Chinatown. In economic terms the Arrows were aware that the opportunity costs of a heritage attraction were higher than other tourism-related ventures.

Over the course of a number of discussions, members of the Arrow family identified a range of less tangible benefits they gain from Pearl Luggers. Stephen Arrow is passionately interested in pearling and maritime history in general. The Pearl Luggers allows him to share his interest. He also has a sentimental attachment to one of the luggers which he served on when he first came to Broome. Fleur Arrow (his mother) sees the project as the Arrow family giving something back to Broome and pearling, strengthening their links with the community. Penny Arrow (Stephen's sister) observes that the Arrows collectively have a strong interest in old equipment and artefacts. She also believes that there are benefits to them in working on such an interesting and pleasant project, that involvement in Pearl Luggers breaks up and varies their normal working routine.

Pearl Luggers opens up other commercial possibilities for the Arrows. Their main business is in cultivating pearls, which are sold to wholesalers. They have no retail shop, nor are their pearls identifiable to the final customer. This contrasts to some of their competitors who do engage in retailing, such as Kailis and Paspaley. Pearl Luggers provides an opportunity for promotion of their name and some small scale retailing. At the conclusion of the tour, visitors will often stay behind to ask their guide further questions. Many of these discussions centre on pearls, for in the last part of the tour they have been shown an Arrow pearl and visitors commonly ask can they buy pearls from Pearl Luggers. In such circumstances the guide will bring out some pearls and the visitor may buy them.

Pearl Luggers works in co-operation with other businesses in Broome's tourism industry. A good example of this is their relationship with another pearling attraction, Willies Creek Pearl Farm. Willies Creek is the only pearl farm regularly open for tours. Pearl Luggers directs tourists interested in pearl cultivation on to Willies Creek, in turn Willies Creek directs visitors interested in the history of pearling to the Luggers. Rather than see each other as competing, both operators see the other as complementary. This integration of the Arrows into tourism in Broome opens up possible opportunities for them to engage in other tourism ventures in the future.

Conclusion

The value of considering Pearl Luggers as a case study of heritage tourism is twofold. First, it is an excellent example of an Australian attraction which considers Aboriginal and Asian interactions with Europeans. In providing this "edgier" perspective, it counters the emphasis in the Australian tourism literature that heritage attractions are preoccupied with providing a conservative Eurocentric view of Australia's history and culture. It demonstrates a trend at Australian attractions to tackle difficult issues of the darker aspects of Australia's history.

Second, it counters the widely held view that tourism is usually destructive of heritage and culture, particularly in coastal resorts. Instead, it demonstrates that tourism may be a highly positive force. Tourists seek the exotic, experiences and places which are different to their everyday. Part of that is translated into the quest for beautiful beaches, sunsets and scenery, but part also is searching for different cultures and historical places and most importantly understanding those cultures, histories and places. While some have voiced their concern that tourism may destroy Broome's cultural and heritage qualities, they have missed the point that tourism has created a value for those qualities and given impetus for their preservation. Pearl Luggers preserves two historic boats and provides interpretation to visitors because there is sufficient demand from the growing numbers of tourists to Broome. Without those tourists it is unlikely that this project would have been undertaken.

A Note on Sources

Field trips to Broome were conducted in 1997, when Pearl Luggers was still at the conceptual stage and 2001, when it was operating. I am grateful to the Arrow family and their staff for their assistance with this research.

References

Altman, J. (1989). Tourism dilemmas for Aboriginal Australians. *Annals of tourism research*, 16(4), 456–476.

Ashworth, G. J. (1998). Tourism in the communication of senses of place or displacement in New Mexico. *Tourism, Culture & Communication*, 1(2), 97–108.

Australian Bureau of Statistics (2002). *2001 Census Basic Community Profile and Snapshot: Shire of Broome*. Canberra: Australian Bureau of Statistics.

Bailey, J. (2001). *The White Divers of Broome: The True Story of a Fatal Experiment*. Macmillan, Sydney.

Bennett, T., Buckridge, P., Carter, D. & Mercer, C. (eds) (1992). *Celebrating the Nation: A Critical Study of Australia's Bicentenary*. Allen & Unwin, Sydney.

Blundell, G. (2002). The Baillieu who took a dive. *Royal-Auto*, 70(7), 28–31.

Bowden, T. (2001). *Penelope Bungles to Broome*. Allen & Unwin, Sydney.

Boyd, B. & Ward, G. (1996). Aboriginal heritage and visitor management. In C. M. Hall & S. McArthur (eds), *Heritage Management in Australia and New Zealand: The Human Dimension* (pp. 208–221). Oxford University Press, Melbourne.

Coombs, A. & Varga, S. (2001). *Broometime*. Sceptre, Sydney.

Craik, J. (1991). *Resorting to Tourism: Cultural Politics for Tourist Development in Australia*. Allen & Unwin, Sydney.

Croall, J. (1995). *Preserve or Destroy: Tourism and the Environment*. Calouste Gulbenkinn Foundation, London.

Curthoys, A. (2001). "Men of all nations, except Chinamen": European and Chinese on the Goldfields of New South Wales. In I. McCalman, A. Cook & A. Reeves (eds), *Gold: Forgotten Histories and Lost Objects of Australia* (pp. 103–123). Cambridge University Press, Cambridge.

Davidson, J. & Spearritt, P. (2000). *Holiday Business: Tourism in Australia since 1870.* Miegunyah, Melbourne.

Davison, G. (2000). *The Use and Abuse of Australian History.* Allen & Unwin, Sydney.

Evans, M. (1991). Historical Interpretation at Sovereign Hill. *Australian Historical Studies*, 24(96), 142–152.

Frost, W. (2001). Golden anniversaries: Festival tourism and the 150th Anniversary of the Gold Rushes in California and Victoria. *Pacific Tourism Review*, 5(3/4), 149–157.

Frost, W. (2002). Migrants and technological transfer: Chinese farming in Australia, 1850–1920. *Australian economic history review*, 42(2), 113–131.

Frost, W. (2003a). The financial viability of heritage attractions: three case studies from rural Victoria. *Tourism review international*, 7(1), pp. 13–22.

Frost, W. (2003b). A pile of rocks and a hole in the ground: heritage tourism and interpretation of the Gold Rushes at the Mount Alexander Diggings. In R. Black & B. Weiler (eds), *Interpreting the Land Down Under: Australian Heritage Interpretation and Tour Guiding* (pp. 204–218). Fulcrum, Golden, CO.

Goodman, D. (2001). Making an edgier history of Gold. In I. McCalman, A. Cook & A. Reeves (eds), *Gold: Forgotten Histories and Lost Objects of Australia* (pp. 23–36). Cambridge University Press, Cambridge.

Griffiths, T. (1996). *Hunters and Collectors: The Antiquarian Imagination in Australia.* Cambridge University Press, Cambridge.

Hall, C. M. (1992). *Hallmark Tourist Events: Impacts, Management & Planning.* Belhaven, London.

Hall, C. M. (2000). Tourism, national parks and Aboriginal peoples. In R. W. Butler & S. W. Boyd (eds), *Tourism and National Parks: Issues and Implications* (pp. 57–71). Wiley, Chichester.

Hutchins, B. (2002). *Don Bradman: Challenging the Myth.* Cambridge University Press, Cambridge.

King, B. (1997). *Creating Island Resorts.* Routledge, London.

Lennon, J. & Foley, M. (2000). *Dark Tourism: The Attraction of Death and Disaster.* Continuum, London.

Lowenthal, D. (1998). *The Heritage Crusade and the Spoils of History.* Cambridge University Press, Cambridge.

McAlpine, A. (1997). *Once a Jolly Bagman: Memoirs.* Weidenfeld and Nicolson, London.

Mercer, D. (1998). The uneasy relationship between tourism and native peoples: the Australian experience. In W. F. Theobald (ed), *Global tourism*, 2nd edn (pp. 98–128). Butterworth-Heinemann, Oxford.

Mercer, D. (1999). Tourism and coastal zone management: the uneasy partnership. In K. J. Walker & K. Crowley (eds), *Australian Environmental Policy 2: Studies in Decline and Devolution* (pp. 142–165). UNSW Press, Sydney.

Moscardo, G. and Pearce, P. (1986). Historic theme parks: An Australian experience in authenticity. *Annals of tourism research*, 13(3), 467–479.

Mowforth, M. & Munt, I. (1998). *Tourism and Sustainability: New Tourism in the Third World.* Routledge, London.

Richter, L. K. (1999). The politics of heritage tourism development: emerging issues for the new millennium. In D. G. Pearce & R. W. Butler (eds), *Contemporary issues in tourism development* (pp. 108–126). Routledge, London.

Ryle, J. (1996). *Jilli Binna*–To look and listen: Creating a cultural past. In J. Friedman & J. Carrier (eds), *Melanesia modernities* (pp. 10–33). Lund University Press, Lund, Sweden.

Staiff, R., Bushell, R. & Kennedy, P. (2002). Interpretation in National Parks: Some critical questions. *Journal of Sustainable Tourism*, 10(2), 97–113.

Timothy, D. J. & Boyd, S. W. (2003). *Heritage Tourism.* Prentice Hall, Harlow.

Trevor, N. (ed) (2000). *Why Broome?* Noel Trevor and Associates, Broome.

Trotter, R. (1992). Pioneering the past: A study of the Stockman's Hall of Fame. In T. Bennett, P. Buckridge, D. Carter & C. Mercer (eds), *Celebrating the Nation: A Critical Study of Australia's Bicentenary* (pp. 160–174). Allen & Unwin, Sydney.

Wells, J. (1996). Marketing indigenous heritage: A case study of Uluru National Park. In C. M. Hall and S. McArthur (eds), *Heritage Management in Australia and New Zealand: The Human Dimension* (pp. 222–230). Oxford University Press, Melbourne.

Venbrux, E. (2000). Tales of Tiwiness: Tourism and self determination in an Australian Aboriginal society. *Pacific Tourism Review*, 4(2/3), 137–147.

Waitt, G. (2000). Consuming heritage: Perceived historical authenticity. *Annals of tourism research*, 27(4), 835–862.

Weiler, B. & Ham, S. (2001). Perspectives and thoughts on tour guiding. In A. Lockwood & S. Medlik (eds), *Tourism and Hospitality in the 21st Century* (pp. 255–264). Butterworth-Heinemann, Oxford.

Wheeller, B. (1994). Egotourism, sustainable tourism and the environment: A symbiotic, symbolic or shambolic relationship? In A. Seaton (ed), *Tourism: The State of the Art* (pp. 647–654). Wiley, Chichester.

Emerging Issues and Directions of Cultural Heritage Tourism in the Asia Pacific Region

Dallen J. Timothy and Bruce Prideaux

The chapters in this book have made abundantly clear how important cultural heritage is in the Asia Pacific as a resource upon which much of the region's tourism is based. Parts of the region are among the world's fastest growing tourist destinations, thanks in large part to cultural heritage. This collection of essays spans a wide spectrum of countries and brings to the fore many empirical examples of living and built culture that draw visitors from around the globe in both the developing and developed areas of the Asia Pacific. The book highlights many issues that are of considerable interest to heritage and tourism scholars and which directly affect the management of heritage resources and heritage tourism.

Several conceptual foundations underlie the chapters in this book: the vast array of heritage resources, the idea of impact and unacceptable change, heritage branding and demand, and power/politics. Each of these is examined below in greater depth and ideas are formulated regarding future trends and research needs.

One thing is certain with regard to heritage resources in the region – there is a huge diversity of cultures and constructed heritages that form the foundations of tourism. Indonesia, for example, is commonly cited as the world's most ecologically diverse country, spanning several climatic and vegetative zones. The same could be said about Indonesia in terms of cultural heritage, although this depth of richness and diversity is multiplied many times over when the entire Asia Pacific region is taken into account. Hundreds of cultures have adapted through human history to varying climates and other natural conditions, thus creating unique cultural landscapes. This vast array of indigenous architecture, dress, food, urban morphology, music, dance, land tenure systems, agricultural products, languages, belief systems, and a multitude of other markers of culture, together with the imprints left behind by European colonial powers, provide most of the tourist appeal of countries in the Pacific Islands, Southeast Asia, South Asia, East Asia, and even into the Americas.

This diversity of peoples and their cultural pasts provides an extremely rich and flourishing laboratory for future scientific inquiry in cultural heritage and its tourism uses. There is considerable work to be done, for different cultures are known to react differently to outside influences, including tourism. Likewise, we still know relatively little about the manifestations of relationships between tourism and religion, agriculture and land tenure, language, urbanization processes, migration, and poverty. All of these can be addressed in the realm of heritage tourism and bear fruitfully on current knowledge about culture and tourism. Additionally, there are destinations in Asia and the Pacific Rim that are still relatively unknown to tourists and therefore off the beaten research path as well, including eastern Russia, Mongolia, North Korea, Bhutan, Tuvalu, Papua New Guinea, Nauru, the countries of Central Asia, and some remote areas of China. These have not yet developed into major tourist destinations for a variety of socio-political and geographical reasons. Research into the politico-spatial variables that advantage some countries and regions, while disadvantaging others, in the realm of tourism, would be valuable in understanding the dynamics of culture and cultural policies, international relations, and domestic constraints to tourism development, of which cultural heritage plays an important part.

Since the Second World War several countries of the Asia Pacific have become the most visited destinations in the world. Unfortunately, a great deal of tourism growth has been characterized by unplanned mass tourism, which has brought with it many severe consequences. While the 1990s saw the beginnings of better and more sustainable planning away from the boosterist approach to mass tourism development, the traditions of spontaneous, uncontrolled growth and their consequences still plague most of the region. The notion of carrying capacity has been overly ignored by governments and other elitist tourism developers, who have in the past favored unsustainable forms of growth as noted above (Mowforth and Munt 1998; Timothy 1999; Tosun 2000). This has resulted in many harmful socio-cultural and ecological changes, some perhaps irreversible, throughout the entire region (Gormsen 1997; Sulaiman 2006; Wood 1980).

Many authors have recognized various socio-economic changes brought about by tourism, although there is a tendency to shy away from harsh criticism of the industry and rather discuss it as a positive social and economic force (Bowden 2005; Chon 2000; Prideaux 1999). This is particularly so in the area of cultural preservation and the potential for tourism to revive lost traditions (Goodwin *et al.* 1999). In many cases, tourism has been noted as a force that causes destination people to become more aware of their own heritage traditions and cultural forms. Likewise, there is a recognized need for destination officials and managers to have a more active role in managing change, whether tourism-induced or brought on by other forces of modernization.

In many parts of the world, including the Asia Pacific, there is a movement toward using cultural heritage as a destination branding mechanism. This is also the case outside the realm of tourism, as is witnessed by the superfluity of institutions that utilize the buzzword in their titles and marketing efforts – Heritage School for the Gifted, Heritage Town Square, Heritage Bank, and Heritage Real Estate, Inc. The designation of cultural resources by UNESCO as World Heritage Sites (WHS), for example, is a large part of this, as the UNESCO label is often seen as a natural image boost for tourist destinations, especially in the developing world where marketing budgets are in short supply (Boyd and Timothy, 2006). One of the perceived benefits of such a prestigious title is that places will receive more global visibility and that the designation will demonstrate to the world that a place truly worthy of such a 'brand' is also truly worthy of a visit. In reality we know relatively little about what kind of bearing this has on visitation and global recognition, and to assume that WHS designation automatically delivers increased visitation and economic benefits may be a dubious assumption (Buckley, 2004; Hall, 2006; Hall and Piggin, 2001). It is unlikely that countries that do not have well established tourism images will become significant destinations simply by having a site or two inscribed on the World Heritage List. There is a clearly defined need to understand better the relationships between WHS status and tourism in a variety of contexts, particularly in countries whose WHS have traditionally not been a significant focus of tourist attention.

Place branding is also often associated with indigenous people, whose culture becomes symbolic, often stereotypically so, of what a destination ought to be – at least from the perspective of outsiders. For example, many cultural elements of Maori, Native American, Aboriginal Australian, and Chinese and Thai minority group heritage have been adopted and incorporated into the commercial development of tourism in their respective countries. Unfortunately this typically happens without the approval of the groups whose heritage symbols are being exploited, which often results in conflict and questions about intellectual rights of ownership and fair trade in culture (Johnston, 2003).

This book also has touched on several aspects of demand – an important topic in heritage tourism that has long been of interest to scholars. However, Ross in this volume points to a less-studied perspective: aging populations and heritage. Elderly populations

have been overwhelmingly ignored in tourism studies, and especially in the realm of heritage tourism, where most visitors are seen as younger or middle-aged with young children and working in white-collar jobs. This neglect is remarkable given that the aging population is becoming ever more concerned with its sense of well being, competence, and understanding of completedness – many underlying motives for travel to historic places (Lowenthal, 1996). It is known, however, that people have a tendency to wax more nostalgic for the simpler times and places of the past as they grow older (Goulding, 1999; Lowenthal, 1979; Tannock, 1995). Needed in this regard is a more concerted effort to understand various populations that consume the heritage product at a micro level, rather than simply amalgamating all heritage tourists into one broad category or even separating them by age and motivation. Clearly there are life cycle-related factors that come into play in relation to experiences and desires.

This also leads to a realization of how important socialization processes are in determining people's interest in their own genealogical past (Otterstrom, in press; Timothy, in press). There is a significant movement now among diasporic communities to travel back to their homelands in search of themselves and in an attempt to discover their roots, to see and experience the places seen and experienced by their forebears. Most documented cases are people of European origin traveling back to Europe, or people of African roots traveling back to Africa. There is, however, a long established and growing interest among Asians and Pacific Islanders of various diasporas to travel to their ancestral homelands (Karlsson, 2006; Lew and Wong, 2002; 2004; Louie, 2003; Nguyen and King, 2004). It would be interesting to pursue this trend further to understand how different groups interact differently with their home-lands and how cultural differences play out in diasporic people's linkages to the lands of their ancestors.

Perhaps the most pervasive of all underlying ideas in this book is the notion of power, which can be manifest in many ways, includ-ing political control, authenticity, societal amnesia, empowerment and disempower-ment, conflict, and marginalization of min-ority groups. A persistent theme in this volume has been community empowerment and the control of tourism among indigenous groups. Even in well developed destinations such as Alaska (USA), community residents have not always had opportunities to control their own fates in relation to tourism growth. This is a particularly salient issue in the devel-oping world as well. There has been, however, a move toward more empowerment in recent years as decision making for tourism growth has devolved from the top to lower levels of government and empowering community members and all interested stakeholders (Timothy 2007).

This devolution of power is a new concept in traditional societies where decisions were almost always made at the top ranks of the political order and imposed or dictated to lower order administrators. Despite tra-ditions, bottom-up development is now the new order in many areas of Asia Pacific. This allows local communities to thrive, promote their unique advantages and decide for themselves what is in their best interest.

In the context of heritage, perhaps the most important element of empowerment as regards destination residents is their right to interpret their own heritage and determine what elements of their cultural past will be utilized for tourism purposes (Johnston, 2003; 2006). This self determination is an important prin-ciple of sustainable development because it

incorporates unique indigenous cultural values and practices into the commercial side of tourism. The Maori of New Zealand have received a great deal of coverage in heritage tourism research owing to their empowered situation whereby they are able, for the most part, to establish their own criteria and cul-tural values for Maori tourism development.

The growing empowerment of local com-munities has resulted in a growing new trend in the heritage product: heritage of the ordi-nary. Traditionally, heritage tourism has cen-tered on the built patrimony (e.g. mansions, castles, cathedrals, palaces) of the gentry and higher classes in society. However, a bigger picture is nowadays being revealed as more ethnic minorities and other community cohorts are enabled to tell their stories, result-ing in a heritage of the commonplace, includ-ing mines, villages, sheds, harbors, farms, schools, folklore and cemeteries. There is a pressing need for tourism scholars to under-take more evaluations of ordinary landscapes and to reveal more about proletarian heritage rather than the aristocratic past that has tra-ditionally dominated the heritage tourism sector.

Related to this is the political 'whitewashing' of heritage in many colonial societies, wherein history is told above all from the perspective of white European colonialists at the expense of portraying the pasts of indigenous peoples. In some cases, indigenous heritages were written out of history entirely, or at best significantly played down in official recitations of the past. Sometimes, as Frost expresses in this volume, the growth of tourism might exacerbate this situation. This societal amnesia has been a common problem in places such as North America, Great Britain, and Australia, and a great deal has been said about this issue in these contexts (Heneghan, 2003; Morrissey, 2006; Paul, 1997; Perera and Pugliese, 1998).

Having received much less attention is the idea that this kind of official disinheritance (Ashworth 1995) may be found in countries that were either not colonized by European powers or that are governed by post-colonial, non-European administrations. These situations, however, are no less pervasive and no less significant when it comes to cultural heritage. In the Asia Pacific region, China, Malaysia, Myanmar, and Indonesia are good examples, where ethnic minorities are often disinherited through official legislation or via less official channels, such as intimidation or re-written histories (Brown and Ganguly, 1997; Esman, 1995; Richter, 1989). There is much scope for researching the various power relations that exist in Asia Pacific between various stakeholders in tourism and the people who exercise power over them.

Another manifestation of power relations in the region involves the political justification of a site's existence and continued funding. In many cases WHS status, or standing as an otherwise important tourist attraction, is commonly used as a way of acquiring funding from public agencies. Similar to this in many ways is the control often exerted by powerful national government officials at the local level by giving certain privileges to destinations and attractions, such as some kinds of official designations or financial assistance if the destination advocates official discourses of nationalism and modernity promoted by the state. Thus, heritage is often used as a political pawn by national governments to promote nationalism or patriotism, to spread ideological propaganda to foreign visitors, to compel obedience, and to coerce devotion to national leadership.

Authenticity is another highly political issue that is being dealt with a great deal by tourism and heritage scholars within the Asia Pacific context. After years of debate among heritage and tourism specialists, it has become well accepted that authenticity is a subjective notion (Littrell *et al.*, 1993; Timothy and Boyd, 2003). While many destination leaders, attraction managers, and handicraft makers view authenticity from the perspective of supply, believing that products and places in themselves can be authentic or authenticated, research has demonstrated otherwise many times over, that authentic products and experiences are in the eye of the beholder. This is despite the fact that some ethnic associations, handicraft cooperatives, and museum alliances have established their own standards by which they base their definitions of authenticity.

Based on place and culture, true authenticity is virtually impossible to achieve in the modern world, because nobody knows precisely what life was like in the distant past (Burnett, 2001; Lowenthal, 1985). As well, there were and are many versions of history that conflict and overlap to such a degree that only fragments of many histories can be told (Timothy and Boyd, 2003; Tunbridge and Ashworth, 1996). Thus, there will always be elements of inauthenticity in the material culture and heritage places that tourists visit and gaze upon. However, because people are socially conditioned into thinking about the world a certain way, and they bring with them their own ideas of reality, what is authentic to one person may be inauthentic to another. Creighton (1997) documented how in some Japanese heritage villages, traditions and events are intentionally created for tourists so that villagers can keep their real customs and practices concealed from the gaze of tourists. For visitors, these places represent 'genuine' rural Japan, but for the villagers they are nothing more than pseudo places and contrived events to satisfy their visitors. Understanding authenticity and its meaning in diverse cultural contexts and from different official or organizational perspectives would be a worthwhile endeavor as researchers and tourists continue to search for 'authentic' experiences.

In conclusion, the Asia Pacific region is a rich laboratory for investigating the multifarious relationships between cultural heritage and tourism. Outside of Europe, the region has provided some of the most abundant and profitable examples of heritage tourism to be utilized by tourism researchers, and many of the concepts that underlie heritage scholarship have derived from work in the Asia Pacific. It is our hope that this book sheds light on many of the more salient issues facing the communities, industry representatives, and academics involved in heritage tourism, thereby contributing to a better understanding of critical cultural matters in the region, and in the process inspiring others to investigate the existential heritage of Asia Pacific.

References

Ashworth, G.J. (1995) Heritage, tourism and Europe: a European future for a European past? In D.T. Herbert (ed.) *Heritage, Tourism and Society*, pp. 68–84. London: Mansell.

Bowden, J. (2005) Pro-poor tourism and the Chinese experience. *Asia Pacific Journal of Tourism Research*, 10(4): 379–398.

Boyd, S.W. and Timothy, D.J. (2006) Marketing issues and World Heritage Sites. In A. Leask and A. Fyall (eds) *Managing World Heritage Sites*, pp. 55–68. Oxford: Butterworth-Heinemann.

Brown, M.E. and Ganguly, S. (eds) (1997) *Government Policies and Ethnic Relations in Asia and the Pacific*. Cambridge, MA: MIT Press.

Buckley, R.C. (2004) The effects of World Heritage listing on tourism to Australian national parks. *Journal of Sustainable Tourism*, 12: 70–84.

Burnett, K.A. (2001) Heritage, authenticity and history. In S. Drummond and I. Yeoman (eds) *Quality Issues in Heritage Visitor Attractions*, pp. 39–53. Oxford: Butterworth-Heinemann.

Chon, K.S. (ed) (2000) *Tourism in Southeast Asia: A New Direction*. New York: Haworth.

Creighton, M. (1997) Consuming rural Japan: the marketing of tradition and nostalgia in the Japanese travel industry. *Ethnology*, 36(3): 239–254.

Esman, M.J. (1995) *Ethnic Politics*. Ithaca, NY: Cornell University Press.

Goodwin, H., Kent, I., Parker, K. and Walpole, M. (1999) *Tourism, Conservation and Sustainable Development: Case studies from Asia and Africa*. London: International Institute for Environment and Development.

Gormsen, E. (1997) The impact of tourism on coastal areas. *GeoJournal*, 42(1): 39–54.

Goulding, C. (1999) Heritage, nostalgia and the 'grey' consumer. *Journal of Marketing Practice: Applied Marketing Science*, 5(6): 177–199.

Hall, C.M. (2006) Implementing the World Heritage Convention: what happens after listing? In A. Leask and A. Fyall (eds) *Managing World Heritage Sites*, pp. 20–34. Oxford: Butterworth-Heinemann.

Hall, C.M. and Piggin, R. (2001) Tourism and World Heritage in OECD countries. *Tourism Recreation Research*, 26(1): 103–105.

Heneghan, B.T. (2003) *Whitewashing America: Material Culture and Race in the Antebellum Imagination*. Jackson, MS: University Press of Mississippi.

Johnston, A.M. (2003) Self-determination: exercising indigenous rights in tourism. In S. Singh, D.J. Timothy and R.K. Dowling (eds) *Tourism in Destination Communities*, pp. 115–134. Wallingford: CAB International.

Johnston, A.M. (2006) *Is the Sacred for Sale? Tourism and Indigenous Peoples*. London: Earthscan.

Karlsson, L. (2006) The diary weblog and the traveling tales of diasporic tourists. *Journal of Intercultural Studies*, 27(3): 299–312.

Lew, A.A. and Wong, A. (2002) Tourism and the Chinese diapora. In C.M. Hall and A.M. Williams (eds) *Tourism and Migration: New Relationships between Production and Consumption*, pp. 205–219. Amsterdam: Kluwer.

Lew, A.A. and Wong, A. (2004) Sojourners, *guanxi* and clan associations: social capital and overseas Chinese tourism to China. In T. Coles and D.J. Timothy (eds) *Tourism, Diasporas and Space*, pp. 202–214. London: Routledge.

Littrell, M.A., Anderson, L.F. and Brown, P.J. (1993) What makes a craft souvenir authentic? *Annals of Tourism Research*, 20: 197–215.

Louie, A. (2003) When you are related to the 'other': (re)locating the Chinese homeland in Asian American politics through cultural tourism. *Positions*, 11(3): 735–763.

Lowenthal, D. (1979) Environmental perception: preserving the past. *Progress in Human Geography*, 3(4): 549–559.

Lowenthal, D. (1985) *The Past is a Foreign Country*. Cambridge: Cambridge University Press.

Lowenthal, D. (1996) *Possessed by the Past: The Heritage Crusade and the Spoils of History*. New York: Free Press.

Morrissey, M. (2006) The Australian state and indigenous people 1990–2006. *Journal of Sociology*, 42(4): 347–354.

Mowforth, M. and Munt, I. (1998) *Tourism and Sustainability: New Tourism in the Third World*. London: Routledge.

Nguyen, T.H. and King, B. (2004) The culture of tourism in the diaspora: the case of the Vietnamese community in Australia. In T. Coles and D.J. Timothy (eds) *Tourism, Diasporas and Space*, pp. 172–187. London: Routledge.

Otterstrom, S. (in press) Genealogy and religious practices: the doctrine and practice of family history in the Church of Jesus Christ of Latter-day Saints. In D.J. Timothy and J.K. Guelke (eds) *Geography and Genealogy: Locating Personal Pasts*. Aldershot, UK: Ashgate.

Paul, K. (1997) *Whitewashing Britain: Race and Citizenship in the Postwar Era*. Ithaca, NY: Cornell University Press.

Perera, S. and Pugliese, J. (1998) Parks, mines and tidy towns: enviro-panopticism, 'post' colonialism, and the politics of heritage in Australia. *Postcolonial Studies: Culture, Politics, Economy*, 1(1): 69–100.

Prideaux, B. (1999) Tourism perspectives of the Asian financial crisis: lessons for the future. *Current Issues in Tourism*, 2(4): 279–293.

Richter, L.K. (1989) *The Politics of Tourism in Asia*. Honolulu: University of Hawaii Press.

Sulaiman, Y. (2006) Thai social workers bracing for rise in child sex tourists. *eTurboNews*, 14 December: 1.

Tannock, S. (1995) Nostalgia critique. *Cultural Studies*, 9(3): 453–464.

Timothy, D.J. (1997) Tourism and the personal heritage experience. *Annals of Tourism Research*, 34: 751–754.

Timothy, D.J. (1999) Participatory planning: a view of tourism in Indonesia. *Annals of Tourism Research*, 26: 371–391.

Timothy, D.J. (2007) Empowerment and stakeholder participation in tourism destination communities. In A. Church and T. Coles (eds) *Tourism, Power and Space*, pp. 199–216. London: Routledge.

Timothy, D.J. (in press) Genealogical mobility: tourism and the search for a personal past. In D.J. Timothy and J.K. Guelke (eds) *Geography and Genealogy: Locating Personal Pasts*. Aldershot, UK: Ashgate.

Timothy, D.J. and Boyd, S.W. (2003) *Heritage Tourism*. Harlow: Prentice Hall.

Tosun, C. (2000) Limits to community participation in the tourism development process in developing countries. *Tourism Management*, 21: 613–633.

Tunbridge, J. and Ashworth, G.J. (1996) *Dissonant Heritage: The Management of the Past as a Resource in Conflict*. Chichester: Wiley.

Wood, R.E. (1980) International tourism and cultural change in Southeast Asia. *Economic Development and Cultural Change*, 28(3): 561–581.

Index

Note: **bold** page numbers denote references to Figures/Tables.